rivers' edge
the weezer story

john d. luersson

ECW PRESS

Published by ECW Press
2120 Queen Street East, Suite 200, Toronto, Ontario, Canada M4E 1E2

NATIONAL LIBRARY OF CANADA CATALOGUING IN PUBLICATION

Luerssen, John
Rivers' edge : the Weezer story / John Luerssen.

Includes index.
ISBN 978-1-55022-619-5

1. Weezer (Musical group) 2. Rock musicians — United States — Biography.
I. Title.

ML421.W399L94 2004   782.42166'092'2   C2004-900616-9

Editing: Jennifer Hale
Cover and Text Design: Solo Design
Production and Typesetting: Mary Bowness
Printing: Transcontinental

Second Printing

This book is set in Century Gothic and Janson.

With the publication of Rivers' Edge ECW Press acknowledges the generous financial support of the Government of Canada through the Book Publishing Industry Development Program (BPIDP), the Canada Council for the Arts, and the Ontario Arts Council, for our publishing activites.

  Canada Council for the Arts / Conseil des Arts du Canada ONTARIO ARTS COUNCIL / CONSEIL DES ARTS DE L'ONTARIO

DISTRIBUTION
CANADA: Jaguar Book Group, 100 Armstrong Avenue, Georgetown, ON, L7G 5S4
UNITED STATES: Independent Publishers Group, 814 North Franklin Street, Chicago, Illinois 60610

PRINTED AND BOUND IN CANADA

ECW PRESS
ecwpress.com

table of contents

acknowledgments

Input: Giles Anderson, Jen Hale, Jack David, Justin Fisher, Matt Sharp, Jason Cropper, Michael Stanton, Kris Stanton, Ric Ocasek, Anna Crean, Jim McGuinn, Travis Keller, Fat Mike, Vanessa at Fat Wreck, Ken Allardyce, Brian Bell, Linda Menasco, Kevin Stevenson, Scott Pittman, Cherielynn Westrich, Drew Parsons, Karen Wiessen, Kevin Kennedy, Brendan Bourke, Ever Kipp, John Horton, Pam Nashel, Dave Leto of Rye Coalition, Rob O'Connor, John Kieltyka, Steve Manning, Mike Gent, The Figgs, Jessie Tappis, Kristen Driscoll, Mikey Welsh, Rick Ross, Ben Eshbach, Heather West, Brian Diaz.

Encouragement: Waleed Rashidi, Hilary Okun, Angelo Deodato, Bill and Michelle Crandall, Andrew Dansby, Christina Saraceno, Jonathan Cohen, Dan Yemin, Chris and Tim and Bill Boyle, Mike McKee, Ann and John Crowther, Ben Forgash, Matt and Fran Azzarto, Doug and Karen Luka, Tom Jardim, Karen Fountain, Brad and Tammie Kear, Jimmy Walsh, Steve Sharkey, Mary Jane and Ray Aklonis, Jen Luerssen, Jimmy and Jamie, Liz, Mom and Dad, Marie, Sally and Rhoda, Meredith, Hayley, Jack and most importantly, my punk rock girl, Heidi Luerssen.

Thanks anyway: Karl Koch, Pat Wilson, Pat Finn, Sarah C. Kim, Rivers Cuomo.

Send comments, corrections, diatribes, and hate mail to weezerbook@hotmail.com.

why bother?

In the spring of 1994, I took my weekly pilgrimage to Vintage Vinyl, a stellar record store in Fords, New Jersey, with my younger sister Ann. Not yet a music writer, but just a music junkie feeding my need for something new each week, I recollect picking up an import-only CD called *The Urge Overkill Story*. Still on a high after their epic rawk disc *Saturation*, I needed a track like "The Kids Are Insane" to keep me going. (I miss Nash, King, and Blackie.) Anyway, on the way out the door, Ann saw — in among the boxes of freebie promo cassettes that always cluttered the floor by the register — a Geffen sampler by a band called Weezer.

As we exited the store Ann goofed, "Gee fellas, I can't play right now, I've gotta stay home and grease Weezer," which was something straight out of the *Li'l Rascals* reruns we'd watch on television as kids in the 1970s. We got in her aquamarine VW Golf, she put the tape on, and that was IT. We were transfixed. What *was* this stuff? Power pop? Punk? This shit was hard *and* catchy. I asked her if I could have her copy of it. And Ann was like, "No big brother, you've got to get your own." Later, when she dumped me off at my apartment, I did in fact get in my car and take the ten-mile pilgrimage back to the Strip Mall Hell that is Route 1 just North of the Edison border.

The dude behind the counter with the tattoos and the pierced septum was listening to some crap like Meat Beat Manifesto. He's like, "Forget something?" I'm like, "Yep." So rather than just snag the freebie — one of the last few down there in the box atop the stained gray carpet — I plunked down a few bucks on some blank tapes (how 1994 is that?) and made my way out of there. Twenty minutes later, I ran up the stairs to my new apartment. Listening to it twice through, I put that cassette on full blast, cracked a beer, and had one of those moments. A half hour later, I took a look inside my brown paper bag and saw the aforementioned Urge Overkill disc. And I was like, "Urge. I don't need Urge right now. I've got Weezer."

Flash forward to May 2002, just as Weezer — after a rather tumultuous and complicated history — released their fourth studio album, *Maladroit*. Inspired by their victorious return to form, and still a dedicated fan of their music over the years, I conspired to write a book on the band. I quickly searched on Amazon for any books on the group. When I came across those Hal Leonard music books, but nothing that might rank as a biography, my memory cued to what I thought I already knew about the band.

Didn't Rivers Cuomo live on an ashram? Wasn't he a metal head as a kid? How about Weezer's rise from an unknown band to an MTV staple in less than a year or the Rentals thing causing a rift in the hierarchy of the group? What about Rivers' acceptance to Harvard and the "failure" of the *Pinkerton* album? Then there were the rumors of a pending break-up after Pat Wilson and Matt Sharp's public criticism of Cuomo around the start of 1997. Followed by Matt Sharp's exit and Mikey Welsh's entrance. And, of course, Cuomo's self-doubt in '98 and '99, which eventually begat their amazing comeback, and then Welsh's quick exit.

My first thought was to go the authorized route. I e-mailed Rivers Cuomo, who by this point was handling the band's publicity and management duties. No reply (it turns out he was on vacation in Asia). Next I tapped Weezer's webmaster. Karl Koch had helped me out in the past with music news stories I had written on Weezer for the likes of *Billboard* and *Rolling Stone*, so I e-mailed him after never hearing back from R.C. Did he think the band might be interested in authorizing a biography? I wondered.

"John, good to hear from you. I'll ask around. It's likely that they're just swamped and back burnered it. I don't actually know how they'd feel about it, maybe they don't either, heh heh . . . Thanks! — Karl."

A number of weeks went by, and operating on the "no news is good news" premise, I began to deeply research the book. In early August, I sent an e-mail to Pat Wilson. His reply? "John. I think a =w= book would be cool! Our story is insane. I forwarded this to Rivers to see what he thinks. We're weird. Rock. — Pat." In the interim I had started making contacts, and in some cases, conducting interviews with people who have a history with Rivers.

A subsequent reply came from Sarah C. Kim, assistant to Rivers Cuomo. "Hi John. We received your e-mails regarding the biography you are writing on Weezer. While we are very pleased that you are pursuing this project, the band has declined to participate in the biography at this time. Thank you."

Depression set in as I thought, "I'm already two months into this." Then a little while later, I declared, "I'm two months into this!"

A few more days went by, and I wrote back to the big cheese of Weez (through his helper). "Hi Sarah: I know Rivers has 'declined' to be involved in the biography I'm writing on =w=, but I was wondering if, when the time comes, you/he would at least verify the accuracy of the biographical information I've amassed. Since you mentioned in a previous email that he was 'pleased' I'm pursuing the project . . . Would you also please be kind enough to ask if he'd at least allow me to extend the same courtesy to Brian, Pat, and Scott regarding their pre =w= lives, and their projects outside the group?"

In the meantime, I wrote back to Wilson. "Hey Pat: Listen, I know Rivers — although 'pleased' I'm doing it, according to Sarah Kim — declined on behalf of the band to participate in the biography I'm doing on =w=, but I was wondering if he'd mind if I spoke to you about The Special Goodness and non-band related matters? I'm also piecing together your pre-Weezer existence in Clarence/Buffalo and your move to L.A. and was wondering if you'd be allowed to talk to me about that?"

Replying again, Wilson wrote, "John, I'm forwarding this to Rivers, but I'm willing to talk about SG [Special Goodness]. Rock. — Pat."

Hmmm. That's promising, I thought, hoping maybe things might turn my way.

Meanwhile, Cuomo's assistant wrote back, "Hi John. I think I may have been unclear through my last communication with you. Though the band is very flattered that you are pursuing the biography, I was mistaken in saying they were 'pleased' by the prospect. They would actually prefer and appreciate if the biography was not published at this time. Perhaps after the next album comes out, they might be more receptive to something like this. We just don't feel this is an appropriate time to release a biography. Please let me know your thoughts."

My thoughts? Well, I'm a little too entrenched in this thing now to dump the whole idea. Maybe Rivers really was the controlling personality other journalists have hinted at. Talking down to his bandmates in front of reporters, belittling them. Why would I really want to write an authorized book in cooperation with this guy anyway? The most interesting and controversial parts of what I had already uncovered would certainly be subject to his red pen. Ivy League English student or not, I decided right there that I didn't want his editorial ink all over my project, even if he changed his mind.

The next day I wrote back to Wilson telling him that since my last e-mail, "Sarah sent me a note saying that Rivers isn't down with being involved. I don't want to cause a rift between you guys, [so it's] your call. I'm still writing the book, though."

Eight days later, Pat wrote back, saying, "I think I'm going to chill for now."

And with the exception of Wilson corresponding with me for a *RollingStone.com* news item on The Special Goodness — where he dodged any questions related to his primary band as if he were under strict orders from the boss — and a cordial 2003 interview with Brian Bell to plug his Space Twins project, I had no further contact with the Weezer camp until late February 2004 when I received a surprising personal e-mail from Rivers Cuomo. Sent from a Yahoo! account, just as this book was being typeset, Cuomo inquired about the project and an article I had written about his patching things up with Matt Sharp. "I'm looking forward to reading the book . . . . . . with some trepidation," he explained. "It's weird to have someone write about you. I'm sorry I didn't want to participate. I felt that it was not time for me to reflect. I sensed that huge changes were about to come over me."

While the maturation he hints at is chronicled in the final pages of this book, there is one recurring theme as you read through *Rivers' Edge*. Weezer is indeed Rivers Cuomo's group, and the other members are his players. While he does permit for some creative input from his band, he always has the final say. For most of the band's history, those in defiance of his rules are usually shown the exit as the ink dries on a freshly signed non-disclosure agreement.

Coming away from this project after more than a year's worth of work, I am still as much — if not more — of a Weezer fan than I was in the hours after I cracked the cellophane on *The Blue Album* almost a decade ago. I've done my best to remain neutral, merely documenting the unique and often peculiar history of the band and reporting on the impact of Rivers' actions toward other people around him — some positive, some negative.

This book would not have been possible without the help of Justin Fisher and Michael Stanton. Both gave the deeply candid and informative interviews early on about life in the presence of Cuomo that served as the impetus to trudge forth with this project. Key phone interviews with founding Weezer guitarist Jason Cropper and original bassist Matt Sharp, whom I later had the pleasure of meeting after a Hoboken solo show in 2003, were obviously also critical and much appreciated. The insights of former Rentals member Cherielynn Westrich, plus Drew Parsons and Kevin Stevenson, both of whom played in the Rivers Cuomo Band in 1997, were all inestimable. Equally invaluable were producer Ric Ocasek's revealing recollections and guitarist Brian Bell's thoughts on his own past and the future of the band. Still, my favorite anecdote of all comes from NOFX's Fat Mike, who told me about an unorthodox business meeting with Rivers in the spring of 2001. Read on and see if you agree.

Rock!

John D. Luerssen

March 2004

chapter one

kiss

Were it not for Kiss — the original make-up–clad 1970s version, that is — it's very likely that a Dungeons & Dragons–worshiping, pubescent Rivers Cuomo might have wound up like so many other nerdy kids. But Cuomo's urge to rock saved him from becoming, say, a computer programmer or a college professor. Weezer is actually a brilliantly mutated incarnation of that *Love Gun*–toting troupe. And this isn't just a theory, as Rivers — an unlikely rock god fronting a quartet of improbable rock stars — has long touted the importance of Paul Stanley, Gene Simmons, Ace Frehley, and Peter Criss in both interviews and in song.

Cuomo's obsession with Kiss first surfaced in verse #2 of "In the Garage," from the band's now-seminal, self-titled 1994 debut album. Here, Cuomo sings about the Kiss posters adorning his walls, name-checking Ace Frehley and Peter Criss, the group's lower-profile, underdog members.

Rivers, frequently tagged a "geek rock" icon, also gets to the heart of his early Kiss loyalty in a March 1997 *Guitar World* feature promoting his quartet's second album, *Pinkerton*. "When I was a kid, I definitely related to the music, and I loved it," Cuomo said, despite being in the dark as a child when it came to Kiss' topical fare. "When I was eight and listening to Kiss, I didn't understand what the fuck they were saying. I mean, 'Me, you in the ladies' room'? That went right over my head.

"It's only now that I'm in my mid-20s that I realize the genius of all those lyrics," the rocker said at the time, counting Gene Simmons as his favorite Kiss lyricist. Rivers' devotion to Stanley, Simmons, Frehley, and Criss hit a fever pitch in junior high school when, at age thirteen, he fronted Fury — a Kiss cover band. Some even argue that the reason Cuomo assumed the moniker Peter Kitts was because it was a slight variation on the name of Kiss drummer Peter Criss.

When the sometimes elusive Cuomo ditched out on a 1995 *Rolling Stone* feature by Mim Udovitch, original bassist Matt Sharp stepped up to pinch hit for Rivers in the Kiss loyalty department. "It has to be Ace," Sharp insisted when asked who Cuomo's favorite member was. "He had the best of the four Kiss solo records." It should come as little surprise that R.C. has used the handle "Ace" when posting on the Weezer.com message board.

Cuomo's fascination with Kiss is an interesting gateway to the world of Weezer. In order to examine the band's remarkable history to date — one that has its share of twists and turns and ups and downs and ups — it's important to look at what prompted the lads to bring the rock. And if you think about it, Weezer closely mirrors Rivers' Kiss heroes by having that same persevering spirit. His band's enormous 2001 comeback after a five-year gap between albums is something of a parallel to Kiss' make-up–dispensing 1983 re-emergence.

In the face of self-doubt, band tension, a succession of bass players, and — as you'll learn — a domineering frontman, the members of Weezer managed not to just stare down their uncertainty, but kick its freakin' ass. Now, as one of the most influential and credible modern rock outfits we have, with a rabid, cult-like fanbase, Weezer has become an unstoppable force.

chapter two

rivers

Rivers Cuomo, the creative force behind Weezer, was born on June 13, 1970, in a New York City hospital. According to Cuomo, his father Frank — then a musician and major soccer enthusiast — missed his birth because he was at home watching Italy play in the World Cup on television.

Rivers also contends that there is some debate over the origin of his unique moniker. His mother, Beverly Shoenberger, assures that her first-born son's name came to her when she heard the sounds of the river outside of her Manhattan hospital window immediately after giving birth. Bev didn't give Rivers a middle name at the time because she wanted him to be able to choose his own. (Incidentally, this is something he has yet to do.) Contrary to his mother's story, Rivers' father insists that he was named after three players in 1970's World Soccer Final held in Mexico. This too could be valid, as the players — Brazil's Rivelino and Italy's Riva and Rivera — did oppose each other a week after Rivers' birth.

Frank Cuomo's love of soccer wouldn't be the only thing he would pass along to Rivers, who learned to walk by kicking a soccer ball. He would also hand down his musical prowess. According to Justin Fisher, current Psoma frontman, sometime bassist in Nerf Herder, and one of Cuomo's longest and closest friends, Rivers' dad was "a kick-ass drummer in New York in the '60s. He played for a little while with the Weather Report before their first album." Rivers' father indeed lent percussion to *Odyssey of Iska*, a 1970 Blue Note Records release by modern jazz legend and future Weather Report saxophonist Wayne Shorter. Recorded on August 26 in the year it was issued (when Rivers was merely two-and-a-half months old), the long out-of-print disc — which is home to moody titles like "Wind," "Storm," and "Calm" — is the only known recording to feature the elder Cuomo.

On August 31, 1971, Beverly gave birth to a second son. Named Leaves, Rivers' younger brother speculated thirty years later that his parents named him after leaves that "were changing on the trees outside the hospital." Marveling at the irony, considering summer was still in full swing, Leaves mused, "Maybe they were planning on naming me after the leaves that would be changing in September/October? But I was [born] premature." Leaves also suggested that Rivers was almost spontaneously named Apple, which makes sense considering the city in which he was born was nicknamed "The Big Apple." If anything, the Cuomo children's earthy names help to surmise that their parents were nature-loving hippies with a fondness for plurals.

Rivers' mother — a practicing Buddhist to this day — and his father became part of the Zen Center in upstate New York, where his dad evidently served as a farmer. Reflecting back on his boyhood, Cuomo commented, "If you could just see where I actually came from . . . it was just farmers. I mean, literally, my dad was a cow farmer."

Rivers' family life revolved around the Zen Center until he was five, when his parents split up. His father — largely absent from Rivers' and Leaves' lives after these early years — moved to Germany where he eventually surfaced as a Suffragan Bishop with the Newborn Ministries in Wiesbaden.

Meanwhile, Rivers' mother drifted until she ended up in Yogaville, an ashram located in Northeastern Connecticut and run by the late Sri Swami Satchidananda. Often referred to as the "Guru to the Stars," Satchidananda ministered to Carole King, Jeff Goldblum, Laura Dern, Diane Ladd, Sally

Kirkland, Carole King, and psychedelic artist Peter Max. Max, in fact, was responsible for bringing the swami to the United States in 1966. With disciples in waiting, Satchidananda moved his base of operations to the U.S. from Sri Lanka, feeding America's youthful curiosities about Eastern mysticism, music, and meditation. By 1969, the "Woodstock guru," as he was also known, opened that legendary rock festival, sharing the stage with Jimi Hendrix, The Who, and The Grateful Dead. Challenging the youth of the world to use "the sacred art of music" to bring peace to the globe, the swami declared music "the celestial sound that controls the whole universe."

By the mid-1970s, Satchidananda's secluded eastern Connecticut Hindu community had abandoned any notions of Woodstock's acid rock. The environment was drug and alcohol-free, emphasizing the simple yet profound teachings of Integral Yoga. Subsequently, Rivers and Leaves Cuomo — who were also schooled on the ashram — were met with a remarkably untraditional upbringing. "You have to realize we were living in an enclosed community of Hindus," Rivers remarked years later. "We lived in an ashram. Isn't that insane?"

"Yogaville has been called a 'cult,'" said Rick Ross, an expert on such matters and the founder of the Ross Institute for the Study of Destructive Cults, Controversial Groups and Movements. "Sadly, many children are raised within cults, which they did not choose to join. Instead their parents simply brought them in. Yogaville and the Integral Yoga Institute have a rather typical 'cult' history, which includes a charismatic Indian guru."

It was in Yogaville that Rivers' mother, one of Swami Satchidananda's spiritual daughters, met Stephen Kitts. Together on the Satchidananda Ashram — suitably named for its focus on yoga and meditation — Steve and Beverly both worked as massage therapists and eventually married. In keeping with the teachings of the guru, one of the primary goals for those who resided in Yogaville was to realize the spiritual unity that lay beneath all the diversity in the world. In this environment — where the staff wore Hari Krishna outfits and visitors and residents alike woke to the sound of violins — the staples of young boyhood, like toy guns and tackle football, were taboo. Unlike in the world outside the ashram's acres of serene, wooded land, no one ate meat, raised their voices, or used four-letter words. "It was a very mellow childhood," said Rivers understatedly.

But the isolation began to severely affect young Rivers Cuomo by the time he was a student of Mrs. Anderson's at the rural Pomfret Community School. "I know I was a very somber child," he recollected. "I would never smile. In the second grade my teacher asked my mother what was wrong with me because I never looked happy. So my mother advised her to say, 'Let me see the smile,' and then I would smile. So she did that — in front of the whole class. She got the whole class to turn around, look at me and say, 'Let me see the smile.'"

Life on the ashram also had a significant impact on younger brother Leaves, who grew up to become an assistant professor of sociology at the University of Washington in Seattle. As recently as 2001, Leaves, under his legal name James Anthony Kitts, would offer a course called "New Religious Movements." During a teaching tenure at Cornell University in the late 1990s, he also taught a class titled "Communes, Cults and Charisma," raising awareness among his students while speaking from his own childhood experiences.

"There were also sex scandals and members and families complaining about exploitation and 'brainwashing,'" Rick Ross added of Yogaville. "Satchidananda by some accounts was quite a sleaze who preyed on women within the group. He indulged himself and largely got away with it, though there was a mass exodus after sex scandals broke some years ago. Yogaville appeared to be little more than the guru's ego fulfillment."

Whether any of this had a drastic impact on Beverly or her sons isn't directly known. Still, in this totally secluded setting, a young Rivers — pre-viously sheltered from the bulk of pop music — managed to get happy in 1977 when the daughter of a friend of his parents played him a Kiss record. In doing so, he said, she "directed the course of my life.

"*Rock and Roll Over* was the one rock record I happened to get," he added. "Somehow that album found its way into the commune. I've pretty much based the rest of my life around that record.

"We were all about six or seven years old. And when we heard 'Makin' Love' or 'I Want You' off that record, we just lost our minds," Cuomo remarked. "The guitar was *so exciting!* I remember we'd all just run around the room in circles, playing air guitar and jumping off the furniture.

"There was no real contact with popular culture," Rivers said of his youth at the "very isolated Hindu commune." Despite that fact, the future Weezer leader kept his eyes on the rock 'n' roll prize, imagining his future role as a hybrid of the Satchidananda's cult of personality and Kiss' glam-orous lifestyle. "I had rock star dreams from eight or nine almost nonstop," Cuomo uttered. "I thought it was going to be like being a God on earth, having super powers, being incredibly wealthy, never doing laundry." The sexual aspects of "Ladies Room," a hard rocking Gene Simmons–penned number about the perils of fame and groupie encounters in concert venue restrooms, might have been over Cuomo's head, but the song appealed to him for its description of being a rock star.

Aside from that lone Kiss album, Rivers was missing out on many of the givens of mainstream culture for so many American kids in the late 1970s — Top 40 radio, *Brady Bunch* reruns, Bubble Yum, skateboards, and cheeseburgers. If his early penchant for rock was being, perhaps unfairly, caged by life on the ashram, Rivers' desire to absorb all things Kiss-related was about to be realized as his family left that environment.

Around 1980, Satchidananda announced plans to move Yogaville and the tax-exempt, non-profit, non-sectarian Integral Yoga School in Pomfret Center that Rivers — known by his Sanskrit name "Rama" to his teachers and classmates — was attending at the time. Courtesy of a generous gift from pop singer/songwriter Carole King, the facility would relocate to nearly 700 acres of land along the Blue Ridge Mountains in Virginia. Instead of moving the family to the newly commissioned Light of Truth Universal Shrine in rural Buckingham County, Beverly and Stephen opted to stay in Connecticut, settling Rivers and Leaves into the Hartford suburb of Storrs Mansfield with the hopes of carving out a somewhat normal existence.

chapter three

fury

Making the transition from life on the ashram to life in a new apartment in Warrenville (and soon after to a permanent home on South Eagleville Road in Storrs) was initially difficult for Rivers and Leaves Cuomo. Here, the brothers were faced with the difficult task of assimilating into regular American life for the first time.

"Suddenly Leaves and I had to join the outside world," Rivers remembered of his eleventh year, which saw him transitioned from the private Integral Yoga School to the considerably more chaotic world of public schools. "We even had to teach each other to swear so that we could fit in at public school." In addition to honing the art of swearing, an ashram-free Rivers immediately joined the Columbia Record Club and bought every Kiss album available. He also selected some unpredictable fare: "I bought twelve albums for one penny or something. Within that package was Eddy Rabbit, Abba, Queen . . . I think they all had a tremendous impact."

"Moving was a big shock for Rivers," said Justin Fisher, who befriended Cuomo shortly after he enrolled at Mansfield Middle School. "An ashram can be a really supportive environment. Then suddenly you're thrown into school with grades and kids swearing at you."

As the Connecticut branch of the Integral Yoga School closed, Rivers was advised in a letter of thanks from his teachers to "take what you have experienced in this school, that was also your home, and enjoy life and be free." This advice was easier said than done.

"His family life didn't really prepare him for social situations," Justin continued. "It was his first time in public school. It was really scary for him to hear people insult each other. Kids can be evil, and to be thrust into that is tough." Adds Rivers of the experience, "[Leaves and I] got the crap beaten out of us. I think it made me very shy."

For enrollment in public school, Rivers had assumed his stepfather's last name in place of Cuomo, and then opted to go by the more traditional first name Peter. "In order to integrate into public school, Rivers and Leaves' parents let them select their own names," Justin explained. "Rivers picked Peter, and Leaves was Jimmy. Of course, by the time Rivers got out of high school he realized that the name he had been given at birth was a lot cooler than the name he had been going by and changed back."

With Peter and Jimmy doing their best to endure the awkward adjustment from commune to public school, Beverly and Steve Kitts set about establishing careers for themselves. Together, in 1981, they founded The Connecticut Center for Massage Therapy — now in Newington — and before too long their entrepreneurial drive and expertise in massage and yoga became a thriving business.

In the rural Storrs Mansfield community — also home to the University of Connecticut — Rivers' mother and Justin's mom, Mary Pat Fisher, discovered that they shared holistic interests and became fast friends. "Our moms had known each other and tried to get us together," said Justin.

"Basically, Rivers and I met in the sixth grade right after he had left his ashram and got to our school," continued Fisher. "The first time I really met him he had a bunch of these kind of cool fantasy magazines and there were a bunch of guys crowded around him. We had similar interests like Dungeons & Dragons, music, and sports like soccer." Needless to say, in a short time the pair became almost inseparable.

"I gravitated toward the, uh . . . elven, or half-elven; something with high dexterity," Rivers would later confess, recollecting that he went split-class during his tenure with the twenty-sided dice. "A fighter-thief maybe?"

In his youth, Rivers was very athletic, but by adolescence he began having problems with his leg and was examined and diagnosed by the Newington Children's Hospital in May 1981, just short of his eleventh birthday. "Pretty much all I did was play football and baseball," he said, "which may seem hard to believe — but as I got taller, the doctor told me I couldn't run any more because it would mess my back up."

According to a letter typewritten by his mother to family members and friends explaining the situation, Rivers — who at the time wore a half-inch lift in his right shoe — saw two orthopedic pediatric specialists and was diagnosed with a rare, albeit textbook case of "congenital femur 'something or other,'" as Beverly put it. Indicating she was relieved nothing was diseased, Beverly's letter also explains how happy her eldest was not to have to wear orthopedic shoes, although he was concerned enough to bring along a stuffed bunny named Mark, which he had had since he was six years old.

The congenital condition occurred prenatally, was not genetic, and worsened as he got older, and the situation eventually resulted in one leg being forty-four millimeters longer than the other. The problems with his right leg steered Cuomo — who began studying music at age nine — toward music nearly exclusively by his thirteenth birthday. "I had to drop out of sports altogether. That's when I decided I wanted to be a rock star."

In seventh grade Rivers introduced his new best friend Justin — who had already schooled himself on the Beatles and the Beach Boys — to Kiss. Together the pair also discovered metal and pop as they mined *Blackout* by the Scorpions and *Business As Usual*, the first album by Men At Work. "Men At Work was our first concert," laughed Fisher at the memory of the night of July 30, 1983. "It was on the *Cargo* tour and it was at the Hartford

Civic Center. I remember that they had this really dumb cloud that rose up in the middle of the stage during the show. It wasn't much longer after that when we started our first band, and learned all Kiss covers."

"I thought if we only did Kiss songs we would be huge," reflected Rivers with pride. When some classmates got together to play Quiet Riot's "Metal Health" during an eighth-grade school function, Rivers and Justin got all the inspiration they needed to put that dream into action. "Everyone started freaking out," said Fisher. "The girls were, like, rushing the stage and we're sitting on the side. We all sort of looked at each other, and we're like, 'why aren't we doing that?'"

"Man, it just blew me away," Rivers said of that same performance, prompting him to ask his parents for an electric guitar on his fourteenth birthday. In the summer of 1984, Rivers learned to play Ace Frehley's guitar solos note for note on his first guitar, a "crappy" Stratocaster copy. He even tried turning his mom on to Frehley, but the reformed hippie wasn't very receptive to heavy metal. "I'd play her the 'Shock Me' solo from *Alive II* because I thought that was the greatest. She told me that it sounded like a dying cat."

Still, to Rivers, "[Ace] was just God, because all of his solos were so memorable and singable. They had form to them; they'd start out low and go up high. . . . They were just great, compact little emotional things."

With the Strat copy in hand, Rivers took his first crack at songwriting. "I remember all my life coming up with gay little tunes," Rivers recalled. "The first song I wrote was 'Fight for Your Right,' which was a Kiss-style heavy metal anthem. It's funny that I basically do the same thing now. Come up with a metal riff and sing it. I've barely evolved."

Around this time, Rivers — whose only other nickname had been "Weezer" by kids who teased him for an asthma condition — became known to his classmates as Peter and nicknamed "Schmete." He also began building on his devotion to metal and was an avid listener of *The Crunch Hour*, a metal show on Hartford rock station wccc 106.9 FM "The Rock." Says Cuomo, "Back in 1982 or '83, the classic rock stations would occasionally play Iron Maiden or Judas Priest, and I was like, 'Wow, this sounds great!' So I got those albums, too. Those guitar players ripped my head off."

Rivers was also blown away by Quiet Riot when he discovered them on 'ccc. "When I heard 'Metal Health' on the radio for the first time, it crystallized everything for me. I thought, 'Here's this new sound that belongs entirely to me and my generation. This is how I want to identify myself as a metalhead.'"

The lyrics to "Metal Health," a rallying cry for disobedient, attitudinal, and misunderstood teen headbangers everywhere, were effectively screamed by Quiet Riot frontman Kevin DuBrow and reflected the thirteen-year-old Rivers' rebellious stance. In fact, to Rivers, image-conscious groups like Quiet Riot seemed a natural extension of Kiss. "When I first got excited about hair was maybe '84," he admitted. "I brought the Quiet Riot album to the hair salon and said, 'Make me look like [guitarist] Carlos Cavazo.' And they did. And my mom got so upset, she got in the car and drove home without me, which was, like, five miles away."

The same year, Rivers and Leaves were reportedly graced with a half brother, Gabriel Cuomo, who was born abroad to their father and his second spouse on March 2, 1984. Less than four months later, Fury, steered by a fourteen-year-old guitar-wielding Rivers Cuomo, began practicing. Comprised of Justin Fisher on bass, Rivers' younger brother Leaves (then twelve) on second guitar, and another friend, Eric Robertson, on drums, the dream of rocking out became a reality for Rivers. Ten days after Rivers' birthday, Fury had their first rehearsal.

"When Fury was formed, we hadn't had much instrumental training," admitted Fisher. "I guess Rivers was a little more skilled than I was. We had both been in choirs together, and my dad had been a musician and so had Rivers' dad." With their fathers' gear at their disposal, the Kiss tribute band took flight. "I think Rivers always wanted to be in a band at that point," Justin said.

For their first-ever gig in Southbridge, Massachusetts, in September 1984, the young rockers in Fury — steered by a fourteen-year-old Rivers sporting black streaks under his eyes, parachute pants, and long hair — delivered just three songs. "Cold Gin," "Rock and Roll All Night," and "Strutter" were all lifted straight from *Kiss Alive*, and were the three tunes the boys had learned when they bought their guitars.

At practices and gigs Rivers played his Stratocaster wannabe through a portable Yamaha amp, while Leaves had "something cheesy" amplifier-wise, Fisher reported. Justin himself had a tall cabinet and a Gibson SG bass that had belonged to his father, a musician in the 1960s, and Robertson — who had been playing a while longer than his bandmates — had a nice Pearl drum set. For vocals, the group ran a pair of Radio Shack microphones through a 20-watt Cortez amp. "We still have tapes from those days and it sounds god awful," Fisher laughed then reconsidered, "Actually, it doesn't sound *that* bad."

The Fury line-up methodically set about learning Kiss material album by album starting with all of the songs on the first record. Once those songs were mastered, the band would move along to the next. Rivers, as the older brother and more proficient than Leaves, played Ace Frehley's guitar parts while singing Paul Stanley's rhythm parts.

Rivers' loyalty to Kiss was still strong, but more technical metal players had also grabbed his attention by '84. "I would only allow myself to put up Kiss posters, so each wall was devoted to Kiss," Rivers confessed. "I also had this other little room that was my guitar practice room and in that room I allowed myself to put up other artists, and they were all guitar players. The guys from Scorpions, the guys from Priest . . . Yngwie Malmsteen, Paul Gilbert . . . guys who inspired me to practice my skills."

By now Rivers had been through a bunch of wicked-looking heavy metal–styled guitars, including a Guild Flying Star, which he later dubbed "possibly one of the worst guitars ever made. It kind of looks like a B.C. Rich Ironbird. What a terrible, terrible instrument."

Around this time, Rivers and Justin began attending more concerts, including Kiss' tour supporting *Animalize* and the Scorpions on their *Love at First Sting* trek with Bon Jovi opening. The Scorps would be a major influence on Cuomo. He'd later say, "The guitarist I hear the most in my playing is Matthias Jabs from the Scorpions."

In the fall of 1984, Rivers and Justin had moved up to E.O. Smith High School in Storrs. Rivers' increasing metal look combined with such geek pursuits as comics like *The X-Men* left him wide open to the harassment of his Lacoste and Ralph Lauren–clad schoolmates. As metalheads, Cuomo and his friends were a minority at the school alongside the jocks and the preppies. According to Rivers, he and his small crew were soon the victims of criticism and abuse. "Me and my friends were metalheads and we were a minority at school," he'd say. "And the jocks, and the grits — that was another clique of burnout-type people — and the preppies . . . everybody hated me and my few friends who were the metalheads. And they picked on us.

"It's probably too embarrassing, and too self-effacing, to describe all the times I've been beat up," Rivers spouted. As a result of his mistreatment at school, the longhaired Cuomo — despite his incongruent leg — studied karate, along with Justin, in part to defend himself. "It was as much protecting ourselves as it was an interest in martial arts, karate, and ninja sort of Asian stuff," Fisher remembered. "Back then, in 1983 and '84, there were a lot of martial arts movies out and we were into it, so Rivers and I took karate lessons at a dojo in Willimantic."

Rivers admitted later that the first time he knocked someone out with his karate abilities, he started crying. "It was really powerful. I was afraid of the killer instinct in myself. That's what was really frightening to me. 'Cause I had been trained my whole life to deny that existed. [It] was really difficult for me to turn on that aggressive killer instinct in myself. I was programmed to be really passive. And that doesn't work in karate. I was taking a really intense, full-contact style. After about a year I was at the point where I could actually beat someone else's ass. . . . You're called on to do that sometimes, and that was one of the most difficult things for me, allowing myself to kick somebody else's ass."

Like many adolescents, Rivers had an identity crisis. Unsure of where he fit in, the depressed, misfit Rivers says he pondered joining a Buddhist monastery. "I went to my parents' Zen master and I said, 'Life is shit. I want to shave my head and do this,'" Cuomo recalled. "He's like, 'You know what? Being a monk is shit too, so I can't advise that for you. What you should do is really listen to yourself and see what path would make you the most excited and just go do that, however crazy it seems.'"

Finally reassured that his lofty musical aspirations up to now had indeed been valid, despite his nay-saying classmates, Cuomo said, "It took me about five seconds, and I was like, 'I want to be a rock star.'"

With his hands on a new guitar — a beloved Charvel Model Two — Rivers was drawn deeper into the dark, mysterious world of heavy metal. "Looking back it all sounds so weak," Cuomo conceded. "But at the time it sounded so heavy and powerful and wild. I suppose somebody should have turned me on to punk or music that actually has some of those qualities. But at the time, metal served that purpose perfectly well for me."

chapter four

avant garde

Peter Kitts' musical tastes were gravitating toward more complex heavy metal groups by 1985, and Fury soon gave way to a much different sounding band. With the axe-wielding fifteen-year-old in command, anchored by his comrade Justin Fisher on bass, this new, fledgling outfit might have been without permanent membership, but its axis was nonetheless focused on an intricate, expressive variety of metal.

"There was a period where we really didn't have a name," said Justin. "Members were moving in and out. There was another group we had, called One Night Stand with some guys we had met from Massachusetts. And Rivers had also been playing some Metallica and Fate's Warning covers."

"Nothing gave me a sense of community like metal did," Cuomo said of the days when he wore his hair to his nipples. "It meant everything to me, it was so important. I started out liking Kiss, but I also liked Quiet Riot, Judas Priest, Iron Maiden . . . then of course I discovered Metallica, Slayer, Megadeth, Anthrax, Yngwie . . . I was a guitar player."

"I used to be into Metallica a lot," remembered Rivers. "Up until *Master of Puppets* I was a huge fan." Drawing off that outfit's first two records — 1983's *Kill 'Em All* and 1984's *Ride the Lightning* — and albums like 1984's *Night On Brocken* and 1985's *The Spectre Within* by local outfit Fate's Warning, Rivers and Justin settled on the name Avant Garde. In hindsight Rivers jokes "we were anything but."

"I was a Fate's Warning devotee," Cuomo admitted, explaining that to

him, "Their songs are really complex, and were really hard to figure out."
Rivers even wound up taking guitar lessons from that band's own Jim
Matheos, having met him backstage at an area concert they were playing.
"I told him how much I worshiped him and that I'd love to take lessons, and
he said it was cool. The thing that I really loved about Fate's Warning,
though, was the melodies." But if he and Justin had given up the Kiss covers
by now, they still loved the group enough to cough up $13.75 a piece to take
in a show by the band at the Worcester Centrum on December 20, 1985.

As Rivers was honing his chops courtesy of lessons by Matheos, things
in the Avant Garde camp were beginning to come together. First Kevin
Ridel, a singer from nearby Vernon-Rockville, Connecticut, whom
Cuomo and Fisher had met following a 1985 "Battle of the Bands" competition, joined the line-up. And when the future AM Radio frontman
became a member of Avant Garde in 1986, he brought along his brother
Eric Ridel to fill the second guitarist position. With Rivers' fellow E.O.
Smith attendee Bryn Mutch — whom Justin to this day touts as "an amazing drummer" — already in tow, the quintet was complete.

Rivers and Justin pursued Mutch, but getting him to join the band was
an "easy sell," said Fisher. After all, Mutch was a diehard fan of Yngwie
Malmsteen's *Rising Force* album and although he was a year behind the pair
at E.O., Bryn hung out in the same crowd. "We were like, 'Hey Bryn, wanna
play some Yngwie?'" laughs Fisher. "After that we conned him to stay."

Often rehearsing three to four times a week for several hours at a time,
the members of Avant Garde were extremely serious about their brand of
music, which Fisher describes with fifteen years of hindsight as "bizarre
guitar rock." Avant Garde's founders had become so serious about bringing the noise that they had little patience for members with less dedication.
For instance, when Eric Ridel's partying ways didn't mesh with the group's
serious work ethic a year into his tenure with the band, the other members

began looking for a replacement for the second guitarist, which they found a year later.

This no-nonsense attitude toward music was nothing new to Rivers. It was he, in fact, who had once given Fisher similar treatment when he confronted the then fifteen-year-old bassist for a single partying offense. "We didn't really drink, smoke, or do most of the things that people usually associate with rock music," said Fisher. "We were really focused on being musicians and the people that we saw drinking or getting high back then didn't seem to be as 'serious' as we wanted to be."

So when Fisher himself experimented with introductory vices like alcohol, tobacco, and marijuana, he learned firsthand that Cuomo didn't have much patience for such behavior. Said Justin, "One night I'm hanging with our friend Jim Emino and a couple of girls — ooh! — and I try schnapps, pot, and cigarettes all for the first time — double ooh! Needless to say, I didn't score very well with the ladies, and when I went to Rivers' house the next day I got the third degree from Rivers, Eric Robertson, and Leaves. They were all sitting around the kitchen table — we were practicing in Rivers' bedroom — and saying, 'We heard what you were doing last night — smoking pot — and we need to know if you are going to want to do it again.' The underlying message being, 'We're not really into having a pot smoker in the band.'

"To tell you the truth, it had been an awful night that I hadn't really been planning to repeat any time soon," recalled Justin, who heeded Cuomo's warning. "But it was a pretty weird experience overall."

With that sort of sway over his peers, Rivers spearheaded his own clique of about a dozen heavy metal worshipers by his junior year at E.O. Smith. If Cuomo's long hair, ripped jeans, and Metallica T-shirts earned him the disdain of the VoAg grits and jocks that ruled E.O., he easily had the influence over and respect of his headbanging crew. "He always had cool ideas and was always able to talk people into things," Fisher said of his friend.

Rivers agreed. "I was an outsider, but this may sound crazy, I've always been a leader too. I always had a group around me. I gradually attracted a really close group of outsiders around me. Eventually we came to see we weren't the outsiders anymore."

When he wasn't calling the shots for his outsider faction or seasoning wicked metal guitar licks in the practice room, a sixteen-year-old Rivers found time to obtain a Connecticut driver's license. With a dated, tan Toyota Tercel at his disposal courtesy of his mother and stepfather, he had the freedom to explore Tolland County and beyond.

Surprisingly, metal outcast Rivers mustered up the courage to fill the role of Johnny Casino in an E.O. Smith High School production of the 1950s-based musical *Grease!* late in his junior year. Cuomo was likely egged on by his music teacher Kenneth Holton for the three performances between April 30 and May 2, 1987, as the choral teacher counted Rivers among his favorite students. "He was fascinated by heavy metal," Holton recalled, "but that didn't seem to affect him when it came to my groups. He didn't blow me off because I was a classical theorist. He had very teased long hair all around his head. He was a very noticeable kid because of his appearance. I guess he thought he was playing the part of a rock star. My chorus got a reputation for having a kid with the long hair."

"I was never a rock star in high school," countered Rivers. "I was always a bit of an oddity. When I was in ninth grade, we were picked on and ostracized. By eleventh grade, we were tolerated. And by twelfth grade, people gave us a certain amount of respect. But we were never rock stars, just the weird guys who did music."

Justin claimed that things again came to a head for Rivers during his junior year of high school. "There was a real jock-against-metalhead thing going on for some reason," he said, "and it all came to a head with a few of us facing off against some pretty big ugly lookin' senior jocks. A year later it seemed like every jock in the country was buying the Metallica's . . . *And Justice for All* album. Weird."

By the time he was seventeen, Rivers was finding himself intermittently lured away from metal's dark wrath, and he began appreciating all facets of pop. While it's doubtful he admitted it to his metal clique, he started to discover '60s songwriting icons like Lennon/McCartney and Brian Wilson while keeping his ear on Top 40 fixtures of the late 1980s like Prince and Madonna among others.

"Spiritually I was a metalhead in my teens, which is really sad to say," he continued, "but musically, I've always listened to everything. I've always listened to classical music. All through high school, I was in lots of classical performing groups. So while I was really rallying behind the headbangers' cause, I always had an open mind to everything else that I was exposed to."

From late 1986 into early 1987, the members of Avant Garde had honed their respective instrumental crafts to the point where they would regularly make 4-track demos when they weren't rehearsing in various locations. Among the places they'd congregate to rock included the workshop behind Justin's parents' house (which, he joked, "the neighbors loved"), Rivers' house (which was empty when his mother and stepfather were away), and most importantly, at a place called The Band Room.

Said Fisher, "The Band Room was a small, burnt-out furniture factory in Vernon. The place was falling apart. There was absolutely no adult supervision and bands like ours would just go in there and rent our own piece of floor for three or four hundred dollars a month and build our own walls. We'd practice in there, and kids would just go in there and hang out and listen to other bands. It was really kind of neat and scary at the same time. It was incredibly cold in the winter and we had this 60,000 BTU

MICHAEL & KRIS STANTON

Got Aqua Net (clockwise from center): Rivers Cuomo,
Justin Fisher, Michael Stanton, Kevin Ridel and Bryn Mutch
as Avant Garde, circa 1988

furnace thing. Bear in mind, we're all in high school, and it's 1986, 1987.
Looking back, I don't know how the hell we came up with the rent — it
was insane!"

"We just kind of sucked," Kevin Ridel said bluntly, looking back on this
era less nostalgically. "We were trying to be the kings of our instruments
and just disregarded the idea of writing good songs. We were striving for
technical prowess, but we still couldn't really play."

Maybe so, but in their junior year, Rivers and Justin put an officially
released demo to tape. Recorded in their rehearsal space with the use of a
portable studio, the premiere Avant Garde release was credited as a collaborative songwriting effort. Consisting of three songs — "Tongue of Fire,"
"I Must Be Dreaming," and "Black Rose" — the cassettes were printed on
black-shells with light blue label stickers on one side and circulated

throughout the suburban Hartford metal community.

By the summer of 1987, after applying to and being accepted for a five-week music program, Rivers attended the esteemed Berklee School of Music in Boston. It was here that he met Avant Garde's future guitarist and Texas native Michael Stanton. A year behind Rivers and from Gatesville, near Waco, Stanton had applied to the same program at Berklee and was also admitted.

"I had to send some recommendation letters, stuff like that," Mike remembered. "I got accepted, and was really pleased. In reality, I don't think the selection process was very rigorous.

"There was a small group of 'rocker' people, including Rivers, there, in a sea of jazz/fusion/studio types," Stanton said. "I wanted to hang out with them, but didn't know how to approach. One day, I was in my room, playing *Master of Puppets* on the guitar pretty loud. Rivers heard that and knocked on the door. We hit it off really well, and did everything together. It was a really fun time. We'd record *wicked* instrumental guitar songs on a 4-track. One was called 'Plankton Frito,' and it had a mean sounding Phrygian harmonized riff.

"We spent hours writing out elaborate counterpoint dual guitar solos, then recording them. Along with some other students, we might go out late at night to a pizza restaurant or get on the subway. Once, a movie theater closed down for the night when they saw a horde of us stomping up to watch a midnight *Rocky Horror Picture Show*. That was cool. This trip was one of my favorite experiences as a teenager, especially because I came from a small Bible-belt Texas town that would have burned us all at the stake for such hedonism.

"Another fun time was taking a train to Salem and catching a glimpse of a *real witch* in the back room of a new age bookstore," he continued. "I remember a lot of hysterical laughing during those five weeks. I barely remember the classes, although we were good students. Rivers and I both knew a lot of music theory. He had an especially good ear for relative pitch, and got me into a lifelong habit of practicing that. On the subway we'd hear a major 9th interval between the low engine rumble, and some high squeaking thing. No sound would go unanalyzed. But Rivers was also cool. He was very good at impressing girls, and had at least one girlfriend during that time. I definitely envied that."

With Storrs less than two hours from Boston, Justin went north to retrieve Rivers (who still went by Peter) in his van when the summer session was over. Mike, with a few days to kill before his return trip to Texas, tagged along. "I had met Mike up at Berklee," Justin said of his best friend's new acquaintance. "He was this amazing guitar prodigy from Texas that Rivers really hit it off with, not only because he was a great player, but because they had similar interests and he looked weird. It was kind of when that really crazy, ripper guitarist rock like Yngwie and stuff had become big."

Before returning to Texas, Stanton stayed with Rivers at his parents' house for a few days and even sat in with Avant Garde when the band played a show at a party back up in Massachusetts on a flatbed truck. "We all really liked how it worked out," Justin said of Stanton's six-string augmentation.

"I was in Mansfield for a few days, and we played a show of metal cover songs," said Stanton, who remembered meeting Kevin Ridel and playing tunes by Whitesnake and Judas Priest. "I went back home to Texas feeling absolutely certain I'd see all those guys again, and that they were the coolest people on the planet. Rivers and I had a great mutual respect for each other. His abilities and ambition would eventually outstrip mine, but that was years away."

By September of his senior year at E.O. Smith, Cuomo was skilled enough to give guitar lessons to his friends and he continued his advanced music studies by enrolling in some music classes at the University of Connecticut. Around this same time, Rivers took a menial job working briefly for the state of Connecticut, receiving a note from his boss threatening termination and forfeit of pay for failure to turn in his employment eligibility form.

His obsession with heavy metal provided a much-needed escape from the stresses at home, where his mother and stepfather's marriage had begun to dissolve. Eventually ending in divorce — the second that he would watch his mother endure — the break-up would have such a dramatic effect on Rivers that he would later chronicle the event through the deeply personal lyrics of "Say It Ain't So."

"I opened up the refrigerator and saw a can of beer," Rivers remembered of the matter. "All of a sudden I made the connection that my stepfather was leaving, because my father had started drinking when he left my mother."

The opening verse of the song speaks of how the sudden presence of Heineken beer in the Kitts family refrigerator gives Rivers the chills. Closing his eyes, he goes on to chronicle life in a tension-filled, alcohol-addled household. As things come to a head, he escapes the stresses in his home life by watching television and wrestling with his younger brother. Using a foaming bottle as a metaphor for his crumbling family life, he pours his heart out in a rock 'n' roll letter to his "real" but estranged father, Frank. In the song, he sings of making contact with his cleaned up, newly religious "Daddy" after several years of silence, prompted by the awakening of "ancient feelings" as a result of Stephen's "cold one." Cuomo's cathartic utterance of the final line, in which he finds himself — like his stepfather and father before him — awash in the negative effects of booze, puts his feelings on alcohol in clear perspective.

"I was really afraid of alcohol at the time," Rivers explained. "I didn't drink 'til I was twenty-one — not even a sip. I was petrified of alcohol."

Despite his woes at home, Cuomo began reaping the rewards of local metal stardom during his senior year, when he lost his virginity at age seventeen. While coming of age sexually gave him a needed ego boost, Rivers also managed to cut loose by corralling his metal posse into bona fide athletes in his senior year. He formed a lacrosse team for the fun of it, despite the fact none of this metalhead friends had experience in the sport. As expected, his makeshift team was mauled when it did manage to play a pair of games against his high school's junior varsity teams. Cuomo later described the experience as a disaster.

On December 12, 13, and 18, 1987, Avant Garde recorded six new songs at Trod Nossell studios in Wallingford, Connecticut. Recorded on the facility's six-hour 16-track demo package at a cost of $288.37, the group's first professional demo boasted the Avant Garde logo, had a black shell with a purple label on one side, and featured "You Were Just Using Me," "Renaissance," "Standing in the Paris Rain," "Father Time," "Never Forget," and "Free Fall." Approximately fifty copies of the recording were made, but it is unknown some fifteen-plus years after their production how many still remain in the hands of Avant Garde's miniscule, central Connecticut following.

Within weeks, Avant Garde's demo had made the WHUS 91.7 Heavy Metal playlist at the campus radio station of the nearby University of Connecticut, appearing in the #11 slot, directly above the self-titled Triple X Records debut by Jane's Addiction. And as 1988 unraveled, gigs at U Conn's "Metal Madness" show with headliners Midnight Dawn on April 21 and a headlining slot at the local venue, Bridge's Café, on May 11 kept the group occupied.

Despite being pleased by the achievement of having made a credible demo cassette, Rivers, Justin, Kevin, and Bryn all wanted to boost their

Hair To Stay: A rare flyer promoting an Avant Garde gig —
with Cheeter and Inquisition — at the University of Connecticut

sound, so they began conspiring to get Michael Stanton into the Avant Garde fold full time. Scheming for a post–high school rock 'n' roll life, Rivers — who graduated that June ranked fifty-fifth out of a class of 170 with a final GPA of 3.14 and listed his pet peeves to be "rain & other things messing my hair" underneath his senior class picture — came right out with it in a long-distance phone conversation. "[He] asked me if I wanted to join the band," reported Stanton matter-of-factly. "I had left high school after my junior year, and was going to a commercial music program at a community college in Waco. Rivers and I planned out that I'd move up there, then we'd move to Los Angeles and go to the Guitar Institute of Technology.

"I was pretty star-struck by the whole adventure, and I guess my mom knew there was no way to keep me on the farm," Stanton confessed. "So she drove with me to Connecticut in my Honda Civic and took a plane home. I arrived and it was a little jarring. I'd always known Rivers as Peter, but immediately had to switch to 'Rivers,' which was kind of hard at first. That evening Rivers taught me six or seven songs for our first practice the next day."

"The amazing thing is that here's a seventeen-year-old kid from Texas who moves to Connecticut to hang out with some other seventeen-year-old kids, just to play in a rock band," said Justin. "It's bizarre!"

Mike's courage to head north in mid-1988, just after Rivers and Justin had graduated from E.O. Smith, thrilled the founding members of Avant Garde. Still, he admits he was apprehensive about meeting Kevin's brother Eric Ridel, the guitar player he was replacing. "I had heard that he smashed his hand into a car window when he heard he was 'fired' from the band," Stanton said. "I was like, 'and you guys didn't tell me this?' But oddly, I don't remember if I met him or not. Kevin was okay though, so I figured I wouldn't be beaten to a pulp. They were already a band, and had recorded an earlier demo tape. I was the new guy, and there were many people and situations to get familiar with."

Staying at Rivers' house was "a lot of fun," Michael remembered. "We lived in the basement, and Leaves was there too. Rivers and I worked six hours a day at Domino's Pizza. I never had a Nintendo before, so I fell hard for *Zelda* and *Metroid*. The three of us would play that for hours. Friday nights we'd go to Denny's and an arcade, talking with various locals. But the focus was always on the music. To my circumscribed knowledge, nobody drank, smoked, or did drugs. We were squeaky clean on that front. We talked about girls a lot, and would stay out late on weekends, but weren't very wild.

"I felt right at home with Rivers' mom," Stanton says of life under Beverly's roof. "She is a really nice lady, and my mom and her had in common a kind of new age mentality. His stepdad was nice too, although mostly absent. Rivers didn't talk about his real dad much. I moved to Justin's house because I eventually learned his mom and stepdad were going through a divorce, and it'd be better if I weren't there. And I felt pretty bad about that."

Rivers, then "a rock star in the area" according to Mike, had the attention of a lot of girls. "A favorite pastime was long phone calls," said Stanton, "seemingly lasting all night. Then he'd mope around and feel pathetic. I recently saw an interview with Rivers where he said he writes his best music in an 'emotionally toxic' state. I thought that hit the nail on the head. In my impression at the time, he was making himself miserable quite a bit!"

With Stanton on board, the band again entered Trod Nossel Studios in Wallingford in July 1988. The end result was a third demo which they would title *Somethin' Different*. Retaining "Renaissance," from the previous effort, fresh titles included new, hard rockers like "Judge and Jury," "Bite the Bullet," "21st Century Shogun," "You Were Just Using Me," and "Never Forget."

"It was really exciting when we were recording the demo tape," boasts Stanton. "Every night we'd go in with a wad of cash from Domino's and hand it over! I think it was four or five nights, each time $300 or so." The group played outdoor gigs at Henry Park in Vernon on July 25 and August 1.

Coming up with the material for the *Somethin' Different* demo was largely a collaborative process between Cuomo and Ridel, Mike recalled. "I came up with some short sections of '21st Century Shogun,' and I wrote some laughable lyrics for 'Judge and Jury.' But really Rivers and Kevin were the songwriters. They would stay up late and have three new songs in the morning. That kind of depressed me at the time, because I strongly wanted to contribute creatively. Either I wasn't good or creative enough, or — less likely, though I felt this way at the time — was prejudiced against for some reason."

With a finished demo in hand, and their eyes on Hollywood, the group continued to practice religiously in the basement of Bryn's parents' house, but didn't perform much. "We had many practices," Stanton said, "but I think only one live show planned that winter. We looked forward to it for months. We were opening for a popular metal band in a real concert hall. But on the day of the big show, we saw a sign on the door of the club that said, 'Club Closed.' The club had gone bankrupt. Justin, in a daze, sailed right through a red light in his van. We were incredibly shocked and disappointed, perhaps me especially, since I was keen to prove my metal chops!"

Justin remembered it a little differently: "Our last gig in Connecticut was at a 2,000 capacity club — the same place where we saw Metallica a few years before. Anyway, there was a freak snow storm that had hit New Jersey, it hadn't even made it to our area yet, but they called off the gig for fear we'd be snowbound."

If the unexpected cancellation of Avant Garde's swansong hometown concert — regardless of the actual circumstances that led to it — was disheartening, Rivers, Justin, Kevin, Mike, and Bryn were now anticipating their departure to Los Angeles. With professionally duped copies of *Somethin' Different* in hand to score gigs, their eyes on stardom, and a passion to play metal on the Sunset Strip, Cuomo and his bandmates left for Los Angeles in March 1989 with the hope of being discovered.

Leaving his mother and brother behind in Newington, Connecticut, where they had relocated in the aftermath of Beverly's divorce from Steve, Rivers discarded any notion of a mundane future existence. His final gesture was to donate his old Toyota Tercel, now barely running, to a co-worker at Domino's in exchange for a favor.

"When we moved to L.A. he gave that car to this girl that he was working with at Domino's in exchange for her to airbrush the Avant Garde logo on all of our jean jackets," Justin reported, before exclaiming, "Rock!"

"She was actually our boss, but that *was* an awesome move," Stanton agreed.

Several years later, when Rivers was having his first taste of stardom, he said, "At eighteen, I freaked out and moved to L.A. to become a rock star." But in reality, it was a long plotted and highly calculated career choice.

chapter five

hollywood

In early 1989, the metal musicians from Tolland County had relocated with high hopes of living a glamorous lifestyle. When they arrived in L.A. on March 5 of that year, they were humbled to discover the place at 1825 Cherokee Avenue was a total dump.

"We had stars in our eyes, and Hollywood seemed cooler than Boston or New York. It was further away from the other cities we considered, and the weather was better," Justin Fisher recollected. "Three days before everyone else came out, I flew out and took over this tiny little fleabag apartment so we'd have a place to live. We took it over without even telling the complex managers or anything. The people who had it before us had dogs, so I go in there and there's dog shit everywhere. Rivers and Mike drove out together, and I think Frank Arresti from Fate's Warning and Bryn drove out in Bryn's family's station wagon. We knew the guys from Fate's Warning and they were also relocating to L.A. at the time. Kevin flew out a little bit later."

"We drove in my Civic, heading southwest to my mom's house in Gatesville, Texas, staying there for a few days," Mike Stanton remembered. "Rivers hated this delay, threatening to hire a taxi and take a plane the rest of the way. This was the first time I remember a big fight with him, but we had some fun anyway. Some rednecks chased us down an icy road with their pickup, so we drove to my friend Dale's house. Luckily he had a high barbed wire fence. 'Close the gate!' we were screaming, as the huge truck bore down on the gate. I'm not kidding, that was scary . . . later, the guys in the truck showed their displeasure by spinning out in a field behind Dale's house. Then we watched horror movies and ate BLT sandwiches all night. It was a chance for Rivers to see what isolated Texas metalheads do with their time."

Upon their arrival in sunny California, these five purveyors of "heavy and aggressive" metal — all in their late teens — crammed themselves into the rundown apartment on Cherokee Avenue. "At the time it was this really gnarly, crack-plagued area, with a little bit of gang activity," Fisher said. "So it was a severe culture shock for us to go from the kind of wooded community we came from where we'd ride our dirt bikes along a trail to a scummy, nasty area where bullets are flying and guys are wearing head-bands signifying gang colors. This was right when that movie *Colors* had come out," laughed Justin, "so we were all, like, freaked out."

A few months after settling in Hollywood, Fisher's girlfriend at the time, Lynn, moved out from Connecticut to a nearby complex at 1811 Cherokee. As a result, he would often stay with her, freeing up floor space for Rivers, Kevin, Bryn, and Mike. But eventually their unauthorized sub-let was discovered by complex management, forcing the five members of Avant Garde into even closer quarters.

"I don't know how it happened, but we had to sneak out of that apart-ment and move into Lynn's one-room efficiency in the complex next door," reported Stanton. "Poor Lynn. She and Rivers had great antago-nism — very tense. Really, Rivers seemed to have a natural dislike for girlfriends of any band members, as my own wife Kris can attest. Lynn moved across the courtyard, and we settled into the place we would live for almost a year."

Nineteen-year-old Cuomo was indeed of the notion that girlfriends were a detriment to a band trying to make it on the Hollywood scene; a

belief that was ingrained after a review of an early Avant Garde performance commented on the abundance of thirteen- to eighteen-year-old
girlfriends and hangers-on.

As for the sleeping arrangements, Stanton said, "I got the closet under
a stairway. Rivers took the opposite closet. Kevin slept in the kitchen. I forgot where Bryn slept. Justin slept at Lynn's. We were up until 2 a.m. at
least, and we would wake at 10 or 11 in the morning. The kitchen and
bathroom were disaster areas. Once, Justin put a 'roach motel' in the oven.
Twenty minutes later — it was full."

Stanton's then-girlfriend and future wife Kris concurred that the apartment was "incredibly filthy. There were a few girls that cleaned it up from
time to time — me included — but I got yelled at because they couldn't
find anything."

"With five of us paying $500 a month total, it wasn't too bad to make
the rent. Our parents were kind of taking care of us and we had gotten
some shitty jobs," said Fisher. "But at the same time, the tough part was
trying to play on the Sunset Strip at the height of 'Pay for Play.' Pay for
Play was the only way to get gigs back then. Basically, we had to cough up
$400–800 dollars per show up front — which, to us, was a ton of money.
We'd also buy ads in all the local music papers like *Screamer*, *BAM*, and
some others, and that would cost us even more. Then we'd make phone
calls to anyone we might know trying to entice them to buy tickets just to
make up the money. Somehow we'd pay the rent, have a place to rehearse
and do these Pay for Play shows."

"Pay to Play was the only way to play the Roxy, Troubadour, Gazarri's,
all the big clubs," Mike agreed. "It was a major headache — we were
spending all our time trying to sell tickets. We had phone lists, and we each
had to spend time calling people." Playing tunes off *Somethin' Different*, as
well as songs like "Hold On," "Let Go," "Farmer's Daughter," and the ger-

Goin' To California: Michael Stanton
and Rivers (in a Fate's Warning
shirt and nipple-length hair) at a Texas
stopover in March of 1989

Dig Those Bicycle Shorts:
Rivers takes a unique
microphone turn,
circa early 1990

mane "You Play, You Pay" to often indifferent crowds, the group was learning that the road to rock stardom was paved with broken glass.

"Everyone in the band was so young and didn't look like the other bands at the time, so they didn't have too much of a following," Kris Stanton remembered. "It was very hard for them to sell tickets and break even, but they did have a lot of thirteen-year-old girls hanging off them. They weren't into partying, that I knew of, and were really talented musicians compared to the huge masses of crap [bands] out there at the time."

In order to sustain their meager existence, most of the members of Avant Garde took crappy jobs. "For me, it was a combination of jobs and my grandfather, who paid insurance on my car," Mike recollected. "Kevin and Justin worked. Rivers never had to work; I think his mom sent money."

On the strip, Avant Garde was still honing its live show and looking to set itself apart from the run-of-the-mill pop metal hair bands dominating the scene. Meanwhile, Cuomo did enroll in the Guitar Institute of Technology in Hollywood.

When downtime from their own rock beast allowed for it, the dudes in Avant Garde caught a few bona fide Hollywood rock shows in between playing *Zelda* into the wee hours of the morning. "In L.A. we saw Stryper, even though their cloying lyrics bothered me," Stanton confessed, acknowledging their brand of Christian metal was something of an oxymoron.

"The best concert of my life was seeing Cacophony at Gazarri's. Me, Rivers, and Justin were at the front of the stage, screaming the lyrics. We were all really amazed by the guitar playing of Marty Friedman, who went on to join Megadeth, and Jason Becker. The singer said we knew the lyrics better than he did, and he would sometimes hold the mic up to us. We must have been rabid fans, because you just didn't do that in L.A. at that time. You were supposed to stand at the back and critique everything in a surly manner."

If Rivers and his buddies lacked the censorious outlook that so many jaded people on the Strip possessed, they at least had an appropriate rocker look for Hollywood circa late 1989. "We all had the boomin' metal hair, especially Rivers," Justin remembered. "He had this big, spiky, crazy wild hair." Although Fisher claimed he, himself, never went so far as to use Aqua Net — the heavy metal crowd's hair product of choice — he chuckled at the thought of his lead guitarist prepping to hit the streets or the clubs. "Rivers needed serious amounts of time to get himself ready to go out the door, or else he just wouldn't go out. There were a lot of days we'd be like, 'C'mon dude, we gotta go do this thing.' And he'd be like, 'It's raining. I can't go out.' When he gets an idea about something, he fixates on it."

Just before the dawn of a new decade, Avant Garde transformed into Zoom. Fisher explained, "Zoom was Avant Garde with a new name. Basically, we were trying to make ourselves more commercial."

"They all sat in a donut shop when changing the band's name and came up with 'Zoom,'" said Kris Stanton. "Other names on the long list were 'Prong' and 'Power Chicken.'"

Upon returning to Los Angeles after a trip home to Connecticut for Christmas, Rivers and the renamed, refocused band approached 1990 with a new, two-song demo cassette that was recorded in a Los Angeles–area studio and consisted of titles like "Power Talk" and "Street Life." In addition to this new material, Zoom was integrating some very interesting covers, including Billy Joel's 1982 hit "Pressure," and The B-52's "Love Shack." The songs were given "much heavier" treatments than their original versions, according to Mike Stanton. "But we never covered a song in the metal genre."

"They did a lot of funny things," said Kris Stanton of the ways Zoom promoted their gigs. "Like one time the band was walking up and down the strip with a big spray-painted 'Z' on poster board. I think Rivers was on Justin's shoulders holding it up. When greeting strangers, they would say, 'Hey John.' I have no idea why. And once they wore T-shirts as pants, but it looked like diapers."

By the height of Zoom's success in February 1990, they almost broke even on a Saturday night show at the Roxy. "Their headlining show was the biggest and best," Kris remembered. "They played Twister on stage and Rivers' girlfriend, Lisa, was pulled up to spin the wheel. Michael and Rivers both wore non-matching shoes, and their 'outfit' was Body Glove bike shorts and T-shirts."

Booted from another apartment, the group was forced to camp out with their gear at a seedy Motel 6 until they could find individual housing. Said Kris Stanton, "Four or five of us stayed in one room and for some reason we left the door unlocked; all of the equipment was in the room. I was sleeping nearest to the door and a black guy opened the door and I said, 'Can I help you?' I thought he was a friend coming to visit. He just backed

MICHAEL & KRIS STANTON

Surf's Up!: A Zoom publicity shot ushers in the 1990s

MICHAEL & KRIS STANTON

Goin' Streakin': A 1989 flyer promoting Zoom's September 6th show at Madame Wong's. Check out Cuomo's highlighted, boomin' tresses

out and closed the door. Then maybe an hour later, he came back again and I said the same thing and he just backed out again. After that, I locked the door. Their equipment would have been gone if I didn't wake up."

After a year of L.A. struggles, Zoom threw in the towel out of frustration by the spring of 1990. "A lot of Rivers' and my friends just sort of came and went," Fisher mused. "I give everyone who comes out to L.A. a year to see if they can handle it.

"It was a tough period," Fisher said of Zoom's demise, "because not only did the band start to dissolve, but we didn't have a place to stay. Our apartment in Hollywood had gotten too gnarly, none of us had any money and we didn't want to stay invested in it anymore. We all just split to different places or crashed at different friends' houses. Meanwhile we're still playing, we're still trying to hold it together. Bryn had already packed it in and we were using temporary drummers."

"When they needed a new drummer, they had an advertisement in a local magazine and Frankie Banali from Quiet Riot called — or at least that's who the caller claimed to be," Kris Stanton remembered. But even if Rivers was close to playing with one of his heavy metal heroes, things in the Zoom camp

MICHAEL & KRIS STANTON

Sunset Stripped: In need of a drummer, the Zoom boys' Help Wanted poster promises "Big management" and a "one album deal"

were bottoming out and the collaboration never actually came to fruition.

MICHAEL & KRIS STANTON

Zoom camaraderie in effect (left to right): Justin Fisher, Kevin Ridel,
Rivers Cuomo, and Michael Stanton

MICHAEL & KRIS STANTON

1-2-3-4 Pressure: Fisher, Stanton, Ridel, and Cuomo
punch out a Billy Joel cover

MICHAEL & KRIS STANTON

Precious Metal: Michael, Rivers, and Justin have a riff-roaring good time

"We had this really big show at the Roxy, tons of people came out and we packed the place and we were still kind of stoked, but by this point things were getting harder," Justin remembered. "Then maybe a couple weeks after the Roxy show, Mike said he just wasn't interested in doing it anymore. He said he wanted to be a computer programmer/classical musician guy and that kind of left the rest of us up in the air." By the time of Zoom's last show — which took place at Hollywood Live, a venue in the 6800 block of Hollywood Boulevard on March 14, 1990 — nineteen-year-old Rivers Cuomo was staying in temporary residence at Lisa's apartment.

"The rest of us tried to keep it going but we were all living pretty far apart from each other," said Justin, "so it just sort of collapsed from there. Rivers and Kevin played together for a little bit longer with this new guy they had met, but then Rivers just did his own thing for a little while."

Cuomo — who had been slacking at his guitar studies as the band floundered — was notified in April that he would not graduate from the G.I.T. after failing to complete his attendance, performance, and minimum academic requirements.

"Kevin went back to Connecticut for a spell, and Rivers started working at Tower Records and met a bunch of new people, and so it all fell apart," Fisher concluded of this era. "In hindsight I think we were a little misguided. Our brand of sophisticated guitar metal was in stark contrast with the hair metal on the Sunset Strip. It was really hard to define ourselves and develop a following and it was hard to keep the band together in that environment."

chapter six

only in dreams

Shortly after the turn of the decade, the rock music world began shifting its focus away from the spandex-clad heavy metal acts that ruled in the 1980s toward the raw, punk-inspired alternative rock that began bubbling up. In Hollywood, once a fertile metal breeding ground, changes were also afoot. Updating their sound to give it a California allure, the members of Avant Garde also buckled to the pressures of the Sunset Strip by switching their band's name to Zoom. But these alterations came too late, and shortly after the group recorded a self-titled two-song demo, the band Rivers Cuomo founded in rural Connecticut five years earlier crumbled. "It was real disillusioning," Rivers said of the break-up. "Because it was my dream band from high school."

Upon implosion, Rivers' original bandmates scattered not only across L.A. — in the case of Justin Fisher — but across the United States. Drummer Bryn Mutch had gone back east to Connecticut and hit the cover band circuit; Kevin Ridel also went home, but soon returned to front a Christian rock band called The Truth (and years later Ridel High and AM Radio); while guitarist Michael Stanton returned home to Texas and later worked for Microsoft. Meanwhile, Cuomo remained in the City of Angels, took a year off from performing music, and attended Los Angeles City College part time.

When Cuomo began going to college, he noticed that his interest moved from practicing the guitar to songwriting. Suddenly, "metal seemed kind of dumb, so I consciously repressed it," Rivers explained, adding that the genre "didn't seem very relevant anymore so I locked myself away with an acoustic guitar and started writing my own songs."

After landing a job at Tower Records on Sunset Boulevard, Cuomo — who had split with his girlfriend Lisa — began to open his mind and quickly embraced the surging alternative sound. Rising stars like Nirvana and Jane's Addiction, seminal bands like the Velvet Underground and The Beatles, and influential outfits like Sonic Youth and the Pixies all caught his ear while working at the retailer. According to Rivers, "The Pixies are one of the bands that really blew my mind when I first moved to L.A. and started to discover cool music."

Working at Tower, Rivers might have loathed his boss, but he instantly hit it off with a co-worker and Buffalo native named Pat Finn. "[Pat] was the first really punk guy I ever met," Cuomo said. "I totally admired and respected him — how completely nuts he was. He was always trying to grab my balls, or trying to get fired all the time so he could collect unemployment. He was always trying to get the boss to hit him. We all hated the boss-guy. So I really respect Pat. He played me a lot of great music, and taught me a lot about cynicism. How to talk, how to act. 'Cause I was still fresh out of Connecticut, a complete idiot. And he also introduced me to Matt and Pat." The duo he's referring to, of course, is future Weezer bassist Matt Sharp and drummer Pat Wilson.

In early 1991, Rivers — discouraged because he was between bands — began to sow the seeds of what would become Weezer through Finn, who, in addition to working with Rivers at Tower, also played bass in a group called Bush. Not to be confused with the Gavin Rossdale–fronted U.K. band that rose to prominence in the mid-1990s, Finn's outfit consisted of drummer Pat Wilson and future Wax guitarist Tom Gardocki. Wax would eventually land a deal with Interscope and go on to have a minor radio and MTV hit in 1995 with the song "California."

Pat Wilson

Weezer drum stylist Patrick Wilson was born in Buffalo, New York, on February 1, 1969. Raised in nearby Clarence, Pat was introduced to the sounds of Barry Manilow at a young age and that easy listening icon prompted his first music purchase — 1976's *This One's for You*. "I had heard the song 'Weekend in New England' and I was way into it," Wilson remembered. "I just had a great love of music from the start."

Pat — like Rivers — was a soccer enthusiast growing up, but he was also a hardcore supporter of the local professional football franchise. "God bless the Buffalo Bills," he once inflected. "I hate the Cowboys." In his eleventh year, Wilson got turned on to airwave affable new wave like Gary Numan's *The Pleasure Principle*, which featured "Cars," and Devo's *Freedom of Choice*, which housed "Whip It." He was equally drawn to hard rock, especially Led Zeppelin and Rush, whom he discovered when he was eight.

"I was a huge Rush fan. *Enormous.* I had a cousin who was about seven years older than me, and when he was fifteen he showed up with *2112*," Pat admitted. "That's when I got into Rush, right around when that record came out, which I think is very strange because I was very young. At the same time he brought over *Van Halen* and Aerosmith's *Rocks* so I got into those."

Shortly after his fifteenth birthday, Pat took in his very first concert, seeing Van Halen on the Buffalo-area stop of their *1984* tour. As a result, the ninth-grader began taking drum lessons along with his friend Greg Czarnecki. Counting Alex Van Halen, Led Zeppelin's John Bonham, and Stewart Copeland of The Police as percussion idols, Pat soon mastered the drums and eventually talked the owner of a now-defunct music shop into letting him and Czarnecki teach the instrument. By the time Pat was a senior at Clarence High School, he and Greg had amassed over thirty students, but Wilson says he grew weary of watching "the selling of cheap guitar amps to unsuspecting kids" and resigned.

Aside from music, Pat had a hard time keeping jobs before his rise to fame as a member of Weezer, burning through twenty-five of them before the band took off. "I always got fired," Wilson noted. "The shortest was working in Wendy's. It was horrible. I would rather sell my body — not that anyone would have it. I get really depressed when I see adults working at Wendy's."

Graduating from Clarence High in 1987, where he claimed to be a "troublemaker" and a "smartass," Wilson went to college locally, but dropped out after one semester. "College was such bunk," he opined. "Too much politics and jockeying for favor. I just couldn't do it. College is great if you want to learn, but that's not what college is about, it's about making your professor happy and getting good grades and getting into an IBM. Any place that says that they're only accepting college graduates is not a place I'm very interested in being."

Just short of his twenty-first birthday, Pat — disgusted by his hometown's "lame" music scene, which mostly consisted of "cover bands and bad metal" — ditched his day job teaching drums, exited his Buffalo-area home, and moved to Los Angeles. It was the winter of 1990, and Wilson had gone west at the urging of his friend Pat Finn, who had arrived in the land of golden opportunity a while earlier.

"I met this guy named Patrick Finn, and he had a Wahl bass," Wilson explained. "I had never really played seriously with anybody, because there was just such a lack of talent in Buffalo — or maybe it was my lack of being able to get into some sort of scene. But when I met this guy and we played, it was insane. He was like mister slap, but he was good at it. He could really shred. We found out that we had the same birthday, and that was it. He was like, 'Dude, I'm moving back to California. You want to go?' and I was like, 'I'm there.' I just took one look around the music store and thought, I'm not going to be thirty-two years old and still working here. I don't know much, but I know *that*.

"I was a guy with a bad haircut from Buffalo," joked Pat, describing Buffalo as being "like Chicago only worse." He chalks up his failure in that city's music scene to his uncooperative coif. "And you want to know why I wasn't in Whitesnake cover bands? Because I couldn't grow my hair. I just never grew it right. I never had 'booming' hair like everyone else did.

"Buffalo is pretty much Canadian," Wilson continued. "Toronto is a fabulous place compared to Buffalo. Buffalo, all you want to do is drive through it. I was forced to listen to Bad Company and Lynyrd Skynyrd, that's all the radio stations played in Buffalo when I was growing up."

Shortly after arriving in L.A., the two Pats disregarded all that they knew about Buffalo's tepid metal scene and lousy cover bands and linked up with guitarist Tom Gardocki. The resulting Bush was a "power trio" as Wilson puts it. Fusing "a modern jazz weirdness" with a heavy funk and rock hybrid, the group aped that era's scene leaders like Fishbone, Primus, and the Red Hot Chili Peppers.

Bush was short-lived, lasting from the spring of 1990 until the spring of 1991. Few of the songs the band created featured vocals, but those that did were songs by Finn. And after the two Pats cut their first Bush demo on July 25, 1990, in Hollywood at their friend Mark Kern's house *without* Gardocki, the guitarist exited on friendly terms. For the four-song demo — which was never publicly released — Finn handled guitar, bass, and vocal duties while Wilson did the drumming on a Roland Octopad. The tunes were "M.F. Toe," "Crap," "Furry," and "Lick Paint."

By November of that year the pair continued rehearsing, with their friend Matt Sharp joining in on occasion. Sharp, then a resident of

Westwood, first met up with Wilson and Finn in the spring of 1990 and
the three developed a close friendship in the ensuing months.

Matt Sharp

On September 22, 1969, original Weezer bassist and falsetto provider
Matthew Sharp was born in Bangkok, Thailand, and reared in Arlington,
Virginia. "The first year of my life I lived in Bangkok and my parents traveled
through Europe for a while before we ended up in Arlington," said Matt.

By 1978, nine-year-old Matt joined the record-buying public when he
plunked down a dollar and change of his own money for a vinyl 45 of "Le
Freak" by Chic. Sharp said his fourth grade classmates were the benefac-
tors. "The reason I bought it was we were all supposed to bring in a piece
of music to school that we could roller skate to. So I had to go out and buy
a piece of music that would be good to skate to. When I bought that, I won
the battle. We listened to that song over and over. I have this distinct memory of going in circles and listening to 'Le Freak' on those cheap
elementary school clamp-on skates."

When Matt was fourteen, he "used to spray Right Guard on a cheap
imitation Fender bass, light it on fire, and run around in the front yard and
pretend to be Geezer Butler. The neighbors loved that." Finding himself
drawn to a variety of music, but including thrash bands that would hybrid
punk and metal like Suicidal Tendencies and D.R.I. (a.k.a. Dirty Rotten
Imbeciles), Sharp went from being a follower to participant within a year.

"When I was younger I tried out for a plethora of crossover bands that
were in that D.R.I. sort of place," Sharp revealed. "I always wanted to play
really fast music like that and I never could do it. I could never keep up.
My arm would just tire out and I just didn't have the stamina for music that
was that spastic. There was a band called Rancid Decay and there was a
band called Wreckage when I was roughly fifteen or sixteen. I loved the

name Rancid Decay, that was fucking incredible. But I never lasted and I always got booted really quick."

Sick of an endless radio diet of Pink Floyd, Black Sabbath, and Lynyrd Skynyrd in an era where no alternatives to the album-oriented rock format existed in Arlington, Sharp contended he split to California at age sixteen, ending up in San Diego. "[Classic rock] used to drive me crazy," Matt said. "In Virginia, they had twenty classic rock stations, pounding it into my brain."

In late 1989, around the time Avant Garde became Zoom, and after kicking around up and down the West Coast for a few years, Sharp found himself fronting a goth-like outfit called The Clique. Inspired by The Cure and Joy Division, Sharp and some temporary musical associations laid down a demo that he packaged as a cassette maxi-single. It consisted of three different mixes of the band's lone tune, "Ice Butterfly." Asked about the project more than a dozen years after the fact, Sharp laughed, "I wouldn't call that a band. A band to me would have to be anything that lasts beyond two weeks."

Band or not, six months later, having befriended the two Pats, Matt put his Robert Smith fixations aside and began creating music with Finn and Wilson as a member of Bush. In tandem with Bush and inspired by They Might Be Giants, Sharp and Wilson also began creating a number of "goofy" recordings on Matt's 4-track at an apartment the two Pats shared in the 300 block of Genessee Avenue. It was here that compositions like "This One's for Pat," "Mi Amor Bandito/Kooky Spanish Song," and the divorce ode "Ugh We March" were concocted with guffaws in mind.

By the spring of 1991, Wilson, Finn, and Sharp's primary group, now renamed The Wrong Sausage, had acquired a new guitarist, twenty-one-year-old guitarist and Oakland native, Jason Cropper. Cropper had previously been playing in the Northern California band Brotherhood Groove Grand Junction.

Jason Cropper

Jason Cropper was born on June 27, 1971, and raised in the San Francisco Bay Area. "I lived in Oakland until the end of eleventh grade. When my parents divorced I went to live with my dad in Santa Rosa," Cropper explained.

While Cropper refused to reveal the first record he actually walked into a store and bought ("To tell you that would be so embarrassing," he said), he proudly spoke of "two great, stellar records" he received as birthday gifts. "I think it was for my thirteenth birthday — and this was my fondest memory of receiving records for gifts — that I got cassettes, because I had a Walkman. It was Def Leppard's *Pyromania* and *Back in Black* by AC/DC."

Those hard rock leanings accompanied him into adolescence, although he began playing an instrument much later than his Wrong Sausage bandmates. "I didn't pick up the guitar until I was, like, sixteen," Jason confessed. "At the time, I was into Jimi Hendrix, Led Zeppelin, Deep Purple, Black Sabbath, all of those kind of bad '60s hard rock bands."

After moving to Santa Rosa for his senior year of high school, Cropper began listening to a completely different segment of the rock genre. "When I moved for my senior year in the suburbs, all my friends there were into the Descendents and Dag Nasty, and things like Bad Religion, NOFX, that kind of real American second generation punk rock," Jason remembered. "I had only gone to concerts, where I had seen The Police and Genesis and Iron Maiden, but then I went to see Primus and Victim's Family and Green Day — while they were still on Lookout! Records. And that kind of helped me to realize, 'Oh. You can be like a miniature rock star. You don't have to be larger than life. You can wear normal clothes and turn your guitar up loud and get a distortion pedal, and if you can get enough of your friends to go — maybe some of the other people who show up will think you're something special.'

"I think it's a pretty standard transition for kids on the West Coast," Jason said of his shift from commercial and classic rock to independent punk. "The comparison I can draw is [Nirvana's] Kurt Cobain — who went from being into stuff like Sammy Hagar and then it was something way more anti-social or anti-establishment. Although I was always way more into the melodic punk than the anti-establishment stuff."

By his freshman semester of community college up in Santa Rosa, Cropper was studying jazz improvisation and taking some forestry classes, considering a career as a forest ranger. He took a stab at songwriting in his free time, and although he lacked confidence, he was determined to give it a try. "I didn't know what I was doing as far as writing songs," he admitted, "but I would make up little ideas and record them into a little one-speaker tape recorder thing, and then I would try to play lead guitar solos over the top of these chord progressions."

After bumming around Santa Rosa for a while, Cropper was introduced to Patrick Finn through a mutual friend from Sebastopol named Jesse, who knew the guitarist was looking to meet other musicians. "Pat Finn's mom lived in Petaluma and he had some desk job in Sonoma County somewhere," said Jason. "I had lived in this house I was renting by then with these Northern California types and I knew he played bass. He came by and he was really skilled, so I watched him play my guitar — just sitting around playing on my guitar just hanging out — and I was just really impressed with his technical ability. He played this intricate jazz-funk or whatever, and I just thought that was really cool. He convinced me that it was a good idea that I move to Los Angeles and play with him in a band that he was putting together with a guy named Pat Wilson. And it was gonna be called The Wrong Sausage.

"The whole thing with the name had to do with this Pat Finn guy, who was like this East Coast, many-generation Irish-descent young man becoming a Muslim. The thought was if he ate the wrong sausage he might not get into paradise," laughed Cropper. "I don't know, I never really thought it through at the time. But anyway we started jamming together.

"So Finn introduced me to Pat Wilson over the telephone and he's like, 'Yeah. Come down to L.A. and maybe I can get you this job at this place where I'm a telemarketer and I sell dog shampoo,'" Cropper remembered, still chuckling. "Then he told me it paid like ten bucks an hour, and I was thinking to myself how that was righteous money for a nineteen-year-old. It was too much; I had to do it. Plus, my grandmother lived in Pasadena, so I figured I could fall back on her for laundry or a place to sleep, especially if I didn't dig it and wanted to bail out before coming back to Northern California. So one day we just loaded up all of my personal belongings — which by then was mostly guitars and amps and a couple bags of clothes — into [Pat Finn's] Ford Escort, and I went."

Almost simultaneously, a post-Zoom Rivers hacked off his nipple-length hair and began pouring his heart out into his 4-track recorder. During the winter of '90–'91, the prolific, serious-minded twenty-year-old wrote songs with titles like "You Overpower Me," "Anything for You," and "Xmas in L.A.," the latter a musical letter home about being away from New England for the holidays.

Forming a band called Fuzz as an outlet for his new, post-metal compositions, Cuomo's new group featured Pat Wilson behind the drum kit. Rivaling the heavy crunch of Soundgarden and Mudhoney, Fuzz dissolved after three months, but not before playing two shows and laying down a five-song demo tape. The tunes — "Answer Man," "Ain't Got No Words," "The Biggest Animal," "I Will Not Cross Over," and "Spiderbitch" — were recorded in one session at a rented rehearsal space on Rivers' newly acquired 8-track machine.

"[Finn and I] came out here and just sort of bounced around, tried to start a couple of different bands," said Pat Wilson of this era. "When you're in your twenties you start to find things out, like, 'Oh man, I don't want this, and I *certainly* don't want what that guy wants.' Eventually you wind up meeting people with similar interests, and hopefully you all become focused on a general idea that you can take somewhere. I met Rivers not long after we got out here. He was leaving this kind of prog-metal band, and he was going through a big change in his life too. He had bought a cassette 8-track and was interning in a studio.

"By that time I had met Matt Sharp," Wilson said, "and we were trying to figure out something to do. We had a lot of passion and interest in certain kinds of music, but we didn't know how that was going to translate into what we were going to do. So we met Rivers — 'He's got an 8-track, let's get with *him*' — and we convinced him to move into this apartment with us. Rivers was just starting to write songs and he asked me to play drums on a song for him. That turned into a band called Fuzz, with this girl bass player. That was pretty cool, but it had to die."

"I ended up in this apartment in the Fairfax district of Los Angeles with the two Pats," Cropper says of his pre-Weezer days. "We referred to them at the time as 'Little Pat,' who was the one who brought me, and 'Big Pat,' who was Patrick Wilson. Matt Sharp also lived there, and Rivers Cuomo. So I met those guys, and that was where Weezer started. We all lived under the same roof, but it was very short-lived."

Matt was also briefly involved in the same telephone occupation as Wilson and Cropper. "I did have a short stint of selling 'luxury' dog shampoo — and tanning lotion — over the phone with Pat Wilson by my side slinging the junk to whoever would buy it. That's when we tried to write a song called 'Get People to Buy What They Don't Need.' The only words were, 'get people to buy what they don't need' and 'that's my job!', that's my job!' and it just repeated over and over again."

By the end of the 1991 spring semester, Rivers was pulling straight A's at Los Angeles City College. With his 4.0 average and the recommendation of his English professor — after writing a thirty-three-page term paper criticizing the United States' meat-based diet — Cuomo had little trouble being accepted into Santa Monica College for the fall.

Rivers spent his twenty-first birthday celebrating with Matt at a small drinking establishment and rock club on Melrose at the corner of Gower called Small's. Just days later, in the early summer of 1991, a fresh college graduate named Karl Koch came west in his 1988 Ford Bronco 2. The Buffalo-area native and future Weezer ally, webmaster, band historian, and unofficial fifth member wound up shacking up with the two Pats and Jason Cropper in a newly acquired apartment on Stoner Avenue.

"I was introduced to Pat Wilson in Buffalo by Pat Finn, shortly before they took off to L.A.," remembered Koch. "A year later I followed and Pat [Finn] introduced me to Matt, Rivers, and Jason. [And] Pat and Jason were very messy roommates."

According to Karl, Finn — the man who played him bands like The Clash, Devo, Wall of Voodoo, Talking Heads, and Bob Marley in the eighth grade, and Black Flag, the Circle Jerks, and The Minutemen two years later — urged him to head west to California. "He said, 'You gotta come out here, man. Whatever you want to do, this is the place to do it.' I was like, 'Alright.' So I kinda packed up, against my own parents' wishes."

Just as Koch was making his entrance, Matt Sharp — seeking a break from L.A. — moved north to Berkeley to pursue what Karl calls, "some sorta symphonic keyboard sequencing music." Rivers also relocated to a tiny apartment on Urban Avenue in West Los Angeles, within walking distance of the Stoner Ave. crew and midway between an often-frequented Taco Bell at the intersection of Pico and Bundy.

"When Matt moved to Northern California, and Rivers transferred to Santa Monica College and moved to West L.A., Pat Wilson insisted that we follow him," Cropper remembers of the move. "So we got an apartment over there on Stoner. By this time I did have a job as a telemarketer selling dog shampoo with 'Big Pat' for ten bucks an hour, but that lasted like, three paychecks, and the company started to go out of business. So they said, 'Okay. You're all fired, but you can have your job back at minimum wage' — which was, like, $3.25 an hour. And I was like, 'Screw this.' So I went and got a job as a cook at an Italian restaurant/deli, and we still weren't playing in a band with Rivers, but he was around and there was music going on. I actually got him a job as a dishwasher/busboy/custodian at this place."

"Rivers was in school and we were all having these shitty jobs, just doing our thing and living in this really nasty-ass apartment, and having fun," Koch said. "Everybody had a band with somebody at some point. It was like this band to that band to this band to that band. Like every night it was like, 'Oh, I'm playing with Joe Shmoe and we're playing this show with this band.'"

The guys were involved with a seemingly endless rotation of musical projects at this time, including a punk/glam hybrid known as The Dum Dums and its offshoot undertaking, a joke death-metal group dubbed United Dirt. Featuring former Bush-mate Tom Gardocki, two future Stoner Ave. roommates named Bob and Vaughn, and Matt Sharp and Pat Wilson (and later Pat Finn when Matt headed upstate), The Dum Dums dressed like Hollywood's post-grunge metal holdovers. A goof on the Sunset Strip bands of the time, the group's material included titles like "Junior Is a Skin Head" and "Mommy Is in the Rehab." Sharp and Wilson also incorporated a sidesplitting 'fat man' shtick into performances, where they would cavort around the stage, donning enormous clothes stuffed with pillows.

HEATHER CONLEY

Pat Finn, Tom Gardocki (a.k.a. Soda, later of Wax), and Pat Wilson pose for a United Dirt promo shot in 1990

"I kind of wish I had met up with some of Rivers' new crowd a little sooner," said Justin Fisher, ex–Avant Garde bassist. "He was hanging out with Matt Sharp and Pat and a bunch of people from Chicago who had a cool scene happening. Along with the guys in Wax, they were becoming kind of big in town, reinventing themselves out of the '80s metal scene. The Dum Dums were this great, cool, fun punk band."

Similarly, United Dirt was Finn and Wilson's foul-mouthed spoof on death metal acts like Exodus and Venom. Also featuring Bob and Vaughn, U.D. played out only once, as an encore to The Dum Dums. But with shocking titles juxtaposing religious figures with sexual acts among the group's terribly offensive six-song repertoire, it's probably a good thing.

"I don't know if we even liked each other very much," Matt Sharp said of these early days. "We just kind of lived together for nine months or a year and then we all went our separate ways. I moved to San Francisco and they moved to different places." Sharp was living in El Cerrito, outside of Berkeley.

"I lived on San Pablo Avenue in a studio apartment above a tropical fish store," Sharp remembered. "It kind of looked like a place that Humphrey

Bogart would have used as an office in one of those old detective flicks. I spent nine months moping around listening to the Cocteau Twins, reading depressing books I probably couldn't understand, working at The Berkeley Hat Company, and as Morrissey said, wearing 'black on the outside, because black is how I feel on the inside.' Oh, woe-was-me."

Back on Urban Avenue, Cuomo's portable 8-track recorder resulted in a number of sonic collaborations with the Stoner Ave. crew. Among the results, nonsensical sonic concoctions from Rivers and Pat Wilson like "The Pop Screen" and "What's Goin' On?" plus Rivers' own introspective pieces such as "Sing to Me Slow" and "I Got So Many Problems." These shared efforts evolved into what became Sixty Wrong Sausages with Rivers now officially in the line-up by August of 1991. Bassist Finn, guitarist Cuomo, and drummer Wilson traded off vocal duties, while Cropper and Cuomo alternated lead and rhythm guitar responsibilities. As far as the name change goes, Karl Koch remembered the band deciding, "No, it can't be just one wrong sausage. It needs to be, like, SIXTY Wrong Sausages."

Rather than be bogged down in endless rehearsals and live shows, the Sausages focused on creating a demo tape that September. With no room for drums in Rivers' minute apartment, Wilson had to forgo his actual drum kit and put the drums to tape using his Roland OctoPad, an electronic drum surface. "The demo took several weeks," Koch recollected, "sessions squeezed into school and work schedules." The end product was the four-song *Cholesterol* EP, which housed "Evil Nest," a Finn composition held over from the Bush days, the amusing and infectious "Been Gi," plus two Wilson-sung items, "Mega Man" and "Workplace" — the latter with Cuomo on drums.

Alongside his new primary group, Rivers kept busy by assisting his friends and former Avant Garde bandmates, helping his longtime friend Justin Fisher — who still lived in L.A. — cut demos, including the song "If

You Would," on his 8-track. Cuomo also assisted his former Avant Garde singer Kevin Ridel, who was recording an album of Christian rock that autumn with his band The Truth. Serving predominantly as engineer, Cuomo also aided with back-up vocals and guitars on tunes like "My Salvation," "Eyes of the Children," and "I Belong to God."

Ridel had some vacancies in the line-up and according to Karl, "he asked Rivers to play bass, and Pat Finn to play guitar," as they performed at least one gig at The Whiskey in Hollywood. Certainly for Pat Finn, his participation in The Truth was quite a contrast to his involvement with United Dirt.

Sixty Wrong Sausages held a total of seven practices between October 20 and November 20 of 1991, following the completion of their "full band demo." Honing the live execution of *Cholesterol* material, plus song titles like "The Barnaby Jones," "Run the Gamut," and "Tennis Ball," the group also worked on Bush holdovers like "Beyond Life" and "Crayon Man." Fuzz remnants like "Answer Man" and "Burn My Britches" were also in their repertoire, while the Wilson–Finn-penned "Sheriff Wong" (about a bong-toting member of law enforcement) retained their offbeat sense of humor.

The pinnacle of these efforts came over Thanksgiving weekend 1991, when Rivers, Jason, and Karl drove north to The Phoenix Theatre in Petaluma, where Sixty Wrong Sausages performed its lone gig. Three months later, Finn would be out, Sharp would be in, and an entirely new batch of songs would change the sonic direction of the group.

"Shortly after the first and only Sixty Wrong Sausages show, the band was no more," remembered Koch of December 1991. "Pat Finn was going through some weird times, and Rivers was losing interest in the band, finding more excitement in his own new songs." Cuomo and Wilson, inspired by the sounds of Nirvana and the Pixies, united to write fifty new songs between them that would drive their new, unnamed band.

"Eventually Rivers said, 'Look, we're going to write fifty songs, and then we're going to have our first rehearsal,'" Wilson recalled. "When we eventually got to the rehearsal, it was a historic thing for us. It was like, 'this is so much fun I can't even believe it; let's just make it official.'"

Around this time, Cuomo was wrapping up his first semester at Santa Monica College, where he was taking a music appreciation class. Here, Rivers eventually made such an impression on the music department chair that he was awarded a scholarship recommendation letter regarding his desire to major in English. A similar letter extolling Cuomo's academic excellence was also written by his contemporary European Literature professor.

If Wilson and Cuomo never made it to fifty tunes, they came close by including Rivers' old Fuzz songs. However, old Bush and Sixty Wrong Sausages material was considered off base and discarded as contenders for this new project, which got underway in December of '91. Cuomo's material for the fifty-song project veered from silly fodder like "Cheesewheel," "Wet Dog," and "Make Me a Pallet" to relationship-minded titles like "Why Do We Hurt Each Other?" and "Close Your Eyes and Gimme a Kiss." Although Pat did cook up titles like "Jessica" and "It's Not the Same," Rivers was clearly beginning to dominate in the arena of song craft, cooking up sketches of early Weezer staples like "Thief, You've Taken All that Was Me" and "Lullaby for Wayne," plus the future Weezer classic "Undone." Meanwhile, "The World Has Turned and Left Me Here" and "My Name Is Jonas," both of which would eventually surface on Weezer's 1994 debut album, were bona fide collaborations between Cuomo and Wilson, with the latter also featuring structural input from Cropper.

And according to Cropper, Rivers — who sensed alternative music was about to explode — was obsessed with getting his songs right, even at this stage in the game. When the two worked together at the aforementioned Italian restaurant in Los Angeles where Cuomo washed dishes, he remembers when they both heard Nirvana's "Smells Like Teen Spirit" on the radio for the first time. Stupefied, they both absorbed the song. When it was over, Rivers started to become incensed that it was Kurt Cobain — not himself — who had written the song's contagious, simple, and faultless riff.

"My fondest, pre-Weezer memory is I'm cooking, Rivers is cleaning, and we're both standing in the same kitchen, and that song comes on the radio, in like the first week of its release, and Rivers says, 'I should have written that.' And I'm like, 'Yeah. That's totally true.' Because the music he was writing was improving in quality every day. Every day he wrote a better song."

The musically meticulous Rivers had a game plan. "We wanted to write a bunch of tunes before we even played together, so that we could have an idea of where we were heading before we started wasting our time and money paying for a rehearsal studio," he explained. "I didn't want to get back into a band until I felt like I had a bunch of songs that were good and that had cohesive style. So I just wrote songs and didn't play at all for a long time. 'Undone,' 'Jonas,' 'Only in Dreams,' and 'The World Has Turned and Left Me Here' were all written before we even played together."

Pat Wilson was so pleased with the results of his work with Rivers and Jason that he brought the material from "The 50 Song Project" to the attention of his old friend Matt Sharp as he passed through Berkeley in January 1992. "He said, 'You should listen to this tape,'" recalled Matt. "'It's some stuff that Rivers and I are writing together.'" Sharp liked what he heard and followed Wilson back down to Los Angeles with his bass in hand. By mid-February 1992, following their first practice, Weezer — consisting of Cuomo, Wilson, Cropper, and Sharp — was officially a band.

chapter seven

in the garage

O n Valentine's Day 1992, a day where lovers cuddled globally, four L.A. transplants gathered together at T.K. Rehearsal Studios to practice for the first time. More than just acquaintances, these friends and room-mates were so enthusiastic that they practiced for several days in a row, recording the fourteen songs they jammed on during their third practice. While the band was without a handle at this early stage, names that Rivers, Pat, Matt, and Jason were kicking around included "Meathead," "Outhouse," "Hummingbird," "The Big Jones," and "This Niblet," as well as the previously utilized "Fuzz."

"When we first started practicing, I mean from our very first rehearsal, I thought to myself, 'We're amazing. This is incredible. Everybody's going to love us,'" Cuomo admitted almost a decade after these rehearsals.

"We were doing this just because we liked the music," remembered Matt Sharp. "Not because we were all great at what we did. It was like, 'Wow, we suck. We don't know how to play well at all and we're not together.' When we played it was like everybody going for it and not knowing what they were doing. [It was] just us having fun, butchering these songs that we'd written. But it was probably the most pure experience I'd been through as far as dealing with people. It was great!"

After five weeks of enthusiastic practices, the band made its live debut at Raji's Bar and Ribshack on Hollywood Boulevard, when they were suddenly asked to open for actor Keanu Reeves' new rock outfit Dogstar.

"Apparently there was no show booked that night at all, and when Dogstar asked to, there was a need for some opening acts to try and beef up the draw earlier on in the night," recollected Karl Koch. "Meanwhile the as-yet-unnamed Weezer was itching to start playing out, and started calling around that day to try and book some gigs. The guy at Raji's said, 'How about tonight?' and so it was. They only needed to come up with a band name at this point, and a major brainstorming session ensued. In the end, Rivers stuck with his 'Weezer' suggestion, and everyone else couldn't quite come up with something that sounded more distinctive. The band called everyone they knew and got seventeen people to show up and watch. Not bad!"

"[That was] the first club show I ever played," remembered Matt Sharp. "Raji's — that place went down in the earthquake. Weezer was opening for 'Rico Suave' Keanu Reeves and Dogstar."

Among the songs played during Weezer's premiere gig were "I Can't Forget the Way," "Undone," "The World Has Turned and Left Me Here," and "The Biggest Animal." At Pat's suggestion, the band also performed "M.E.," a cover of a Gary Numan tune, in which he and Rivers traded instruments and roles. Attendees were witnesses to the first public display of Rivers Cuomo's urgently raw songs. Ushered along by the rhythm axis of Wilson and Sharp, the acoustic strums of Cropper, and the blistering riff work of the frontman himself, this fractured pop style — augmented by lyrics that veered from ridiculous to emotionally honest — would eventually be a formula for unexpected success.

"When we first started, we didn't really have any expectations of anything," Sharp later acknowledged. "We weren't in it to get signed or anything. We were just like, 'Let's just do this because we like the songs.'"

But, of these early songs, Rivers confessed, "most of them sucked." Still, he said, "it became a habit that stuck with me. Because I'm so terrible at

HEATHER CONLEY

Jason Cropper, Pat Wilson, Rivers Cuomo, and Matt Sharp
on Weezer's first photo shoot in 1992

expressing my feelings directly, and because no one really cares, and because anything real is impossible to talk about, [I'd] come to rely on music more and more to express myself."

Aside from marking Weezer's live performance debut at Raji's, March 19, 1992, also signified moving day for Sharp, Cuomo, and Justin Fisher, who spent their first night at the "Amherst House" — located at 2226 Amherst Avenue in West Los Angeles. The garage of this house would quickly become home to nearly all of Weezer's rehearsals and demo making, and — some three years later — the notorious shooting location for the band's "Say It Ain't So" video clip.

"Right when Weezer was getting together for the first time, Matt had been called back down from San Francisco and I needed a place to stay and Rivers had been renting a room," said Fisher. "So I said, 'we should all get a house where we can have bands practice and stuff.' Then the three of us found this amazing house in West L.A. that had a garage and we convinced the Japanese landlords that we were UCLA film students who'd make a lot of noise, and for some reason they gave us the house."

But, said Justin, living with members of the newly christened Weezer meant getting hazed for having a passé metal look in between meals of noodles and toast. "At the time I still had super-boomin' long hair from back in the day and I can remember one time where Rivers and Matt were just like jumping up and down on top of me with scissors and they were like, 'Cut your fuckin' hair, cut your fuckin' hair!'"

Subsequent gigs during "No Bozo Jam Nights" at Whiskey A Go-Go in Hollywood on March 30 and April 13 followed, with the first of many acoustic shows also going down at the 8121 club on April 7. For the stripped-down performances, Wilson would play his hi-hat and snare with brushes, Sharp would turn the volume on his bass way down, and Cropper and Cuomo used acoustic guitars as they worked through "Undone," "The World Has Turned and Left Me Here," "Thief, You've Taken All that Was Me," and "Let's Sew Our Pants Together."

In addition to frequently taping and often videotaping these landmark performances, Karl Koch was a handy friend to the band. He had a knack for flyer artistry and a reliable Bronco 2. Said Koch, "I just started driving them all around 'cause nobody had a car and they needed some way to get their gear there. It was just like hanging out with your friends. I mean, they had all these schemes. Everybody wants to get a record deal and be a band but [for] so many of the early bands, it just wasn't gonna happen for them. It just took a long time for a combination to click."

Weezer continued to practice at their house on Amherst Avenue into May and June, playing acoustic gigs at 8121 and introducing new tunes like "Say It Ain't So"; "Simply State (and the Girl Will Follow You)," which housed a guitar riff recycled four years later as "El Scorcho"; and "Paperface" (a "dead" song now widely circulated via the Internet) to their repertoire.

Electric gigs at Club Dump with Wax (then signed to Caroline Records), Joyride, Black Market Flowers, Crash Course, and English Acid were bolstered by their first official demo. Designed to get Weezer booked into other clubs in Los Angeles and distributed as such, the three-song tape consisted of "Thief, You've Taken All that Was Me," "Let's Sew Our Pants Together," and "The World Has Turned and Left Me Here." Produced through Cuomo's 8-track with the whole band recording their parts in layers, Karl Koch called it "the best recording they'd made to date, but they were still a little shaky."

Few people outside of their L.A. clique took notice as the band began to gel in mid-'92. "We would just play, and if we got a following, we did, and if we didn't, we didn't," Matt Sharp said. "And we didn't. It was pretty much no expectations for anything; we just basically didn't have anything better to do. And we all sucked, me especially."

"Nobody would come to our shows, for months and months and months, and it seemed like forever," Rivers remembered. "And I remember just being totally shocked at how little people responded to us, because I thought we were so good. I mean, we were playing the same songs that eventually became big hits, like 'The Sweater Song' and 'Say It Ain't So,' and we'd play 'em out in the L.A. clubs and everyone would just be like, 'Go away. We want a grunge band.'"

In an era where grunge acts like Nirvana, Soundgarden, and Alice in

Chains ruled, the band's assessment of itself was pretty bleak. "We would always be last slot on the bill at 1 a.m. when everyone was leaving. So we had really low self-esteem," added Cuomo. "We weren't part of a happening scene. At the time, there were a lot of pseudo-grunge bands in L.A., and it was hard to find our audience.

"It was really strange at first, because the whole Sunset Strip scene, which was basically bands just arriving from Idaho who play like Poison or Guns N' Roses, was still happening," Rivers continued. "The whole rest of the city was copying the Seattle sound, so it was really hard. We'd end up playing with all these other bands that sounded nothing like us. We'd play a gig every week without fail, and it was really depressing because we just weren't building a following at all."

"We were terrible live," Pat Wilson candidly expanded on these early months. "We were constantly out of tune, the tempos weren't solid, and the singing was naff at best." Playing to empty houses throughout much of 1992, Sharp said, "it was the same five to ten friends who would show up because they felt guilty; they didn't want the club to be completely empty."

"I can remember Rivers and Pat and Matt sitting around in the kitchen until four in the morning after, dissecting those club shows, just trying to tighten things up with the band," Justin Fisher remembered. "Just analyzing who might have hit a bad note here, or who missed a part there. That kind of thing."

"We would just play in our garage and, like, once a week, play a show," said Matt. "Nobody would show up. And then we'd go back to the garage and play more and play a show the next week and still nobody would show up. Maybe seven people would come to see us, but usually it was right around three."

A pair of shows at Hollywood's Coconut Teaszer on July 27 and August 12 — the first of two dates with Transcendental Hayride — sandwiched

Weezer's second crack at a demo tape. Known to those who frequent Internet file-sharing services like Kazaa as *The Kitchen Tape*, the sessions for this demo cassette took place on August 1, 1992. "This was a more serious attempt at getting a demo put down on tape," noted Koch. "The name *The Kitchen Tape* started because the drums were recorded in the kitchen, adjacent to the garage. This sounded good but sure bummed out the neighbors."

The Kitchen Tape was created in an effort to secure gigs and an attempt to make an impact on the local scene. As Koch later reported, "There were no aspirations yet to try and generate real label interest, but the concept of 'creating a buzz' was being thrown around."

Of the eight songs finalized in these sessions for the demo, five — "Let's Sew Our Pants Together," "Thief, You've Taken All that Was Me," "My Name Is Jonas," "Paperface," and "Only in Dreams" — have been bootlegged into MP3s and can be located online. "The World Has Turned and Left Me Here," "Say It Ain't So," and "Undone" were also included on *The Kitchen Tape*, but have yet to surface in bootleg circles. Another track, "I Said So," was also demoed, possibly with Rivers on all instruments, but did not make the final cut and is assumed lost.

Marking Matt's recorded vocal debut, as he added his now legendary falsetto to "Say It Ain't So," Koch reported later that *The Kitchen Tape* was "distributed as is, and with the three songs from the earlier session integrated as well. Most had all eight songs, I think. In any case, only a handful of copies really got out, perhaps ten or twenty total, all copied at home." In 1996, Cropper compared the demo to some of the lo-fi efforts of Guided By Voices, noting Rivers' shift from groups like Kiss and Judas Priest to the Velvet Underground, the Beach Boys, and The Beatles.

Further solo 8-track recordings put to tape by Rivers during July and August 1992 included titles like "The Purification of Water," "Please Sweet Peepers," "Why Do We Hurt Each Other?" and "The Bottle of

HEATHER CONLEY

In The Garden of Weezer:
Rivers, Matt, Jason, and Pat get some shade

Wine Song," the latter which made it to Weezer's live set on one occasion for a Coconut Teaszer gig during the same era. Most notable among these new compositions, however, was "No One Else," which Rivers penned that August. It, too, would later surface on the band's major label debut.

That August the band played its first-ever out-of-area dates. On the heels of a second Coconut Teaszer gig, a four-day trek to Northern California marked dates at Marsuggi's in San Jose on the 13, the Power Station in Eureka on the 14, and an outdoor party with Cropper's former band, Brotherhood Groove Grand Junction, in Gurneville on the 16.

By the 15 of September, after six months and one day of rehearsals and live gigs, the foursome finally began to hit its live performance stride during a repeat gig at the Teaszer. Describing that night's Weezer gig as "a turning point for the band," observer Karl Koch said, "they played tighter than ever before [and] had a better sound."

"I remember Matt and I just finally collapsing, like, nine months into the whole thing and just looking at each other and saying, 'We must be crazy,'" Rivers said in 2001. "'We must have bad taste,' because we thought this was cool and nobody else is getting it. 'We might as well just give up.'"

"We just kind of kept playing in L.A. and just rotating the songs a lot until we figured out what we liked the best," said Sharp, of the band's persistence. "Our theory or whatever that we practiced was *never sell anything, never try to push anything on anybody*. And that's sort of why nobody ever came to see us. We just wanted to do it pretty organic. . . . So we just kept playing and playing until people started showing up."

chapter eight

92–93

Working the Hollywood circuit, the friends and members of Weezer spent the autumn of 1992 posting and handing out photocopied flyers promoting gigs at area clubs like Ghengis Cohen, Coconut Teaszer, Lingerie, Club Dump, and the Huntington Beach venue 5092. With their fanbase on the L.A. club circuit slowly expanding, the band planned and executed a follow-up to *The Kitchen Tape* that November.

Dubbed *The Real Demo*, this four-song cassette consisted of "No One Else," "The World Has Turned and Left Me Here," "Say It Ain't So," and "Undone — The Sweater Song," all of which would later surface on Weezer's 1994 DGC debut. Some copies also boasted an "unfinished" take of "Surf Wax America" on the tape's flip side, but because the members of Weezer were unsatisfied with the way it turned out this addendum was circulated only among friends.

Engineered by Jon Pikus, a familiar face on the L.A. scene at the time due to his participation in El Magnifico (and later The Campfire Girls), *The Real Demo* was recorded over two days at what Karl Koch called "a weird little 16-track studio in Hollywood." According to Koch, the demo was recorded on the cheap, "meaning, give speakers to the engineer," and stated that the band "could have worked faster but the studio was being 'borrowed' without the knowledge of the owner."

The version of "Undone" on *The Real Demo* featured Koch's first-ever studio assistance, as he provided a brief series of snippets for the first two verses of the song that he extracted from "various weird records." Among them, he culled a Darth Vader quote from *Star Wars* in which the character intones, "You are part of the rebel alliance, and a traitor," plus quotes from *The Hobbit* movie and "some other bits of nonsense," said Koch. "The band also did the talking thing and the result was pretty chaotic."

"Jon was a capable, but not gifted, engineer," continued Koch, speaking of future Columbia Records A&R man Pikus. "The tape, while being the best-yet representation of the band, was still flawed by sonic strangeness, such as a snare drum that sounded like a tennis ball hitting a racket at Wimbledon." The result was Weezer's first attempt to land music industry attention, and the group circulated close to three hundred copies of *The Real Demo* to labels, lawyers, producers, talent scouts, and friends. Three printings of roughly one hundred each were made with a succession of light blue, green, and yellow labels for each printing.

Not only novel for Koch's "random and hilarious bits" on "Undone" — the need for which Karl says Pikus failed to understand — the November '92 recording session also birthed the now legendary "=w=" symbol. "Capitalized by Pat and seconds later put into existence by me," Koch remembered the sign was "first drawn into the purple velvet wall rug, then in light blue tape on the back of Rivers' shirt."

Winding down the year with shows at familiar L.A. venues like Club Dump and English Acid, the lads made their debut at the Alligator Lounge in late November. A significant date in the history of Weezer soon followed, when the group shared the stage with Beggars Banquet recording artists Carnival Art at Club Lingerie on the night of December 11, 1992. Making the acquaintance of guitarist Brian Bell for the first time that night, Rivers and Matt came away from the gig impressed with what they heard and saw from Brian, and, as Karl Koch put it, "The memory of this event would play a major role in the band in another ten months."

Ringing in 1993 with more shows throughout January at their typical haunts, Rivers, Pat, Matt, and Jason played their first show at a venue called Music Machine on February 20 with That Dog. The two bands became fast friends, sharing bills throughout Los Angeles that spring at English Acid, Al's Bar, and at a Rhino Records in-store appearance.

On the songwriting front, Rivers was actively working through titles like "Please Pick Up the Phone" (which was an early draft of what would become "Mykel & Carli"), "Afraid of What We Need the Most/Keep Your Distance," "When You're Near Me" (an "a cappella doo-wop style thing"), "Jamie," "Left My Broken Heart In Carolina," and a drastic reworking of "Lullaby for Wayne" during February and March of '93, with the latter making its way into the band's live set by April. Pat, meanwhile, concocted compositions like "Show Me How to Ride This Thing," "I've Thrown It All Away," and "Don't Quit Your Day Job."

Pat and Jason had also put some goofy tunes to tape that spring, recording an amusing rap song, "Techno Ono," under the handle Black Plant Forceps. Another tune, "Song for Los Angeles," fused local news snippets with instrumentation. Later, Wilson linked up with old buddy Pat Finn at his apartment to put some music to tape. The fruits of their collective labor spawned a five-part monstrosity known as "Caffeine Saga."

Throughout April 1993, Rivers kept busy working out covers to The Beatles' "If I Fell," and the Beach Boys' "Don't Worry Baby," altering the pitch settings on his 8-track to reach the high notes his natural vocal range couldn't achieve. He also started carving out new material like "Ode to Pat Finn," which was a barbershop quartet–styled song in honor of his former bandmate, and "Punk Rock Girl," which paid tribute to his gal pals in That Dog. The friendship between the bands was mostly due to the fact that they were both chasing the same thing — a record deal.

Three-quarters female — consisting of singer/guitarist Anna

Waronker, siblings Rachel and Petra Haden on bass and violin, and drummer Tony Maxwell — the members of That Dog succeeded in beating Weezer to the punch, releasing a debut double 7″ in late '92 on the tiny independent Magnatone Records. When the single earned That Dog the courtship of major labels in the spring of '93, attending A&R scouts got more than they bargained for and wound up witnessing impressive sets by Weezer at shared club gigs. This in turn scored Cuomo, Wilson, Sharp, and Cropper label interest of their own.

Much of the hype around That Dog was initially attributed to the fact that, besides being a kick-ass punk-pop band in their own right, the female members already had a music pedigree. Anna was the daughter of the legendary music producer (and, at the time, Warner Bros. Records chief) Lenny Waronker and Rachel and Petra were two of the triplet daughters of jazz stalwart Charlie Haden. Weezer shared the benefits of these associations when both bands would eventually sign to the same major record label within weeks of each other a few months later. Despite the interest of record companies, Weezer's fanbase was relatively minimal at the time, hovering at a core of about twenty-five loyalists.

"Weezer wasn't really popular in town for most of the time they were around until after they got signed," Justin Fisher remembered. "Some of the time [the audience] would be the occasional record company people, but mostly just a few dozen of our friends. They'd play late at night after other, more popular grunge-based bands like Transcendental Hayride and Black Market Flowers. Matt and Rivers used to come home really late at night after their gigs and sit at the table in our house and go, 'Where did we go wrong tonight? Why aren't we a bigger draw? No one seems to be getting it.' They'd talk for hours about how to make it better."

Among the followers getting it were Mykel and Carli Allan, who had been loyal Weezer gig attendees since the previous July. "They were amongst the very kindest, sweetest, funniest, and coolest people on earth," Koch later reported of the sisters who "brought their infectious fun with them when they moved to L.A."

Ardent supporters of Hollywood's developing, post–hair metal alternative rock music scene, the Allans quickly befriended the group and often presented cakes and cookies to the Weezer boys after gigs.

"We moved to Hollywood together in 1989 as parents planned another family move," wrote the Allans in the early *Weezine* issues in 1995. "Carli converted Mykel to seeing live music and since then we have spent most of our nights standing too close to thumping speakers and becoming the 'jaded-scenesters' that we are. While in Hollywood we saw literally thousands of bands, some good and some not so good. It didn't take long to make a list of favorites and meet the people involved. July 9, 1992, we were at Club Dump (Johnny Depp bought the place, called it the Viper Room, River Phoenix died there) to see a good band Crux (no longer a band). At someone's suggestion we stuck around to see the next band Weezer. We were impressed and put them on the mental list of bands to go see again. The following night we were at a birthday party for our friend Bryan Ray. Bryan is the bass player in a band called Black Market Flowers, the first band to write a song called 'Mykel & Carli.'

"At the party we recognized the guy with long hair sitting alone by the refrigerator," the Allans continued. "It was Rivers, from Weezer, and he had his eyes on the birthday cake we had brought. We told him we had enjoyed his band the night before, he seemed amazed that we had liked it so much. The three of us sat on the couch and talked about music, food, and growing up — we had weird names and hippie parents in common. Rivers told us when the next Weezer show was and we remained antisocially on that couch wondering how long it had taken some of the people there to get dressed. We made sure he got a piece of the cake and visited

HEATHER CONLEY

They Might Be Giants (clockwise from top left):
Rivers, Pat, Jason, and Matt

until his ride was ready to go. We continued going to Weezer shows whenever we could. We met the rest of the band and provided a spectator's viewpoint and sideline reviews, whether they wanted to hear it or not. We made cookies and road trips."

"With us, still nobody was showing up to see us play," Matt Sharp said, even though A&R scouts were starting to check Weezer out. "Most of the people coming to see us were people from record companies and our friends who felt sorry for us."

"We'd do gigs where there were fifty people there, and they all had business cards," Cuomo affirmed.

When California-based independent label Restless Records first expressed interest in having a meeting with Weezer, the word got out to other A&R people, resulting in requests for Weezer demos by a number of labels, including Geffen. One Geffen A&R man began courting the group, but soon lost interest.

"Once people started showing up, a couple of record people on smaller labels started showing up," Sharp added. "Then, around L.A., if one key person gets into it, they all go, 'I don't want to miss out.'

"You play a show and if one [A&R] guy says, 'Wow, they're really good,' then everybody's just afraid of losing their jobs, so it's the domino effect. They haven't even heard of you and they're flying out from New York."

Record company scouts flirted with them when they weren't touting the virtues of a Berkeley-based punk band called Green Day. "Every label was flipping out over them," remembered Sharp of Weezer's peers. "We kept hearing their name over and over and over again."

On April 15, 1993, Weezer was invited into the 24-track recording studios at Los Angeles' Loyola Marymount University by Dale Johnson, a music engineering student who had witnessed a Weezer gig and wanted to get the band on tape for his final project. Split between two recording rooms, they recorded six takes of "Jamie," the last of which would later appear on the 1994 compilation *DGC Rarities, Vol. 1*.

Johnson discovered Weezer in the spring of 1993 when he worked the soundboard for an in-store performance by the band at Rhino Records in Santa Monica. Introduced through mutual friends Rachel Haden and Kerry Murphy, who booked that night's show, Dale asked Rivers, Pat, Matt, and Jason to participate in his recording assignment, which wound up being a live to two-track take of "Jamie."

"I guess the guys were happy with the LMU version of 'Jamie,' but I never was completely satisfied," Johnson said. "I mean, there's only so much you can do with a live take and only a few hours. Rivers seemed to be completely amazed when I told him I only got a B+ on the project. 'But it's gonna be on a CD, man . . .' I remember Matt being really adamant that they would do the recording project with me, but that they had to own the master. Smart boys they were, and I agreed to it. I just really wanted to be credited with the recording."

"What sounds like acoustic guitar at the beginning is actually the un-amplified sound of Rivers' pick hitting the strings, picked up by the super 'hot' vocal mic," recalled Koch of the Weezer rarity. "It needed to be way up because Rivers was moving his head around too much. The whole session was full of silliness between takes, inspired by the vast distance between the two rooms. Shouts of 'Karl! Where are you? I'm trapped in the mine and I need my bromo-seltzer!' were frequent. My old tape of the *Rarities*-destined 'Jamie' includes Matt saying 'You better . . .' a split second before the familiar feedback whine that starts the song. There is no telling what he was about to say."

Twelve days later, Weezer went back into the same studio to participate in the final project of one of Johnson's classmates, recording various takes of "Lullaby for Wayne" and "My Name Is Jonas." Johnson recalled, "I hooked them up with another classmate of mine named Sharon when she didn't have a band lined up at the last minute. I tried to get her That Dog — who was the other band I really wanted to record — but they couldn't get it together in time, so I figured the Weezer guys would be down with coming back for a second time."

Plotting to use the fruits of this second LMU session for an independent 7″ single, Weezer's goal was soon quashed by the promise of a major label deal. In between all of this, Matt and Rivers collaborated together for the first time in a writing capacity for Weezer on a title called "Mrs. Young," which would later morph into "Please Let That Be You." While Sharp wrote the bulk of the song, he sought vocal and structural assistance from Rivers. And of course Cuomo continued progressing composition-wise, introducing future Weezer staples like "Buddy Holly" and "Holiday" to the band, while crafting titles like "Negativland," "Chess," and a reworking of "The Purification of Water" on his 8-track.

On May 24, the band landed a high-profile gig at the L.A. venue Jabberjaw opening for Sloan, a talented Canadian alternative pop band then signed to DGC Records. While the performance pulled Geffen executives Weezer's way with real intent, Cuomo later complained, "I never felt like we ever really got one of those hyper-buzzes going. There really wasn't a heck of a lot of industry interest. At the end of the day there was really only one major label that offered us a deal. We never got to a point where there were more than 150 people at our shows. And even then, that was at our peak. We'd been playing a year and would still play to ten people on some nights. It was very, very disheartening. We'd see other bands come up and they'd get a huge buzz instantaneously and get a big deal. We couldn't understand what our problem was. I mean, we were playing 'Sweater Song' and 'Say It Ain't So' in these clubs and passing around our demo tape with those songs, and for months and months no one heard it.

We'd get comments from the industry like, 'We don't really hear these songs going anywhere, but keep writing!' We started to think we were insane, because we thought our songs were so good and we were so cool, but no one was getting it."

Although a number of labels were, as Rivers put it, "willing to take you out to dinner, kiss your ass, and make you feel like a rock star," he added that "Ninety percent of those companies hear your tape and see you live and say, 'You guys suck!' They express all kinds of interest, and suddenly they just turn around and act like they never knew you." Around this time, the group was close to signing with Slash Records — home of classic records by X, Faith No More, and the Violent Femmes — when Todd Sullivan, a different Geffen A&R rep, stepped in to ink the band to Geffen on June 25, 1993, following a three-month on and off label courtship. "Sully" had signed Weezer to DGC, the alternative music arm of Geffen Records, but despite the fact the label was home to Nirvana, Sonic Youth, and Teenage Fanclub, Cuomo still worried about fitting in. "I don't really know how the rest of the company felt about us," Rivers explained. "We assumed they looked down their noses at us. We had a serious inferiority complex."

But, for all Weezer's feelings of inadequacy, the band did indeed pay their dues and were deserving of the contract. "I think the smartest thing we did, as far as success strategy goes, was to hook up with bands that were a few steps ahead of us," he recalled. "Wax and Black Market Flowers and El Magnifico — these bands already had followings and label interest and publishing company interest, and we had none of those things. So we befriended these other bands. They liked our music and let us play on the same bill with them. I think that was the best we could do to forward our career at that point."

As the ink dried on their Geffen contract, Mykel and Carli Allan made and gave the fellas in Weezer a "great treasure" in celebration of the event

— handmade replicas of the necklace talismans given to Kiss in the film *Phantom of the Park*, complete with red velvet–lined cases. In return, Rivers had by then cooked up a special song in their honor, "Mykel & Carli" (which surfaced a year later as the B-side to import versions of the band's "Undone" CD single.)

On July 1, 1993, the band's first record company advances were issued. While it's unknown if all of Weezer's members received the same disbursement, Cuomo was paid a total of $2500 by MCA, the parent company of Geffen Records. The money was divided, with $1250 designated as living expenses and $1250 as an advance against future royalties.

As the members of Weezer turned their collective attentions toward plotting out their major label debut, a couple of challenges would lie ahead. In a little less than two months, the band would be in a New York City recording studio concocting *The Blue Album* with producer Ric Ocasek. In an interesting turn of events, they would also find themselves in need of a new second guitarist.

chapter nine

electric lady

With Geffen's backing, Weezer started practicing beyond the confines of their garage in July and August 1993 on new equipment in the professional facility known as Cole Rehearsals in Hollywood. Running through long-time staples like "My Name Is Jonas" and "The World Has Turned and Left Me Here," plus newer tunes like "Buddy Holly," "Surf Wax America," and the freshly penned "In the Garage," the group was prepping for forthcoming studio sessions, slated to begin in late August in New York City. The band began to focus on their vocal interplay, practicing barbershop quartet–styled songs that helped Rivers and Matt achieve a newfound collaborative comfort during rehearsals.

Sharp, who said he never sang before he joined Weezer, got his falsetto background vocals in check to memorably augment future hits like "Say It Ain't So" and "Buddy Holly." "The trick was that I had to sing an octave higher than Rivers. After a lot of practice, I started to get it down."

After toying with the notion of self-producing their major label debut — which Geffen suits outright objected to — the band selected Ric Ocasek, former frontman for the multi-platinum rock outfit The Cars. According to Rivers, "The record company was really pushing us to work with a producer, so we figured that if we had to have somebody in the studio with us, it might as well just be someone who writes good songs — and The Cars' first record just rules. We sent Ric a tape and he called right back and said, 'You guys are great, I want to work with you.'"

"A day later, two days later, the record company called us up and said Ric's coming to your rehearsal today," Sharp recollected. "We were just like, yeah, right, he's coming to our rehearsal. But that day Pat saw him in a guitar store and he goes, 'Oh my god, maybe he is coming.' So he came to our rehearsal and hung out, and we were all pretty nervous. We'd never really dealt with anybody outside of the band at all."

"I got their demo from Todd Sullivan," Ocasek said over the phone in July 2003. "I had been in L.A. working on another production — I think the Bad Brains' second album for Maverick — when he handed it to me. And I remember putting it on in the car and I was driving around and I just flipped out. I just said, 'God these songs are so great.' But I didn't know what the band looked like or anything. I actually thought they were a heavy metal band, because the guitars were kind of heavy on the demo, and the guitars were nice and muddy. I couldn't pinpoint what they were like image-wise. I thought they'd probably be a long-haired band, but at the same time, the lyrics were kind of too intelligent for that. But I really just didn't have a clue. And then I went to a rehearsal while I was in Los Angeles and I was blown away. They were kind of shy but I just loved what they were doing. Once I learned of Rivers' history with heavy metal it made perfect sense. It didn't have metal riffs, but they had real power. And at the time that kind of approach wasn't really available."

During one practice, on August 6, the band even finalized a cover of The Cars' 1978 smash single "Just What I Needed" in homage to their new producer. A few days later, Rivers, Pat, Matt, and Jason flew to New York City to rehearse in the presence of Ocasek at Manhattan's S.I.R. Studios. Here, Ric — with his assistant Haig and the project's engineer Chris Shaw in tow — recorded Weezer on a 12-track machine to, as Karl Koch described, "get a feel for the sound of the group and try to narrow down the song selection for recording the album."

"I had them in pre-production for at least a week, trimming it down," Ocasek recollected. "I wanted it to be a concise record that had a focal point. In pre-production they did Cars songs, which I thought was pretty cute."

"When we first met Ric, we were so freaked out by everything," remembered Matt Sharp. "We'd never met anyone famous. We were like, 'Oh my god, what's happening?' It was very hard to look at anybody eye-to-eye. But we milked him for all The Cars stories we could because we were all Cars fans." Cars albums released between 1978 and the band's demise in 1987 have sold a phenomenal 23 million copies so far in the United States alone, according to the Recording Industry Association of America.

"I'd always admired The Cars and Ric Ocasek's songwriting and production skills," enthused Rivers. "I wasn't worried about him handling the band's heavier side. He'd produced Bad Brains and they're a lot heavier than us."

"We picked him . . . scratch that. *I* picked him because I liked and respected his songwriting," Rivers later said of Ocasek. "What we learned from him is actually kind of boring and technical. Before we met him, we always had our guitars on the rhythm pickup, which has a bassy, dull sound to it. That was the sound we liked at the time. But he convinced us to switch to the lead pickup, which is much brighter. I think when I wrote those songs originally, I was just sitting in the garage by myself and it sounded great when you're all by yourself, because it sounds heavy and bassy. But in the context of the full band, playing at Club Dump, that pickup just sounds really . . . dull. And he got us to brighten it up. It made a huge difference, I think, in the way we sound."

At Ocasek's urging, the band left the comforts of Los Angeles to record in New York City. "[Ric] was saying your first record should be an experience," Sharp said. "You should get away from L.A. and get away from all these people and really just get into the making of a record. His wife [model Paulina Porizkova] was in New York, and she was pregnant, so he couldn't leave so he said, 'Let's go to New York.'"

Fifteen songs were tracked during Weezer's first New York practice session, but four songs — "Lullaby for Wayne," "Getting Up and Leaving," "I Swear It's True," and an alternate version of "In the Garage" — were eliminated as contenders for *Weezer*. A fifth tune from this session, "Mykel & Carli," would be attempted but abandoned only to be recorded the following year when it was relegated to B-side status. For the album, Ocasek and the band came to agreement on ten songs. They were: "My Name Is Jonas," "No One Else," "The World Has Turned and Left Me Here," "Buddy Holly," "Undone — The Sweater Song," "Surf Wax America," "Say It Ain't So," "In the Garage," "Holiday," and "Only in Dreams."

The actual recording of Weezer's debut got underway at Electric Lady Studios in late August 1993. While in New York, the band stayed on the ninth floor of the Gramercy Hotel on Gramercy Park and as they put work to tape, the "tracking roughs" (or immediate results of their efforts) were put on cassettes for listening and scrutiny at the end of each day.

"The plan was to do a quick record over the span of just three weeks or something," said Ocasek. "The real fun came when we started to record at Electric Lady. That's where the personalities developed and I got to see just how artistic Rivers really was. A lot of times we had little talks about which songs we should do. I remember at one point he was hesitant to do 'Buddy Holly' and I was like, 'Rivers, we can talk about it. Do it anyway, and if you don't like it when it's done, we won't use it. But I think you should try. You did write it and it is a great song.' He was up for doing almost anything. I had a good relationship with him, because I wouldn't make him do anything he didn't want to do. I was just sort of there to guide him."

In the midst of all of this, Jason Cropper received some deeply personal news that not only caused anxiety for him, but for everyone in the band.

What transpired was never made clear, but by the first week of September, Cropper was "asked to leave" Weezer. When pressed on the issue, Koch digressed, "due to the expressed wishes of privacy on everyone's behalf."

Some speculate that Cropper was forced out of Weezer by Rivers, Matt, and Pat when they learned from Jason that his girlfriend and future wife Amy had become pregnant. But if the three were taking the position that they had real concerns about Jason's newfound family responsibilities detracting from his role in the band, the need for a confidentiality agreement well before Weezer had ever achieved stardom — and which the guitarist was required to sign upon his departure — is, depending on how you look at it, either deeply puzzling or remarkably clever.

Cropper said he is contractually forbidden to talk about his time in Weezer, even though he would like to. "My exit contract with them was pretty strict," Cropper said a decade after the separation. "I don't remember the exact language, but I don't want to make myself liable. If it matters, at this point I have nothing but the fondest of memories of my time in Weezer. I would never say anything disparaging."

In a 1999 Internet interview with *O Flageul* he reportedly stated, "It was always very difficult to work with those guys. They're very particular. It was very stressful and I was glad when it was over — it was a relief." When asked if these acrimonious comments were true, Cropper simply said, "There's some funny stuff online." So what about this text from the same interview:

"[Weezer] paid me for what I did on that record just like if I was in the band. And on top of that, I didn't have to hang out with those guys anymore and we weren't really friends anymore when I left the band. So, I could stay and be with a bunch of guys that I hated, or go out on my own and do my own thing and still make the money. So I don't regret [the split] at all. I mean maybe a little bit in that I could have, you know, been a bigger rock star or something, but you know, I've got to be with my family."

Or this comment he made about sustaining a friendship with Rivers Cuomo:

"I don't know if anyone is [friends with him]. I mean, he's not any easy person to be friends with. He's extremely talented and he makes great records and he writes great songs, but things like friendships or whatever just get in the way with him in making records and making songs. He's a professional, and it was a business relationship. It wasn't a friendship. And that's the funny thing about being in bands — a lot of times you're in bands with people who you're friends, a lot of times you're in bands with people where it's just for business and with him it was business."

Cropper only spoke to the second statement. "It's hard to be friends with someone who is so intellectually stimulated," he said of Rivers. "The guy is really creative. He's an artist and he's following that path really intensely. Could you imagine being best friends with Van Gogh or Mozart or somebody like that? It's just probably not possible to share a one-on-one, 'Hey buddy!' relationship for a long time. Especially if you're working for, or with, the guy; whatever you want to call it. The guy's a genius. When you meet him, talk to him, or you read his personal writing, it's just mind-blowing what the guy can do with the written word. He'd be a great author someday."

When probed as to whether he opted out of the band or was forced out during the Electric Lady sessions, Cropper asked inquisitively, "Has Rivers ever said anything about that?" Then, after pausing for a moment, said, "Whatever Rivers says on my exit from the band, that's what the word is."

After laughing at the absurdity of what he just said, Jason became serious. "Rivers makes his living in the public eye and if he does well it benefits me," said Jason, who still earns royalties from the band, and is concerned about breaching his confidentiality agreement with Cuomo, which governs his public relationship with the group. "So, I only want the best for the guy." Cropper went on to have three children with Amy. He fronted the band Chopper One for the release of 1997's *Now Playing* on Restless Records before retiring from performing to run a vintage music gear rental company based out of Southern California's world-class Ocean Way Studios.

So, what really went down? Rewind to September 1993 as producer Ocasek remembered the whole ordeal a little differently. "They weren't like a happy-go-lucky band anyway," said Ocasek, who has gone on to man the boards for the likes of No Doubt, Guided By Voices, and Bad Religion. "In the middle of that record he fired the guitar player," Ric divulged. "He called me when the record was finished, the day before we were supposed to start mixing, and said, 'Listen, I just fired the guitar player.' So I said, 'What are you gonna do now?' He's like, 'I want all of his parts off the record. I don't want *any* of his parts on the record.'"

So with Jason Cropper now out of Weezer and the circumstances surrounding his departure effectively thought to be buried in legal documents, Cuomo and his remaining business associates found themselves in a self-inflicted quandary. To smooth the introduction of their debut album, Weezer concocted a story about making a desperate call to Brian Bell, a guitar-playing acquaintance and seasoned veteran of the L.A. alt-rock club scene, asking him to fly to New York and join the group for the sessions. While Bell *did* join Weezer, it is now apparent that he became the second guitarist after the debut album was wrapped.

Brian Bell

Born in Iowa City, Iowa, on December 9, 1968, Weezer guitarist Brian Bell was raised in Knoxville, Tennessee. Bell gravitated to music early, when at age four his parents, Tom Bell, a geography professor at the University of Tennessee, and Linda Menasco, now an assistant principal at

an elementary school in nearby Powell, took him to an Elvis Presley concert at the Knoxville Civic Auditorium.

"That kind of changed my life, seriously," said Bell of his early exposure to "The King." Soon after Brian became obsessed with his dad's pile
of records, which included such treasures as the Rolling Stones' "19th
Nervous Breakdown," and he "managed to scratch and destroy most of
Dad's valuable 45s.

"You know, it was like, 'What else do you have like this, Daddy?'" Bell
remembered. Among the stacks of wax was a copy of an Elvis LP that Brian
took into his kindergarten class. Listening to it on headphones, he began
to sing along loudly. Although his teacher thought it was cute and laughed,
Bell claims he became so embarrassed by the moment that he refused to
sing for anyone again for years.

Linda Menasco said that her son was always shy, "But his kindergarten
teacher still talks about his singing 'The Ballad of Davy Crockett' for his
entire class." After forcing Brian to take piano lessons, she refused to let
him take guitar lessons until high school because she "wouldn't believe that
he would practice."

Intrigued by guitar pickers he witnessed on television from "such fine
Eastern Tennessee programs as *The Barneyloo and Buster Show* and, of course,
Hee Haw, Little Brian learned how to pick 'n' grin on a ukulele his grandma
won at a bingo game," according to the first DGC press release on the band.
Bell, along with his sister Leia, who was born when he was two months short
of his ninth birthday, was raised near the intersection of Cordoba and
Granada in the Spanish Trails section of Karns, outside of Knoxville.

"Outside of The Beatles and the Stones, there's this live Cream record
my dad had that blew me away," Brian said. "But *Combat Rock* was the first
record I bought with my own money through the Columbia Record and
Tape Club, where you get a bunch of music for a penny. Along with that I

also got *Led Zeppelin IV*. But I remember being so intrigued with the lyrics of that Clash record. It's almost like calligraphy the way they're written out on the sleeve. There was so much there that I didn't understand. I just thought it was the coolest thing ever. Soon after that, I thought I was punk — a twelve- or thirteen-year-old punk. It made a huge impact on me. Putting it on, I can't remember much more than studying the lyrics and looking at these guys on the cover with their mohawks."

In his teens, Brian was torn between metal like Iron Maiden and hard-core punk like the Circle Jerks, and like his future bandmate Rivers Cuomo, Bell had a Kiss phase before discovering the Velvet Underground. In the ninth grade, Bell's parents finally softened and allowed him to take guitar lessons from a Knoxville musician named Ben Bolt. "My mom assumed that a guitar meant long hair, rock 'n' roll, and drugs," said Brian. "But she said it was okay if I bought the guitar with my own money. So I sold my Atari when I was fourteen to my uncle for his kids — all my cartridges and everything. I thought to myself, 'It's time to get serious. I'm not a kid anymore.' So that's what I did."

"He just blossomed," said Menasco of her son's interest in guitar. "But he thanks me now for making him take piano."

"I wasn't really that into piano," Brian admitted. "The recitals were the most petrifying thing in the world. My mom asked me if I wanted to take piano, and I said I'd love to do it, but the actual bit of going to lessons she sort of had to force me into."

"When I was in ninth grade I switched high schools," said Bell. "I was zoned to go to County School and my mom taught in the city, which meant that I could go to a more privileged school. In doing that I was surrounded by snobs. I was kind of finding myself at the time, so I decided to go to the school I was zoned for. The bus came around and picked me up which meant that I didn't have to wait on my parents to pick me up or take me to school. I wanted to be completely independent. Unfortunately it was a completely backward, country set-up. I don't like to use the word redneck because it's derogatory, but there were a lot of farmers. And while I did have some friends from my neighborhood that I hung out with who were kind of cool, school itself was pretty terrible.

"But when I met Tim and Glenn Maloof, my whole world changed," Bell remembered. "The Maloof brothers were these half-Lebanese kids that had moved to Tennessee from Los Angeles that year. They, too, were at this country school and they were skaters and artists and had earrings and long hair. So it was really funny. They introduced me to punk rock and I befriended them right off, but they were not accepted at all at our school. I was going through an odd transition at that time where I was wanting to fit in, but then I didn't. I realized I wasn't fitting in and sort of decided I didn't really want to anyway. So freshman year was when I sort of found myself and got a guitar. The Maloofs and I all got instruments at the same time and started jamming and ditching school. Their parents were, shall we say, less conservative than mine, and they let us set up drums in their downstairs den and we pretty much jammed our way through that first year of high school. We were a basement band. We were not good at all, just learning Black Sabbath songs, and Black Flag songs, and I think the first Metallica record came out that year. So we learned those riffs. We would jam, like, [Metallica's] 'The Four Horsemen' going into [Sabbath's] 'Sweet Leaf,' things like that. Then they ended up starting a band the next year, but I went back to the city school. I wanted to become much better at guitar before I could play out, but they started playing out as a band called The Bloo Shrooms, which was like Pink Floyd-meets-The Stooges. Right away, in my eyes, they were rock stars. I always felt sort of upset at them that they didn't ask me to join that band. So, in the back of my mind, it was always a goal of mine to play in a band with the Maloofs." (He would get his wish a few years later when his old friends returned to Los Angeles to join his side band the Space Twins.)

As a result, Brian became a "closet guitarist" who didn't want to play in bands. "I didn't see the point in Knoxville," he said. When he wasn't practicing the guitar, a sixteen-year-old Brian washed dishes at the local Red Lobster for a spell, so that he could "save enough money to get a car stereo — a cheap one that was just loud as fuck, that's all I cared about. It was for my '74 Capri.

"Working there was like being on the deck of a whaling boat," Bell remembered. "It's insane how many dirty dishes that place had. There was this forty-year-old guy that was working with me that was on crack or something. Seeing him just made me realize that I didn't want to do this, that I had to get my act together."

Bell calls Knoxville's music culture of the day, "really a dead scene, except that since it was such a small music scene, everybody knew everybody. I was hanging out with people who were my friend's brother's friends, who were about four years older than me, and were 'out of their mind' crazy. That's because the scene was so small and anyone that was into punk music, skateboarding, or anything out of the ordinary would come to these parties. You couldn't really select [your friends].

"It was like, 'I know these people are bad, but I'm forced to hang out with them because there's nobody else that's interesting in this town,'" Bell said. "I had a lot of wild times, I saw a lot of good bands — Dead Kennedys, Circle Jerks, Scream, Black Flag. All those bands came through. It was wild at the time but then I realized for myself that to join a band there was kind of a pointlessness, because nobody had the dreams that I had, the same visions."

Clearly beating to a different drum, Bell says he refused to go to his conformist senior prom, "much to the eternal chagrin of my mother and my high school sweetheart Linda Jendencko." And despite the fact both his parents are educators, they respected his decision not to pursue higher education.

"I did want Brian to go to college first but he told me I'd be wasting my money," said his mom. "I believed him. So we spent our money on guitar school and room and board in L.A. for four years. After that time, he was on his own." Settling on Yucca Street in Hollywood, the 1986 Farragut High School graduate refined his skill on guitar for three years and oddly enough wound up playing bass in the band Carnival Art.

Moving to L.A. when he was eighteen, Bell had a number of jobs, most of which involved delivering. "Delivering pizza, delivering movie scripts to Frank Zappa and Penny Marshall. Delivering flowers to some eighty-year-old woman on her birthday," Bell recounted. "Flowers are the hardest thing to deliver because you have to keep them nice and the water is spilling all over you. The first time I ever delivered flowers I get way up in Beverly Hills somewhere and I get them to this old lady's house and she said, 'these roses are crushed.' I had to go all the way back and get new flowers. That was pretty depressing, but I felt sorry for her. She seemed so lonely. It was also bad going to the hospitals and places like that."

When not delivering perishables, Bell and his mates in Carnival Art managed to secure a deal in 1989 with prominent New York independent label Beggars Banquet, which was then home to The Fall, Love & Rockets, and Peter Murphy, and distributed through RCA Records. The band received decent college radio airplay, and through some touring successes as well as his day job efforts, Brian was able to buy a brand new Volkswagen Fox in 1990. Purchased because it was roomy enough to house his guitars and amps, the car also managed to take a beating on endless deliveries.

Life in a semi-prominent band on a high-profile label wasn't enough to sustain Carnival Art, however. Despite the best efforts of Bell, guitarist Ed (no last name needed, evidently), drummer Keith Fallis, and frontman

Michael Petak, the quartet's sales were non-existent. After two full-length albums, 1989's *Thrumdrone* and 1992's *Welcome to Vas Llegas*, which paid twisted tribute to Bell's beloved Elvis, the outfit parted company with Beggars Banquet, and changed its name to Jerkwater. They worked out a new sound in hopes of landing another record deal, but Brian had grown tired of that arrangement and soon gave up on his band of five years.

"I gained a lot of knowledge and experience recording and touring and all that," said Brian, "but the sad fact is if you're on a major label and you don't sell enough records, you'll get dropped."

Around the time his own band was disintegrating he became acquainted with the guys in Weezer. "They started playing on the scene, and I instantly saw something unique in them," Bell recalled. While grunge was at the height of its popularity, Bell remembered Weezer was playing more "happy-go-lucky" songs.

"I didn't necessarily want to be in their band," Bell added. "They, for some reason, were in with the wrong crowd and playing at the wrong venues. I wanted to help them out any way I could and I wanted to play a show with them."

One of Weezer's songs, "Say It Ain't So" was memorable enough to Bell that he couldn't escape it. "I would go home after shows and sing it. And I'd think, 'God, that's a timeless song. I can't believe a modern band wrote that song.'

"At this point, I was pretty much fed up with being the small guy and constantly struggling," Brian revealed. "I was sick of starving." Then, one night in the late summer of '93, when he was driving home from a disastrous "rave" show in the desert, Bell decided once-and-for-all to quit Carnival Art.

What Cuomo and company contend happened next now appears to be something of folklore. Reportedly that same night, waiting for him on the answering machine back at his apartment, was a message from Weezer bassist Matt Sharp.

"I had no idea why he was calling me," Bell said. "We hardly hung out together at all in Los Angeles. We just exchanged numbers to play a show together, and I knew that they got a record deal and were recording in New York City."

Sharp called again the next day, or so the story goes.

"Matt was just beating around the bush, and Rivers took the phone from him and said, 'Do you wanna join our band?'" Bell contended. "And I thought about it for a couple of nanoseconds and said, 'Yeah.' And he's, like, 'Well, can you sing?' And I kinda lied and said, 'Yeah, I can sing.'"

The next day Bell reportedly received a hand-delivered package from a Geffen Records employee containing a demo tape with four of the songs the band was working on with Ocasek. Brian added his vocals and guitar to "No One Else," "Undone — The Sweater Song," "The World Has Turned and Left Me Here," as well as "Say It Ain't So," and on September 14, 1993, he allegedly overnighted his audition tape back to New York City by Federal Express. Rivers, Pat, and Matt called him back to inform him that he was in the band. Travel arrangements to New York supposedly followed, placing Bell with his new Weezer bandmates and Ocasek for the remaining days of studio sessions at Electric Lady.

Bell contended his arrival was hardly a celebration, though, as the falling-out with Cropper left the founding members of Weezer feeling dejected. "Everyone was so pessimistic about the whole ordeal," Bell said. "It was just about to fall apart and never happen. Rivers played me a rough mix of some of the songs I hadn't heard yet, like 'In the Garage,' 'Holiday,' and 'Only in Dreams,' and I was, like, 'Oh my God, this is really good.' I definitely saw the potential when I heard those songs for the first time. So I think I brought a sense of optimism to the band."

And Bell said that when he first joined Weezer, he was an ideal fit for the group because of his and the band's shared metal roots. Aside from the fun that most alternative bands sought at the time, Brian — also a Kiss fan — also gleaned the same drive for success that Cuomo did from his boyhood heroes.

Despite Bell's story and the album credits, it was experienced guitarist Cuomo — not Bell — who re-recorded all of Cropper's previously-tracked guitar parts. According to Ocasek, "After he fired his guitarist, I said, 'Rivers, who is going to do his parts?' And he said, 'I'm going to do them all.' And he did them all. In one day. *All in one day!* And he did them perfectly. *In one take!*"

While Koch reported that Bell did supplant some of Jason's backing vocals, "except when Brian was too unfamiliar with the material to get it just right, in which case Rivers stepped in," such vagueness only serves to support the notion that Bell doesn't perform on the debut.

Interestingly enough, the Weezer camp still adamantly insists that "Brian plays and sings on every released recording except for 'Jamie' on the DGC *Rarities* CD." But Cuomo's six-string capabilities and the little time remaining on the sessions when Bell joined the band makes this seem ridiculously doubtful.

Using an old 50-watt Mesa Engineering amp and Ocasek's late 1950s Les Paul Junior, it was Rivers who achieved a forceful guitar crunch on the record. And interestingly enough, the early-1980s style keyboard sounds on some tracks were also Rivers' idea. "Everyone thinks that's Ric's fault, but it's really mine," Rivers later said. "In fact he hated the keyboards and asked me to take them off. I said, 'No way. I know they suck, but they're staying on there.'"

Ocasek was mostly hands off for the sessions, except for keeping Weezer hard at work while they made their way through the guitarist transition. "We had figured out where the songs should go, the form and arrangement, so Ric wasn't very heavy-handed," remembered Matt. "He wanted to keep us excited about doing it, but not too stressed out, and just sort of be there for us."

According to Cuomo, besides putting lava lamps throughout the studio to set a proper recording aesthetic, Ric played the band his old demos of Cars songs. "It was just him and a drum machine in his living room. And then they sold millions of records. It really made us feel good about what we were doing.

"We were just looking for somebody to give us advice if we needed it, and to not get in the way," Rivers continued. "And that's what he did. He was always right behind me, to my right. And if I was ever stuck, and needed an idea, I'd say, 'Ric, what should I do here?' And he'd always have a good suggestion."

"Rivers was always good," Ocasek says, "and everybody else in the band played pretty tight. You know, he was running the show, even then. It was always Rivers' group. My impression was just that they should be recorded the way they were. I didn't really want to tamper with it much.

"That whole experience was one of those mind-boggling recording trips. Rivers wanted to do a lot of things against the grain, which I was impressed by. On his guitar and his amps he would always have the treble turned all the way off. It would always be really muddy and he wanted it that way. At first I was really skeptical about that, but as time went on I thought it was a cool idea. It made that sound, with just the drums peaking through. He didn't want any effects on his vocals. There, in fact, were no effects — no echoes or reverbs — used in any way on that record. Which was great.

"Now, the label had no idea what was going on or they might have objected," added Ocasek, who in April 2003 became a senior vice president of A&R with Elektra Records. "But when I produce records I never have anyone from the record company at the session. Odd that I'm an A&R guy now, but I never wanted to have A&R guys in the studio. I just wanted things to come naturally, so Geffen never heard anything while we were doing it. Todd would come in and listen but he never interfered."

"Ric definitely had something to do with how it ended up sounding," said Sharp. "But it was more like he was just there to protect us and make sure that nobody came in from the record company or anywhere because he was worried about that for us. He's like, 'You're a new band and people can screw with you. I want to make sure you get what you want.' He just was more like an executive producer in the fact that he was there to make sure everything was okay. To make sure we relaxed."

And Pat Wilson added, "Ric's biggest contribution was that he put us in a position to do well. He gave us a good studio, a good engineer. He let us make the record we wanted to make.

"I think [the band] produced it," Wilson continued, saying Ocasek — who, for instance, chose the recording engineer for the project — was involved "not as much in a hands-on way, but in more of a macro kind of way."

Bringing his enthusiasm for the band and expertise to the project, Ocasek brought Weezer out of the garage and into the 24-track studio. Despite the commotion within the band during the two-month process, they wrapped the record in early October and went back to L.A. According to Karl Koch, "the ten-song album was barely completed on time and did in fact go a bit over budget [by $20,000 according to reports], mainly from increased studio time." A few weeks later, Cuomo — having clearly assumed the band's domineering role — returned to New York alone for final mastering and track sequence of Weezer's DGC debut.

One snag with "Undone — The Sweater Song" resulted from Karl Koch's new and improved samples, which he said, "Got as far as a 'final, unmastered' cassette of the album." As with the demo version of the song, Karl compiled snippets of dialogue, this time by Humphrey Bogart, Charles Schulz's *Peanuts*, and excerpts from the motion picture *The Black Hole*, that were "mixed in a way so that the left side was all enthusiastic happy stuff, and the right was all bummed, depressed things."

It was all deemed unusable by DGC executives, whom Koch reports couldn't be bothered to legally clear the material. "Geffen didn't even want to try," he claimed, "as there were thirteen different old record labels to ask." In its place the band, already back in L.A., hurried to come up with some new dialogue. Recording a new script that was executed on Rivers' 8-track in the garage of their house on Amherst, these newly scripted speaking parts featured Sharp, Koch, and Mykel Allan preceding the verses with club dialogue about beer, favorite local bands, and catching rides to after-parties. The words that would end up being memorized by countless Weezer loyalists were subsequently mixed down on a DAT machine and brought back to New York by Rivers when he returned to master the album. According to Karl, his, Matt's, and Mykel's conversations "were 'flown in' both literally and in recording-speak."

In between pizza slices at Ray's on 6th Avenue and aside from recording at Electric Lady, Matt Sharp and Pat Wilson kept busy in their spare time during their New York stay by recording 4-track demos in their respective hotel rooms. Wilson titles — some which would end up on his *Suburban Advantage* EP — included "Buying and Selling," "I Wouldn't Say It," "Old and Wise (Aliens in my Hometown)," "Commercials for Levi's," "Scare You Off," and "Aren't My Friends." Meanwhile Sharp began carving out a number of demos, including skeletal takes of future Rentals tunes like "California," "Stupid Girl," and "Friends of P."

With the highly eventful recording of their debut album behind them, Weezer, upon returning home to Los Angeles, began to work on breaking

Brian into the band by scheduling a long series of gigs in the area. They played old haunts like Lingerie and Raji's in between venue debuts at On The Roxx, The Anti Club, and The Blue Saloon.

Following a long Christmas break, the group reconvened for more club work in mid-January, unaware of the kind of success they would reap as 1994 played out. With Weezer's finished debut "in the can," Geffen executives had no way of knowing they were sitting on a pot of gold.

chapter ten

weezer

Weezer's self-titled debut album was released on Tuesday, May 10, 1994. Although the ten-song disc was met with little fanfare initially, DGC was an imprint well schooled in building music industry buzzes on up-and-coming bands.

The disc's commercial release came during a suddenly uncertain time for the alt-rock world. Music fans were still mourning the recent suicide death of Kurt Cobain, frontman for DGC's biggest band, Nirvana. Cuomo, not just a fan of Nirvana's but a student of Kurt Cobain's songbook, was deeply impacted, and listed the news of Cobain's death that April in the diary that he'd post online years later.

Prior to the release of Weezer's debut album, Rivers had already written a number of new, high-quality songs and in January 1994 he committed "I'm Tired of Having Sex" (which later became "Tired of Sex"), "Susanne," "Waiting on You," "Gitchoo" (which would morph into "Getchoo"), "Longtime Sunshine," and "Why Bother?" to 8-track. However, with the anticipation of his band's first album release and the work surrounding the launch of Weezer's career, the songwriter/frontman wouldn't revisit the bulk of this material until late 1994.

Rivers' bandmates' creativity also flourished, yielding a solo outlet for each respective member. Brian's project, the Space Twins — which was essentially himself with then-girlfriend Susan Fox — recorded its first demo, the seven-song *Craterface*, in the weeks leading up to the release of

Weezer. Started in late 1993 as a Saturday afternoon time-killer, Bell later described the duo by saying, "It was meant to be nothing more than a cute project; something where we would play children's parties. We had monikers: I was Space Helmet and she was Moon Boot and we wrote crazy, wacky songs about Snuffleupagus and Bo Peep counting sheep. We made our own antennas out of headbands and wire and Styrofoam balls with glitter, and I would wear a blue Star Trek–looking shirt at the gigs."

Meanwhile, Pat Wilson's Suburban Advantage put a number of songs to tape in the Amherst garage around the same time, including three that are only now making the rounds on Internet file-sharing services: "If You Move Away," "Let's Go to the Mall," and "New Wave Lullaby." The group, which later evolved into Huge Guy and subsequently became The Special Goodness, was basically Pat and a Dr. Rhythm drum machine at this stage.

Concurrently, Matt Sharp was amassing a substantial number of demos for his side outfit, That's Incredible!, which would become known as the Rentals. And somewhere between April and June of 1994, Matt landed his first real "solo" recording session at Tom Grimley's small Poop Alley facility. With Sharp on guitar and bass, Rod Cervera on rhythm guitar, principal bandmate Pat Wilson on drums, and backing vocals by That Dog's Rachel Haden, the group put down several songs. Additional "after hours" recording work resumed later at a television voiceover studio known as "Hellcentro" in Hollywood that belonged to Cervera's father. Ten completed songs emerged, including "Stupid Girl," "Waiting," "I Don't Want This, Babe," "Crumblin'," "Friends of P," "Mrs. Young," "California," "These Days," "The Love I'm Searching For," and "Say Goodbye Forever," the last featuring Brian Bell on melody guitar. Although real progress was made during these sessions, the tracks wound up being shelved due to Sharp's increasingly busy Weezer itinerary.

Elsewhere, Cuomo was wrapping up another semester of studies. "I was still in school when the record came out," Rivers humbly remembers. "I brought it to class and said, 'Look everybody.' They were all like, 'Yeah, cool, whatever.' I was at community college in Los Angeles. [The plan was] I'd finish up my two years and was going to transfer to U.C. Berkeley, but I got a record deal."

But this wasn't just *any* record deal. With the meteoric rise of Nirvana, DGC had — in just three years — become a leader in the industry, counting Beck and Hole among its successes. Clearly, the company knew how to get the support of the music industry, and that was the game plan with Weezer's forthcoming release.

An article in *Billboard* on February 12, 1994, titled "Geffen's Modern Rock Methodology Pays Off" extolled the label's ability to succeed. And three months before the release date of their debut, Weezer even managed to get a mention in the story, which mostly focused on its aforementioned labelmates but touted the group as "L.A.'s tart punk-popsters."

Product development managers, publicists, and the radio promotion staff at Geffen sent advance promotional copies of *Weezer* to modern rock retailers, music writers, and radio programmers several months ahead of the street date. The inlay card for these CDs and cassettes consisted merely of a track listing on a white background. The plain wrapper gave little hint of what the disc contained.

Jim McGuinn, program director for the Weezer-friendly Philadelphia alternative rock station Y100, remembered the first time he heard the advance: "I got a cassette of the band's first album and I remember thinking, 'what the heck is this?' It was definitely different from what was happening in early '94. I was working at a modern rock radio station called KPNT, The Point, in St. Louis at the time, and I remember hearing the cassette while I was in temporary housing, waiting to move into my apartment. Pretty quickly after that I embraced the band, and we knew we

JAY BLAKESBERG

"Pull this thread as I walk away . . ."
Rivers dons his sweater, Matt averts his gaze

were going to support the album as soon as it came out."

Aside from the advance, a four-song giveaway cassette sampler was also sent to radio and retailers that spring. Housing "My Name Is Jonas," "Buddy Holly," "Undone," and "In the Garage," this rarity — now highly collectable — featured a picture of the band's feet, which were cropped out of the photo on the cover of *Weezer*.

Dave Leto, drummer of New Jersey–based indie punk band Rye Coalition, remembers picking up the sampler at Pier Platters in Hoboken. "I remember the day like it was yesterday," Leto says. "I just got my driver's license and I was driving around in my mother's 1988 Ford Tempo. Pier Platters was the place where you bought all of your 'cool' records, and they had a box of free tapes. Usually, it was a bunch of crappy tapes by bands you never heard of, or one song off some band's new album. I used to take them all and stick tape over the holes so that I could re-record over them with my own hot mix tapes or something. But I took one that had a black and white photo on it that said *Weezer*. It had four songs on it. The first one was 'Buddy Holly' and from the first line, my brother and I were laughing out loud. We were amazed that the opening line of the song by these average white dudes were like 'gangsta' rap lyrics. Then I noticed that the song was super catchy and that it kinda sounded like The Cars. Upon further inspection of the tape, it turned out that it *was* produced by Ric Ocasek. Needless to say, the tape became part of my regular listening rotation. Until I bought their album when it came out."

The actual CD booklet itself, which hit record racks on the second Tuesday of May 1994, featured Patrick, Rivers, Matt, and Brian standing left to right in front of a blue backdrop. The simple packaging, which was also used predominantly in advertising for the disc, sent many record collectors digging into their album crates to compare artwork with the Feelies' similarly presented *Crazy Rhythms*.

Inside the booklet, Rivers paid tribute to his metal past with a photo taken inside the group's garage on Amherst. Perusing the artwork, a poster for the 1980 Judas Priest album *British Steel* sits to the left of the shot, while a concert poster of Quiet Riot's Carlos Cavazo and Kevin DuBrow hangs to the right. The album credits list the title of Rivers Cuomo's publishing company as E.O. Smith — an homage to the high school he graduated from six years earlier.

Running down the track listing, Rivers himself summed up each song, respectively, in the wake of the record's release. Of the roaring set-opener "My Name Is Jonas," Cuomo said that, "it's a good introduction to the album," and reveals that the song "explains how 'the plan' is reaming us all. Especially my brother."

Interpreting what he means by this requires studying the lyrics to

"Jonas," in which Rivers speaks directly about receiving troubling news from his little brother, Leaves. In the song, Cuomo sings of an injury that likely correlates to a motor vehicle accident that James Kitts (a.k.a. Leaves) had been in on September 22, 1992, while enrolled at Oberlin College in Ohio. Seriously injured as a passenger in a friend's car, Leaves put in an insurance claim under his mother and stepfather's Connecticut Center for Massage Therapy, Inc. corporate policy with Utica Mutual. Unfortunately, the claim was denied because the vehicle he had been riding in at the time of the accident was not listed in the policy. Leaves contended that he was covered as a "family member" of his mother's household, so in an effort to circumvent his aforementioned 'reaming,' James Kitts filed a lawsuit against Utica Mutual. His position was ultimately rejected by the court and sadly, after playing out over several years, Rivers' brother lost all hope of being compensated for his injuries when the case lost in appeals court in late 1996.

Less dramatic, but no less personal was "No One Else," which Rivers simplified as "the jealous-obsessive asshole in me freaking out on my girl-friend." In the song, as he sings about wanting a girl who will only laugh for him and who will hibernate indoors while he's away, Cuomo reveals a misogynistic need for control set to an infectious punk-pop backdrop. Yet with the next track, the mid-tempo rocker "The World Has Turned and Left Me Here," the same control freak ends up getting his just desserts when the song's love interest up and leaves him. As Cuomo succinctly put it at the time, "The World Has Turned" chronicled "the same asshole wondering why she's gone."

As for "Buddy Holly," Rivers explained, "it's about a particular girl I knew. . . . It's about my commitment to her . . . our relationship . . . and, er, my willingness to defend her. It's very platonic. Not a romantic thing at all." The tune, aside from its future hit status, breaks ground by integrating hip-hop language into alternative rock with the utilization of phrases like "homies" and "dissing." Followers later uncovered that the tune is about a protective relationship Cuomo had with a Korean girl named Cung-He, whom people made fun of in high school. The song's subject — sensitive to suburban American assimilation — protectively looks after the "slit"-eyed, English-fumbling female. Of the ironic use of hip-hop slang in his lyrics, Cuomo later confessed to going through a rap phase in 1991, where he listened incessantly to bands like Public Enemy, NWA, and Ice Cube. An NWA album autographed by Eazy E — who died of AIDS in 1995 — would later reportedly become one of Cuomo's favorite personal items.

Regarding "Undone — The Sweater Song," Cuomo likened it to "the feeling you get when the train stops and the little guy comes knockin' on your door. It was supposed to be a sad song, but everyone thinks it's hilarious." Using a sweater unraveling as a euphemism for heartbreak, the song soon became Weezer's breakout hit. As Brian Bell once commented, "The whole irony of 'The Sweater Song' is that people sing along and don't catch what Rivers is talking about: a relationship break-up."

Moving along to "Surf Wax America," Cuomo noted in 1995 that the composition is "a total sarcastic call to hedonism, so sing along, drink and be merry. I hate drinking and only do so when I absolutely have to — which in these days, seems to be quite often." Rather brilliantly, the song gives the middle finger to day jobs and the rat race in general, instead opting for the surfing life. Cuomo — who, like one of his idols, Brian Wilson of the Beach Boys, doesn't surf — notes in his lyrics how "the sea is foaming like a bottle of beer," and "rolling like a thousand-pound keg."

Less celebratory, but "also about beer" according to Rivers is "Say It Ain't So," which, as previously mentioned, chronicles the influence of alcohol over his mother and stepfather's separation and eventual divorce.

Closing out the disc are "In the Garage" and "Holiday," two relatively upbeat tunes written after the group had inked with DGC. While the latter flirts with escapism in an upbeat manner, it's the former that revisits Rivers' youth with notable exuberance. Giving nods to pubescent boyhood interests like Dungeons & Dragons, comic book heroes, and his much beloved Kiss, "In the Garage," is arguably the centerpiece of *Weezer*.

Summing up the record, Rivers confided, "None of these songs are perfect, but I think you can hear that we're trying hard to be honest and real. Pat really kicked ass on the drums and Brian, Matt, and I sang with a lot of feeling. The record sounds kind of weird, but if you turn it up extremely loud and lie down, it can be rewarding."

In the bio sheet sent to media along with promotional copies of *Weezer*, three of the four members took the opportunity to scribe revelatory, albeit humble personal information. Here's some of what they had to say:

Rivers: "Because I'm so terrible at expressing my feelings directly, and because no one really cares, and because anything real is almost impossible to talk about, I've come to rely on music more and more to express myself."

Patrick: "The record sounds the way it does because the drums aren't the loudest thing in the mix. Somehow, Phil Collins' style of recording has taken over, and we didn't want that. The only effects used are fuzz bass on 'In the Garage' and a little compression here and there. Certainly not as much as they put on Ringo."

Matt: "This is the first band I've been in and the first album I've played on, both of which mean a lot to me. I also sang the falsetto vocals on the record, which is probably most recognizable on 'Say It Ain't So.' These were, oddly enough, the first notes I sang in front of anyone. Singing can be pretty rewarding even when you're not that good at it. For me, it filled a gap in my life that was there until the band started. I'm not exactly sure what we four have in common, but I do consider Pat, Brian, and Rivers to be good people and good friends that I am glad to be associated with."

Oddly, the band's newest member, Brian Bell, wrote his entry in the third person: "Raised in Tennessee, little Brian knew he wanted to be a rock star at an early age. Lucky enough to catch an Elvis (Presley, that is) concert at the age of four, he wanted nothing else than to be a hound dog."

With those disclosures behind them and in celebration of their debut album's commercial release, Weezer's leader was no doubt stoked when he heard "Undone" on the radio for the very first time that month on the local, influential college radio station. "I was living in an apartment with not one piece of furniture, " Cuomo remembered. "[I was] just sleeping on the floor, and my roommate at the time was sleeping on the other side of the room. And he started screaming, saying, 'Rivers, wake up!' And he ran over to me — we didn't have a stereo, but he had a little handheld radio with a single earpiece earphone — and he stuck it in my ear, and it was 'The Sweater Song' on KCRW. And I woke right up and started jumping up and down and screaming."

Days later Weezer hit the road in their newly acquired used black van — christened "Betsy" — for a month of West Coast dates, playing at notable venues along the way like Rckcndy in Seattle (May 17), La Luna in Portland (May 18), and the Troubadour in L.A. (June 4). Despite having a major label debut on the shelves of record stores nationwide, the band was met with a humbling moment in Berkeley, California, when no paying customers showed up for a performance at Berkeley Square on May 22. Six days later, however, *Billboard* profiled Weezer in its "Popular Uprisings" column, calling the group's debut "full of humorous and fun lyrics about simple things in life, like beer on 'Say It Isn't So' and jealousy on 'No One Else.'" DGC released the first single, "Undone — The Sweater Song," on June 7, aiming it at modern rock radio and trying to get it added to playlists. Explaining the allure of *Weezer*, the band's A&R man Todd Sullivan rather accurately told the music industry trade, "It's a very unknown band and a very strong record. It's not a matter of forcing it right at radio. Once they hear it, they will latch onto it and it will develop by word of mouth."

For all the song's airwave affability, one problem — especially for a startled Rivers — was when the promotional CD single version of "Undone" was shipped to radio stations with an erroneously short edit of the song. His blistering guitar solo in the middle had been drastically trimmed — by twelve seconds to be exact, shrinking the tune from 4:10 to 3:58. Luckily, few people noticed outside of those in the band, and when most radio outlets began gravitating toward the lovesick anthem in the wake of influential Los Angeles station KROQ debuting it on May 23, they played the album version.

By June, a short West Coast tour was underway, supporting Chicago power pop trio Material Issue — known for minor alternative radio hits like "Valerie Loves Me" and "What Girls Want." A two-week break from the road followed early the next month, but by late July the band was on to Ohio for a one-off gig with popular New Jersey rock outfit The Smithereens. If living on Taco Bell and Mylanta hardly seemed glamorous, it far exceeded reporters' textbook early questions to the still largely unknown band: "What was it like working with Ric Ocasek?" and "Did you get the opportunity to meet his supermodel wife Paulina Porizkova?"

The roadwork helped generate live previews and reviews in regional newspapers, and noted pop music critics like Jim DeRogatis of the *Chicago Sun-Times* wrote favorable reviews of *Weezer*. DeRogatis gave the disc three and a half stars on July 3, calling the debut "lean and mean, with 10 short, punchy tunes," and referring to the band as a "group of poppy slacker wiseguys that you just have to love."

More critical love came from the Windy City the same month when Dan Kening of the *Chicago Tribune* called the chorus to *Weezer* extract "Buddy Holly" "a hook so insidious it replays in your head time and time again. And the rest of the album isn't bad either."

Meanwhile in the *Miami New Times*, critic Greg Baker took an opposite view, slamming the record. "They sound like Nirvana," he wrote. "They sound like Hüsker Dü. They sound like Meat Puppets. Somehow, this is not necessarily a good thing. In fact, it can be downright tedious."

Rye Coalition's Leto didn't agree. "I liked the album a lot," he says. "I think 'Say It Ain't So' is the standout track. Everything about that song is cool. All the chord progressions, the feedback, the emotional vocals, it almost reminds me of Hall and Oates. You felt like they had some other emotion other than 'happy all the time.' It's the one song on that album that had some soul. As far as the album goes, I can't remember anything that was out that was like it at the time."

On July 5, the members of Weezer found themselves in the company of high-profile labelmates like Counting Crows, Beck, Hole, and the sadly bygone Nirvana, when Geffen dropped *DGC Rarities, Vol. 1*. The compilation CD, housing rare or never-before-heard tracks by the aforementioned artists and others like Weezer friends That Dog, boasted "Jamie," a song penned about Weezer's lawyer that marked the only commercially released recording with founding guitarist Jason Cropper.

Released just as the band was wrapping up six weeks of touring the country by van, the issuance of "Jamie" proved one thing — that Weezer lacked studio-quality rarities. Fresh off their first national trek as a major label act, Rivers, Patrick, Brian, and Matt went straight into Ocean Way studios in Los Angeles for a two-part session with Paul DuGre, who had previously engineered records like Bad Religion's 1993 album *Recipe for Hate* and Toad the Wet Sprocket's *Pale*. The motive was B-sides, which Geffen clamored for to append to international versions of CD singles for "Undone."

"The session was to last one day," remembered Karl Koch, "but the studio they were in went haywire, prompting a last-minute second session the next day, which happened to be the day before a ten-day break when Brian went to Australia with his family. Needless to say the sessions were hectic."

With the studio time, the band cut a new version of "Mykel & Carli," because the version attempted at Electric Lady was determined to be far too difficult to salvage. "My Evaline," a traditional barbershop-quartet–styled tune, was a spontaneous thing that wasn't intended to be issued commercially but wound up being something deemed good enough to use.

Upon completion of the sessions, the band had three new songs in the can: "Susanne," "Mykel & Carli," and "My Evaline." Meanwhile, a second attempt at "Jamie" was left incomplete. (Interestingly enough, "My Evaline" wound up mistakenly listed as "Sweet Adeline" when it later surfaced on the Australian version of the CD single for "Undone," in February 1995.)

The whole import flip-side game actually irked Koch a bit. "Why do U.S. record companies think U.S. kids don't care about B-sides?" he asked. "I fully sympathize with the kid forced to hunt down foreign imports for new songs — I've done it myself and think it sucks that it's happening to Weezer fans."

"Susanne," incidentally, did eventually find a stateside release in the fall of 1995, when it surfaced on the soundtrack to the teen flick *Mallrats*. Written for Geffen A&R representative Susanne Filkins, who worked with The Stone Roses and Guns N' Roses among others on the label's roster, the members of Weezer stunned Filkins when they rushed into her office to debut the song.

Following the two-day session and with Bell in Australia, Rivers used the two-week respite from touring obligations to lay down some 8-tracks. Among them was a cover of the Beach Boys' "Little Surfer Girl," which included his own complete and extensive backing harmonies, plus "There Is No Other One," which would shrink its title when it appeared on Weezer's second album as "No Other One." Cuomo also flew home to

Connecticut for a long weekend during this period of downtime, catching the World Cup Final between Brazil and Italy with his stepfather Steve.

Once Bell returned to his native soil, and with Rivers back in L.A., Weezer jumped on a tour with shoegazer pioneers Lush. "They were awesome," Pat Wilson later said of the headliners on Weezer's first big tour. "I would watch [Lush] every night and they just sounded amazing. We did that for a month. At first it was hell because we did not know anything about touring. We had a van, we didn't know what it was all about. In fact, I guess we were just like most bands starting out."

Brian Diaz, bassist and vocalist with The Reunion Show, a band inspired by Weezer's musical approach, said, "The first time I saw Weezer was in 1994, at what is now known as the Hammerstein Ballroom in New York City. They were opening for Lush. I had heard of them before but I never listened to the band. My friend Tommy was with us, and he was a big fan of the first album at that point and he insisted we get there early to check them out. I'm glad I did because it really changed my life. It restored my faith in guitar-driven, hard pop rock."

The support slot took the band to new terrain in the Midwest, Deep South, and East Coast and kept them busy throughout August of '94. In tandem with the trek, the group began drawing radio support from alternative outlets, and in turn listener response was remarkably good. "I remember going to see them at Mississippi Nights in St. Louis on their first tour. They were the opening band for Lush and I just really liked them right away," Y100 program director Jim McGuinn remembered of the August 2 gig. "We were already playing 'The Sweater Song,' and my wife at the time was working for Geffen's distributor, Uni. There was, like, no local Geffen representative in the area and she wound up driving the band around in her little Volkswagen. So they were all pretty willing at the time to do just about anything. They were really working it in the sense that they came to the station and played acoustic for us at KPNT. There was something different about Weezer right from the start — you could sense that. And I was totally into it but it fit my sort of vibe. It just harkened back to this sort of Beatle-ish, punky power-pop sound but there was a new and different twist on it too. It was a lighter moment amid the [Smashing] Pumpkins and Soundgarden, much harder airwave favorites of the day. The record was fresh. The record stood out and people reacted positively, even in a meat and potatoes market like St. Louis. Looking back on it now, it feels like those were the glory years of alternative radio."

Still, for all the promotional backing necessary to propel the song — which eventually landed at #6 on the *Billboard* Modern Rock chart — Cuomo felt that Geffen could have been more supportive. "I don't recall anyone at the 'corporation' — that is, the record company — having *any* faith in us whatsoever," Cuomo complained in hindsight. "They totally ignored us. I'm sure they had no idea that we were going to have any success at all. They just put out the record, and when our song actually got on the radio, they were utterly shocked."

"They came up with this pop sound that was very unlike grunge," said Lisa Worden, music director of influential Los Angeles radio station KROQ and an early endorser of the band, describing the allure of "Undone." "It stood out like a sore thumb in a great way." But despite the hit, the entertainment trade publication the *Hollywood Reporter* couldn't help but take some potshots at the group during an August 8 hometown gig at Glam Slam. "Caught in a bit of a creative rut, Weezer seemed musically clouded — not quite sure whether to take their sound and style in a pop or true punk direction," wrote Marc Pollack. "Straddling that musical fence, Weezer fell short on both sides. Lacking aggressiveness, the DGC four-piece band is not heavy or combative enough to be punk, and its material isn't hooky enough for pop. The hybrid, which works for other bands like Green Day and to a lesser extent Offspring, fails to come to fruition for Weezer."

Regardless of Pollack's jaded observations, music fans began to take note of this group called Weezer. At the request of the band, Mykel and Carli Allan, who had already been handling the large number of fan requests for lyrics to *Weezer*, upped their involvement in the Weezer organization with the formation of the outfit's official fanclub. "We wanted to share what we knew about them with other people who care about them," the pair professed.

While in L.A., the band shot their first-ever music video with band acquaintance Spike Jonze. "This was not a day we were looking forward to," Rivers acknowledged. "Until they put our video into Buzz Bin, we all hated MTV. It seems like a shame to confine a song to one interpretation. For example, I'll never hear Aerosmith's 'Cryin'' again without thinking about that lame chick bungee-jumping off the bridge."

With their single beginning to ascend the charts, Rivers spoke of how DGC "thought it would be a smash if it had a video." Hesitantly, Weezer agreed to make one under the condition that the clip for "Undone" would contain absolutely no visuals of an actual sweater. The label's video department subsequently solicited treatments from over twenty-five directors.

"Every single idea featured — you guessed it — a sweater," Rivers said. "Whether we were playing in a sweater factory, knitting a gigantic sweater, or blowing up a sweater with five megatons of TNT, every single director had his or her own vision of the great sweater. Nauseated, we almost gave up on doing a video — until we got a call from the messiah of video-making, Spike Jonze."

Spike, coincidentally, had been an old friend of Brian's dating back to the director's days as a photographer for the skateboard magazine *Thrasher*. Bell — who continued working day jobs up until the DGC debut was released — ran into Jonze in the fall of 1993 when he was delivering food to the director's Propaganda Films office.

"I was going around the corner, and Spike was sitting there," Bell explained. "And he's like, 'What are you doing?' I said, 'I'm delivering food. What are you doing?' And he was making all these calls, and he was in charge of Propaganda Films in this area. And I say, 'I'm in this new band Weezer.' And he's like 'Hmmm.' And we're both thinking, or I *think* he was thinking, 'Well, maybe I'll make your video one day,' and I was thinking, 'Maybe you'll do our video.'"

Jonze, known for his directorial work on the Beastie Boys' action-packed "Sabotage" clip, pitched a video involving a blue room in an empty warehouse, a pack of dogs, and couple of guys hanging upside down from the ceiling. The concept, deemed "vague" by Rivers, wound up costing $60,000 to lens. "Somehow, Spike took a video with no editing, no cast, and no set to speak of, and gave it a budget I would have thought purchased major explosions, extraordinarily beautiful women, and MC Hammer–like choreography. Apparently $60,000 is only an average price for a video these days," Cuomo said soon after the filming.

"When we started shooting, I had that terrible feeling of regret that comes only when one sees dollar signs floating uncontrollably skyward," Rivers confessed. "Everything was going wrong. First of all, in order to achieve the slow-motion effect that makes the video so dreamy, we had to perform the song twice as fast as normal. This also means we had to sing like the Chipmunks."

"The treatment for the video was ten words," Joy Ray, who produced the video for Jonze, recalled. "It said, 'A blue stage, a Steadicam, a pack of wild dogs.' We had Bernardo Bertolucci's Steadicam operator. We had about twenty-five dogs that were released onto the stage and we filmed the whole thing in one shot." As for Weezer themselves, Ray observed that, "they were very unassuming. They were like, 'Oh golly gee whiz. A live video.'"

"The cameraman had to run around the set twice as fast as it appears he did while wearing this immense apparatus known as the Steadicam," said Rivers, describing the experience. "Following him were a number of assistants, and behind them, Spike, yelling commands at the cameraman, the lighting guy, and me. The cameraman was yelling commands at the assistants, who were in turn yelling at each other. And then the dogs ran in at double speed. Across the set from the dogs were the trainers, all yelling at the dogs: 'Buddy! Scrappy! Here, Buffy! Good doggy!' The dogs got so confused by all the screaming and the monitors blasting the Chipmunks version of 'The Sweater Song' that they turned around and ran directly away from the band. The trainers, in an amazing display of ignorance, told us we had to turn down our instruments because we were 'scaring Scrappy.' So we pretended to turn down the instruments — which weren't even plugged in — and continued on."

Playing the song and lip-synching twenty times in a row at high speed while racking up a $60,000 bill was not only tedious, but a little depressing. Fittingly, one of the dogs actually ended up defecating on Pat's bass drum pedal — a move which the frontman later tagged "an act of great symbolism." While the dog's trainer extended apologies, Cuomo details how the band "snapped."

"A dog had crapped on our $60,000 video," Rivers complained. "From that point on, our lip-synching wasn't quite as accurate. Matt would take time out from playing the bass to snap his fingers or to sit down. Despite the importance everyone placed on it, we didn't care about our video anymore. We saw it not as a significant work of art depicting the anguish of Generation X, but as it truly is: a piece of dog shit."

Canine excrement or not, the video was an instant hit on MTV by late summer. It was even arranged for the band to stop by the network's New York studios to tape a live performance of "Undone — The Sweater Song," for the channel's Sunday night alternative music program *120 Minutes* that

August. Further promotional duties in between live dates included performances at WHFS in Washington and an acoustic "unplugged" spot on
WNNX in Atlanta. In regard to the tune's increased profile, Cuomo marveled
at the time about the public's misinterpretation of it. "It's supposed to be a
sad song," he said, "but everyone thinks it's hilarious."

On August 25, Weezer touched down in New York to mark its debut
in the late night talk show arena. Making their first nationally televised
appearance on NBC's *Late Night with Conan O'Brien*, a day after launching
the first leg of their World Domination tour at the Fast Lane in Asbury
Park, the group cranked out its fast-rising single. Rivers, exhibiting his
love of all things soccer, sported a jersey endorsing the sport, and as Koch
remembered, "After the song was over, a 6'4" Conan came over and
dwarfed all members of Weezer. In the clip, you can see Conan trying to
pick a fight with Matt."

Spin magazine's Jac Zinder was there to tag along with the "unabashedly
pop" Weezer for a feature on the group which ran in the January 1995 issue.
Observing the band in the green room before their performance at 30
Rockefeller Center, Zinder found Matt chilling with a childhood friend;
Brian pacing, wrought with nerves; and Pat cracking jokes.

Wilson told the room, "I'm so nervous, I'm probably gonna crap my
pants when we play." Rivers, meanwhile, was found in the fetal position,
but rose to remind his cohorts, "It's just 1-4-5, basic three-chord guitar
pop. No big thing." Later, after a performance that found 1960s television
fixture Adam West — the original Batman — looking on from the guest
couch, Cuomo said, "That was so surreal. TV, a studio audience full of
squares, and Batman! I mean, Batman gave us the thumbs-up! I guess that
there aren't many mysteries left now."

chapter eleven

holiday

Three nights after rocking Conan, Weezer made the transition from opening act to headliners when they launched their first-ever club tour on August 27 in Fredericksburg, Virginia. The month-long trek with openers the Figgs included three high-profile CMJ convention showcases at venues like New York's Academy, the legendary CBGB's, and Maxwell's in Hoboken. Performing before music industry executives and college radio staffers alike, the band played its style of rock unabashedly and won over each respective audience before wrapping the jaunt the following night with a gig at Local 186 in Boston.

Figgs guitarist/vocalist Mike Gent distinctly remembered the start of the tour, reciting notes from his 1994 tour diary. "We did a show on August 28 at this place called the Peppermint Beach Club in Virginia Beach. I remember we both played early and then there was a nine-piece reggae band or something that played after us. The cool thing was that the show was right on the beach.

"Weezer's first record was just coming out, and we didn't really know anything about them, but as soon as we got on tour with them we swapped records," Gent continued. "The album we had out at the time, *Lo Fi at Society High*, through Imago Records, was gaining momentum, and although we were different, our records had a similar sensibility. I always thought we were a great double bill and the fact that they had a single on the charts helped to make certain that the venues were usually full. Their audience was really open to us. The crowds were great and it was a fun tour to be aligned with, because Weezer really gave a great set every night."

On August 31, the band touched down in St. Louis for the second time in a month, this time as headliners at a venue called The Other World. "They came back and did a club tour with this great band called the Figgs," McGuinn recollected. "And there was like an industry reception for the band with distributors, radio, and retail. It was one of those classic scenes where everyone was talking to each other and schmoozing a little bit, but Rivers was, like, over hanging alone in the corner. Here's the first time most people are meeting the guys from Weezer, they've heard the record, but they don't know who is in the band. And people are like, 'the front-man's over in the corner, that's really odd.'"

"We didn't hang out with those guys too much," Mike Gent said. "They kind of kept to their van and we kept to ours. But I do remember I played drums with them at a sound check and we did 'Metal Health' by Quiet Riot. Which was wild because Rivers is a total shredder, and he tore into it."

People also dove into the record, if Weezer's warm reception during the CMJ convention a few weeks later was any indication. Despite the growing success, the event was met with Rivers' own fixation about fan adulation — no doubt fed by the notion the group was on the verge of something very big. "When I go to sleep, I see all these hands reaching out to me, trying to shake my hand," Rivers said the week of CMJ. "You know how when you play a video game for a real long time, you start playing it in your sleep? That's how I feel about shaking hands."

Dave Leto saw the CMJ show at Maxwell's in New Jersey that month. "The capacity at the club is around 200 people," he said of the infamous venue. "It was an awesome show. Bands are always better in small clubs; it was cool to hear the songs I had listened to so much at this tiny club. It was probably the last tour they did in small clubs because they blew up after that. They were great, they sounded amazing, and they were really comical, too."

In between the various CMJ dates, Weezer and the Figgs played their final show together during an unusual bill on September 22 in Rhode Island that found them sharing the stage with up-and-comer Sheryl Crow and hard rocker Joan Jett. Throughout September and October, "Undone" gained drastic momentum on the radio, bolstered by a second national television appearance on *The Jon Stewart Show*. Earning Buzz Clip honors on MTV in the first week of September, the video — issued at the height of alternative rock's popularity — soon became one of the top requests on the channel. Less than a year earlier, the song was in danger of being scrapped altogether due to legal clearances, but it was now a runaway hit. Had the new intro dialogue not been presented by Rivers during final mixing sessions in October '93, the song would never have been given the chance to succeed and the outfit's newfound ascent might never have happened.

With his rock star dreams beginning to come true, Cuomo himself was starting to have mixed feelings about the song's popularity. "'Undone' is probably my least favorite song on the whole album," he said that September. "I hope it's not the only song people will know us by. I guess the record company is choosing the catchy songs." Minutes later, Rivers countered, "I'm happy with how everything's going. We're still in the van six hours a day, doing shows, and then catching some rest. Stardom has been non-stardom so far."

Despite Buzz Bin status for "Undone," there were detractors like the *Boston Globe*'s Michael Saunders. "Inane lyrics, a doofy song and presto: an alterna-teen hit," Saunders wrote in his "Video Vibe" column. Calling Weezer a "band unencumbered by talent yet marginally interesting for about as long as a dropped $20 bill will stay on the sidewalk," he trashed the video, claiming that it "falls short of recent directing by Spike Jonze. Here, he's on a mission of mercy. Marrying a pack of dogs to this dog of a song was a rescue befitting the Coast Guard."

JAY BLAKESBERG

Getting Down To Business:
The *Blue Album* takes off

Countering this position in the *Orlando Sentinel*, Eric J. Larson succinctly wrote of *Weezer*, "this CD kicks butt," calling *Weezer* a "thoughtful mix of punk, slow rock, heavy guitar, good basslines and lots of musical variety. The tone is always changing, the lyrics are straightforward yet thought-provoking, and beyond all that, the vocals are unbelievable."

On the week of September 24, *Weezer* placed at number 82 on the *Billboard* Top 200 album chart, with its impressive sales jump qualifying the act as a Heatseekers Impact Artist. A week later, the disc hopped to number

70, topping the Heatseekers chart of new and developing artists, counting 71,000 copies sold, according to SoundScan. The October 1 issue of *Billboard* magazine also boasted an extensive feature on the band.

But the music trade's coverage of the band caught Rivers in defeatist mode. "We're probably the most pessimistic group of people ever assembled," he said. "There's always different voices in my head. One is saying, 'This is so great, this has to be huge.' But that's not the louder of the voices in my head, especially when we looked at what's popular. It was hard to imagine Weezer fitting in there."

Yet "Undone," which *Billboard* reporter Carrie Borzillo dubbed "a pop ditty about emotional unraveling," was indeed a hit at modern rock format. Having peaked at number six on that survey, the article marveled at how the track was crossing over to the album rock and Top 40 radio formats.

Although Geffen's hopes were high from the outset, the public's overwhelming response to the band was clearly a surprise. "There wasn't a big bidding war," said Robert Smith, then head of marketing at Geffen. "[Weezer] didn't come from an indie scene. They had nothing out before this album. We started from scratch."

But as many in the industry learned by this point, the power of Los Angeles' leading modern rock station KROQ was epic in breaking an artist and Weezer was no exception. "[Sales of *Weezer*] definitely exceeded our expectations," said Bob Bell, new-release buyer for the 350-store Wherehouse Entertainment chain. "Once KROQ put it on, we saw an increase in sales. Geffen has really been aggressive in terms of advertising and discounting this, as well. They really made sure it was upfront, even before airplay."

"We felt it was important to build a base with college radio and indie retail and have a truly credible indie development," Smith said. "We put them on the road a few months before the album came out. They did small retail stores and some college radio to build interest and a base before the label sent the track to commercial radio."

Still, MTV arguably deserves the most credit in terms of getting Weezer out to the masses. "We see it selling well in some markets where it's in between airplay, and we know it's because of MTV," the Geffen marketing chief assured. "This is your typical case of radio, video, live appearances, press, and a good profile at retail helping to sell an album."

And the band members themselves were not above hard work. In fact, the mere suggestion by Borzillo that Weezer might be classified a "slacker" band made Rivers mighty upset. "Today, we have three radio shows to do, one instore, this interview, and tonight we have a show," Cuomo argued in *Billboard*. "We're not slacking off at all. Whatever I'm doing, I want to be working as hard as possible. Even in school, I was a super-hard-working student." Speaking of school, it was in the *Billboard* piece that Cuomo first made public his desire to return to college as soon as Weezer could secure some time off.

Touting his baby band's debut on-the-rise, A&R rep Sullivan said, "It's a very honest and real record. The band's philosophy from the get-go was to make it honest in every aspect of how they present themselves." Of his personal songwriting approach, Rivers added, "I couldn't write about anything too abstract, or about politics or current issues, because I couldn't write honestly about it."

The same day the *Billboard* article ran, Weezer took to the road again with York, Pennsylvania–based headliners Live, who were then reaching their commercial apex with the album *Throwing Copper*. Opening at the Orvis Activities Center at Alfred State College in Alfred, New York, and wrapping on November 23 at the Tower Theatre in Upper Darby, Pennsylvania, the seven-week excursion saw the band move from a van to a tour bus, but according to Wilson, the experience was marred because "[Live's] crew was a bunch of dicks."

Leaving Betsy — the shoddy black van with the leaky sunroof, inoperable air conditioner, and iffy radio — to rest back home in Los Angeles, the bus was a newfound luxury. Following the success of the "Undone" video, Spike Jonze had already been tapped in September 1994 to direct the clip for Weezer's next video, "Buddy Holly," which was filmed on September 29 and 30. In its planning stages, few could predict that the song and its resulting video would send Rivers, Matt, Pat, and Brian's music careers into orbit.

"I don't know what it's going to look like," Cuomo said of the new clip — which was still in the early editing stages — to his hometown paper the *Hartford Courant*. "I can tell you that the Fonz is in the video. That's about all I can say." Cuomo clearly had no idea what was to come.

But Brian Bell knew the clip was going to be a hit from the moment he walked on the set and spotted Al Molinaro and the extras already in costume. Blown away by the shoot, Bell called it "one of the most surreal experiences ever."

Concurrently, support from MTV continued to be phenomenal throughout the fall, with "Undone" elevating the band to headliner status again in time for some shows in the Midwest during Thanksgiving week 1994. Several sets were taped during this jaunt, including one at the Horizontal Boogie Bar Show in Rochester, New York, which gave birth to the live takes of "My Name Is Jonas" and "Surf Wax" that eventually were used as bonus tracks on the U.K. CD single of "Buddy Holly."

Meanwhile, reviews from the road kept on improving, as evidenced by Troy J. Augusto's review of the band's October 29 gig at the Ventura Theatre in the November 1 issue of *Daily Variety*. "The young, DGC-signed L.A. band, whose Everly Brothers-meet-Nirvana sound fueled recent MTV hit 'Undone — The Sweater Song,' have a knack for sweet pop melodies and searing, modern guitar sounds that translate well to the stage," Augusto wrote.

Although critics were increasingly supportive, after six months of non-stop touring and plugging, the group was road weary — especially frontman Rivers. "Touring's a necessary evil and mostly a pain," he said by late November. "Every day a new city, a new hotel which looks the same, all kinds of people that you're obliged to deal with, the ongoing craziness of it. I hate all that."

Much of this was exacerbated by the fact that life on the road was stifling to Rivers creatively. "I can't write songs on the road," he confessed. "So that's another drag about touring. I guess I'm only here to support the album. It's part of the deal; you make the album, you have to go out and support it.

"The actual playing's the only neat thing," Cuomo continued. "Sometimes, we're flat and it doesn't happen. Or the audience is not into it and the gig doesn't happen. But mostly, we put on a strong show and we play the tunes just like they are on the album, but with more passion."

Becoming more and more disillusioned with his newfound fame, a dejected Cuomo started to defer to Matt, Pat, and Brian when it came to tour publicity. "Whatever adolescent rock 'n' roll fantasies I had are long gone," he said. "I don't want to sleep with a different girl every night, I don't do cocaine and only drink in self-defense. I'm not getting much out of it, I guess.

"I guess I don't have the brightest outlook," Rivers continued, sounding like a mope. "I'm excited about the songwriting, I'm excited about the playing sometimes. A lot of the time I'm numb about the whole thing. I don't know that I would tour if I didn't have to."

By December, an increasingly despondent Rivers had handed the publicity reins over to his bandmates altogether and rarely picked them back up over the next two years. The decision was probably a wise one, as his gloomy perspective on life as a rock star probably would have been lost on his newfound and exuberant fans.

In Rivers' place, a comical Matt did the best job he could. "One day nobody wants to hear you and then when you turn around you are on the radio and the clubs are jammed," he marveled to a reporter from the *Plain Dealer*. "There is always something weird going on. We recently played Pittsburgh and the entire crowd started chanting 'Brian Bell! Brian Bell!' I can't understand our popularity, but I'm glad it's happening."

Sharp's sense of humor, however, sometimes careened with his low self-esteem. One minute he'd jokingly tell reporters, "I've met David Hasselhoff from *Baywatch*, so things must be good." The next, he'd serve up self-deprecation like "I don't think *Bass Player* magazine would have much to ask me. If you listen closely, you'll find I'm a pretty lousy bass player. The Weezer sound is straightforward power chords. I think that hides that I can barely manage a note."

When he wasn't knocking himself, Matt began using his time with the media to voice his frustration about the band's creative arrangement, saying that Weezer's music speaks for itself and reflects songwriter Cuomo's vision. "There is very little creative interaction between us," Sharp said unhappily. Wilson, too, was apparently bothered by Rivers' lock on all things creative. "Rivers writes pretty much all the music. I used to give him the music and he would write the lyrics to it, but he does it all pretty much now," stated the drummer. And so, fans began to get a glimpse into the discordant world of Weezer.

If Sharp's touring observations ("It gets so that you can't remember what town you are in when you are in them") spoke for the band, it was clear they all needed to recharge their batteries. But with the newly completed "Buddy Holly" video an instant sensation on MTV and with tours of Europe, Japan, and Australia planned for the first half of 1995, there was little time for rest in the Weezer camp, save for a brief break at Christmas.

The video for "Buddy Holly," which seamlessly fused new footage of the band with vintage reaction shots from the 1970s sitcom *Happy Days*, became an overnight smash on the music video network in late 1994. Featuring actor Al Molinaro — who for years played Al Delvicchio, the proprietor of Arnold's — making a cameo in the new stock alongside the band, the clip begins with Al plugging his hometown in the band introduction, saying, ". . . from Kenoah, Wisconsin: Weezer!"

As Weezer performs the song dressed in 1950s garb, the video's savvy editing intersperses new footage of the band with a wicked dance sequence by the Fonzie character, played by Henry Winkler. "All of a sudden, I'm cool with my three children because I'm in the video," bragged Winkler that December.

"The idea of it being on the set of *Happy Days* came pretty early," Spike Jonze remembered. "My editor Eric Zumbrunnen and I went through hundreds of episodes, pretty much every one that had anything in Arnold's, and when we found the footage of Fonzie dancing, it was like a goldmine."

"We rebuilt the inside of Arnold's — the restaurant on *Happy Days* — and we dressed up and we would film a scene," Pat Wilson explained at the time. "We bought some film footage of *Happy Days* and just put it all together. When they filmed us they processed it and made it look a little grainy so it matched the quality of the old footage of *Happy Days*. I mean, you can tell when Fonzie does his dance, then you see us, you can tell it's a different guy and not Fonzie. But for the most part it looked really good. I think the thing that makes it really come off is the fact that Al is in it also."

Featuring footage from *Happy Days* episode #53, otherwise known as "They Call It Potsie Love," and including snippets from several other episodes, the video was also an immediate hit with critics. Although it didn't air until the last month of 1994, the "Buddy Holly" clip made a number of year-end "Best of 1994" lists. For instance, Chris Willman from the *Los Angeles Times* loved the video. He wrote, "*Happy Days* are here again — quite literally in this ingeniously silly clip, which has postmodern Weezer bewigged at Arnold's pre-modern '50s malt shop, doing a set for Richie, Joanie, et al. By the climax, Fonzie is so moved by this untimely alternativeness that he breaks into a precursor to the break-dance, right in cue with the tune."

Willman also remarked how Jonze's new photography meshes with the old footage in such a way that viewers "may come away with the delusion that Weezer was digitally inserted into the '70s footage." Elsewhere, veteran *Baltimore Sun* critic J.D. Considine touted the video with the following sentence: "As dazzling as it is to see this band dropped seamlessly into an episode of *Happy Days*, the video's real achievement is the way it underscores the latent pop appeal of the song itself."

"'Buddy Holly' was so catchy," said Rye Coalition's Dave Leto. "It was pretty much a perfect pop song. You felt happy as soon as you heard it. Nothing sounded like that at the time, which I think definitely worked in Weezer's favor, but there is no doubt that Spike Jonze's video propelled this record to its status. Everyone loves *Happy Days* and the song and the visual fit perfectly together. It was funny and smart. It was one of the first, if not *the* first time someone used the *Forrest Gump* technology for a music video."

"The song was on MTV incessantly," said The Reunion Show's Diaz. "But that's what people were ready to hear in 1994, because it had become such a bland time for rock and roll and just pop culture in general."

Wrapping up their triumphant first year in the limelight with a series of highly publicized performances, the downhearted men of Weezer initially touched down at the third annual Q101 Twisted Christmas Concert in Chicago on December 1, playing with notables like Dinosaur Jr., Bad Religion, Korn, and labelmates Hole and Veruca Salt. At Madison Square Garden on December 5, Brian, Matt, Pat, and Rivers played alongside luminaries like Bon Jovi, Melissa Etheridge, Sheryl Crow, Indigo Girls,

Toad the Wet Sprocket, and again, Hole, as part of New York radio station z100's Jingle Ball.

Less than a week later, on December 11, Weezer played another holiday radio gig, performing before a sellout crowd at KROQ's "Almost Acoustic Christmas" show at the Universal Amphitheatre in Los Angeles. This time, joining acts like Liz Phair, Luscious Jackson, and the Cranberries, the band were met with a roaring crowd already amped by Winkler's introduction. Unfortunately, Cuomo, who was sick with a sore throat and worn down, spent the day preceding the show in a Universal City hotel on bedrest.

A few days later, the members of Weezer took a break from their frenzied ascent. Rivers hopped a plane home to Connecticut, where he spent Christmas with his mother and brother. His aim during his break from the band was to "play piano, take long walks in the snow, and hopefully write some songs."

Shortly after Christmas, Stephen Thompson of the *Wisconsin State Journal* ranked *Weezer* as one of the year's best albums. Beating out one of Rivers Cuomo's favorite songwriters at the time, Lou Barlow, who ranked at #5 with Sebadoh's *Bakesale* (Sub Pop), *The Blue Album*, as it began to be known, came in at #4. "If you like 'Undone — The Sweater Song' and 'Buddy Holly,' you'll feel the same way about the other eight songs here," the critic penned. "The album is full of buoyant, sing-along guitar rock that lifts your spirits like no record since Urge Overkill's *Saturation*."

Aside from the glowing regional press, *Weezer* finally earned its due from the granddaddy of all rock rags, *Rolling Stone*. In the December 29 issue, contributor Paul Corio gave an overall positive review of the disc. "Weezer's Rivers Cuomo is great at sketching vignettes (the Dungeons & Dragons games and Kiss posters that inspire the hapless daydreamer of 'In the Garage'), and with sweet inspiration like the waltz tempo of 'My Name

Is Jonas' and the self-deprecating humor of lines like 'I look like Buddy Holly/You're Mary Tyler Moore,' his songs easily ingratiate."

Putting a lid on 1994, the increasingly elusive Rivers looked back on the year his life changed forever by downplaying Weezer's success. "As to how well [the album] did, that was a total surprise," Cuomo said. "I knew we were a good band; I just didn't know how many people would get what we're doing. It's more of a relief that they do. It means we can carry on."

chapter twelve

blast off

On the heels of a crazy year, and with a sorely needed respite from touring and the music business in general, Rivers Cuomo escaped home to Connecticut for a month-long Christmas break in late December 1994. He visited his paternal grandmother in Rochester, New York, during his stay, and when he wasn't in the presence of his family, the Weezer front-man — having brought his 8-track recorder and guitars along — had a prolific songwriting spell back east. Rivers also began piecing together new song ideas with previously demoed tunes on a cassette to test his track sequencing ideas for the group's next album, which he was tentatively titling *Songs from the Black Hole*.

Mostly consisting of new 8-track demos — with the exception of a couple that dated back to 1993 — *Songs from the Black Hole* was conceived as a rock opera. The zealous plan was built from titles like "Blast Off!," "You Won't Get with Me Tonight," "Maria's Theme," "Come to My Pod," "This Is Not for Me," "Tired of Sex," "Superfriend," "She's Had a Girl," "Good News!," "Now I Finally See," "Getchoo," "I Just Threw Out the Love of My Dreams," "No Other One," "Devotion," "What Is This I Find?," "Longtime Sunshine," and "Why Bother?" And according to Cuomo, *SFTBH* was "supposed to be a whole album of songs transed together." The plan was to have each song flow together seamlessly, using a technique akin to Side Two of The Beatles' *Abbey Road*.

While looking ahead to Weezer's sophomore album, January 1995 found the band reconvening to remix "Say It Ain't So" for radio, trimming a second off the original 4:18 running time and tweaking the drums and vocals. Rivers also had his first-ever magazine article published that month when *Details* ran "Road Worriers: 24 Hours with Weezer." Chronicling a day in the life of a modern rock band on the rise, the happenings of the day were rather tame. Cuomo prefaces the piece by writing, "A couple of months ago, I though it would be a good idea to write a description of a typical day in the life of Weezer. Unfortunately, it turned out to be one of the lamest days of my life."

In the piece, he affirms the notion that the life of a popular touring band is pretty mundane stuff as he describes waking up late in a Houston hotel room and brushing his teeth with the PBS children's show *Barney and Friends* on the television in the background. Later, after the band misses their plane to Seattle for a radio station–sponsored event, he explains how the group wound up in Albuquerque with an unplanned night off. It's not exactly cocaine and strippers when the lads partake in oddball tomes like *The Book of Leviticus* and sub-par Hollywood sequels like *Terminator 2*.

When not trying his hand at magazine articles, Cuomo found time in early '95 to prep Weezer for their first international dates. En route to London with plans to launch the overseas installment of their World Domination Tour at the city's Splash Club on January 30, the band was on a high, having just scored their first major chart achievement a day earlier. *Weezer*, on the strength of "Undone" and "Buddy Holly," peaked at #16 on the *Billboard* album survey on its way to eventual U.S. sales in excess of three million copies. Ironically, "Buddy Holly," the album's breakout hit, according to Brian, "was the song that nearly didn't get on the album."

The day of the Splash Club gig, Weezer — like The Beatles, Jimi Hendrix, Led Zeppelin, and The Who before them — took advantage of an invitation to record at the British Broadcasting Corporation's 24-track recording studio. For the BBC session, the group re-recorded two takes of "My Name Is Jonas," as well as performances of "No One Else," "In the Garage," and "Surf Wax America."

Three days later, and in tandem with Weezer's European tour, the band's "Buddy Holly" CD single was released in the U.K. Featuring a picture of a school-aged, bespectacled Rivers sitting beside his younger brother Leaves, the disc housed live takes of "My Name Is Jonas" and "Surf Wax America" that were recorded live in Rochester the previous fall. Also appended was the *DGC Rarities, Vol. 1* version of "Jamie."

Tour stops abroad included Amsterdam, Rotterdam, Stockholm, Oslo, Milan, and Paris in addition to a number of cities in Germany, England, and Spain. Sadly, during the trek, Matt Sharp had to rush home to Virginia after learning that his father had suffered a stroke. Aside from canceling the remaining shows on the European jaunt, the most frugal choice for the band was to remain abroad until Matt returned. This left Pat, Brian, Rivers, and Karl stranded in Hamburg, Germany, for a week.

Making the best of their time, the group rented a mid-priced recording studio to work on some demos. Pat and Karl laid down some material as Southern Fried Swing, including a tune called "The Complete History of Techno," which Koch said, "was done solely to make fun of the nasty music being created in the studio next door." Rivers, meanwhile, worked on material from *Songs from the Black Hole*, putting down new versions of a few tracks, including a new take of "Blast Off!" that included a robotic voice effect provided by a rented vocoder.

Although the *SFTBH* concept was eventually abandoned later that year, Karl explained that during the winter, spring, and summer of 1995, the band "debated the semantics of how to pull [*SFTBH*] off, and indeed, if it should even be done. Some of the songs were in fact rehearsed as a band, some were played out live, and some made it all the way to the second Weezer album

JAY BLAKESBERG

No One Else: Cuomo copes with
newfound fame

— although by then the album concept was quite different."

"Blast Off!" — which Rivers himself has called "one of the greatest melodies *anyone's* ever written" — is one of several songs that have made it to the Internet with the advent of MP3s and file-sharing technology. But the version now widely available possesses splices that Karl called "Scotch tape edits." The song finds Cuomo's personal happiness at odds with newfound fame as he juxtaposes his nouveau riche rock star status with bouts of depression.

So far, there are four other songs available as downloads from the *Black Hole* concept: "Come to My Pod," "Longtime Sunshine," "Tired of Sex," and "Oh No This Is Not for Me." With "Longtime Sunshine," a beautiful and revelatory escapist piano ballad that rivals the finest work of Ben Folds, Cuomo sings of his desire to leave L.A. for a state "back east" like Vermont or Maine, where he can settle down with a good woman and build a home with a wood stove. Rivers also sings of finding satisfaction in the simple things. Predicting his future, Cuomo would get his wish in the fall of 1995.

Upon Matt's return to Europe, the band taped a performance for the Paris radio show known as "The Black Session" on February 21. Opening for critical favorites Radiohead, who were supporting their acclaimed second album *The Bends*, Weezer ran through six of the debut's ten tunes, including obligatory versions of "Buddy Holly" and "Undone."

During Weezer's five weeks overseas, Pat Wilson and Brian Bell both spoke to London's *The Independent*, in respective pre- and post-gig stories on the band. Two days before their second gig in the city, Wilson explained the band's fan appeal by cracking, "Who can relate to David Coverdale?" With this one inquisitive remark, Wilson dismissed all that is bloated and boring about the cock rock that once ruled the charts. Describing the group's appeal to fans, the piece put it simply: "People can relate to them. Evidence? Their popularity is spreading like a virus."

Assessing his bandmates that month Wilson opined, "Rivers is not without humor, Matt is a porn star, Brian is a prince and our fashion consultant, while I'm . . . married." Here the Weezer drummer revealed for the first time that he had tied the knot with his fiancée, Jen.

In the second article for *The Independent*, Cuomo, by then clearly sick of doing interviews, ditched the London press in favor of taking in an opera. In his absence, Brian explained, "He's gone to the opera because he wants to study opera at university."

With the emergence of those details, Weezer were not only solidifying their image as rock nerds but becoming comfortable with the designation. "If someone's paying attention it doesn't worry me, no matter what the reason is," Bell said at the time. "We're nerds compared to a typical rock band — none of us are big drinkers or partiers. We're not concerned with picking up girls every night."

Weezer gave the impression they were a new, largely wholesome breed in the post–Kurt Cobain music world; they were the anti-grunge rock alternative. "Nirvana opened doors for bands like us to get exposure on MTV, and now major labels see potential for making money off us," added Bell. "But there was definitely too much grunge — it was too dark and everyone started to sound like Pearl Jam. Some of our songs are about depression. 'The Sweater Song' is about a relationship break-up. Although maybe you couldn't tell that from the happy-go-lucky, catchy chorus and the party atmosphere."

In March 1995, *Guitar World* ran one of Rivers Cuomo's most candid early interviews, which actually took place the day of the band's Madison Square Garden gig three months earlier. In the piece he divulged his desire to abandon his English studies in favor of classical music, and revealed that he had applied to the University of California at Berkeley for the fall of that year. Speaking candidly about being a metal devotee in his teen years, Cuomo even joked about calling the group's next record *Weezer II* or *Back for More, Back for the Attack* in tribute to outfits of his youth like Ratt and Dokken. Rivers also professed to being tired of playing the same ten songs off *Weezer* day in and day out.

"I was sick of playing them before we did our record," he said. "We practiced every night and played them out for a year before we even got a deal. Once you play a song a hundred times, you're pretty much sick of it. But tonight we're playing Madison Square Garden — there will be twenty thousand people singing along to 'The Sweater Song.' It doesn't bother you so much when you hear all those people getting excited."

Cuomo balked at the "overnight success" tag the media was hanging on Weezer, as stardom was a goal of his from youth. And in its early stages, Rivers was bittersweet about his fame, revealing concerns that Weezer might be perceived early on as a joke band because of the "quirkiness" of "Undone" and the "goofiness" of the "Buddy Holly" video. "That would be a bummer," he said. "The thing is, when you go to do a video, you start out with a serious idea and you think the song is serious. But then something happens, and your video just goes crazy and ends up being really funny. If you take a video too seriously, it just comes out like crap. I don't know if there has ever been a good serious rock video. I guess some people like 'Jeremy' by Pearl Jam, but that couldn't be us. If we did that it would be terrible."

But the instantly popular "Buddy Holly" video, part of the continued wave of alternative music in general, still managed to piss off some of the on-the-outs metal bands Rivers worshipped as a teen. "I mean, we sold ten million records," Cinderella frontman Tom Keifer bitched at the time. "You can't tell me they're all listening to Weezer now."

Ironically, it was Rivers and his bandmates who were out-of-the-closet on their metal past. "At least Weezer is really on the table about being into Crüe and Ratt," said labelmate Jim Shapiro, drummer for Veruca Salt, at the time.

During their ascent, Weezer's members' attempts to fill those hard partying rock star shoes from a behavioral standpoint were a bust. From their Las Vegas hotel room on March 10, for instance, before a gig to launch both that city's brand new Hard Rock Café and their spring 1995 U.S. tour, the Weezer guys threw perishables into the pool below rather than the lamps, televisions, and furniture that music fans might expect. "We were in a nice hotel room, and it was the first time we actually threw stuff out of the window," said guitarist Bell describing the incident. So what did they heave into the pool below? "Oranges, apples, and a pineapple. It was nothing Keith Moon would do, but I finally felt like a rock star."

Meanwhile, Weezer's concert set at the new Hard Rock resulted in further national television exposure, as excerpts from the show were filmed and later broadcast on an MTV special. Performance footage of "The World Has Turned and Left Me Here" and "My Name Is Jonas" stood in stark contrast to live clips by soul icon Al Green and recently resuscitated new wavers Duran Duran.

If Duran Duran's new wave hairstyles were a fashion no-no by 1995, then shaving one's eyebrows was certainly a questionable rock 'n' roll move. Brian realized his mistake as soon as he'd done it, and wound up wearing glasses to hide the peculiar look until they grew back in. But after years toiling in an unsuccessful band, the guitarist was more than happy with his newfound roles as a rock star and player of Rivers' songs. "He pretty much writes a song, brings it to the band, and we'll screw it up — make it a band song," Mr. Bell said at the height of MTV's loyalty to "Buddy Holly."

But for Pat, who had co-founded the group with Rivers and was in on the early songwriting, such a diminished creative role was clearly a continued source of soreness. Rivers writes pretty much all the music," Wilson complained at the time. "I used to give him the music and he would write the lyrics to it, but he does it all pretty much now.

"Basically, this is just Rivers' band," Pat added. "It used to be different. It used to be more of a band 'band,' but Rivers isn't down with that idea. He says he's not interested in playing anybody else's music. And the idea that he would say, 'This is all about me' — it hurts me. Sometimes I'm so sympathetic to Rivers, and sometimes I'm so antagonistic. It's the most amazing thing, and I just can't figure it out."

Despite his frustrated existence as Weezer's drummer, Pat Wilson did his best to accept his supporting role in the band. And every now and then, the founding member would get the opportunity to come out from behind his kit to play guitar. During the band's spring tour of the United States, for instance, when the men of Weezer performed an all-acoustic set at the Cat's Paw Studios for Atlanta radio station WNNX, Wilson himself picked up a guitar to augment Rivers, Matt, and Brian's "unplugged" jamboree. Two songs from the set — "No One Else" and "Jamie" — wound up as B-sides on import versions of the "Say It Ain't So" CD single later in the year.

During the spring leg of the World Domination tour, Rivers caught himself — and no doubt his bandmates — off guard when he learned that he had been accepted to study English, not at UC Berkeley as he hinted at in interviews, but at Harvard. The previous fall, Cuomo, who up to this point had only studied part time, took a self-guided tour of the prestigious university's campus following a Weezer sound check at a nearby venue, Local 186. On a whim, he dropped by the admissions office, picked up an application, filled it out, and submitted it. Tired of playing the same dozen or so songs each night, the twenty-four-year-old songwriter and guitarist began to imagine himself in the post-graduate nine-to-five world.

"I wrote my application essay on how disillusioned I was with the rock lifestyle," Rivers revealed. "They'd probably never received such a thing before. I don't think [the others in the band] were really that surprised. I was a weird, anti–rock star, capable of doing something so lame all along. It was just a matter of time."

Putting the dream that inspired the demo for "Longtime Sunshine," one of his post-*Weezer* compositions, into action, Cuomo later confessed, "I had this fantasy of moving to New England, going to an Ivy League school, getting married, and having a family. I wanted to be a boring person."

Meanwhile, Weezer had just landed their biggest magazine write-up yet, as *Rolling Stone* covered the band in March 1995. Oddly, the story found Rivers blatantly defying his own rock star dreams by avoiding reporter Mim Udovitch as she chased the band around Europe. And by leaving Matt, Pat, and Brian to handle his press duties again, the story didn't quite pan out in the camp's favor. Rivers' "shy" and "elusive" routine is rumored to have bumped the group from a sure-bet cover story to a lower profile piece. Dubbed "They're not punk, they're not pop, they're not pretty, but they're huge — Weezer, Revenge of the Nerds," Udovitch's story was damn near sabotaged by her subject's main character.

In the article, Brian marvels at the fact that Weezer's debut album is a chart hit. ("It's so amazing that suddenly we're, like, No. 16 on *Billboard*.") Matt points out that the band's sound is dry because "reverb is not good for the kids." Pat even theorizes that the band — at that time all the rage with the eight- to twelve-year-old demographic — "could have [their] own TV show," but then discounts that suggestion because if "the kids met Rivers he'd make them really depressed."

For all the revelations and pranks in the story — concluding with Cuomo himself apologizing to the reporter over the P.A. system during their London gig for his refusal to talk to her — the feature somehow succeeded in putting the weird world of Rivers Cuomo on display to millions of magazine subscribers. Evasive and sealed, the frontman's silence and his bandmates' thoughts on the group say as much about Cuomo, arguably more, than his own words might.

Perhaps *Weezer* producer Ocasek summed up the piece, and Cuomo himself, most articulately when he chronicled the "Buddy Holly" bard this way: "You know, socially, Rivers would stand in a corner, but I don't know if that's a weakness. Andy Warhol did that, too. And having to have too much control can be a weakness, but looked at in a different way, it can also be a strength. And America should be proud that they have a Rivers in the pools of records coming out. He's writing intelligent lyrics, he's writing melody. I feel pretty certain that Rivers is a real force. He's writing songs, and whatever happened to songs? Please, let's have some more."

With fans' noses still deeply ensconced in the March 23 issue of *Rolling Stone*, the band, hot off the triumphant "Buddy Holly" clip, set about lensing its follow-up with a new director, Sophie Muller. Muller, who would go on to make videos for No Doubt ("Don't Speak") and Blur ("Song 2"), took Weezer home again by filming "Say It Ain't So" at the Amherst House where the band had lived just a year before. The clip was shot on April 9, 1995, the day after the quartet wrapped up their spring North American dates at the Hollywood Palladium.

Shot in the same garage pictured inside the CD booklet of *Weezer*, and where the band regularly rehearsed between 1992 and 1994, the performance video finds band assistant Karl Koch doing his laundry as the band rocks out emotively around him. Elsewhere in the video, a close-up on the washing machine reveals a picture of one of Rivers' Kiss heroes, Peter Criss.

Re-enacting the past for the clip found the Weezer frontman reminiscing about meals of noodles and toast. "It definitely has a very homey vibe for me," Rivers said of the Weezer house that day, before offering up some arguable comments about being a shy musician. "I'm not much of a performer at all. It's something you're born with or not, and I'm not. Put me in front of a camera and I just turn off and try to hide. Some people turn on and it's really entertaining. But that's not me." Could this be the very same bicycle shorts–donning Zoom guitarist that was largely flash over substance just a few years earlier?

Responding to the hype-sensitive alt-rock community's backlash surrounding Weezer's meteoric rise on MTV and their Ramones-meets-Beach Boys sound, Cuomo succinctly snapped, "I've heard backlash against us since our first show. When people talk bad about us now, it doesn't strike me as this new trend."

As the band wrapped work on their third video in just nine months, there was little denying they had achieved more success than they ever could have imagined. "Everything has been a surprise — and kind of weird," Matt admitted in April of '95. "We've never had this ridiculous dream of being on MTV and taking over the universe."

"When you're touring, I don't think you really notice any growth," Sharp continued. "You don't listen to the radio so you don't have any sense of your record getting big." While the video for "Say It Ain't So" failed to surpass the frenzy of "Buddy Holly," it received regular MTV airplay. Alternative radio followed suit, bumping the album excerpt to #7 on *Billboard*'s Modern Rock Tracks survey in the summer of '95.

"Weezer had become enormous," Amherst housemate Justin Fisher remembered. "The whole thing when they started to get big was to down-play their worth. There was a strong focus on teaching each other just to be cool — and *don't* think you're the shit. What they did was take on these fake names, which they'd call each other just to keep their egos in control. I don't remember all of them, but I think Pat was 'Winky Smile,'" Fisher laughed.

As *Weezer* continued to fly off record store shelves, Cuomo followed up the "Say It Ain't So" video shoot and the Hollywood Palladium gig with a painful leg operation. Designed to stretch out his right leg, the unique sur-gery required doctors to deliberately break his limb and attach a brace to it that slowly stretched it so that bone could grow in between the gap. While music publications like the U.K.–based *Vox* were touting Rivers as the "king of post-grunge nerdcore," he was much closer to the king of pain for the bulk of 1995. "It hurts but it will be worth it," R.C. assured shortly after the operation.

The surgery had become necessary because Cuomo's leg and joints connected to the leg were becoming so painful for him that walking had become a chore.

Throughout the late spring and early summer of '95, a post-op Rivers sported a lethal-looking metal cage that was bolted directly through his leg halfway down his right thigh. "I have to keep the cage on until the bone is completely solid, which probably won't happen until the end of the year," he said at the time.

"See this scar?" he continued, revealing the wound just above his knee. "That's where they went in and broke the bone in half. They took a ham-mer and chisel and cracked it all the way around. Now, this frame is bolted on to either side of that crack, so the bone can't move either way or col-lapse. Each day, I have to turn each of these four cranks and extend the screws, separating the bone by a millimeter a day."

According to Cuomo, the unorthodox surgical technique surfaced in error, when a patient in Soviet Russia attempting to reduce his overlong leg with a similar device cranked it the wrong way by mistake. His doctors were startled to discover that his bones began growing as a result of his actions. "It was an accident," Rivers chuckled. "Like every other great discovery. They used to just cut the bone and stick some other bone in there, from some farm animal or something. When I was around ten that was what they offered me. I said: 'No thanks, I'll wait until something better comes along.'"

Still, Rivers, who demand-fed himself painkillers in the months that followed the surgery, endured such excruciating post-operative pain on the twenty-second day after the operation that he chronicled it in a notebook and vividly spoke of the agony. "I remember that day well," he recollected. "I was having a muscle spasm all day long. Without warning, it would seize up and I would just scream." This sort of misery didn't come cheap — the operation cost Cuomo in the neighborhood of $50,000 — and he acknowledged that without the breakout success of the debut, financing the corrective surgery wouldn't have been feasible. "I couldn't have had the operation before Weezer," he assured weeks after the procedure. "I wouldn't have been working, I wouldn't have had time to recuperate, or the money to pay for it."

Rivers "recuperated" by honing material for the band's forthcoming second album, reportedly writing a song for Vegas legend Tom Jones, and firming up plans to move to Cambridge, Massachusetts, that September to study at Harvard. Meanwhile, his Weezer bandmates sought out creative outlets of their own. Brian Bell — along with bandmates Susan Fox (his then-girlfriend) and drummer Mike Elliott — cut a new Space Twins demo. "We Are the Space Twins" was the name of the project, which boasted six tunes: "Vacation States," "Here Comes the Sun," "My Love," "Smells Like . . . Hot Dogs," "Thoughts of Lust," and "Space Twins Theme." The demo landed the indie-pop trio gigs of their own in the Los Angeles area and also begat the "No Show" single on World Domination Records.

Meanwhile, Matt Sharp's side outfit, the Rentals, recorded their "Poop Alley" sessions during several outings at that studio. A track called "California" found its way onto the Win Records compilation *The Poop Alley Tapes*, which housed tunes by other rising stars on the L.A. scene like Beck, That Dog, and Spain.

These Rentals recordings consisted of contributors Pat Wilson (drums), producer Tom Grimley (Moog synthesizer), Rod Cervera (guitar), Jim Richards (keyboards), Cherielynn Westrich (vocals), and That Dog's Rachel Haden on vocals and Petra Haden on vocals and violin. The collective's sessions were so productive that they spawned the full contents of what would later become the group's Maverick Records debut *Return of the Rentals*.

Despite the success of the side projects, Weezer took precedence for everyone. In June 1995, the band had a brief studio outing. As Cuomo was now able to stand and perform with the help of his pain medication, Weezer entered Bearsville Studios in Woodstock, New York, for a quick 24-track recording session in late May with producer Rob Cavallo. Riding the success of Green Day's major label debut *Dookie*, which he also produced, Cavallo was an in-demand studio hand by the time the session took place. He also happened to be the son of Bob Cavallo, joint-founder of Atlas/Third Rail Management, the outfit that handled Weezer's affairs.

The end product was the first studio version of "You Gave Your Love to Me Softly," a song that wound up on the soundtrack to the teen movie *Angus*. "The whole thing was a bit incestuous," Karl Koch remembered of the soundtrack session for the film, as the younger Cavallo was producing the song for a film produced by the elder Cavallo's Third Rail. "Rivers was on strong medication and his leg brace was still quite freshly implanted. [He] struggled with his vocals and was never really satisfied with his performance on this one. Of course, the rest of us all think it sounds fine."

When the European tour launched on June 12 in Barcelona, Spain, the band had begun taking the stage to the *Battlestar Galactica* theme. The trek took them to England, Scotland, Belgium, and Germany before wrapping on July 9 in Stockholm, Sweden. "Rivers is dealing but he's in a LOT of pain," Koch reported from the tour. "We are always looking for ways to reduce the distances he has to walk as he's very slow and it's very hard for him."

A twelve-day break from the road followed, during which time "Say It Ain't So" — already a U.S. alternative radio and MTV favorite — was released on July 13 as a commercial CD single in the United Kingdom. Slightly tweaking the A-side as a remix, with minimal vocal and drum alterations, the single also boasted a pair of B-sides, including acoustic versions of "No One Else" and "Jamie" from the aforementioned Cat's Paw studio session earlier in the year. Utilizing Rivers' own childhood art, the CD cover cleverly reverses a photo negative of the picture. According to Koch, the scene depicted is that of a "young soccer player scoring the winning soccer goal as the father roots the lad on." Completing the picture is a young Rivers' misspelling of the word "goll."

When the group resumed their North American tour in New Orleans on July 21, they were headlining above DGC labelmates Teenage Fanclub and That Dog. But their old pals in That Dog, veterans on the L.A. scene compared to Weezer, expressed a little animosity in interviews about the headliners. "We were friends with Weezer a while before they signed, and they were actually opening for us," marveled Rachel Haden. "Now they've got Teenage Fanclub opening for them. How many records has Weezer put out? One?"

Despite such mild resentment and the severe discomfort of his leg, Rivers led Weezer to fulfill another touring commitment. Midway through the trek, while in town for a concert in New York's Central Park, the band revisited CBS-TV's *The Late Show with David Letterman* to bang out a scorching version of "Say It Ain't So." Introducing the band, Letterman described the group as "a peppy power pop quartet" before handing the reins over to the mighty =w=.

The performance found a post-surgery Cuomo donning the same short haircut he sported in the song's video and wearing baggy khaki pants to mask his metal leg cage. Largely stationary near his microphone stand, and in noticeable pain, Rivers leaned on his left leg for most of the song. In contrast, the bespectacled Matt Sharp and his shortly cropped counterpart Brian Bell could barely contain their exuberance. As they careened around the stage, displaying an assortment of rock 'n' roll poses, a close-up on a green-haired Pat Wilson found the drummer all smiles as he pummeled his metallic blue drumkit with reckless glee. What is most remarkable about the appearance is how Rivers diligently trudged forth in such a severe state of discomfort. And although the bulk of Weezer's fans at the time were probably unaware of his suffering, instead probably assuming he was pissed off about something, it certainly helps to explain his inability to smile amid the glorious mayhem.

Earlier that day, Weezer's rhythm section found time to drop by MTV's studios to shoot their guest-host spot on the channel's Sunday night, alt-music program, *120 Minutes*. Sirs Wilson and Sharp were as loose as ever while talking up new videos from Hum and the Jon Spencer Blues Explosion, and a live performance by the pre–"Bittersweet Symphony" Verve.

Their appearance on the video network notwithstanding, Matt's position on the medium — regardless of the success it had yielded his band — was pretty amusing. "If you write music and you think videos are a serious art form, then you're an idiot," he observed. "We treat them like they should be treated. We just want to do things for videos that are fun for us and kind of poke fun of the whole video thing of being super-dramatic and serious and

'I'm this tortured artist.' If we did that it would just look ridiculous."

Later in the week, on August 8, *Weezer* earned a multi-platinum award from the RIAA for U.S. album sales in excess of two million. "None of us really expected any of this, so we're all handling it in different ways," Brian Bell said just days after the band received the double-platinum award. "It's not like I think we suck or anything, it's just that it's such a surprise. Personally, I know we've worked hard for what we have, but I also know that only a fraction of good bands actually make it this far, so it's cool."

Sharp reflected the same sentiment by saying, "Everybody in the band thought the songs were good and we wanted people to hear them, but we expected the record to fail. We were shocked when we were up around a thousand records. We were going, 'Oh, my God, all the people who own this record, we don't even know who they are! Wow, somebody went out and bought our record, somebody who does not know us and is not a friend, not even a friend of a relative or anything. It's just somebody who heard it and liked it.' That absolutely is the weirdest thing in the world to all of us."

In spite of the band's ascent to popularity and wealth, Sharp confessed little had changed in Weezer's day-to-day lives as road dogs. "We haven't had time to think about anything. We've just been on the road constantly. You get in your van and go. The food is the same. We don't eat meat, we're vegetarians, so we end up getting, like, the same junk back in the clubs. They give us cheese sandwiches or something. So it's not too extravagant or too glamorous."

If cheese sandwiches were Weezer's baseline as celebrities, perks for the band included Cuomo meeting one of his biggest musical heroes, Kiss' Gene Simmons. The encounter with the tongue-exposing, hard-rock bassist followed a KROQ-sponsored performance on August 18, the closing night of Weezer's World Domination Tour at the Universal Amphitheatre.

Following a gig that saw Cuomo bat audience-tossed beach balls back into the audience with his cane — a much tamer move than an earlier Ohio show where he dropped his trousers to show the audience his post-op leg contraption — he met the man so influential in his quest for rock.

"I couldn't tell him how much he meant to me," a star-struck Cuomo later reported. Sadly, meeting Gene — a self-professed ladies' man — failed to help Rivers (or so he said) when it came to scoring with the opposite sex and tasting the fruits of the rock star life.

"We somehow seem to have avoided that whole groupie thing," he sighed that same summer. "If I could see how I'm living now when I was fifteen and dreaming about being a rock star, I would be so disappointed because I thought the whole point of it was to get chicks. But now I'm in the position to live like that, it's no longer appealing. If I could have had this when I was fifteen, that's the time to do it. But now I'm twenty-five, I'm an old fart and my values have completely changed. I feel like I've been robbed."

But the truth is that Rivers probably could have scored with any lady in the house at the MTV Video Music Awards on September 7, as his band dominated the 12th annual event held at New York's Radio City Music Hall. However, the Weezer frontman passed on attending, instead opting to dive headfirst into his new identity as a Harvard University undergrad. Pat was also conspicuously absent from the event, with Koch, old band ally Pat Finn, and "Buddy Holly" director Spike Jonze filling in for the drummer and frontman by joining Brian and Matt onstage for the collection of trophies in the categories of Best Alternative Video, Breakthrough Video, Best Direction, and Best Editing. If few people noticed the substitutions, even fewer clued into Matt Sharp's puzzling use of an Eastern European accent during his turns at the microphone.

Cuomo's and Wilson's absence — along with Matt Sharp's upcoming Rentals album through Madonna's Maverick label — did little to help quell talk that the band was imploding. "We're definitely not breaking up," Brian Bell told the press around this time.

"I know there have been some rumors."

So with Rivers off to study at a college that at this point he'd reveal as "one of those expensive ones" where he could "disappear, grow a beard, not talk to anyone [and] not make any friends," fans wondered how someone so much in the public eye could walk away from it all. Clearly, few understood the anonymity Cuomo craved. "I just want to disappear and study," the fame-addled rock star proclaimed. And that's exactly what he did.

friends of p

Whenthe World Domination Tour came to a close in August 1995, the members of Weezer took a sorely needed break. It lasted seven days. On the twenty-fifth of the month, just days before Rivers Cuomo was to head north to a newly acquired home in Cambridge, Massachusetts, and his educational pursuits at Harvard University, the band gathered for two weeks of recording in the same studio where *Weezer* had been made just two years earlier.

"The album's already done in our heads," Brian Bell promised earlier in the month. "We're going for the deeper, darker, more experimental stuff, but we'll always be the Weezer you know and love." Achieving that fresh, conceptual sound meant forgoing Ric Ocasek's glistening production hand in favor of producing album #2 themselves. In these very early sessions for what would eventually become the quartet's 1996 *Pinkerton* album, the band attempted to record a "special coda" of several overlapping songs — including "Waiting on You," "Blast Off!," "Why Bother," and "Longtime Sunshine" — at Electric Lady.

"I think Rivers was trying to emulate a technique in classical music, where all the major elements of a musical piece are briefly recalled at the end," Karl Koch reported. Although Cuomo still retained hopes that *Songs from the Black Hole* would come to fruition at the outset of the sessions, after a few days of experimenting with the technique the foursome went back to its traditional methods of song structure. From August 28 to 31, the band tracked "Why Bother," "Getchoo," "No Other One," and "Tired of Sex."

In September, the group recorded "Devotion," a version of "I Just Threw Out the Love of My Dreams," a second and third take of "Getchoo," a second runthrough of "Waiting on You," a recording of "You Gave Your Love to Me Softly," and a repeat performance of "Longtime Sunshine."

In addition to the new recordings, "Suzanne," a song tracked in the summer of '94, was mixed elsewhere in the Electric Lady facility for the upcoming *Mallrats* soundtrack, which would be released on October 17. Meanwhile, Patrick — facing large gaps of free time due to Rivers' pending Harvard schedule and inspired by the fact that Matt's Rentals project inked a deal with Maverick — was working hard on his own, non-Weezer music in a different part of the studio. Putting himself out in front of a band he'd dub Huge Guy, Wilson booked studio time in tandem with Weezer's own at Electric Lady and cut what Koch later described as "some fairly slick demos." The drummer spent his time trucking up and down the facility's hallway between sessions for both bands. When Rivers wasn't in need of his services, Pat was a few doors away, crafting 24-track recordings with titles like "A Song of Healing and Transformation," "You Know I'd Like to Think," and "It's All So Simple."

As for the Weezer material, it was impressive to think that Cuomo was trying to deliver his new songs under miserable conditions. "Rivers was on painkillers," Bell said. "He had this painful contraption on his leg. It was painful for him to hold his guitar a certain way, so most of the songs are written in the first position [on the fret board]. I would almost have to egg the songs out of him."

In addition to the pain, he was also short on new material, having discovered that he was incapable of writing on the road. With only half an album on his hands, the pressure was on to find a new way to create songs. "That time touring was really terrible for me," he later admitted. "I kept trying and everything I wrote was terrible. I couldn't come up with anything."

For Rivers, Harvard offered him an opportunity to withdraw from stardom and recharge his batteries. "I had an all-consuming obsession with the idea of moving back to the Northeast, going to an Ivy League school, practicing piano a lot, not partying, not rocking, and finding a really nice, pure girl to settle down with," Cuomo said. Aside from scholarly reasons, Cuomo says he was also drawn to the school because it had "lots of cute Asian girls" and was close to where his mother lives and where he grew up.

Although he originally intended to study literature, thinking that he might end up an English teacher someday, the riches that *Weezer* yielded in 1995 changed his mind. "As soon as we became successful, I realized that I probably wouldn't have to get a job for a long time, so I changed to music."

So, following the MTV Awards, Koch helped Cuomo, still in his leg brace, migrate north to Cambridge. The members of Weezer and the master tapes from Electric Lady also left New York for Boston's Fort Apache Studios. Recording at the New England facility during the week of September 9–15, the group again ran through "Why Bother?," "Getchoo," "No Other One," "Tired of Sex," "Waiting on You," and "You Gave Your Love to Me Softly," before putting their second studio album on hold until they could reconvene during Rivers' winter break.

After an intense eighteen-month run, and with their first extended break in over two years, the remaining members of Weezer dispersed to various locales. Pat Wilson moved to Portland with his wife, Jen, aiming to restore his '67 Chevrolet Chevelle; Brian Bell, having declined an opportunity to play bass for labelmates Elastica, returned to Los Angeles to focus on work with the Space Twins; and Matt Sharp kept tremendously busy promoting the Rentals' forthcoming debut album.

On September 19, 1995, Matt Sharp unveiled the first Rentals single, "Friends of P," on San Diego's leading alternative music radio outlet, 91x. But the song selected to launch the band was just one of ten contagious, Moog-laced potential singles on *The Return of the Rentals*.

"I didn't play any of the Moog on the Rentals record," clarified Cherielynn Westrich, despite receiving the credit. "And I'm not sure how much was Matt and how much was Tom Grimley. I think Tom played and wrote and came up with ideas for a lot of the Moog stuff. I'm sure it was Tom's Moog that we used originally."

"Basically, Matt called me one day and asked if I would pretend to be in a band with him, and I was like, 'Okay,'" explained Westrich, who, along with Cervera, hung out in the Weezer circle of friends that also included the Croppers and the guys from Wax. "He had a meeting in San Diego with a small record company — I don't remember the name of it — and he was just trying to get a 7" single put out or something. He wanted to give the impression he had a band. So Rod and Matt and I went down there, and I had never even heard the Rentals music at that point. So we did that and they were interested, but nothing ended up happening with it. A few weeks later he called me and he wanted me to re-record the songs Rachel [Haden] already had sung, and then, from that point, really be in the band. So I agreed to it and we went through most of them. I know on the album there's a song or two Rachel is still on."

"The demos Matt did originally were very different, and I think Tom Grimley had a lot to do with the sound of the album and the Moogs being added on," said Westrich. "I know a lot of the ideas came from Tom, but he didn't get credit for those ideas. I don't think anybody did, except Matt [chuckles]."

Westrich even helped pen one of the album's strongest numbers. "He gave me 'My Summer Girl,' just the music, and said, 'Could you do something with it?'" Cherie remembered. "So I just took it home and I rewrote the melody line and then I wrote the words." However, a look through the album's credits shows no mention of the fact that she gave the song its life.

And for all of the involvement of Sharp's friends in helping him realize the project, sources say he pretty much tried to take credit for everything that anyone would let him. "I don't think Matt's a really nice person," Westrich said with many years of hindsight. "At first, Matt was really great and we were good friends. We'd go to parties and stuff and hang out. But I think he got a little full of himself at some point. I can't really point out where it happened, but when it started to come across in his behavior I just thought it was kind of odd. I was just surprised every time. Maybe I'm a little naive but every time he would do something mean I would just be surprised again."

Although she didn't want to disrupt what she had going with Supersport 2000, who were beginning to cause a buzz of their own in Los Angeles in 1995, Westrich said, "Matt convinced me to come on tour, because Matt said he wanted it to be me and him in all the publicity, that we would be in the pictures and do all the promotional stuff together. He said, 'Look, everywhere we'll go you can talk about Supersport, and maybe you can play some shows on the road,' because it was also Rod, and later Mike from my band with us. But right near the beginning of it all, Matt put an end to that. He quickly decided that he didn't want me involved in any interviews and stuff. He kind of cut me off, so it didn't work out as I was promised."

If it sounds like they might have been personally involved at any point leading up to his curt behavior, Westrich said, "Heck no. If it were true it would be more exciting, and when he started treating me this way I thought maybe there was a crush, but I didn't see it. I almost wonder if there might have been some jealousy at the beginning because I was a girl and when we'd walk into places, people noticed me and I think that might have bothered him. I remember we were in some radio station in Southern California just before the album came out and we sat down with a microphone in between us and Matt just grabbed the microphone and turned away from me. So I'm at a radio appearance without a mic, which I thought was sort of silly. So I sat there for a couple of minutes and the DJ was looking sort of uncomfortable. He would ask me a question and I would have to stand up and lean over Matt's shoulder to answer. I sat there for about two questions and then I thought, 'This is embarrassing.' I was shy and a little upset so I just got up and left. Then, I was standing out in the hallway waiting, and interestingly enough, I was near some office and a fax started coming in. And I saw pictures of the Rentals album. I peeked in and looked at it, and it was just Matt on the cover. I was like, 'What the heck?'

"They had already put the cover together and it was reportedly done, with both me and Matt together with a look similar to the video. And then I saw that, so when we got down to the limo outside the radio station I was like, 'Did they change the cover?' And Matt said 'Yeah.' And I said, 'Why wouldn't you say something to me about that? That's weird.' And he said, 'You know, Cherie, honestly, I thought it was more honest that way.' And I said, 'Okay Matt. Considering you asked me to pretend to be in the band in the first place.'

"I think that was the same conversation where he confided to me that after having dated a model he could never date a regular girl like me, ever. And I was like, 'Okay.' I don't know what model he was supposedly dating," Cherie said, starting to laugh.

Out from behind the scenes of the Rentals, and speaking of the debut single at the time, Matt informed the media that, "P. is whoever or whatever you want P. to be." Quickly added to heavy rotation at KROQ, the song soon took off at alternative radio when outlets nationwide followed suit.

Sharp later revealed that the song was written in homage to onetime super-model Paulina Porizkova, the wife of *Weezer* producer Ric Ocasek.

"I found out later that [Matt] had written that song about my wife," said Ocasek. "I thought the song was okay, although I thought it was a bit silly. The truth was that Rivers and P were actually the ones that got along really well. They both played classical piano and they always talked about girl and boy problems. Rivers was at my house a lot when we did that first record, and it was like Paulina was the psychiatrist. He used to come over to practice piano at my house for like hours when he was in New York. Their relationship was kind of different, and kind of nice."

But as for the Rentals' first single, Ocasek said, "I thought it sounded a lot like Weezer, which, right there, was pretty telling to me about how much individual creativity Matt actually had. I thought, well, if that's the best you can do outside of Weezer, then you sound just like your own band. I wasn't too fond of that part, actually. But the song was cute."

In late September, album advances were shipped to the media, complete with the band's oddball biography. In the one-sheet serviced with the disc, it is alleged that the members of the Rentals are the offspring of American embassy employees in Prague and that the band was founded in 1978. At that time, the Eastern Bloc group's "icy synthesizer anthems" were sabotaged when guitarist Rod Cervera was imprisoned for espionage. Twelve years later, he was released, and three years after that, during the outfit's first performance in fifteen years, pop diva Madonna supposedly discovered the reunited act in Prague. In receipt of such materials, Matt's use of Eastern European dialects earlier that month at the VMAs suddenly became clear to North American music scribes.

On October 24, 1995, Maverick Records officially released *Return of the Rentals* to an immediately warm reception. MTV, loyal to Sharp because of Weezer's VMA victories, put the video for "Friends of P" in "Buzz Bin" rotation, airing it several times a day. In stark contrast to the high-budget clips on the channel, the Rentals' black and white video was shot for a mere $400 — cheaper than the catering on most others. Featuring members of Sharp's side band — most noticeably the attractive Westrich — performing in a rigid and aloof manner with glasses and stodgy clothes against a plain white backdrop, the amusing film was directed by the Weezer bassist with his longtime friend Jason Ruscio.

"Rod shot the video for him," says Westrich, "and we all pitched in and that was the black and white 'Friends of P' video. I think that is what got the interest of Maverick Records. At that point, Matt had to really get it together or else. We all were friends [in the band] and so we all just pitched and said we would help him out."

Describing the video on a Rentals press junket, Matt called it "cold and removed," and added "it's certainly not the most high-tech video ever made." Shot with an old camera of Cervera's dating back to World War II, the Rentals' brainchild marveled that they "didn't have any professional editing equipment" when they put it together. "When we tried to edit it, the music would always be two or three seconds out of synch."

Sharp initially deemed all the footage from the shoot to be unusable. "I was bummed out because I thought that we had wasted the $400," Matt admitted. "The weird thing is that I don't know anything about making videos. We just sort of made this for fun. It wasn't made to sell records. We didn't think anyone would ever actually see it. It flips me out that MTV is even playing it."

In addition to the music channel's enthusiasm for it, the clip — maybe the most unlikely MTV hit of the year — earned critical praise in that week's *Entertainment Weekly* when it received a grade of B+ in a piece by David N. Meyer dubbed "Back in Black (And White)." "Weezer bassist Matt Sharp employs off-kilter close-ups, holds his edits an extra beat, and tosses in

Russian subtitles (huh?)," wrote Meyer. "Sharp isn't as funny as he thinks he is, but his Devo-esque wit is endearing nonetheless."

Sharp was thrilled with the music industry's immediate response to the single, and told *Billboard*, "It's very fulfilling to be able to completely do your own thing with no influence from the record company. That's what the Rentals are about." The album, recorded on the cheap by industry standards — for approximately $10,000 — received warm reviews as well. *CMJ New Music Report* touted the disc as "super pop," and declared "all of the songs are equally fun," before professing that the record's "dominant Moog synthesizer adds even more depth to the songs."

Meanwhile, a few weeks after running a feature on Sharp's unique musical outfit, *Billboard* again wrote of the Rentals: "In the tradition of ground-breaking bands like Suicide, the Cocteau Twins, and Polara, the Rentals make great power pop that happens to shatter the sonic boundaries between instruments."

Those retro-European pop references, likely spawned by the heavy presence of vintage Moog synthesizers throughout the record, were hardly a calculated move. "I think it's just coincidental," Sharp asserted. "I don't think the record sounds like an '80s record at all. Nobody would have played it in 1980. I love a lot of music from that time, but it wasn't pre-meditated on this record."

If early Rentals demos were extremely similar to Weezer's sound, those productions lacked most of the flourishes that the end product possessed. Clearly Sharp was concerned about being too derivative of his primary group. "After we had recorded the record, and it was really a straight-ahead thing, I listened to it for a while, and didn't really like a lot of the singing," Matt admitted. "Time went by, and then we went back into the studio to re-record some things, and there was a Moog there. I decided I wanted to use it for a couple of things, and then we just really started enjoying that. We decided to change everything and layer it with four or five Moogs in every song."

So what started as a bare-bones punk-guitar album evolved into a fun, new wave–derived keyboard disc. "We got into this Jeff Lynne thing where more is more," Sharp said, comparing the recording to those helmed by the Electric Light Orchestra founder.

Despite the heavy keyboard presence, Matt was unwilling to bill the Rentals as a keyboard band, due to the negative connotations. "U.S. audiences are too used to hearing just two guitars, bass, and drums," he concluded. "When you say music has synths and Moogs, people think the band plays Top 40 or mellower music, or European music, or something like Depeche Mode."

If Matt was a little surprised by the breakout success of the single, he was clearly enjoying all of the attention and accolades he was receiving during his hiatus from Weezer. The Rentals marked Sharp's freedom from the confines of merely playing bass and providing falsetto vocals. But any speculation that he might be splitting from his duties with the quartet that launched his career was quickly quashed. "We're all enjoying our break from the band," he declared, but said of his Weezer comrades, "We are all getting along better than ever." It was an odd proclamation he volunteered, as no one had asked if any infighting existed.

Although his participation in Weezer was still guaranteed, Sharp's Rentals were anything but a lark to him as the group set to embark on its first tour. "I've spent more time on the Rentals in the last year than I have on Weezer," Sharp insisted. "I had to sell guitars to make the Rentals record, but people still can't grip the concept that I can possibly be in two serious bands. They say, 'Uh, you're in Weezer and now you're in this other band. Uh, like, what's going on?'

"Most people tend to think of a band to the point of a marriage — to the point where people don't think you can do anything else," he defended. "I know that most people were like, 'Oh, great, a bass player wants to do a record.' I understand that. But it's not like, 'This is what Weezer has been holding me back from — I've always wanted to do this tribal record. . . .'"

"Rivers knows where I'm coming from, and I don't really have to explain much to him anymore," Matt asserted, acknowledging Cuomo's chief role in Weezer. "We have a very good understanding between the two of us. He's one of my best friends in the world, so I just say, 'Whenever you need me, just let me know and I'll stop and I'll do what you want me to do.'

"I love working with Rivers. He's very influential on me, he's my favorite songwriter. We work really hard and have a lot of fun — all that corny stuff — but he writes the songs in Weezer. Those are his songs; now these are mine." One of the key points Sharp insisted upon when he shopped the Rentals record to labels earlier in 1995, with the permission of Geffen Records, was that the group's debut album be released in the fall to avoid interfering with Weezer's schedule.

"Geffen was cool to let us take the project elsewhere," the bassist said at the time. "They have the first chance at all of our work, and Geffen was great with Weezer. But I wanted to have another label for the Rentals that would really fight for us.

"[Geffen] basically did me a very big favor, and they were extremely nice about it," Sharp continued. "I didn't want them involved in it because I wanted it to be thought of on its own and not thought of as, 'we'll please him by letting him put out this little thing.' I wanted people to be focused on it and backing it and believing in it and for it to be important. And Maverick's a much smaller company, so I just figured they would be ready for that. DGC has done a great job with the whole Weezer thing, but my thing definitely needs its own voice."

Sharp says he basically handed everything over to Madonna's A&R man Guy Oseary in its completed state. The record, the video, the songs — including potential B-sides — and the artwork were all delivered en masse. "[Maverick] didn't have anything to do with it," he bragged. "I wouldn't do anything unless I could do it my way."

Describing the personality of the Rentals' A&R man at the time, Westrich says, "Guy, for me, was someone who I knew from around town. I'd see him at a Supersport show or I'd run into him through friends. And I had been to dinner with him. He used to just come up to me and try to convince me that I'd made out with him before and that I had a piercing in my tongue. And I kept telling him, 'You've got the wrong person, it isn't me.' Every time I would see him, that's what he would say to me, coming on to me. The truth is he was just some young punk to me you'd see out at a show, and then one day he called me on the phone and he said, 'Do you know who I am?' And he tried to explain it. I said, 'You're that annoying guy.' And he said, 'No, I'm your A&R guy.' And I said, 'What's an A&R guy?' But I know one thing to this day, I've never had a tongue ring and I never made out with Guy Oseary. And you can print that."

Speaking of his "Vogue"-touting label boss, Sharp said at the time, "I'm a big fan of [Madonna's]. I didn't get to meet her until after we were signed, but when I did, I told her I was glad she was my boss, and she said she was a good one."

Meanwhile, Sharp's other boss was having mixed feelings about the Rentals' sudden attention. "Initially I understood [Matt's] need to express himself apart from Weezer," Cuomo confessed later about the project. "Who, better than me, could understand it? But the dictatorial part of me also regretted its implication, because the Rentals seemed to weaken Weezer. The reaction of a spoiled child says, 'Hey man! You want to play in my group? It's out of the question that you exhaust yourself elsewhere.'

But I succeeded in keeping that aspect of my personality under control, looking at it as a positive step for Matt. However, I think that the Rentals made a remarkable disc."

As Matt Sharp's solo star continued to rise, Weezer frontman Rivers Cuomo was busy recovering from a leg operation, studying mostly music classes at Harvard University and — as the rock star in hiding — constantly worrying about being recognized. "I was always expecting somebody to come up and harass me," Rivers said about his low profile.

If he was at first worried about keeping his anonymity, he soon learned Harvard was a place for strict academia, not fan adulation. "After a month, I realized no one knew who I was, and no one cared," Cuomo added. "That was both a relief and also kind of depressing.

"I was totally anonymous and that was completely important to my ability to write songs," Rivers continued. "I saw people with Weezer shirts on walk right by me and not even notice me. And while that was probably for the better, and I'm glad it was like that, it was like a hard crash coming down from being a rock star to being a normal person again — having to wait in lines and stuff." In fact, Cuomo — who claimed he "looked like a crippled, homeless rabbi" — was without a car at the time and took public transportation despite the fact he was a multi-platinum recording artist.

Cuomo acknowledged that the transition from rock star to "scum bag" was a tough one. With his long beard as a mask and the corrective apparatus on his leg, he felt freakish, clutching to his cane on campus. If he desired new friends, he made little attempt to make them, acting like a timid, peculiar loner.

"For the previous year and a half, I'd done nothing but hang out and do photo shoots and play shows and drink," he rationalized. "And I just wanted to crawl into a hole and be alone and think and write songs for a while. Plus I was probably in a really anti-social mood because I was crippled and felt very strange about meeting people under those conditions."

Cuomo added the decision to embrace academia didn't sit too well with his mom. "My mother bitched at me for dropping out of my rock band and going back to college. She was like, 'What are you doing? Think of your future!' It was ironic." And Rivers later confessed, "I was in school for all of three days before I realized, 'School sucks. I want to go back and be a rock star.'

"I blend in wherever I go, I never get noticed," he complained while an undergrad, admitting that the temptation was there for him to blow his cover. "'Hey, it's me! Give me some attention!' But they didn't notice. It's really bad for my ego, but it's probably good for my homework and my ability to write.

"I've sold two million records," Cuomo added. "I've toured around the world singing in front of thousands of people. And there's a girl sitting across from me in English 101, and I just look up at her every once in a while and put my head back down. I'm still a pathetic fool. No matter how many records I sell, I'm never going to be in Kiss."

If his social life during that first year at Harvard was non-existent, Rivers also cut himself off from the rest of the world. "I didn't have a television. I never read magazines. I despise any type of periodical. I always get really depressed when I read them, newspapers or magazines. It just kinda feels like a waste of time, 'cause in a year or two, everything in that magazine is pretty much gone.

"It was a very sweet-and-sour experience," he said of studying Bach chorales. "I was really lonely, it was cold, and my leg hurt. I was a 'nobody' again, instead of a star. But at the same time I was happy to be alone and in touch with my creative self."

In Harvard's competitive environment, Rivers revealed that he "became very unsure of [his] instincts." Unsure of how people would react to him, "whether they were going to ridicule me or harass me or fawn all over me or whatever," Cuomo was taken aback when none of his scholarly peers noticed he was among them. "I was shocked and disappointed to find out that they all ignored me completely. Eventually, I got to the point where I was like, 'Shit, doesn't anyone want an autograph?'"

Adding to that — or perhaps as a result of it — Rivers was having a tough time getting the ball rolling again as a songwriter. "There was a lot of false starts," he later confided. "A lot of pulling my hair out." A song written midway through his first Harvard semester called "Pink Triangle," about an ill-fated relationship with a lesbian, was the song that got him out of a painful eight-month–long writer's block.

With Rivers' attention turned to textbooks on music theory and new Weezer material, Matt Sharp's Rentals project — in a rather odd pairing — was "personally selected" by 1995's breakout diva Alanis Morissette as tour openers on a twelve-date December jaunt. It is interesting to note, however, that at the time the Rentals were chosen by Sharp's labelmate (no doubt at the encouragement of Guy Oseary) he had never met the Canadian native. "Apparently she likes the record," he mused. "A lot of people seem to want to pit me against her, which is really weird.

"I've only heard a couple of her songs on the radio," Matt continued. "I figure you write songs, and if people like them, good." But Alanis fans were slow to pick up on the Rentals' Moog madness. Recalling the Denver stop on the trek, Sharp said the crowd was perplexed. "I know nobody knew who we were, because they were yelling, 'Who the hell are you?' It was weird. I thought we were playing at Bennigan's."

"[Alanis] was really kind of a dud," Rentals vocalist Westrich says. "She would sort of only talk to Matt, and that was about it. She went out of her way to avoid us, actually. I mean, Maya [Rudolph, a member of Sharp's touring band and later a *Saturday Night Live* cast member] and I saw her on the street and she tried to turn the other way and pretend that we weren't there. So she wasn't that great, but we had the best time on that tour with the guys in her band. Her drummer then, Taylor Hawkins, who is in the Foo Fighters now, he was so funny, we just hung out with him and the others in her band every day. That tour was big places and lots of kids in it. And the kids were really nice; they didn't even boo us."

Morissette, a late-'80s/early-'90s teen pop sensation akin to Tiffany and Debbie Gibson in her homeland, was signed to Maverick Records and promptly ditched that dated image in favor of a new one as the angry young woman of alternative rock. The move made her a household name with hits like "You Oughta Know," "Hand in My Pocket," and "Ironic" from her Glen Ballard–produced *Jagged Little Pill* album, but while the label bought the rights to Alanis' back catalogue and buried it to help preserve her image in the Lower 48, they overlooked the music videos she made.

"The only thing they didn't do was buy the rights to the videos," snickered Sharp on the eve of their shared tour dates. "Now MTV's got a hold of them and they're going off on it. MTV made her, then they try to knock her down. What are they gonna say, 'Well, Alanis used to be like Debbie Gibson'? Well, so what? MTV used to play Debbie Gibson. And I like Debbie Gibson."

Luckily, such un-hip declarations didn't hurt the Rentals' critical exposure on American alternative radio. "Friends of P" quickly became a *Billboard* Top 10 Modern Rock track that fall, and Sharp and his band weren't shy when it came to working their promotional magic, making four live appearances at L.A.'s influential KROQ in the span of a month in late 1995. The Rentals even lent a Moog-laden version of the Christmas staple "Silent Night" to the *KROQ Kevin and Bean's Xmas Tape '95* after rocking the station's "Almost Acoustic Christmas" event at the Universal Amphitheatre, playing alongside the likes of Bush, the Foo Fighters, Garbage, the Goo Goo Dolls, Lenny Kravitz, Morissette, No Doubt, Oasis, Radiohead, Sonic Youth, and others. In between live dates in November and December, the group also gave radio performances for KNRK in Pat Wilson's new home-town of Portland and at Washington D.C.'s WHFS, just within the airwave radius of Matt's Arlington, Virginia, hometown.

Incidentally, Pat, who played drums on *Return of the Rentals*, opted out of the Rentals' touring commitments in favor of rest and relaxation, a keen interest in the continued restoration of his Chevelle, and the adjustment to married life. Wilson also pursued his own songwriting, crafting acoustic Huge Guy demos with titles like "I'd Like to Know," "Fatigue," "Much Better Thank You," and "Conquistadors of Nothing." A number of those compositions got the full instrumental electric demo treatment, as did tunes like the apropos "Muscle Car" — which he recorded with the help of Skiploader's Tom Ackerman (now a member of Sunday's Best) — and "I'm Not Too Proud."

Happy to have relocated to Portland, Sharp conceded, "L.A. is terrible for me, nasty. It's a great place to go if you have something to do but I had ceased doing things and wanted to live somewhere pretty."

For Rentals roadwork, Wilson was replaced by Mike Fletcher, who had also played with Rod Cervera and Westrich in Supersport 2000. Rounding out the touring band, which Sharp described as "more aggressive" than the studio version, were keyboardists Jim Richards and Rudolph.

With Weezer on extended vacation, it was important for Matt to keep busy. "Keep moving before you get depressed," he said succinctly, express-ing a unique motto. "You might as well work while you still want to." But for all his motivation surrounding the Rentals, he grew increasingly frus-trated with the media calling the band his "little side project."

"How would you feel if you put a lot of time, a lot of thought, a lot of money into something, and then you finally put out the final product, and people say, 'That's cute — that little side project'?" Sharp balked. "Interviewers can be sort of rude without even knowing it. 'So how's this dinky little thing you're doing?'"

"I'm not shocked by the skepticism," he added. "It's just that inter-viewers were referring to the Rentals as a teeny, miniscule side thing. In the long run, it won't be difficult to get by that. I want to write, record, and release music, and that's as important to me as anything." Still, the Rentals' trumped-up backstory of how they had been discovered by Madonna in Prague was downright ridiculous and Matt knew it. In order to be taken more seriously, he dumped the bogus band biography.

"The Eastern Bloc backstory was just this joke that we all thought was funny at the time," said Westrich. "Some people actually believed at first. We realized very soon after doing it that it wasn't really that funny and we just stopped doing it immediately. It was kind of neat on the video, but it was kind of silly after a while."

"I just didn't have the energy for it," Matt admitted. "I think people get really offended when they don't understand your humor, and then you have to do interview after interview with all these people that are really put off by you because you're being sarcastic."

But the truth is, Matt plotted the whole scheme himself in an effort not to lean on Weezer. "I really wanted the record to stand on its own," he said. "Besides, legally we could not use Weezer's name at all. I figured it would be better if we just pretended we were from another country for a while. But everybody knew right away. It was just kind of pointless."

The fall of '95 was far less hectic for Brian Bell, who casually worked on material with the Space Twins and eventually took that band out for one performance mission at the similarly titled Los Angeles venue Spaceland

RICHARD BELAND

Czech It: Sharp's Eastern Bloc backstory tanks,
but The Rentals land a hit anyway

on November 15. Meanwhile, 3,000 miles away in Boston, Rivers had demoed tunes like the aforementioned "Pink Triangle," and another tune, "El Scorcho," yet he was still having trouble coming up with songs for Weezer's hotly anticipated second record.

By the time all of Weezer regrouped in January 1996 for a two-week recording session at Sound City Studios in Van Nuys, California, the focus was on wrapping up the songs they had first worked on at Electric Lady late the previous summer.

"Most of the songs had very little preparation going into the studio," Rivers remembered of the spontaneous sessions. "I flew out to L.A. for Christmas vacation, we rehearsed for a couple of days, I taught the band a few songs, we worked out our basic parts and then just went into the studio and pressed the record button."

"Rivers goes to college and he didn't have any songs," Pat Wilson recollected, "so whenever he'd get a batch, like in his breaks, we would [record them] then." After knocking out new takes on previously tracked tunes like "No Other One," "Getchoo," and "Tired of Sex," plus new recordings of "El Scorcho" and "Pink Triangle," the Weezer men again parted company as planned so that Rivers could attend his spring semester at Harvard and attempt to finish writing the album. Meanwhile, Pat and Brian went back to relatively low-key demo and gig activities, respectively. Matt hit the road again with the Rentals opening for Blur, before taking on support stints with the Red Hot Chili Peppers and Garbage in the U.S. and abroad.

"In America, most people thought the Rentals were crap," says Cherie Westrich. "When we did the Chili Peppers tour, we'd get booed. Sometimes with Blur, we'd get booed too, but not as often. It was actually kind of fun, because I'd stop playing and just start doing cartwheels across the stage. I figured if they didn't want to hear us, I'd give 'em something to look at. When people would come backstage, they'd ignore us and pay attention to someone else who was more famous."

In an effort to keep publicizing the Rentals' album, Matt resumed doing extensive tour press. With the number one question from journalists being, "Is Weezer breaking up?" Sharp cleared the air by insisting things were well within the band. "We've recorded half of the Weezer record," Sharp reported in February 1996. "We're just trying to figure out how to complete it, and [see] if Rivers and I are going to write together. A bunch of questions are up in the air with us."

Despite his songwriting drought, Rivers quickly dismissed any suggestion of co-writing. He put such notions to bed that year by succinctly proclaiming, "This band plays my songs." In doing so, he quashed Sharp's, Wilson's, and Bell's hopes for an increased creative role in the band. In making such a public declaration, a line had been officially drawn between Weezer's frontman and his subordinates, with the other founding members forfeiting control. Describing the material being readied for Weezer's upcoming album as "autobiographical," Cuomo concluded, "It would be very strange for one of them to help me write my autobiography."

While Rivers was shutting Matt and Pat out of the songwriting process for Weezer, he seemed to be growing more comfortable with his band members' auxiliary roles. He went so far as to praise them as songwriters, even if he was keeping them out of the Weezer creative process. "There's surprisingly little tension about solo projects. We all understand that everyone is going to do their thing when the Weezer tour is done. I don't think anyone has a problem with that."

"Rivers has these songs and we just play 'em," Pat explained matter-of-factly, seeming to have accepted his reduced role with the band despite having helped craft early Weezer favorites. "We get to play what we want as long as Rivers likes it. If he doesn't like something it won't be that way."

"Playing with Weezer has been great," Wilson remarked that year, actually sounding satisfied with Rivers being the boss of the group. "I love it, I mean there is a certain part of the population that wants to buy something that I've created. The last two years have been the best education of my life; there are so many over-educated, under-experienced people. I'm so glad I dropped out of college after one semester and became a rock star. It's the best."

Meanwhile, Cuomo asserted, "There's a certain amount of executive rights that I have because I write the songs. If there's a disagreement that we can't resolve, I think that there's just a general understanding that I have the ultimate right of approval."

Matt Sharp's own creative success with his "Friends of P" purveyors meant that he could continue on down his own musical road, even if he was left out of any co-writing credits in Cuomo's band. "I'm planning to devote a lot of time to the Rentals, and hopefully, we'll be making records for a long time to come," he said as he found time for additional promotional stops during the band's U.S. touring commitments that February. Included among these were radio visits and retail store performances.

Having become fast friends with Blur's Damon Albarn, Sharp's Rentals re-joined that U.K. quartet as openers on a six-week trek through Europe that launched in Madrid on February 26, 1996. "Opening for Blur was great," said Cherie Westrich. "We went almost everywhere you can think of in Europe. It was pretty much like being in The Beatles. I mean, even though we knew the screams weren't for us, we were experiencing them. We'd come out the back door after playing a show and they'd whisk you away and these security guards would shove you into a van and you'd be driven off to some exclusive European nightclub and you'd have your VIP area and there were all of these other famous European people who didn't speak English who would be there. And it would be crazy, so I could see how you could take it personally and really get wound up in it. We'd be on the bus and girls would just be pounding on the bus and screaming. And then we'd come down off it and they'd realize we weren't Damon Albarn and they'd just sort of walk away. It was super fun though."

That is, until Sharp stopped paying Westrich a salary, while, oddly, continuing to pay everyone else in his touring band. "Money issues were horrible," Cherie says today. "He didn't even pay me for touring. I was literally borrowing money from the other people on the bus to get a sandwich. We had per diems, but it was tough sometimes when you're traveling. Everyone else was coming on the bus and saying, 'Look at my new leather jacket' and all this stuff. And I'd be like, 'Do you think you could spot me, I spent my money last night.' It was really pathetic. He did pay everybody else, to the best of my knowledge, which I thought was good. I mean, this is all long ago, and for a while I did pursue my options about trying to get paid the money he owed me and then I just thought, 'Oh, forget it.'

"Aside from the money, it was more meanness in other ways," Westrich continues. "I remember when we first got our tour bus and we were all excited and me and Maya — because we're girls — we were first on the bus to arrange everything. And we put all of our stuff in bunks across from each other. And then, she got off the bus and I was still on it and Matt just came in and started throwing all of Maya's stuff on the floor. I was like, 'Why are you doing that?' And he's like, 'I want this bunk.' And I'm like, 'Matt, Maya picked it,' and his answer was, 'It's my bunk, I had this bunk when I toured Europe with Weezer and this is where I'm going to sleep. I paid for this bunk. It's my bus. It's my money.' And I remember Maya was very hurt. But it was his general rudeness like that that I was floored by."

By early spring 1996, Westrich says the mistreatment began to overshadow the fun that had kept her involved with Sharp's group. "We had gone to do the Garbage tour in Europe and we did one or two shows and it was annoying for me because I couldn't just have fun anymore. It was super fun all the time and then I'd have to be on the phone with my lawyer trying to get the money part sorted out. And that was creepy. I'm on this big tour, but my rent hadn't been paid in two months and my phone was about to be shut off. And so being in the Rentals, for me only, meant that I couldn't even provide the bare essentials for myself that I needed to live. It wasn't even a job because there was no money. So we're in London, and we're playing those shows and I put in a call to Pat Magnarella, who was the Rentals and Weezer manager guy. He said he was putting money in my account. So two days after the day he said the money should be in my account, I called again and there was no money. My account had zero dollars by this point. And I was bouncing checks. So after I spoke to my mom, she's like, 'Look, if you aren't having fun, just come home.'

"Then, I just called Pat Magnarella again and said, 'Hey. I think I'm going to go home,'" Cherie said. "And he's like, 'What?' So I told him that I was really upset and, acting surprised, he said, 'What? I put money into your account. I did it yesterday.' And I thought, I can't believe how mean this all is. And I said, 'Pat, you're lying. Why are you lying to me? You're hurting my feelings. I had lunch with you and your wife and you wore overalls and you looked so cute, and now you're telling me lies over thousands of miles of phone line?'

"The next morning, after I said goodbye to Rod, the tour manager calls my room just before they're all leaving on the bus. He called me specifically to tell me they canceled my plane ticket home. And I said, 'You're kidding.' And he's like 'No.' And I said, 'You know I have no money and I'm stuck in London, what shall I do?' And he's like, 'Well, Matt wanted it canceled, so I canceled it.' So quickly, I said, 'Someone's at the door, can you hold on?' While he was still holding the phone, I ran downstairs and went to the bus and I told Rod what had happened. So he stood up for me and went to Matt and said, 'Look. If you don't give her a way to get home, then I'll stay with her, this isn't cool.' So Matt was forced to give me my ticket home. And I just thought that was so mean. Here I am, down and out because of him and he was going to leave me trapped in a foreign country.

"I don't want it to sound like I'm bitter about it," Cherie said of the whole ordeal. "Even up until that moment it was an exciting thing for me. I could have been working in a factory, but I was running through hotels trying to get out of Europe. That's fun.

"I was on the phone with my mother and I was thinking that I really didn't want to talk about this because even though it's all true, I'm sure I come off like a complaining, bitter person about it," Westrich said of her time spent in the presence of Sharp. "And that's not really it at all. But at the same time, it's the interesting, gossipy part to people. But aside from all that, I really had good times with Maya and Rod and Mike."

Which makes one curious. If Sharp was so mean, not just to her, but the others in his circle, why does she think everyone else stayed with the Rentals? "Money," she said. "I know Rod got a ton of money for his part. And I know when I was going through all this I was pretty naive about business and lawyers. The others were more savvy. Their parents had money, whereas my parents live on a farm. So I confided in the others, and they were really supportive and annoyed with Matt. Everyone was kind of in different stages of not liking being around him. But once I made the decision to walk away, a lot of them turned on me because I think they were worried how it was going to affect them personally. They wanted to continue the tour, so — with the exception of Mike and Rod, who were just great to me — they all sided with Matt. As I got off the bus I remember Jim saying, 'If I never see you again it will be too soon.' And I thought, 'Really?' And he just looked at me. I just instantly thought, 'Wow. Money and fame must mean a lot to you. This is a person, who — one week before — was rubbing my feet and staying up all night drinking with me."

Several weeks after Westrich's departure, after wrapping the dates in

Luxembourg, Belgium, on April 6 — and playing a radio station gig in Paris known as "The Black Sessions," where his group paid tribute to Blur by covering "Tracy Jacks" — Matt wound up in London, where he initiated the recording of the Rentals' second album. Over the next two and a half years Matt would devote most of his Weezer-free time to the project that would eventually emerge as 1999's *Seven More Minutes*.

While she and Sharp were obviously no longer on friendly terms, Westrich says Sharp's ego wreaked havoc over most of those involved in the Rentals' long-delayed second disc. "I remember Petra Haden went over to England and recorded with Matt, and I know Rod did, but everyone who did ended up regretting it," she said. "They'd tell me, 'You were right, this is awful, I shouldn't have gone.' Petra called me and asked me for advice before she went, so I told her that it would probably be a nightmare. And it was. She told me how she went running out of the studio crying, and she left early. And it was terrible, but maybe it was a lot of money he was offering. Rod said the same thing, that the experience was kind of awful but he was being paid a nice amount so he hung in there for a while. But I think Matt had a lot of trouble there for a while, where people started helping him and then backing out."

Conceding that during his days with the Rentals, he was "kind of an asshole to people who probably didn't deserve it," Sharp, when first probed, opted not to elaborate. Although Westrich wasn't ever given any credit or royalties, Sharp did finally publicly concede that she indeed wrote the words to the Rentals' song "My Summer Girl" before playing it during an April 2003 solo performance at Maxwell's in Hoboken.

When asked what she made of all this, shortly after Sharp's gig, Westrich said, "I think honestly, that his humbleness now is due to the fact that he still wants to be famous. But now that some of his behavior has found its way into the public eye you can't go on denying it, you just have to admit it and then somehow try to cover up for it. I don't believe in his sincerity with trying to be humble. I think if he reached a certain level of fame again, he'd turn right back into being a jerk. I don't buy it. He was too mean in the way he treated me and some of the others to have just been some fluke accident. I think it's in his person to be that way."

Interestingly enough, Sharp did speak fondly of Westrich in a lengthy November 2003 interview. Making no mention of the money issues or the tension surrounding the 1996 European tour, Matt did acknowledge that Cherielynn was integral to the development of "My Summer Girl."

"I was a bit lost on [that song] and Cherie was the first person from the outside to really support me," he admitted. "So I gave it to her, the music was already recorded, and she brought the cassette back a day or two later with a bunch of ideas revolving around this melody that she came up with. And what we did was we took the lyrical ideas and her melodic idea.

"If you look at the original bios for *Return of the Rentals*, it completely credits her for the song," Matt continued. "I think the only reason it got omitted from the artwork for *Return of the Rentals* is because I was really trying to make the credits and the layout really clean and precise and not full of thank-yous and all sorts of things, which was a mistake on my part. But Cherie has always had the writing credit on the song, always had the publishing [rights] on the song, and I tried when I initially put out the record to credit her as much as possible. When we did radio interviews I tried to talk about her involvement on the song because it's probably my favorite on that whole record. I think the big misconception is that somehow I tried to take full credit and I never tried to do that.

"In no way did I ever mean to hurt her," Matt added. "I was just a dumb kid who overlooked something because I was so concerned with not having anything in the credits. I don't think I've ever had a problem with crediting people and making sure that their contributions are really well known. So since it has come up, I do try to credit her when I perform it, although I don't think it's worth all that much. I look very dearly upon that time that she and I spent together and she really was a very important part of my life. If she feels upset about it, she has nothing but my deepest apologies for that and I guess it's not much of an excuse to say you were a dumb kid, but I was a dumb kid."

If things behind the scenes were rather quarrelsome back then, Sharp never let on, carrying himself off well in the public eye. Looking back on his triumphant two years, Matt would later comment that he found "the whole scenario surreal. Whether it was the Rentals or what was going on with Weezer. It was just an enormous cluster of surrealism. One minute, you're at the MTV Awards talking to Madonna about new wave or whatever. And then, a few months later, we're in Portugal opening up for Blur, and you're going, 'How the hell did we get here? What happened to the past couple of months?'"

As the Rentals overseas tour ran out of gas, Pat Wilson's outfit — now known as The Special Goodness — spent March and April of 1996 recording at his newly finished Portland studio. Fittingly titled the Special Land, the facility was christened with the production of ten tunes, which counted Pat playing almost every instrument with the exception of a pair of numbers where Sixty Wrong Sausages alum Pat Finn played bass. Producer Tony Lash (Cardinal, Pond, Eric Matthews), who played drums in Elliott Smith's pre-fame outfit Heatmiser, manned the boards for the record and was even Wilson's roommate for a spell.

Tracks like "Congratulations," "Pay No Mind," "Conquistadors of Nothing," and "A Fortunate Mistake," were among the ten songs completed under The Special Goodness banner. The self-titled set that became known by fans and Wilson himself as *The Bunny Record* — due to its cartoonish CD cover — was only ever released commercially by Japan's Rock

Records in 1996. A planned release through DGC in North America was delayed several times and ultimately abandoned by 1998, although Wilson was finally planning a U.S. release of the album in 2003.

"I played all the instruments on it," Pat said of the project at the time. "It sounds awful when I tell that to people. I don't want to make it sound like I'm Prince, like I'm the white Prince from the suburbs," but in comparison to his bandmate Sharp's rock star behavior at the time, Wilson couldn't help but sound downright humble.

chapter fourteen

the good life

The spring of 1996 found Weezer re-grouping in Los Angeles to continue work on what would become the *Pinkerton* album at Sound City Studios in Van Nuys. On a week-long break from his Harvard studies, Rivers flew in from Boston with three new songs needed to round out the halfway-finished project. As with "El Scorcho" and "Pink Triangle," the compositions — "The Good Life," "Across the Sea," and "Falling for You" — were scribed during Cuomo's "strange months at Harvard," according to Karl Koch, when the Weezer frontman "had some major [songwriting] breakthroughs." With a strong desire to get back to the good life, Cuomo's need to rock again gave birth to one new song idea, "The Good Life." And by his spring break, with the bulk of the album tracked, Cuomo's cabin fever found him cutting loose on his overdubs.

Rivers flew back to Cambridge for the remaining weeks of his second semester at Harvard and his university finals, and returned in the early summer of 1996 to put the finishing touches on *Pinkerton* in Los Angeles with Pat, Matt, and Brian. After writing the acoustic "Butterfly" that June, additional time was spent recording B-side contenders "Devotion," "Waiting on You," "I Just Threw Out the Love of My Dreams" (complete with vocal augmentation from Rachel Haden), and a new version of "You Gave Your Love to Me Softly."

During this time the Weezer leader — without a permanent L.A. residence at this point and staying at Le Parc Suites in West Hollywood — fretted about an uneasy reversion from textbooks to tour bus. "I was a little worried that I was going to have a hard time making the transition back into the rock life. My life the previous year was very different, but I slipped right back into it like I'd never left." Cuomo even went so far as to suggest to a journalist later in the year that he was bipolar, citing his cycle between "lame-o" and "partier" being about six months.

Looking back on the grueling campaign to support *The Blue Album* in the summer of '96, Wilson conceded, "It's true we got pretty burnt. We played the same songs for two and a half years. The desire to stop touring was definitely there. We weren't prepared for that level of success and it was difficult to get a perspective on what was happening to us."

"We needed to take some time off to regain the eye of the tiger," Cuomo said. "When you think about it, the normal thing to do when you're done touring behind an album is to take some time off and write songs for the next one. That's all I did. If I hadn't gone to school — if I had stayed in Los Angeles and hung out at the Viper Room and partied — I surely wouldn't have written [these] songs, and the songs I would have written probably would have sucked. I wouldn't have found the inspiration."

A superstitious Cuomo, however, hadn't yet set foot inside L.A.'s infamous Viper Room since it had been known as Club Dump and vowed that he never would, due to the fact that another celebrity with a very similar first name and background died at the club. On October 31, 1993, twenty-two-year-old actor River Phoenix — who Rivers Cuomo was planning to meet through a mutual friend just days later — overdosed in the club. In the years that followed, Rivers refused to go to the popular venue, in spite of the fact that he never saw any of Phoenix's movies and knew little about the film star, but "felt some weird connection." He cited their close names, the similar names of Leaves and the thespian's brother Leaf (now Joaquin), the idea that they were the same age, and the fact that both were reared on communes by hippie parents.

Better prepared and optimistic about what the new album, to be titled *Pinkerton*, might bring, Wilson insisted, "We won't have any problem dealing with any future success. In fact we just want to make sure that it happens as much as possible."

In the final *Pinkerton* session, two additional tracks — "I Swear It's True" and "Getting Up and Leaving" — were attempted and nearly finished, but left incomplete just prior to the mixing process. Koch said that "it's nearly certain that they would have been the B-sides to 'Pink Triangle,' if that had been put out as a 'for sale' single." As a result, the songs never saw official release. But it's important to note that all of these new songs, both for *Pinkerton* and its respective B-sides, were penned exclusively by Rivers, and completely quashed any of Matt Sharp's previously chronicled hopes for a collaborative role in the band's future.

"Was there tension? Absolutely!" Wilson said, echoing Sharp's dissatisfaction with Cuomo's autocratic approach to making the album. "There was total lack of communication. We all had our own ideas and we all write stuff, so things got very frustrating because we were unable to contribute. But we've reached a position where we accept Weezer is the product of a single vision and it's probably better for that."

Interestingly enough, Rivers' perception of his group's interactions during the making of *Pinkerton* was much different. In one interview he spoke of the group's working relationship being the best it had ever been, citing Pat, Matt, and Brian as his dream band and explaining that he was open to input. Describing the sessions as healthy and productive, Cuomo's observations made fans wonder if he was even talking about the same band.

Not that he was denying conflicts existed, but he sugarcoated his message just the same. "We all just argue incessantly until we come to a

JAY BLAKESBERG

Who You Callin' Nerd? Rivers taps his inner Fonzie

compromise, and it almost always works out where everybody's reasonably happy. I think everyone feels like their voice is heard in this band," he rationalized. And while "Weezer" was to be billed with the production credit on *Pinkerton*, Wilson belittled his contribution by saying, "all I did was play drums and I recorded the drums. Rivers is the auteur behind this record. He's definitely responsible for the way it sounds."

"I do feel an enormous amount of pressure to write good music and to make a good album," Cuomo said at the time. "I've never really wanted to be a producer. I just feel that the best way for us to sound like ourselves is to record on our own. For the first album, the record company felt very strongly that we needed somebody, so we asked Ric Ocasek, who I really view more as a great songwriter than some hot-shot producer guy."

The band's plan all along was to keep a big-name knob-twiddler away from its sophomore set. Said Patrick, "with the first album, Ric allowed us to sound how we wanted. This time around we simply chose good engineers because we're all students of music and sound and we know what we want."

Now capable of handling a big studio and producing an album on their own, the members of Weezer acknowledged they had earned the right to such artistic freedoms after the success of their debut album. The intention the second time around was to make a raw record, one that better resembled the band's live sound. Using benchmarks like the Flaming Lips' releases to date, plus Steve Albini–produced epics like the Pixies' 1988 classic *Surfer Rosa* and Nirvana's 1993 swansong *In Utero*, Weezer's goal was to achieve a big drum sound and abrasive guitar sounds. Cuomo realized the latter by connecting multiple distortion pedals to create a thunderous six-string attack.

"I just figured that he wanted to do *Pinkerton* himself," says Ocasek, when asked why he was absent from Weezer's second disc. "But I did see him in L.A. when they were recording the record. I did go into the studio with them and Rivers asked me about the guitar parts he did. I think he was getting hung up on the lead guitar parts to some of the songs. He was working with an engineer who was taking a little too long for his liking and putting the music through a lot of stuff, and I don't think Rivers had the kind of control he wanted to have. So I went in and I was telling him I loved the guitar parts he already had on tape and I told him that he should just go for it. He was having second thoughts, I think, because he didn't really have any direction. You know it's hard to make your own record and be an outside ear at the same time. But I knew he wanted to hold the reins himself."

Still, Rivers also believed his strong compositions would persevere without the gloss of *Weezer*. Looking to get away from the gimmickry that bolstered "Buddy Holly" into the public's consciousness, under his watchful eye the band remained true to its live sound and deliberately shed anything that could be construed as contrived.

At just under thirty-five minutes, *Pinkerton* was, according to Rivers, "short by design." In recording the album over four respective sessions, the band would traditionally spend two days on rehearsals and then head into the studio to track the tunes. "I think that's when we play the songs best," the band's domineering force proclaimed. "Patrick, especially, is just an amazing, spontaneous talent. So we like to capture it when we first learn the arrangements." To give the record a live feel, Brian, Matt, and Rivers recorded the vocals in tandem around three microphones, which fostered interaction, and according to the twenty-six-year-old Cuomo, this meant that "we couldn't go back in and punch in more vocals."

That approach had its good and bad points, according to Rivers. "If one of my band members sang a really sour note, it also ended up bleeding heavily onto my track, so that in order to keep some of the tracks of myself that I really liked, I had to accept that there would be some pretty strange stuff in the background. But I think that overall it was way worth it, because there's such a live, fun vibe about the whole recording. I feel that all the different influences — metal and other — in my guitar playing are starting to come together more. I don't feel like I have to control my playing so much anymore. I can let it all hang out."

Pinkerton was considerably different from its predecessor, marking a shift to more sophisticated songwriting and playing. If it was less immediate, serving as a greater challenge to listeners, even at the risk of alienating fans, Weezer's sophomore album still managed to resemble its debut by being a concise ten songs in length.

Launching *Pinkerton* with the stick of rock 'n' roll dynamite that is "Tired of Sex," a roar of distortion gives way to a cathartic, Pixies-inspired rant about Rivers' meaningless groupie sex encounters. Reciting his list of conquests, the singer wonders why true love eludes him, but like any man in his position, he "can't say no." It's a damn honest and contagious opening statement with pummeling drum work by Pat, thumping bass by Matt, and the first real evidence of Brian's studio-tracked guitar abilities with the group.

Speaking about the track, Rivers confessed to cringing at the thought of his mother hearing the song. "I always hope that she can't understand the lyrics," he said. "I want my female relatives to think I'm perfect."

Perhaps this explains why the Weezer frontman found himself drawn to feminist author Camille Paglia around this time in his life. Down on himself after writing some of the more despicable songs on *Pinkerton*, feeling guilty and even referring to himself as an asshole in interviews, Cuomo was bolstered and soothed by her books. Paglia helped him to understand where some of his feelings were coming from, and that it was natural — as a male — to feel the way he did.

Cuomo also admitted that the guitar line for "Tired of Sex" was derived from his metal roots, telling *Guitar World*, "I think that's the lead from the Scorpions' 'Rock You Like a Hurricane' — note for note if I remember correctly. It's either that or 'No One Like You.'" Thinking about this disclosure, Cuomo half-jokingly asked, "Can I get sued for that?"

Buzzsaw guitars washed in distortion kick the second cut, "Getchoo," into gear with more revelatory words about abusive, dysfunctional love from Rivers, who sings from the perspective of a lovelorn, self-professed "freak." Its follow-up, the emotively delivered ballad "No Other One," finds the song's subject, presumably Cuomo himself, in a twisted relationship with a woman who has an affinity for drugs, tattoos, and snakes. Matt Sharp's falsetto here is dynamite, augmenting the pensive track.

The immediately infectious "Why Bother?" finds the band capably rocking on all four cylinders with Cuomo's heartfelt vocals arguably as skilled as his (and Bell's) dexterous guitar riffs. Here Rivers debates whether to attempt having a relationship with a woman, but ultimately determines he'd rather "keep wackin'."

"Across the Sea," the album's centerpiece, is accomplished rock music. Piano-laced with a brilliant melody, the revelatory song is one of the finest in Cuomo's songbook. "I feel like, probably more so than any other song ever that I wrote, I managed to capture a really complicated, beautiful feeling with melodies," Rivers said of the song, which was prompted by a female fan letter from Japan he received during months of isolation in Cambridge.

"She basically wrote the lyrics to the first verse and part of the chorus, too," he continued, promising that the fan would earn some royalties from the song. Yet, interestingly enough, a quick check of *Pinkerton's* liner notes reveals no songwriting credits outside of Cuomo's own. Whatever the mechanical royalty arrangement might or might not have been, Rivers was smitten with the Japanese letter-writing lass. "When I got the letter, I fell in love with her. It was such a great letter. I was very lonely at the time, but at the same time I was very depressed that I would never meet her. Even if I did see her, she was probably some fourteen-year-old girl who didn't speak English."

The fan's lyrical help aside, the final verse of the song was possibly the most confessional Cuomo had written to date. Reflecting back on the ashram experience in which he shaved his head like a monk when he was ten years old so that older women would like him, he also sings of his mother being at fault for something, but doesn't clarify. He then goes on to tout himself as a good little boy in search of a hand to hold onto.

The roaring rocker "The Good Life" chronicles the rebirth of Rivers the celebrity after an identity crisis as an Ivy League loner. Speaking about one of *Pinkerton's* more accessible tunes, Rivers said, "It's basically me saying, 'I wanna go back on tour and this time I wanna have fun.'" Cuomo contended that at the time he wrote the song, it was the middle of the winter, he had been out of the spotlight for eight months, his leg was very painful, and he had no friends to speak of, let alone a girlfriend. "I was becoming frustrated with that hermit's life I was leading, the ascetic life.

And I think I was starting to become frustrated with my whole dream about purifying myself and trying to live like a monk or an intellectual and going to school and holding out for this perfect, ideal woman. And so I wrote the song. And I started to turn around and come back the other way."

Pinkerton's first single extract, "El Scorcho" opens to a stomping floor tom, acoustic picking, and Matt's falsetto stylings before morphing into an unusual love song that incorporates hip-hop lingo. Balancing rough riffs with an undeniable chorus, the opening line's use of "Goddamn" looked poised to hinder airplay in the Bible belt. Speaking about the lyrics later he said, "We meant to record a single version, without the 'Goddamn,' but we forgot. I probably would have said 'hot damn' or 'gosh darn.'"

Confronting his fetish for "half-Japanese" women on "El Scorcho," Rivers revealed the song "is more about me, because at that point I hadn't even talked to the girl, I didn't really know much about her. The song is more about my shyness and inability to say 'hello' to her." After asking his crush to accompany him to a Green Day concert and meeting with rejection, the song's subject sneaks into the girl's room to read her diary. "I didn't have access to her room," he admitted of the exaggeration, "but I had access to some of her writing, and actually put some of the lines in the song. See I can't say too much about the song because I don't want people to know who it is, 'cause she would get really pissed off."

If "El Scorcho" was a rather odd choice to launch their second album, then "Pink Triangle" — complete with xylophones — was the obvious selection for a single. The record's most alluring tune — named for the upside-down pink triangle used by Nazis in World War II Germany to single out homosexuals — is painfully revealing. It's also the song that got Cuomo past his songwriting drought, a problem exacerbated by the distractions of fame, his inability to write songs while on tour and his first semester at an Ivy League school.

Rivers said, "You can hear, the very first line sounds like a guy sitting down to start writing songs again: 'When I'm stable enough, I start to look around for love.' That was the first line I wrote post-success. Because for that year and a half, my life wasn't stable enough for me to write." In the song, the subject falls in love and wants to get married, but soon discovers the object of his devotion is a lesbian.

The Nirvana-like riffs of "Falling for You" drive an expertly played and hard-bopping rocker that sees Rivers falling in love with a girl who leaves a cello in the basement of his Cambridge home. When he attempts the instrument, and is startled by how bad he is at it, he wonders what she sees in "little ol' three-chord" him. He also testifies how he wants to trade in his "rock star card" to grow fat and old with her. That tune makes way for the acoustic album-closer "Butterfly," which too finds Cuomo at his heartfelt and vulnerable best. A breathtaking ballad titled after Madame Butterfly's namesake finishes the disc, the song existed essentially as the musical equivalent of an open wound.

The completed album put to rest real fears at Geffen Records that the band might be a flash in the pan after the success of the "Buddy Holly" video and Cuomo's long spell of writer's block. "When we saw the video, it was like, 'Wow, this is great,'" Weezer's A&R man Todd Sullivan admitted. "Then we thought, 'Oh God — what sort of light does this put the band in?' It could have been interpreted as them being a highly disposable pop band. Fortunately, they proved they were more durable.

"It's a very brave record," Sullivan continued, hyping the disc. "The spontaneity shows. There's a lot of anticipation for this record and no one's going to be disappointed."

Calling *Pinkerton* a "subtle" concept album, Rivers admitted, "I really wanted the album to tell a story, so any song that I wrote that didn't further the story didn't really fit. It's not like *2112* by Rush or anything, but there is a story. The songs are sequenced in the order I wrote them, so you can kind of hear the evolution of my personality over the two years. I wrote some songs that were about totally random things, so I didn't include any of them. They're good, but they just weren't part of the whole *Pinkerton* saga."

In actuality, "El Scorcho" and "Pink Triangle" are exceptions to the sequential rule Cuomo followed for Weezer's second album. But overall, the project told the story of someone who was having real difficulty connecting with anyone on a deep, emotional level. Cuomo assured the record was indeed a reflection of himself. "That's pretty much what my life is like," he said of his own hang-ups and relationship issues. "It's probably what life is like for a lot of people, actually.

"The frustrating part about becoming a rock star," Rivers continued, "is realizing that the loneliness doesn't go away. Then you start to think, 'If I can sell a couple million records and I'm still really lonely, that just makes it all the more depressing.' Especially when I still have all the exact same problems. I'm still really shy. I can't talk to girls. That was particularly frustrating this past year at school. It was like, 'I've got a platinum record and I can't even say hello.'"

Adding to his esteem issues, Cuomo tried out for but failed to make the choir at Harvard. "I wanted to be in it so bad," he said in 1996, blaming his "average voice" for the fact he didn't make the cut. The same day, the music major also self-deprecatingly proclaimed, "I really have no special talent in music."

Not to mention the metal cage he was still sporting, his Percocet habit that nearly became an addiction due to the pain from his leg surgery, or the fact he clutched a cane and wore a long beard. Cuomo remembered, "I looked really weird, and people gave me a fair amount of distance in the hallways."

chapter fifteen

el scorcho

After getting back to the good life, Cuomo and his Weezer bandmates set an international release date of Monday, September 23, and a North American release date of the 24th for *Pinkerton*. With work on the disc finished, Matt Sharp hopped a plane back to London in July 1996 to resume recording on what would eventually become *Seven More Minutes*. But within a month, work on the second Rentals album would get put on hold again indefinitely, when his Weezer duties began to overtake his schedule. Back in Los Angeles in early August, the group shot a video for the new album's first single, "El Scorcho," with director Mark Romanek. Having dismissed a treatment proposed by Spike Jonze to the perplexity of many — he had helped raise Weezer's rock 'n' roll status to platinum sales levels in 1994 and '95 — the director's lone involvement in *Pinkerton* was limited to shooting some promotional photos for the record's liner notes.

Romanek, who had lensed videos for Nine Inch Nails, Beck, and Madonna, oversaw the filming of "El Scorcho," but the clip wound up without his credit due to a director–band disagreement over the production. Filmed over the course of fourteen hours at La Cosa, an assembly hall in downtown Los Angeles, the video was not only distinct for unveiling the giant, notorious light-up =w= sign, which became a fixture on future tours, but for boasting a smaller, flashing "weezer" light sign that was altered to read "weerez." If Wilson and Sharp seem disgusted onscreen, it's reportedly not acting. They were as upset with Rivers as Romanek, who quit the clip after a verbal duke-out with Cuomo, leaving the Weezer principal to edit the thing himself. (Romanek declined to comment on the matter for this book.)

The band took a straight approach to videomaking because, according to Pat, Rivers was "against doing another 'Buddy Holly'–type video. He feels it adulterates the *Pinkerton* experience, which is ludicrous. Nobody watches *Help* and says The Beatles suck and their records are awful. Yeah, it's a stupid movie, but whatever."

After all, Rivers was never a fan of music videos, despite the fact that without them mass popularity and wealth would have likely eluded him. "I think videos are evil," he said. "I wish we didn't have to make them. But we do. You can [be like] Pearl Jam [and not make them] when you sell ten million records, but I think if you want to be in this game at all you have to make videos. It helped out with sales — I don't know if they helped out with an appreciation or understanding of our music."

Despite having won 1995's Alternative Video of the Year for "Buddy Holly," Cuomo was unimpressed by the honor. "It means nothing to me," he proclaimed of the Moon Man. "It's like getting awarded for something you have no interest in. It's something I wasn't really involved in, besides lip-synching. It wasn't really an artistic endeavor, for me. If we'd gotten an award for the record, or a song, it could've meant more to me. I mean, of course, our success is due to that video."

With such expensive stupidity out of the way, Weezer traveled across the sea for a series of pre-*Pinkerton* festival dates and some intermittent headlining gigs throughout Europe, beginning at the Arena in Vienna, Austria, on August 15. Switzerland's Winterthur Festival, Germany's Bizarre Festival, England's Reading Festival, Belgium's Pukkelpop Festival, and Holland's Lowlands Festival put the band in the company of Rage Against the Machine, the soon to be defunct Stone Roses, Sonic Youth,

Garbage, and the Butthole Surfers, to name just a few. For these appearances, the band played an abridged, ten-song set, which fused material from *The Blue Album* with songs from their forthcoming second LP.

Fat Mike, co-founder of the West Coast punk band NOFX and head of the enormously popular indie label Fat Wreck Chords, remembered the gigs in Austria and Germany, and said he picked up on tensions between Matt and the rest of the band. "This was right before *Pinkerton* and we did two shows. Their bass player at the time, he was the guy that everyone had a problem with," Mike says. "One of the shows we did with them in Europe, we were on the stage, and it was a big festival, and I don't know why I said this, but I go, 'Those guys in Weezer are fucking cool, what a great band, except for that asshole bass player.' The rest of the band started cracking up, but the bass player just sort of shuffled away, you know?" Still, few outside the inner circle were aware that things were becoming increasingly strained in the group.

A review of the band's headlining gig at The Garage on August 21 in London by Stephen Dalton of the *Times* described Rivers as "diminutive" and "looking every inch his nerdish cartoon image" as he blinked "like a startled rabbit." Still, Weezer's "anthemic, highly melodic bubblegum grunge" image was taken to task by a wicked, albeit stunted cover of Iron Maiden's "The Trooper" at the outset of the show's encore. Versions of the yet to be released "Tired of Sex" and the rarely utilized oldie, "Jamie," closed the gig.

A show at Revolver in Madrid bowed the European obligations on September 8, but just five days earlier, the U.K. single for "El Scorcho" was released. Preceding *Pinkerton* by three weeks and featuring a cover photograph of a Japanese geisha, the CD single hosted two non-LP tracks: a remixed version of "You Gave Your Love to Me Softly" and the heartfelt waltz "Devotion."

Although the "El Scorcho" video — which found Rivers, Matt, Brian, and Pat performing in a circle and facing one another — debuted on MTV's *120 Minutes* and received moderate play on the channel during the early fall of 1996, it was Weezer's least successful outing in the medium to date. Around the time the video aired, rumors that Rivers insisted on having himself in 70% of the footage surfaced (a careful review of the perform- ance clip actually supports this speculation). Such a move helps explain why Wilson and Sharp were having problems with Rivers on the shoot, sparking a rift that would eventually resurface in the national media.

Expressing his opinion of the "El Scorcho" clip shortly after filming, Pat Wilson spoke of it as "a lame concept. We sat around a room with lights and spent way too much money on stupidity, basically." But aside from Wilson's opinion, Cuomo still pushed for the straight performance clip, even though Spike Jonze had written a great treatment for the "El Scorcho" video that would have featured Public Enemy's colorful rapper Flavor Flav emphasizing one of the song's key lyrics.

"I really want the songs to come across untainted this time around," Rivers said of his decision to ditch Spike's idea. "So when I went to write the songs, I was very careful about being really straightforward and sincere. And not being so ironic or using weird metaphors or imagery. I really want to communicate my feelings directly and because I was so careful in writ- ing the songs that way, I'd hate for the video to kinda misrepresent the song, or exaggerate certain aspects. Spike's idea was a pretty limited inter- pretation of the song, like the 'Buddy Holly' video was. Although I think it is a hilarious video, and it's brilliant and probably responsible for our suc- cess, I think there's a chance that people would have heard the song with a little more of an open mind if they hadn't seen the video first. I'm embar- rassed of that song now, and I wasn't when I first wrote it. It was inspired by a powerful feeling, just like the other songs were. And it has really nice

melodies, and it was in line with my sensibilities at the time, which contain
a lot of irony. But by the time it came out on video, it became something
that didn't really represent my feelings anymore. I take total responsibility
for that, too."

"El Scorcho" was gaining momentum at radio and MTV when *Pinkerton* was
released for public sale on September 24, 1996. But a day before the CD
hit the racks at North American retailers, a restraining order was obtained
against Weezer by the internationally known Encino, California–based
security firm, Pinkerton's Inc. The 116-year-old company was suing both
the group and Geffen Records for alleged federal trademark infringement,
claiming that Weezer was trying to capitalize on the company's reputation.

Under the terms of the Pinkerton's restraining order, which also had
them seeking $2 million in damages, Weezer would be kept from "selling,
distributing, or advertising an album with the name Pinkerton." The security outfit — which had a trademark on the names "Pinkerton" and
"Pinkerton's" — said that it had contacted Geffen about one month ahead
of the September 24 release date. Pinkerton's claimed that at the time
Geffen's attorney David Berman allegedly told the company that a resolution was possible, even though the album and CD covers had been pressed.
But just prior to the album's street date, Pinkerton's was told no changes
would be made to the title or album art.

The move irked Pinkerton's enough to seek a court ruling. "Other
avenues were not successful and we were left with no alternative," said the
company's spokesperson Dereck Andrade. Because the album had been
advertised on national television, the suit alleged — somewhat absurdly —
that the use of Pinkerton's name on the record had created the false
impression that it has a business relationship with the album's creators. So
there was Weezer, playing a KROQ-sponsored gig in the parking lot of

Tower Records on Sunset — where Cuomo once worked — as attendees speculated whether they would be able to purchase copies of *Pinkerton* past the first day of release.

"The morning our record came out I woke up feeling pretty excited, like it was Christmas morning or something," Rivers remembered of the situation. "And I checked my messages, and there were about five messages from my manager saying, basically, 'We're going to court. You're being sued. Some detective agency has got an injunction. You can't print or ship any more of your albums.' This is the day our record came out. And I got really sick to my stomach and really sad. So that whole day was just shot, I was in a weird mood all day."

"To Weezer, Pinkerton is a character in Puccini's opera *Madame Butterfly* — a favorite of singer Rivers Cuomo," responded Geffen spokesman Dennis Dennehy. "Rivers' choosing to use the name Pinkerton came strictly within an opera fan's frame of reference. It was not meant to be aimed at any sort of corporate entity. It was merely a musician paying homage to an inspiration, and hoping to enlighten a few fans in the process."

"It sucks!" Pat Wilson declared when asked about the Pinkerton's suit. "There was never any warning that Pinkerton's was going to sue us," Brian Bell continued. "It wasn't until the day before the record was released that we got a very official document stating that we couldn't use the name."

Still, Andrade called the interpretation of the CD a "subjective call," insisting that someone not familiar with *Madame Butterfly* might mistakenly think that Pinkerton's Inc. had something to do with the record. "The First Amendment does not give anyone any right to trample on the trademark rights of a corporate entity," Andrade contended. "The Pinkerton name is a valuable trademark that Pinkerton's vigorously protects. We certainly are not looking to create a brouhaha with Geffen Records. All we are asking is that they not utilize the name Pinkerton."

Following the Tower Records parking lot gig, Cuomo spent the remainder of the day working on the suit. "I wrote up, basically, a six-page paper defending my choice of *Pinkerton*," he said at the time of suit, "explaining why I chose it, and how it works for the album, and how it's essential. My understanding is their name is so famous they're worried about it becoming diluted by other people using it, even if it's in a completely unrelated use. They wanna have exclusive rights to the name. It's so . . . famous. I guess. I've never heard of it before."

Although a federal court hearing had been initially set for October 3 in Los Angeles, the seriousness of the legal and financial ramifications surrounding the record — complete with a cover depicting a snow-capped mountain scene and a Japanese woman on the back cover akin to the heroine from Giacomo Puccini's tragic 1904 opera — forced the case to be expedited to September 26. Based on the artwork alone, Weezer's case looked strong, and Judge John G. Davies dissolved the previous court order to have the CDs pulled after determining that the hardship of not issuing the *Pinkerton* disc would be greater for Geffen than any hardship Pinkerton's or its shareholders might incur from consumers who mistakenly presume the company has anything to do with the album.

When Davis threw the case out of court, Pinkerton's declined its option to continue with the litigation. "I'm just relieved it's over," said Rivers afterward. But for Cuomo, altering the title to keep it on the shelves was never an option. "I had lists of names as I was writing the songs," Cuomo said. "But as soon as I realized what I wanted the album to be about, what the title was gonna be, then I wrote the rest of the songs in support of that title. So at this point, there could be no other title. There is no second choice."

According to Bell, the band was required by Pinkerton's to abide by a non-disclosure document in an out-of-court settlement that allowed the group to keep the album title. "[We] had to sign something saying [we] wouldn't talk about it," the guitarist revealed. In doing so, the security firm put the members of Weezer on the receiving end of a confidentiality agreement akin to the one they had required Jason Cropper sign upon his dismissal three years earlier.

Whether the publicity around the lawsuit sent record buyers into the stores any quicker is debatable, but the fans that snatched up copies of the disc were soon intrigued with and/or perplexed by Rivers Cuomo's obsession with both Japanese women and the opera *Madame Butterfly*, as well as his sad emotional state and his lust for a lesbian. To fans of "Buddy Holly" and "Undone," *Pinkerton* — taking its name from Butterfly's American lover — was clearly a much different record than its predecessor. But to Rivers, such an opinion was just based on misperception: "People took those songs [on *Weezer*] as funny and fun, goofy and lighthearted. But I never thought so. I don't feel like I'm being more serious now, just more literal, more direct."

With litigation stresses behind them, the band knocked out a pair of glorious hometown shows at Whiskey A Go-Go on September 26 and 27 before hopping a plane for three weeks of tour dates in Australia, New Zealand, and Japan. Meanwhile, reviews of the new album were initially mixed.

Critic J.D. Considine of the *Baltimore Sun* noted, "The songs on the quartet's sophomore effort, *Pinkerton* are certainly tuneful enough, [but] it would probably take an *Unplugged* performance to get a real sense of how hummable the material is. As it stands, what we hear are roaring guitars, whooshing synths, and bashing drums — a great rock 'n' roll noise, but one that tends to obscure not only much of the melody but a good bit of Rivers Cuomo's singing."

Elsewhere, *Entertainment Weekly*'s Jeff Gordinier was a little harder on the record in a feature review titled "Weezer's *Pinkerton* Could Use the Sweet Relief of Their Debut." "Sadly, academic life has turned Cuomo into even more of a hermit," the critic wrote, opining that the sophomore effort "sounds like a collection of get-down party anthems for agoraphobics." Giving the disc a B-, Gordinier knocked Weezer for bypassing *Blue Album* producer Ric Ocasek to handle the duties alone. "As such *Pinkerton* should please all those indie-rock purists who like their pop sloppy and raw," he critiqued, "but it'll disappoint anyone who prefers a candy coating on the bubblegum."

Rob O'Connor of *Rolling Stone* gave the record three stars, but he seemed to mistake the deeply personal and emotive mood of the record for what he categorized as "true to the sun-'n'-fun aesthetic of great jangly pop." O'Connor also took aim at Rivers' songwriting, calling it "a juvenile tack on personal relationships." Later, he slammed "Tired of Sex" as "aimless" before he praised "Butterfly" as "a real treat, a gentle acoustic number that recalls the vintage, heartbreaking beauty of Big Star."

More affirmative were the accolades of the *Austin American Statesman*'s Chris Riemenschnieder, who described Weezer as "an amazing, tight band" that "backs up Cuomo, through these amusingly self-absorbed, sensational love songs." Riemenschnieder added that, "on *Pinkerton* the geek-rockers have refined themselves from a smarty-pants, goofy, tongue-in-cheek band to one of the most wildly-orchestrated, catchy and original groups banging away today."

In the October 5 issue of *Billboard*, which also found the *Pinkerton* debut at a respectable #19 in the album survey, the music trade championed the band for "avoiding the sophomore slump in a major way," while heralding the disc as "a real step forward" thanks to "great rock writing from enigmatic leader Rivers Cuomo and a 'live' band sound."

The criticism — whether good or bad — had become one of the most painful parts of the songwriting job for Cuomo. "It's really difficult to take [constant criticism] because it's really myself that I'm putting out there for everyone to judge," he said. "And usually when someone doesn't like it, it's because they don't really understand it or haven't really looked into it deep enough. But it's so difficult to be criticized so constantly and to be under the pressure to perform well or be criticized again. It's really not in my nature."

Criticism aside, the album probably didn't debut as well as it might had influential radio stations like KROQ in Los Angeles — then programmed by a powerful man named Kevin Weatherly — been more receptive to "El Scorcho." While wrapping up Weezer's European dates on September 6, startling word made it to Cuomo through Magnarella that KROQ wasn't behind the record. At the time, Weatherly also programmed the station's New York–based sister station K-Rock (WXRK).

Jim McGuinn, program director at Philadelphia's WPLY–Y100 clarified the band's position at radio this way: "They're obviously the two biggest markets in the country, so even though you have a top ten single at the format — 'El Scorcho,' by the way, was a huge hit here in Philly — you're still missing New York and L.A. So you're missing a lot.

"I think the record was also hurt by 'Popular,' by the band Nada Surf, which was a big radio hit in '96 that sounded like Weezer," said McGuinn, who also fronts the band Cordalene. "And you had 'Sucked Out' by Superdrag, which also tapped the same vein, so it was kind of an overload of that sound. And there's no question that *Pinkerton* was a denser, thicker, more kind of ragged and fucked-up production-wise kind of record."

Pat Wilson blamed the indifference on a new modern rock trend fostered by bands like Sublime, No Doubt, and the Mighty Mighty Bosstones. "We don't fit in. Right now ska is the big thing in America. We're an anomaly." Rivers himself later blamed it on the rise of female artists like Sarah McLachlan and others who headlined the Lilith Fair tours of the mid-to-late 1990s. "It was the year of the woman," he ruefully declared in hindsight. "That rudely interrupted our whole scene."

Cuomo and Wilson might have been on to something, because the presence of "El Scorcho" on both the airwaves and MTV was short-lived. But despite lackluster results on the video channel, Weezer had managed to retain a relatively large and loyal audience. "We have a really good base of hard-core fans that are all nuts," Rivers said proudly. "They're very devoted and they hang on every word in the lyrics and they really get the music. They really understand. And on top of that there's a lot of people who just saw the video and bought the record and don't really give a fuck."

"*Pinkerton* will always be one of my favorite rock records ever," said Brian Diaz of the Victory Records band The Reunion Show. "It's exactly what I wanted the second Weezer record to be. More dark, more personal, better songwriting — in my opinion anyway. I liked it instantly. I got it shortly after it came out and played it non-stop. I had to know every word and every little nuance, every drum fill, every little scratch of the strings. It was like the bible for that style of rock 'n' roll. I had my fill of the fluffy, easy-to-swallow Weezer. I knew they had it in them to lay their souls out on the table. So, for the second time, my perception of music was changed by the same band."

Said Dave Leto of underground rockers Rye Coalition, "I bought *Pinkerton* right about the time it came out. It is, without a doubt, my favorite Weezer album. I think I listened to it every day at the time. Right now, it's in the CD case in our van. And it is the only album the whole band can agree on. The drum sounds on that album are the best they've ever had. The guitar solos were crazy, like that of, say, early Mötley Crüe, the lyrics on it seemed more personal — it felt like you were getting to know them or something silly like that. It is completely different-sounding than the rest of their albums. It just felt real. I would say I was obsessed with it when it came out. Many musicians that I know feel the same way I do. It is the 'rocker's' album of choice."

Trimming the gimmickry of *The Blue Album* from *Pinkerton* was essential to Cuomo, and he understood it would not be without its costs. "I think we're also going to trim some of our audience," he predicted that fall. "[It] is unfortunate. We were never one of the top bands like Green Day or Offspring anyway; we were always a notch below. Maybe now even two notches below. Yeah, it's a bummer, but I don't really feel like I have a choice in the matter. I've got to do what I've got to do, and right now that means not making the gimmicky video and not using language that's quite quirky. It means speaking more directly. Maybe the audience will be smaller, but at least they'll be liking us for the right reasons."

The band forged ahead, while Rivers mulled over whether he might again handle press duties, something he had shied away from since the autumn of '94. After all, having Pat, Matt, or Brian answer questions about his deeply personal songs just didn't make a lot of sense. For instance, when Pat was asked what Rivers meant in the opening line of "El Scorcho," he vaguely responded, "All I can say is if you're inferring Rivers has an obsession with Japanese women, well, I won't deny it."

"So who's the girl he writes about?" a journalist asked.

"I don't know exactly. All the songs are written from Rivers' perception," Wilson remarked. "Evidently, he had connections with these Asian women."

"One girl or several?" the reporter probed.

"I honestly don't know but there's something funny going on," Pat said reservedly. "We let him write the songs — we don't talk to him too much about it."

"Did she turn out to be a lesbian?" the music scribe inquired.

"Evidently he's had experiences with a lesbian." Clearly, Pat either didn't know, wasn't willing to spill the beans about Rivers' songwriting inspirations, or more likely, didn't care. Either way, Wilson was hesitant to follow in Cuomo's opera-fascinated footsteps. "I'm not a fan of the form," Pat declared indifferently.

"Rivers doesn't like talking about the music, he'd rather people interpreted it," Todd Sullivan complained early into the *Pinkerton* publicity drive. "It can be very frustrating, but we have to respect that."

Cuomo himself admitted that by not talking to the media, he managed to retain some of his privacy. "I don't want to become bigger," he said, explaining his motive. "I like being anonymous. I think not doing interviews really helped maintain my anonymity. I want a lot of people to hear the record, I don't know if I really want to be a celebrity." But when Cuomo eventually spoke out to the media about the project and the origins of the concept, his explanations were far more logical and detailed. "I'm basically an opera fanatic, and especially a fan of Puccini."

"Pinkerton is the ultimate macho rock star kind of guy," Rivers Cuomo elaborated, helping to explain the lyrical direction of Weezer's latest album in a manner that was lost on Pat Wilson. "Actually, he's a U.S. sailor in *Madame Butterfly* and he goes from port to port, hooks up with various women and uses them, and then goes to the next port."

Rivers' tour behavior wasn't much different, as he had become prone to picking up members of the opposite sex on various tour stops. "Of course it's easy meeting girls who come to my shows," he rationalized. "If I'm at a bar or school it's different. I can't just walk up to a girl and say, 'Hey, I'm in Weezer, do you want to fuck me?' It doesn't work that way. You still need cool lines and I don't have any."

Like any rock star with an average-or-better sex drive, Cuomo took advantage of his fringe benefits. And for their own amusement, his bandmates and road crew took to spying on him when he hooked up with groupies. In one incident, the tour bus play by play went this way:

"Rivers just got here."

"Does he have some hot little number?"

"She's not really hot. She's not even Asian."

"Man, he's slipping."

"It's funny, when we were touring for the first album, I didn't tap into my inner Pinkerton at all," Cuomo said of his behavior, which also began to include imbibing Jack Daniel's whiskey. "I totally withdrew and didn't go out and meet anybody. I just stayed in the bus and moped, basically. I don't know what happened, but I just got really freaked out. Anti-social. That's not the case now, though."

"On the road, there's no chance to begin a relationship," the singer/ guitarist added, defending his promiscuity while responding to accusations that beneath it all he was becoming a rock star whore. "I don't respect her," he said of one groupie conquest, "but I also don't think she really likes me. She's objectifying me as a superhuman rock star."

Looking back on the *Pinkerton* tour and Rivers' behavior when it came to the pursuit of Asian women on the road, Patrick said, five years after the fact, "I think [Rivers] tried so hard back in the day to be such a debauched rock star, but he just couldn't, you know? It wasn't like a natural scene you know. It wasn't like backstage at a Van Halen concert in 1981, it was a pretty forced thing."

When pressed by a reporter who once observed Cuomo backstage in the act of seeking out a female companion who was of age, didn't have a boyfriend, and was half-Asian, Patrick — a married man — conceded, "Yeah, that kind of creeped me out. Like shopping."

From his own perspective, the twenty-six-year-old rock star had been devoid of a solid relationship since Weezer's infancy. "I was so consistently critical and condescending and jealous that eventually she couldn't take it anymore and broke up with me," he said of his ex-girlfriend Lisa. When asked why he was unattached, Rivers confessed, "I guess I'm running out of excuses. For a while, it was because I was on the road, and it was impossible to get a girlfriend on the road. I'd never talk to a girl for more than five minutes, and then I'd never see her again." When pressed for further details, Cuomo eased off the discussion by saying, "it's probably just stupid to talk about relationships and stuff. I mean, who cares?"

Rivers believed that his life was unremarkable, despite the fact he was a wealthy, young, multi-million-selling rock star. He went so far as to tag his life and his experiences as mundane, describing songwriting as an outlet for his emotions that still allowed him to retain some privacy. Through the forum of songwriting, he claimed to have "found a way to express the full intensity of [my] feelings. If I talk about the details of the experience, then it takes away from the feelings."

His mission was to clarify matters surrounding *Pinkerton*, and although he desperately wanted to steer the public in the right direction, being misinterpreted was a real source of aggravation for Rivers, who was quick to rebut Rob O'Connor's *Pinkerton* review from *Rolling Stone*. "It says we're something like a fun and sun band that sings 100% happy songs to make people feel better," he griped. "These songs were written in the dead of winter when I was in a lot of pain and very lonely. When I listen to the records, I don't get that feeling of happy pop at all. I don't feel like we're lugubrious or wallowing in our sorrows at all or entirely pessimistic. There's some kind of blend of pessimism and optimism but I think it's really easy to overlook that. And a lot of people have, including *Rolling Stone*. Instead they see us as just a one-dimensional, silly pop band."

In defense of his review a number of years later, O'Connor says, "I wrote [it] from an advance cassette before the album was released. If my memory serves me right, I'd wanted three and a half stars for the album. I do remember liking it quite a bit more than I originally anticipated. In my review I was responding to the impressions the album made on me; how the album felt at the time. Obviously, there's angst and longing, all real emotions, happening in those songs. However, Cuomo's persona, his delivery, and the band's presentation shades things humorously, lightening things up in the process — much the way, say, 'Happy Together' hides its troubles in an optimistic arrangement. No one's going to mistake Weezer for those sadcore bands. American Music Club they ain't. As a rock musician and pop performer, Cuomo chose this pose, or it was genetically chosen for him. But it seems to work for him."

"It's a strange field I've gotten into," Rivers admitted at the time. "It's so commercial, and it's so personally important to me at the same time. It's a weird juggling act. But it's pretty interesting." Being commercial also meant accepting a sponsorship with sneaker maker Vans, Inc., which resulted in a new pair of shoes arriving on his doorstep each month. "I love it, it's so great," Cuomo said, thrilled with the arrangement. "Until this past year, I wasn't able to wear normal shoes. I always had to wear this dorky-assed shoe with a big lift on it. I hated it so much. One of the greatest things about having even legs is that I can wear whatever shoes I want."

While he had grown comfortable with his even legs, Cuomo was still askew when it came to traditional rock star roles. Showing up on time for appointments, sipping on apple juice, and having nervous reactions to video cameras present in interviews without warning clearly set him apart from the more relaxed rock stars. While his sincerity was rare for a multi-platinum artist, he was a far cry from the David Lee Roth personality type so many rockers embodied.

But through his songs Rivers was able to resolve a lot of inner conflict. Often a personal problem would give way to a new composition that examined all facets of the problem. Working through his conundrums with music, Cuomo regularly found himself able to evolve after achieving a successful resolution.

Rivers approached songs from a deeply personal space, and during the creative process he tried to forget that millions might actually hear them in their realized state. "Essentially all these songs are just parts of myself," Cuomo contended, "so how they're perceived is kind of irrelevant to what these songs really mean. But really, I'm trying to communicate how I feel so it's important to me to try and do my best to communicate in a way that people can understand."

Influenced lyrically at the time by the likes of Sebadoh's Lou Barlow and Brian Wilson's efforts on the Beach Boys classic *Pet Sounds*, Rivers was drawn to the honesty and unpretentiousness of these artists. Cuomo deemed Wilson "a very rare talent," regarding him as one of the finest talents of the 20th century. Rivers acknowledged emulating Wilson, but denied any comparisons to him, dismissing his own abilities as minute when matched against one of his favorites.

Cuomo also cited comic books, including Joe Matt's *Peepshow*, as a strong influence over his own lyrics. Rivers — a comic devotee since grade school — was such a fan that he jumped at the opportunity to be interviewed by his hero in a *Cake* feature at the time. Cuomo let his guard down during the piece, opening up even further about his general view of women and his sex life on the road, boasting nearly forty conquests in just two years in the limelight.

"It doesn't bother me [that I've slept with forty girls]. It doesn't seem like a lot to me," he told Matt of his inner Pinkerton. "If I'm in a new city every night and playing for thousands of girls every night, and I have sex with, say, thirty girls in two years, that's not a lot at all." When Matt countered that the rocker was averaging only one partner every three weeks or so, Cuomo confessed, "Yeah, that's terrible."

Admitting that he had a hard time coming to terms with his new lifestyle in his first year of stardom, Rivers said he used alcohol to overcome his inhibitions and eventually found himself capable of taking advantage of situations involving multiple sex partners. He also expressed hope that his groupie conquests might involve partners that were with him because of physical attraction or actual sexual desire, rather than just because of his fame.

"I'd been in Japan for a week and every night there were ten or fifteen girls in my room and nothing happened because I wasn't confident enough to say, 'Let's have sex or get out of the room,'" he explained. "So finally, at the end of my stay there I said, 'Whoever wants to stay in the room has got to take their clothes off and get on the bed.' And most of them left but four of them stayed. It was a difficult step for me to take but I had to take it. It was the truth about what I wanted."

In fact Cuomo believed that he could achieve all of his *artistic* goals in his basement. His sole purpose in going out there to rock at this point in his life was to meet and ultimately have sex with women. And while Rivers endorsed his own behavior, he had a double standard that found him negatively judging women who achieve a similarly high level of promiscuity.

"I think the two sexes are very different," he rationalized, explaining that men in his position were largely going for quantity over quality when it came to sex. "There shouldn't be one standard for both. Men and women are entirely different and for a woman to have sex with loads of guys is different. There's an evolutionary argument. A woman can have, say, ten babies in her life, so for her to risk one of those opportunities on a meaningless fling, it's a much bigger risk than for a man who can have thousands of babies in his life."

If Pinkerton's character was the ultimate example of macho, Cuomo evidently had little trouble slipping in and out of the sailor's shoes when it suited his needs. If he was worried how his mother might take some of the songs on his second album at the time of its release, by the time of this interview he seemed to hold little concern about how she might perceive such sexist principles. Into the fall of '96, in ports of call in Japan and beyond, Cuomo tried to squeeze in some concerts between indiscriminate conquests.

chapter sixteen

who you callin' bitch?

Touring the Far East in October 1996 meant concert appearances in Australia, New Zealand, and Japan. During the trek, Rivers had become intent on meeting the female fan that helped him scribe "Across the Sea," but just as soon changed his mind after having fears of embarrassment. Some of those feelings may have come from the fact that he was having a lot of dire interactions with women of Japanese descent.

"Halfway through writing the album, I started to realize or become aware of a pattern in my life that I seem to be having a lot of disastrous encounters with half-Japanese girls," he confessed. "And then it developed into disastrous encounters with Asian girls of all sorts. I suppose it's fair to say that I'm fascinated by Asian girls. For some reason, they're particularly beautiful to me. I don't know why. And when I became aware of that and also the fact that it was the masculine part of myself that I was learning about in these songs, I remembered the story of *Madame Butterfly* and the story of the character Pinkerton in that opera. And I decided to use or refer to that story as a means of unifying the record. And so I kept that in mind as I wrote the second half of the record. Pinkerton is the ultimate character representing male id who goes to Japan as an American sailor and hooks up with this fifteen-year-old Japanese girl and gets her pregnant and then abandons her. He's thoroughly despicable. But I can't deny that there's some of that in me."

Meanwhile, Pat Wilson's take on the jaunt through Japan was mostly favorable. "The people were extremely polite," Wilson observed, "but it was really polluted. Tokyo is just insane. When you order a large fries at a McDonald's, I've never seen people so excited to give me my fries. Which in no way is an endorsement for McDonald's. Here, you just get the people behind the counter who are just waiting for their shift to end because they hate their job so much."

After wrapping up the tour of the Pacific Rim, the band flew home to Los Angeles. Wilson and Sharp joined up for a promotional appearance on the nationally syndicated radio show *Modern Rock Live* on October 28, making a concerted effort to give *Pinkerton* some renewed life on the U.S. album charts. A few days later, on November 1, Weezer launched the North American *Pinkerton* tour at the Ventura Theatre in Ventura, California.

Still, sales for the disc were slipping, and it was soon evident that the record buyers who had propelled *Weezer* to multi-platinum sales weren't as eager to buy into Rivers' fixations with Japanese women, opera, and Pixies-styled distortion. Looking back on the band's frenzied *Blue Album* era in late 1996, Brian marveled at Weezer's unexpected ascent. "We saw our audiences change from intelligent, hip-looking people to complete jocks who just came because they saw the video. That's the price you pay if you want to make a living at this."

In his life and his writing Cuomo had been trying to get in touch with the masculine side of himself he had been denying for so long. He believed the first record was wimpy and damn near emasculated, while the second found his masculine side pushing through. *Pinkerton* was a knee-jerk reaction to the slicker disc that preceded it and Cuomo was content to fuck a bit with the pop formula that had made him a millionaire by his twenty-fifth birthday.

"I think with this album, we got a lot better as a band — [after] all the touring we did on the first album," Cuomo said. "When it came time to do the second, we trusted ourselves more. We had the attitude to just record how we sound, naturally. On the first record, we sucked so bad. It's just impossible to exaggerate how bad we sucked. We were really concerned with getting things to this listenable level. So it sounds really artificial. I think the vibe on this record is so great. That's more important to me than radio play. It's always nice to be on the radio, though."

But the reality was that *Pinkerton*, in comparison to Weezer's debut, was starting to tank without radio and television exposure. Despite Rivers' unwillingness to do a video akin to "Buddy Holly," the straight perform-ance clip for "El Scorcho" did little to ignite interest with the powers that be at MTV, so the band reached a compromise in the hopes of rekindling album sales with their next single and video, "The Good Life." Speaking on the matter, Bell said, "I, for one, know that we'll never make another video as good as 'Buddy Holly.'" Just the same, the band forged ahead with a concept video featuring a pizza delivery girl. Commenting on the story-board, Bell said, "I was a pizza guy for years, so I know the ropes."

The band postponed a scheduled gig on November 9 in Salt Lake City in order to film the video. Hatched and directed by the award-winning pair of Jonathan Dayton and Valerie Faris, who were notable at the time for The Smashing Pumpkins' acclaimed "Tonight, Tonight" clip, the concept cen-tered on a seemingly depressed pizza delivery girl in a mundane job and longing for "The Good Life." It was an existence that not just Bell, but for-mer Domino's employee Cuomo knew all too well. Interspersed with studio performance clips, it included one riotous shot of Matt and Pat running around the room pretending they were airplanes, shots of Brian posing for the camera, and — no surprise here — plenty of close-ups of Rivers.

"We kinda had to compromise," Rivers said of "The Good Life" video. "For example, the 'El Scorcho' video was just us performing, and the sec-ond video off the record is more MTV's style." Unfortunately, the video deserved more exposure than it was given following its debut on MTV's *120 Minutes* some six weeks later. After the premiere date of December 15, 1996, it aired rather infrequently. Clearly, loyalty from the music tastemakers at radio and MTV had waned, regardless of the band's efforts to be true to Cuomo's vision.

Three days before the shoot, Weezer performed an acoustic lunchtime concert at Shorecrest High School in Seattle that was broadcast on the city's commercial alternative outlet KNDD. Resulting from a contest to have the group play an acoustic set in the winner's school cafeteria, a student by the name of Ladd Martin was responsible for his schoolmates being witnesses to unplugged renditions of "Undone," "No One Else," "The Good Life," "El Scorcho," "Pink Triangle," and "Buddy Holly." In the acoustic format, Pat joined Rivers and Brian on guitars, while Matt sang harmony vocals, but one wonders what the principal at Shorecrest must have thought about Mr. Cuomo's infamous ode to lesbians.

On November 29, as the band's U.S. tour wound eastward, Weezer was forced to cancel a gig in Old Bridge, New Jersey, when Matt wound up over-medicated on painkillers for an abscessed tooth he had developed. Meanwhile, five days later, Rivers again found himself with anxiety about playing in his home state. "I've tried to avoid it," Cuomo said, explaining why it was only Weezer's second appearance in Connecticut. "It's incredibly nerve-racking." Part of it had to do with the thought of "people I know judging me," he continued of the gig planned for Toad's Place in New Haven. "I just feel more pressure in Connecticut than anywhere else in the world."

Brian Diaz of The Reunion Show caught two of these East Coast gigs and says, "The onstage chemistry was amazing. Matt Sharp was a show in and of himself. The crowds were wildly enthusiastic and I pretty much figured they were poised to be a band that consistently sold millions of records."

The band worked to keep audiences happy, touring up until just before Christmas and playing dates in the Northeast, including one holiday gig for Philadelphia's WDRE as headliners at the Electric Factory on December 5. Shows throughout the Southeast, Texas, and the Southwest closed out their 1996 concert obligations, wrapping with a hometown gig at The Palace in L.A. just four days before Christmas. While Matt took care of his tooth and Pat and Brian retreated to their respective loved ones, Rivers spent the bulk of his 1996 Christmas break back home in Connecticut, as he put it, "bored."

Although the *Pinkerton* tour was largely successful, bringing the group to mid-size venues like the House of Blues in New Orleans and Austin's Liberty Lunch, the fact that the album kept slipping down the Top 200 album survey wasn't helping the band's morale. Infighting between the band members was growing increasingly common. Outwardly, Brian and Rivers were giving the media the impression that everything was hunky dory, as they'd go off to shop for clothes or practice piano respectively, but original members Matt and Pat — who largely holed up on the bus playing video games like Sega Soccer — had no qualms about rolling their eyes at Cuomo's egocentric behavior. Sharp, who had a powerful personality of his own, and the sarcastic, wisecracking Wilson began to take Cuomo's "selective democracy" to task in front of reporters whenever it suited them.

Pat was first to publicly knock Rivers by citing his own participation in Weezer as strictly fiduciary. "Rivers thinks I'm here to support the concept of *Pinkerton*, but I'm here because the concept of *Pinkerton* should support me," Wilson cracked in a *Details* piece that hit the magazine racks as Weezer embarked on a short two-week tour of the East and Midwest in early 1997. Responding to the comment that year, Cuomo retorted, "He can be an old grump sometimes."

When the tour resumed after Christmas at the Chameleon Club in Lancaster, Pennsylvania, on January 9 (and wrapped at the Barrymore Theatre in Madison, Wisconsin, on the 24), the short run of gigs would be the last Weezer concert dates for four months. By late January, Cuomo was back in Cambridge to resume work on his studies, having deferred his fall 1996 semester and shifting his major from music to English after he became unhappy with the classical pieces he was required to study.

"I'm starting to feel melancholic," Rivers said as his return to studies loomed. "The *Pinkerton* tour is almost over. As this tour ends, I'm actually bummed that it's over. I've had such a great time these past six months playing, partying, meeting girls. Never have I felt this unlonely. I don't want this feeling to end. Soon I'll be back at school, however. The Bad Life. It's cold in Boston and I have no close friends there. This semester, however, with my newfound quasi-social skills, I think I'll be able to make friends and enjoy life."

But enjoying life was a challenge when just days earlier, a long feature article on the band, titled "Happy Days Canceled: The Unraveling of Weezer," surfaced in that month's *Alternative Press*. Written by journalist David Daley and documenting the friction in the band on the previous October's trek through Australia and New Zealand, the piece informed fans that sweaters weren't the only things unraveling in the Weezer organization. As a result, what should have been a quiet few months apart for the members of the group, wound up being a time of deep frustration, disillusionment, and ultimately, re-evaluation.

Cuomo's depiction as a sad sack — someone whose wealth and fame were overshadowed by his lack of real friends and low self-esteem issues — wasn't exactly a revelation to fans. Speaking to Daley, Rivers dismissed the "Buddy Holly" video, Weezer's most successful, as his least favorite because it was entirely Spike Jonze's idea and had nothing to do with him.

He said the video was a method of trickery used to get his album into the hands of those pining for *Happy Days* nostalgia.

More insightful is the turmoil chronicled in the *AP* piece, which pitted Cuomo against Wilson and Sharp. Pat countered Rivers' stance, arguing that the "Buddy Holly" clip was the best thing they'd ever done. Wilson also contended that without a similarly alluring video, the large success of *Weezer* would never be repeated.

"I know [Rivers] has a little bit of a complex about that," Sharp chimed in. "Did we sell two million records because of that video? Are we a flash in the pan? If I were him I would probably have a complex about that too. I just think we were lucky we made this video and people got to hear all the other songs. Maybe he thinks of it as trickery, but if we made a good record, and we're proud of the record, we should get people to hear it. To me, videos are not a serious art form."

Pat told Daley that because of Rivers imposing the 70/30 split regarding frontman/band video exposure, he was at an impasse with Cuomo over the making of another performance video. Wilson said, in all seriousness, that if it were up to him he would wear a bear suit in the band's next clip and Sharp would sport a big bunny rabbit suit. Meaning that if the others were forced to forfeit camera time, they would have to be allowed to ham it up in return.

But the rift went deeper than music videos. Sharp, in a drunken interview from his Auckland hotel room, balked that in Weezer his only real job was to play the bass capably and keep his falsetto from going out of tune. "I think we're settling into something now that's much different from what we started," he said. "In that period, I felt a bit more involved with what we were doing. In most cases with most bands, you see that the whole is better than the sum of its parts. I'm not so sure if this is the case with us. We're getting more towards supporting a single vision than incorporating

JAY BLAKESBERG

Strained Times: As Pinkerton stalls, bad vibes infiltrate the band

the wide range of personalities. I don't think that we're not important, but the name of the band *is* Weezer. It's [Rivers'] name, you know."

Wilson was more direct with Daley in his one-on-one interview as he made it clear that things had been strained between Cuomo and himself for quite a while, confessing that he had almost quit the group on several occasions. The tension stemmed back to the way Cuomo structured the division of mechanical royalties on the songs that Pat and Rivers had written together for their debut album. Wilson called Cuomo's dysfunctional arrangement, which split the royalties into three parts — music, lyrics, and melody — to give himself two thirds of the money, "fucked."

Despite his feelings of bitterness, Wilson never actually handed in his resignation. Each time he was at his breaking point, the band's success became greater, making it harder and harder to walk away. So while Patrick was committed to playing in Weezer because he made "a shitload of money," he made it known that he wasn't down with Rivers' lyrics and had objections to the "selective democracy" set-up that gave Cuomo the ultimate veto power over the band.

"If you're asking the $64,000 question — would I be doing this if it didn't make me any money? — I don't think I would," Wilson reasoned. "I guess my experience in this band can be best summed up as 'good thing happens, turns into bad thing, becomes successful, [and] perpetuates.'"

Meanwhile, Rivers — despite proclaiming that the other members of Weezer were all talented players and songwriters — dismissed any notion of ever performing Rentals, Space Twins, or Special Goodness songs in the context of Weezer. Cuomo simply explained that he was averse to performing cover songs.

As the piece wound down, Cuomo defensively proclaimed, "I'm not the dictator of this band." But the damage was already done, and rumors of an imminent Weezer breakup, fueled by a four-month break where Rivers returned to Harvard, did little to prolong the life of the band's second album.

Despite Weezer's infighting, guitarist Brian Bell kept a low profile, clearly just happy to play in one of alternative rock's best-known bands. Still, Bell was frustrated with the public's reaction to *Pinkerton*. And although *Pinkerton* was arguably one of the finest records of 1996, the public criticism rang out loud and clear when *Rolling Stone* readers ranked it in the year-end readers' poll as the second worst album of the year, right behind Bush's sophomore let-down *Razorblade Suitcase*.

"There is a magazine stand in Hollywood and I was feeling really lonely, so I walked down there," Bell remembered. "It's a horrible place to walk when you're lonely. I was looking at magazines and seeing if there was any-thing on Weezer and I came across this *Rolling Stone*. It had this poll on worst records and *Pinkerton* was listed as one of the worst. It just felt really shitty."

Aside from lackluster sales and mixed critical response, the controver-sial *Alternative Press* article had Weezer's frontman crying foul. "I was bummed when I read the article," said Cuomo shortly after the piece ran. "What's even worse is the fact I knew the guy too. He lives in Connecticut. It just seems like journalists are always trying to get the hot story. We were mad at each other then, but not as mad as he made it out to be."

Just the same, it is interesting to note that after the *Alternative Press* article emerged, Pat and Matt were noticeably absent from subsequent interviews as Brian and Rivers attempted to put a positive spin on things. "It's a relationship like anything else," Bell said, doing damage control at the time. "We're four extremely different people and each of us is talented in our own right, and very smart. We try to be a democracy, but there's bound to be problems. So, you just have to talk about things. Maybe it's because we know we have a long break coming up, but all four of us are communicating better."

As the spring of 1997 approached, Weezer was still largely inactive. Cuomo and his opposing forces Wilson and Sharp took some time apart and cooled off. Meanwhile Bell focused on the Space Twins, now featuring the aforementioned Maloof brothers, who had come back to Los Angeles at Brian's urging. One of the first songs Brian crafted with the new line-up in mind was "Osaka Aqua Bus," a song written after Weezer's initial jour-ney to Japan.

"When I was there on tour with Weezer, everything I ate had the taste of fish . . . fish shavings, fish eggs, fish heads," Bell said laughing. "It was impossible to get by! It was a mix of things. One day I was walking back to the hotel in Osaka and I saw a sign, and I had woken up really early that day so I thought I was hallucinating, but it said, 'Osaka Aqua Bus,' and that name! I wrote the song the next day because the word just stuck in my head."

"We've had this line-up since, like '97, and the first thing we did was a six- or eight-song demo to sort of try and find our own sound," Brian said in 2003 of his own band. "As you know we had quite a bit of free time — and a lot of room for disaster — then, because Weezer was inactive. The first initial demo had this really cool song on it called 'Goddess of Love' that was put out as a single. But the other songs were my first attempt at songwriting. I think what a lot of people do when they first start writing, primarily if they are a musician, is to put so many musical ideas and intricate changes [into songs]. This makes them very interesting as pieces, but not necessarily as popular songs. We were almost verging on prog, which is very difficult to play, because the band had to be so in tune with my vocals and body language. Almost like the way Frank Zappa would conduct his musicians — not that I would consider myself of that caliber. But then I realized I wanted to have an audience that wasn't only musicians. So I started to simplify things. We just kept demoing and rehearsing and each segment of demoing would prevail."

While Bell drove the "Osaka Aqua Bus," the Weezer camp as a whole kept relatively quiet that spring as *The Good Life OZ* EP was issued in Australia. Consisting of that single's A-side, as well as two bonus tunes from the *Pinkerton* sessions, "Waiting on You" and "I Just Threw Out the Love of My Dreams," the EP also boasted two acoustic tracks, "Pink Triangle" and "The Good Life," both recorded at the Shorecrest High School promotional appearance. If the picture on the cover — taken from Weezer's Tower Records parking lot gig the previous September — was no big deal, the inner sleeve displayed a downright creepy x-ray of the leg that Rivers underwent surgery on.

Around this time, Weezer — traditionally a headlining act — was approached and accepted a support slot on a summer tour with California ska-pop act No Doubt, who had just shifted seven million (on their way to ten million plus) copies of their breakthrough album *Tragic Kingdom*. But there was speculation as to whether Matt could leave the Rentals' ongoing studio obligations alone long enough to participate, fostered by Bell's announcement that Weezer "might have to hire another bass player" for the No Doubt jaunt.

In April 1997, the band indeed auditioned two bassists to substitute for Sharp at Boston's Fort Apache studios. Matt was frustrated and behind schedule on the Rentals' second album due to a dispute over studio fees. As a result, the London facility housing the work in progress had refused to fork over the tapes to Sharp, who was planning to pick up work on the project in Los Angeles in early 1997. So while Maverick Records balked — but eventually managed to get the tapes released to Sharp — Matt was left in limbo.

The bassists auditioned were a musician named Alex (whom Cuomo only remembers as a "bald dude with earrings") and former Letters to Cleo member Scott Riebling. Although Riebling was actually selected to play for Sharp, Weezer's founding bassist had miraculously cleared his schedule by the time the tour bus started rolling. If the step back to opening act was indeed a humbling one, it was a decision that proved the group could reconcile their differences and hang together to preserve the future of the Weezer.

Discounting all of the infighting, Cuomo quashed continuing rumors of a breakup. "I'd be more likely to believe all those rumors I heard growing up about how Rod Stewart supposedly swallowed a gallon of cum," he said. "We haven't fought for a while, but there was a point where we were beating each other up constantly. But we're pretty much hitched for life. We did fight a lot [over egos]. It's like a marriage between four guys. It's unholy.

"It sucks that [*Pinkerton*] hasn't done as well," added Rivers matter-of-factly just prior to the tour launch. "We've tried really hard to promote it. We're opening for No Doubt, we're doing everything we can." The No Doubt trek through North America — which Brian Bell described as the band "going for that stadium rock thing" — was slated to begin at the Gorge Amphitheatre in Washington State on May 24 just after Cuomo closed the book on his third semester at Harvard, and was to last two months, eventually wrapping on July 20 at the Galaxy Concert Theatre in Santa Ana, California.

Just prior to the No Doubt dates, Weezer appeared on May 19, alongside Reel Big Fish, Nerf Herder (pre–Justin Fisher), Guided By Voices, the Gigolo Aunts, and others at the Best Music Poll Festival on Boston's Lansdowne Street, sponsored by Boston alternative radio fixture WFNX and its affiliated music publication *The Phoenix*. Cuomo told the paper, "It's the first time we've played together since January, so we'll be busting at the seams. I'll have just finished my last final. It'll be the beginning of a summer-long party for us."

In between his studies and dismissing those pesky suggestions that Weezer had temporarily dissolved, Rivers found time to devote to his beloved sport. With his healed leg, Cuomo joined a Bay State League soccer team.

Realizing that his and Bell's previous attempts to diffuse the media's presentation of dissension in the Weezer ranks weren't entirely believable, Cuomo conceded in May that "there's an incredible amount of friction" within the band. Although he was hesitant to blame it on any one thing, Rivers made it clear that in his mind the struggle surrounding songwriting for Weezer was resolved on the first record.

"It's an open door for whoever wants to write songs," he attested, perhaps broadcasting such a falsification to promote a perception of harmony in the group. "But they all have their own bands, so when they write a great song, they think, 'Why give it to Rivers to sing?' *Pinkerton* was a very unified record, so it would be bizarre if suddenly there were a 'Friends of P'–type song in the middle of it. Hopefully on the next record it will be mixed up more."

Reacting to the slow sales of *Pinkerton*, which had yet to go gold (and wouldn't until July 3, 2001), Rivers said, "I don't think we were choosing to do something different because we wanted to be different or because we were reacting to success. It's just that I was writing about different things and, because of that, other aspects of the record changed also. Production changed, the marketing changed, the venues changed. But it all came from the fact that the songs were different, the lyrics were more direct. Instead of being couched in strange language or weird metaphor or ironic nostalgia, my heart is much more on my musical sleeve."

"The lyrics were all very personal," Brian rationalized *Pinkerton*'s weak sales. "And I think sometimes when you get too personal people just can't latch onto it."

"To me, the anomaly was the success of the first album," Rivers added. "That was pretty much a shock. This level of success feels much more understandable to me." Blaming *Pinkerton*'s lackluster chart performance on a changing musical climate, he theorized that "popular taste has left the white-male-playing-electric-guitar genre and moved on to other things."

The band released "Pink Triangle" as the album's last-ditch attempt at the airwaves. As the song went for modern rock radio playlist adds on May 20, Cuomo mused how bizarre it was that the word 'lesbian' was popping up everywhere, largely due to the popular film *Chasing Amy* and the Ellen DeGeneres sitcom *Ellen*, which both focused on the alternative lifestyle. Rivers denied seeing either, but joked, "Hopefully, we can ride the lesbian wave, like we rode the alternative wave."

In addition to that notion, Cuomo was extremely grateful for his core audience and acknowledged them for their support in issue #10 of their fan quarterly *Weezine*. "I want to thank all of you who have supported and defended Weezer in the media," he wrote. "We've really had a terrible time between the magazines that say terrible things about us and the radio stations that don't play Weezer as much as they ought to. Sometimes I get so bummed at all the criticism but I feel a million times better when I see you sticking up for us."

R.C. went as far as directly praising the Weezer fan club member who wrote a devoted letter to a certain controversial magazine and "ripped *Alternative Press* an alternative asshole in their April issue. Journalists have an amazing knack for twisting a story around till it's scandalous enough to sell copy. And sometimes the things we say don't come out how we mean them to. Sorry."

chapter seventeen

mykel & carli

Remixed for radio by airwave gloss expert Tom Lord-Alge, the version of "Pink Triangle" that sought radio airplay housed a reworked guitar solo, the addition of a synthesizer, plus a different vocal performance. And although Weezer was now at the point where they'd do whatever was necessary to regain some love on the FM dial, the promo CD single — which also featured the acoustic version of the same song from the Shorecrest High School performance — stalled, killing any chance at a CD single or a video.

Although radio wasn't receptive to the song, Weezer continued on into July, plugging away as openers for No Doubt. "It was kind of a really unfortunate time for the band," Justin Fisher remembered. "They had all been arguing, and it was a bad scene for a while, until the tour with No Doubt. Then they all kind of came together and were having fun again. Although, by then it was a little too late for the album."

But as morale soared in the Weezer camp, the quartet was dealt a tragic hand on July 9, 1997, when Mykel and Carli Allan — longtime loyalists and founders of Weezer's official fanclub — were killed with their younger sister Trysta in a motor vehicle accident five years to the day after they caught their first show by the band. Following the group's show at the Ogden Theatre in Denver on July 8, as the trio was caravanning on to their parents' home in Orem, Utah (and the next night's Salt Lake City, Utah, gig), their car careened off the road just after midnight on I-70 near Rifle, Colorado.

According to reports, the sisters died instantly, but because the single vehicle accident was not visible from the road, they were not immediately discovered. With the Allans' whereabouts unknown, the members of Weezer played the next night at Salt Lake City's DV8 venue, in spite of concerns and worry over their friends' noticeable absence. On July 10, 1997, en route to a pair of dates at the MacEwan Hall Ballroom in Calgary, Alberta, the band learned the disturbing news. The Allan family had called Jennifer Wilson — whose cell phone number was in Carli's personal journal — to notify her of the tragic accident, and in turn, Jen notified the Weezer organization. Managing to play the Calgary gigs on July 11 and 12 in a state of disbelief, Rivers, Brian, Matt, and Pat canceled a concert planned for July 14 in Vancouver, British Columbia, and caught a plane to Salt Lake City to serve (along with Karl Koch) as pallbearers in the memorial service. At the end of the funeral, Karl placed a Weezer hat on the graves of both Mykel and Carli.

In a letter to the fanclub immediately after the event, Karl informed the 4,000-plus members of the tragedy and revealed plans for a benefit show. "It is beyond words, beyond reason how shocking this is and how cruelly unfair it feels," he wrote, acknowledging that they were continuing the tour, although it was very, very difficult doing so. "We have lost three of the most loving, giving and wonderful people we could ever be lucky enough to know. Mykel and Carli were the cornerstone of Weezer fandom and an inspiration to band and fans alike. Though I knew Trysta less than them, she quickly impressed me with the same wonderful qualities. We are all much poorer without them."

Following the July 14 funeral for the three Allan sisters, and with the group still in mourning, they resumed the final week of their North American touring commitment, which was followed by ten days of dates in Japan, Thailand, Bangkok, and lastly, Hawaii. On July 27, Weezer's first performance in Japan at the Mt. Fuji Festival was canceled due to an expected typhoon, as the entire event was rained out. In an effort to kill time, Matt, Pat, and Karl eroded their sadness by purchasing fireworks at a nearby 7-11 store and setting them off behind a nearby trash dumpster.

Of the Thailand gigs that followed, Brian would later recollect, "It felt like we were The Beatles. The crowd rushed the stage. Army guys with machine guns were in the [venues]. I kept wondering if this was because they really like us, or that they're just so completely starved for live music."

On August 9, the quartet rocked the crowd at Honolulu's Nimitz Hall in what Koch calls "a spur of the moment" gig, followed by a few days of rest and relaxation in Hawaii that culminated with the group attending a performance by the legendary Don Ho. During the Ho show, Brian was even invited up onstage to strum along with the band.

But upon returning to Los Angeles, such lighter moments were again met with sadness and ultimately the acceptance of Mykel, Carli, and Trysta Allan's passing. In a benefit concert planned for The Whiskey in Los Angeles on August 15, 1997, Weezer — alongside That Dog and Black Market Flowers, other bands the Allans championed — took the stage for an emotional set in front of fans, including celebrities from the rock world like Green Day's Billie Joe Armstrong, Ben Lee, Jeff and Steve McDonald from Redd Kross, and No Doubt's Tony Kanal and Adrian Young. Hollywood types like Clare Danes, Jared Leto, Sofia Coppola, and "Buddy Holly" director Spike Jonze also caught the gig. MTV gave substantial coverage to the benefit, which was designed to assist the Allan family in paying for funeral expenses and help endow the Weezer Memorial Fund, a college fund for the Allans' nieces and nephews. Mykel and Carli had been more than mere acquaintances; they were close-knit friends of the band who helped the group mend wounds during the infighting that came to a head in the *Alternative Press* cover story.

"I'm happy that we have this opportunity to do something — to show them how much we love them," Rivers added the night of the show. "And for the other bands that they worked with, it's that same opportunity for them. And all the fans here tonight too, I think are also Mykel and Carli fans. And I think everyone's here just to show them how much we love them and . . . show them what kind of impact they had because they were definitely a big part of everything that's happening tonight, keeping all these bands going and getting all these fans together. They were really the strong force holding the whole community together."

"Even when we've had our bad times," Matt Sharp chimed, "which we've had a short period of that, they were the one great positive thing that kept everything together. I mean, if they can make us look good they can make anyone look good. They had the ability to make a positive experience out of harder times. And so it's a really strange thing they were doing, they were starting a trip with us to go across the country and, for me, it's a really sad thing they couldn't have been a part of that because this is the time where we've finally gotten it together and we're all very happy with being with each other. We just wanted them to be with us and to celebrate and have a wonderful time. I think that's all of what the show's about, about a certain period that they couldn't be with us and now we feel like they can be."

Following That Dog's performance, Rivers, Pat, Matt, and Brian took the stage to the *Family Feud* theme. As their sixteen-song set got underway, reportedly played with "drunken abandon," Matt Sharp picked Rivers up and spun him around roughly ten times before launching into "My Name Is Jonas." Prior to the last song, the Allan family took the stage, with father Wayne holding up a picture of his daughters. "They died doing what they loved," he said to the packed crowd, choking back tears. "Thank you for your love and support. They are here in spirit with us."

Five weeks after the sisters' passing, the show had brought Weezer fans and Mykel and Carli's family — including their parents and siblings —

together in the same venue for some closure. "We feel very fortunate that they went together," Wayne Allan said before exiting the stage to an ovation. Then Rivers picked up his guitar to perform the tribute song he had written for them years earlier, his voice cracking with sadness as he sung their namesake number, "Mykel & Carli."

Looking back on the Allans' efforts, Karl Koch said, "They set the precedent of how to treat fans and how to be nice to them." And in fact Rivers didn't just write a song for them, he bestowed the girls their own island on the antique map buried beneath the black CD holder on the inside of *Pinkerton*. And after lending the track "Mykel & Carli" to the benefit compilation *Hear You Me*, which was released later in the year by Vast Records and featured Black Market Flowers, up-and-coming act Ozma, and Justin Fisher's band Shufflepuck, the members of Weezer attempted to put the tragedy behind them.

Immediately after the No Doubt tour, it was Rivers who wanted to resume roadwork, but the rest of the group wanted to pursue their individual creative sides. "After a while you just want to do what makes you happy," Wilson explained. So Patrick returned home to Portland to write songs, Matt went back to work on the Rentals second album, Brian hooked up again with the Space Twins, and Cuomo headed back to Cambridge.

Just before they broke apart, Cuomo made optimistic statements in the press about the future of the band, but deep inside the camp, things were as bleak as ever. "Everything just fell apart," he later reflected. "We talked about trying to fight onward, but it just seemed like the gods were against us, and we'd better give up while we were still alive."

Bell said the loss of the girls, coupled with internal tensions, "just kind of made us all really question what we were doing. There was a big black cloud over us. We just had to get away from it." Parting again, the group stayed away from the public eye for what wound up being several years.

Having experienced high points like platinum album sales and playing in front of thousands each night, as well as the lows of insignificant record sales, bad press, and being at odds with one another, Weezer's post-*Pinkerton* future was in serious doubt again. When asked what was next for the group shortly before the members scattered in different directions, Rivers said, "I have no fucking idea, I'm really scared. Hopefully, we will make another album. We will just cross our fingers and hope it flies."

chapter eighteen

fun time

Upon returning to Cambridge after the *Pinkerton* tour, Rivers Cuomo spent the fall of 1997 becoming more actively involved in the Boston music scene. At the last minute, he dropped out of Harvard when he began a fertile songwriting spell and didn't want to derail the process. Without curriculum interference, Rivers also found more time for soccer that autumn. As the starting left-midfielder on the Brestchester United team — which was part of Massachusetts' Bay State League — the quick and agile Cuomo scored a pair of goals that season.

Living something more akin to a rock star life in Boston than his earlier educational pursuits would allow, Rivers was becoming more and more comfortable with his even-legged self. Describing his typical day at the time, he would "wake up at 10, lie in bed and listen to Howard Stern for a half hour, get up, pee, have a cup of coffee, practice piano for an hour, work on songs all afternoon (or alternately procrastinate and accomplish nothing), play music with friends or go to soccer practice, and finally, at the end of the night, call up a girlfriend for some affection before I go to bed. Although I make sure that the girl is at least 3,000 miles away so as to avoid the risk of actually forming some type of real relationship."

While a typical day for Cuomo in late 1997 was pretty mundane, he was productive. Playing with a rotation of musicians between September 1997 and January 1998 in his first-ever side outfit from Weezer, one constant in the Rivers Cuomo Band was Kevin Stevenson, vocalist and guitarist for local punk outfit The Shods.

"At the time, The Shods were just starting to headline at T.T.'s, a small club in Boston," Stevenson remembered of his first encounters with Cuomo in 1997. "We'd be playing T.T. the Bear's and I'd look out in the audience, and I'd see Rivers standing out there watching us. You know, he probably came to two shows or something. The second time I saw him out there he approached me afterwards with his idea to start a solo band. And I said, 'That sounds good. Call me when you get it arranged.' And he called me like a day later, or something. 'I got it. We're all ready to go.'

"My band had recorded an album called *Stop Crying* at Fort Apache for the studio's label, which was to be distributed by MCA. That later fell through, but Rivers liked our stuff. He had a cassette of it. So many times I'd come into his house and he'd be sitting at his table in the kitchen with his boom box playing that album. So he knew what I could do.

"The first time I went down to practice at Rivers' house I knocked on the door, and no one answered," Stevenson chuckled. "It was a nice, small house in West Cambridge, but not how you'd expect a rock star to live at all. I knocked on the door again a little louder. No one answered. So I edged open the door a little bit to see if anyone was there and Rivers was sitting at his kitchen table eating a bowl of cereal. And I said, 'Rivers, it's Kevin,' and he didn't say anything. So I just walked in and stood around in his kitchen while he ate his cereal. He had milk to his right and cereal to his left and he kept filling his bowl. And I said, 'Hey Rivers, what kind of stuff do you have planned that we're going to play?' No answer — just eating his cereal. I said, 'Rivers, when are the guys getting here?' No answer — eating his cereal. I said, 'Okay Rivers, I'm gonna go home.' I'd had enough of that shit.

"So I turned on my heel and then Rivers came to life," Stevenson said in his demonstrative Boston accent. "He's like, 'We're gonna practice — in a half hour!' And I said, 'That's cool. What kinda stuff are we gonna do?' And he starts dribbling a soccer ball all over the house. I'm like, 'Rivers, who are we gonna be playing with? What kinda songs are we gonna be doing?' Dribble, dribble, dribble. I said, 'Okay Rivers, I'm going home NOW.' And he said, 'No, come on, let's go downstairs.' So we went down to his basement where we would rehearse, and he showed me some stuff. But that's how he is, really strange. He gets himself wrapped up in anything and it's hard to make contact with him. He's a strange guy.

"So I go downstairs and he had a really nice set-up," Kevin recalled. "But as soon as I got down there, Mikey Welsh and Zephan Courtney came in, the other guys Rivers had first brought in. And I already knew of them, but they were kind of bad news among my friends. I came from the Boston punk scene, and we're not into that showpony stuff. We always put substance above style.

"So we're down in the rehearsal space and I said, 'Hey what do you say we loosen up a little bit and play something? What do you guys listen to?' So Mikey says in an affected voice, 'Stereolab.' And I said, 'Well, that's not exactly jamming music.' I wanted to play some rock 'n' roll. 'What else do you like?' I ask. He says, 'I like Kiss.' I say, 'Okay, that's good, I know all of the Kiss songs.' I start playing 'Detroit Rock City' and Zeph, the drummer, never came in. And Mikey never started playing. So I'm playing by myself. I finally stopped what I was doing and said, 'What is up with you guys, don't you know this song?' He replies, 'No, I never learned this one.' I'm like, 'Learn it? It's friggin' two chords. It's not a matter of learning it.' So they had minimal ability to jam. Basically, Rivers and I would have to coach them through every song we wanted to play."

After a few weeks of jamming, Cuomo, Stevenson, bassist Mikey Welsh, a veteran of Chevy Heston and longtime New England favorites

Heretix, and drummer Courtney, also of Chevy Heston as well as Stompbox, made their live debut at Boston nightclub T.T. the Bear's on October 8. Billed as the Rivers Cuomo Band, the group played new Cuomo-penned tunes like "Rosemary," "1,000 Years," "Prettiest Girl in the Whole Wide World," "Baby," "Fun Time," and "American Girls."

"I've been playing live shows with some of my Boston friends," Rivers informed *Weezine* readers. "Trying out songs that may appear on the next Weezer record. They're very different from those on *Pinkerton* and ol' *Blue* but I'm not going to tell you how."

Of the solo material, Stevenson said, "There wasn't really any room for input with the songs Rivers brought to the band. They were kind of finished. And I was fine with that. I would just say to Rivers, 'Do you want me to play some bass around the chords or do you want me to play something more sparse?' And he'd say [with a whiny, curt affectation] 'I don't know.' I'd go, 'Okay.' I'd just keep on trying stuff until I got a good reaction from his face — he has these facial expressions. I wouldn't say he's hard to please, but he's either just got such a firm idea of how the song has got to sound or else he really just has no freakin' idea how he wants it to sound. It's one of those two, because often times we'd end up going with something that was nothing like what he was playing.

"When I joined the Rivers Cuomo Band," Stevenson confessed, "I didn't even like Weezer. I was fed up with pop bands using so much distortion, so I kind of dismissed them. I was on a different trip back then. I was into the Rolling Stones and a lot of early rockabilly stuff. Anything with distortion and power chords I thought was an easy way out. I told him all the time that I didn't dig it. I'd be like, 'Oh, we're playing *that* Weezer song, I hate that song,' which surprised him. Everybody else was kissing his ass and I was the only one who stood against him. I told it just the way it was. 'Rivers, I never liked that record.' He'd respond in his little voice 'Really?

CHRISTINA RADISH

Fun Time: Cuomo signs autographs in 1997, sporting a new look

You didn't like it? Wow, you're the first person I ever met who didn't.' I'm like, 'Wow! I feel proud.' I think he liked the fact that I wasn't some adoring fan. I told him what I thought.

"What's funny is, when I was in the middle of my run with his group, I started listening to *Pinkerton* and the first record," Stevenson laughed, "and I friggin' loved it all. I heard so many brilliant elements of songwriting. I don't know why that didn't occur to me before that point, but when it became apparent, it really struck me. Maybe playing some of those songs with Rivers opened my eyes to them. 'My Name Is Jonas' for instance, is fucking brilliant. I love that acoustic introduction. One thing I discovered by working with Rivers is that he truly is a musical genius. And to be honest, that's kind of hard to beat."

A second Rivers Cuomo Band show took place in late October at The Paradise in Boston. The gig consisted mostly of the same songs but added a new number, "Baby." Two *Blue Album* tunes, "Say It Ain't So," and "Undone — The Sweater Song" were also utilized as crowd pleasers.

While the shows were pretty successful, the rhythm section underwent some alterations after the Paradise gig. "We played together for a while, but it didn't work out," Kevin remembered. "We played a few gigs and I called Rivers up and told him, 'Look, I'm not gonna play with Mikey and Zephan anymore. I'm just not enjoying it.' I said, 'Man, I don't want to quit your band but that's what I'm doing.'

"So Rivers hung up on me," The Shods frontman added. "I figured I pissed him off and that was it. But five minutes later the phone rings and it's Rivers. He's like, 'Okay. We've got a new band, we're all set.' I said, 'What do you mean?' He says, 'Yeah, I found a couple of new players.' I'm like, 'In five minutes? How the hell did you do that?' And those guys were great musicians. That was a great band. It was Fred Eltringham, who drummed in the Gigolo Aunts [and now plays with Ben Kweller], and a friend of his, Drew Parsons, who was with Traci Bonham and is now the bassist in American Hi-Fi.

"Drew and Fred were super guys," Kevin recollected. "We all hit it off instantly and jamming with them was a breeze. We played everything. Kiss — Rivers loved Kiss — or I could break out a Stones song, or a Who song and those guys were right on top of it." Parsons and Eltringham, Boston-area transplants who grew up together in the Philadelphia suburb of West Chester, Pennsylvania, ended up playing together with Rivers rather naturally.

"Fred's wife had been hanging out with Rivers and he had been talking about how he was going to be playing with a bunch of different musicians in Boston because he wanted to work on a bunch of solo stuff," Drew Parsons remembered. "She was actually the one who recommended me and hooked me and Fred up with the gig."

Excited to participate, Parsons said he was a big Weezer fan. "I loved the first two records, especially *Pinkerton*. I thought that was just amazing. But the stuff he wanted to do was a little different than the first two Weezer records, it was more like a '90s version of '50s-era pop songs. Like, really poppy stuff, but he was open to our input. I hadn't really known him at all before that — I had met him when we did a couple of shows with Traci — but I hadn't really hung out with him. So it was my first hang with him, but while he was open to our ideas, he still had a pretty strong vision of how he wanted the music to sound in his head."

Rehearsing nearly every night in Cuomo's modest and extremely neat house and subsisting exclusively on pizza, Parsons said playing in Rivers' band was a lot of fun. "We hung out a lot at his place. We rehearsed in his basement and it was good times — hanging out and drinking beers and stuff. Rivers was very into the fact that Fred and I could make this cricket sound — we could both make cricket noises for those moments of dead silence. Like when a bad joke goes over poorly. So, for months, Rivers would try to do that. I think he finally learned how to do it, because when I saw him a few years afterward, he showed me he could finally do it."

On November 5, the Rivers Cuomo Band, Mach II, hit the stage for a gig at the Middle East, bringing forth eight new compositions Rivers had in mind for a countrified solo project he was calling "Homie." The quartet premiered "Autumn Jane," "Hey M'Darlin'," "Sheila Can Do [It]," "Think About," "Wanda," "Sunshine O," "Stay There," and "Hot Tub." "No One Else," an obligatory Weezer number, was served to the audience in appreciation for its attentiveness.

The show, billed as "The Save Central Square" benefit, featured ten bands including the Willard Grant Conspiracy, Nan, and headliners the Rivers Cuomo Band. It was organized with the aim of protecting the Boston neighborhood's diversity and character against the encroachment of big-money developers and retailers like The Gap and Burger King. Looking back on the event, Parsons laughed, "I think we agreed to play the event and then later we found out we weren't even necessarily down with the cause, but it was a fun gig."

Meanwhile, Cuomo had become uncomfortable with fans viewing his Boston efforts as "solo projects." "The word project makes it sound like I'm working with construction paper and paste," he attested in an issue of *Weezine*. "Or that I'm dispassionately pouring hydrochloric acid on rocks to see if they fizzle. I'm not doing anything like that. I'm rocking out. This is a way of life, not a project. Also there's nothing 'solo' about what I'm doing, I'm playing WITH other guys. I have no interest in playing music by myself. That would be as much fun as playing tennis by myself or simply playing with myself (which seems to suffice in a pinch). 'Side project' seems a bogus term too, as if the music I'm making now is merely cranberry sauce alongside the roast turkey of Weezer. There's no need to divide music up into meaningless categories like 'side project' or 'solo project' or 'the Alan Parsons Project.' We're all just singing along like one big dysfunctional family. So relax. There's just a lot of new songs and I want to play them while Pat, Matt, and Brian are busy working with their, um, other bands."

A second performance with the same line-up went down on November 21 at T.T. the Bear's. At the outset of the concert, Cuomo informed the crowd at T.T.'s that the night's set would be comprised largely of country songs, which didn't thwart the audience's exuberance. The gig incorporated some of the same titles from the Middle East show, plus another stab at "American Girls," and a version of another Weezer staple. "We covered one Weezer tune, 'The Good Life,' and the rest was all these new songs," Parsons said, beginning to chuckle. "A lot of his really die-hard fans came out. Like, the whole front row was young Asian girls who didn't speak any English."

In between time spent rehearsing for these shows and executing home and studio demos, Parsons said he was very impressed with Cuomo's work ethic. "He was working on a lot of piano at the time, and he was really focused on these classical pieces. He is a really hard worker, and based on what I could tell, he was really focused on anything he set his mind to. Whether it was music or school or whatever."

"I think because he's such a genius, he's also sort of socially retarded," Stevenson explained. "When you talk with Rivers you realize just how brilliant he is. He's a very, very smart man. But as you continue talking to him, you realize, 'Oh my god. He's like a child.' He has no social abilities at all. He really doesn't. He can't really hold a conversation." Stevenson recalled hanging out with Dicky Barrett from the Mighty Mighty Bosstones at the Middle East when Dicky asked to be introduced to Rivers. "So we went over and Rivers was with one of his young Japanese girlfriends that he's known for and we're standing there. So Dicky just starts busting his balls. Then I jumped in and we were tag-teaming him, just laughing until we were crying. We weren't ragging on him but just sort of poking fun at the fact he was with a girl who looked like she was thirteen years old. So we just had some fun with it. And Rivers just like curled up into a ball. He didn't know what to do. He's just no good in social situations like that. I called him up the next day, and I'm like, 'Rivers, man, I just wanted to introduce you to Dicky.' And he was like, 'Oh. Please don't ever do that again.' Because Dicky is a South Boston guy, he's been busting balls his whole life, that's just the way he was brought up. If you're gonna hang around with him you gotta learn how to bust balls. I was laughing my head off, but I sort of felt bad once I realized how Rivers is just no good in those kinds of situations."

Barrett confirmed this story, while insisting on pronouncing Cuomo's first name incorrectly. "*River* is a little too fragile. And I think *River* figured out he better toughen up or get the hell out of Boston."

"You've got to figure that if Rivers could get into Harvard at the same time he's fronting one of the biggest bands in the country, he's gotta be doing something right," said Stevenson. "And to play with him was a great, but bizarre, experience."

Cuomo was not above wild, erratic behavior, either, as John Horton, the one-time owner of Boston's Cherry Disc Records and a longtime associate of Mikey Welsh's, remembered Rivers' presumably drunken behavior at the 1997–98 New Year's Eve Party thrown by Morphine's manager Deb Klein. "I was standing around the keg and Rivers is standing there talking to about four or five really attractive women," said Horton, now the proprietor of Hearbox Records. "And he made some really foul, off-color sexual comment about eating pussy. And the four women are just standing there smiling. None of them blinked. None of them said anything. They were just standing there, like 'Wow.' It was absolutely bizarre."

But the winter of 1997 to 1998 largely found Rivers in a very productive frame of mind. With the second RCB line-up Cuomo recorded an album of goofball songs he'd written over the past six years that were never recorded by Weezer. "Most of them are acoustic and almost country-ish," he informed *Weezine* readers, "but don't worry, it's still a cool record. Unfortunately I don't know when it's coming out."

According to Parsons, the group recorded a bunch of basic tracks at nearby Fort Apache Studios and some others at Cuomo's house on a 4-track. Several of the tunes wound up being demoed professionally with local engineer Ross Humphrey at Fort Apache for possible future use with Weezer or Homie, including "Lover in the Snow," "Rosemary," "American Girls," and "The Prettiest Girl in the Whole Wide World."

"I don't know what his plans were for the stuff," said Parsons, "but I was definitely hoping for a solo album." It seems that Cuomo, at least for a time, had similar intentions, by compiling what is now known as the lost Homie album. Along with Stevenson, Eltringham, and Parsons, Rivers recorded what he considers to be a complete disc, although it was never mixed down and sadly remains unreleased.

A fifth live "solo" show went down at T.T. the Bear's on January 14,

1998, with Rivers, Weezer drummer Pat Wilson — who had flown in to Boston from Portland to participate — and guitarist Jake Zavrachy of local act Quick Fix, who was brought in to help out as Stevenson had a performance obligation with The Shods.

While in town, Pat — who had come east to see if he and Rivers could still find some common ground — joined Cuomo in a Boston studio to professionally record "American Girls" for the soundtrack to the upcoming movie, *Meet the Deedles*. Operating as Homie, the session was produced by Matt Sharp, who had since returned from Rentals recording work in London to co-produce (and provide backing vocals). Sharp, who had become increasingly obsessed with his solo venture, was actually working on it in Beantown and staying at Rivers' Cambridge home.

That recording also featured Cake guitarist Greg Brown, as well as Soul Coughing's Yuval Gabay (on drum loops) and Sebastian Steinberg (on bass), Weezer's own Brian Bell, the band's A&R rep Todd Sullivan, plus Justin Fisher and Adam Orth (both formerly of Shufflepuck) on backing vocals. And although no one knew it at the time, the Homie session, which surfaced when the soundtrack album hit the racks on March 24, 1998, would be Matt Sharp's last studio collaboration with the members of Weezer.

Brown would make an enormous impression on Matt Sharp, who said he knew the two would end up collaborating in the future. "Todd Sullivan was a huge fan of Cake and especially of Greg's," Sharp explained from an Omaha hotel room in November 2002. "He's really into guitar players. He had tried to get me to go see them a bunch of times, but I never did. So I was working with Rivers, trying to help him produce a song for the *Meet the Deedles* soundtrack. And it was a tune where we were going to be using a whole bunch of different people. We got Sebastian Steinberg from Soul Coughing and some different other people, where I wasn't really into their bands, but I liked where their heads were. So Todd said to me, 'Listen, if you're going to use all of these outside people, you should think about Greg Brown.'

"So Rivers and me, we're working on the song and the song's okay, you know, and it's going alright, but it's not great," Sharp continued. "And then Greg comes in and doesn't say anything to anybody. He just takes a cassette of the song into the other room and comes back out a little later and just adds the perfect part and makes the whole thing work. Then, he doesn't say anything to anybody and he leaves. But the whole feeling about the track changed. We turn around and he's gone. We couldn't thank that masked man, you know?"

By February 1998, Cuomo had again left his educational pursuits dangling indefinitely, heading back to Los Angeles to get cracking on Weezer demos. Although, in doing so, he left the members of the Rivers Cuomo Band high and dry. "He never called me to say anything," Kevin Stevenson maintained. "He had Angie C. — a mutual friend of ours who was on the radio here at WFNX — call me up to tell me he left. 'Well, Kevin, the Rivers Cuomo Band is all done,' she said. I said, 'Why did you call to tell me that?' She says, 'Well, because Rivers is in California right now.' I'm like, 'Well he still has my fucking phone number. There's such a thing as long distance, right?' But he didn't bother. It was pretty lame, the way he ended it."

Parsons was less bothered by the way it fell apart. "I ran into Rivers a couple of times in L.A. and things seemed like they were going well. I had actually left an old amp of mine in his house in Boston and he had moved out before I got it back. I just figured, 'Oh well, I lost that amp,' but I was kind of bummed out because it was my grandfather's guitar amp. And I figured, 'Oh well, I don't know how to get in touch with him. It's gone.' This was like 1997 or '98. So five years go by and then, like, two months ago, one of his assistants called me out of the blue, and she's like 'I have an amp I need to send you.' I was pretty impressed that he actually remembered it was mine and I was able to get it back."

Of his few months playing with an auxiliary band, Cuomo once said, "It was a totally different experience." And while the shows consisted of completely unique material, Rivers advised that there was little chance those songs would ever surface on a Weezer album. "I never finished those songs," he added. "In classic Rivers style, I just lost confidence and dropped it."

chapter nineteen

turn it off, now

By late February of 1998, Rivers was back in Los Angeles, the city he once called "congenial to his nature," living in the executive condos at Park LaBrea and working with Brian and Patrick on future Weezer demos. Matt Sharp was noticeably absent from these efforts, in which the group cut the RCB holdover "The Prettiest Girl in the Whole Wide World," at the home studio of a friend. Despite Matt's absence from Weezer's new demo recordings, it is interesting to note that he and Rivers still remained close at this point. Social calls continued, with Sharp — who was on the fence about whether he wanted to remain a part of the band or devote his full attention to the Rentals — hanging out with Cuomo and Justin Fisher to watch the U.S. vs. Brazil Gold Cup soccer match.

Although Cuomo had exited Harvard the previous autumn, reportedly just three semesters shy of his diploma, he somewhat surprisingly called his tenure at the school "one of the best times of my life" and added that while "the people were amazing — genuine, interesting, intelligent, humble, and focused," he ultimately realized he wasn't cut out for the Crimson world. "[It] was kinda stupid, in retrospect," Rivers later explained. "I think I have two semesters left, but I'm never going back."

In just a few short years, Cuomo had gone from knowing absolutely nobody to knowing a lot of people in and around the Boston music scene. With his mother and former stepfather under two hours away by car, he found himself too much at ease there to create the type of material he had become known for.

"At a school like Harvard, every waking moment is spent doing what somebody else told you to do," he explained. "As long as you do that well, you get your A's and you feel good about life. Then, after a while, you get the same feeling that you get on drugs, like 'Oh man, I'm just wasting my life away. I should be doing something more productive.'"

In March, Rivers, Pat, and Brian used a *Meet the Deedles* promotional appearance on the syndicated program *Modern Rock Live*, to remind folks that Weezer was still alive and kicking. Sounding upbeat, Wilson and Bell revealed plans to put their respective other bands to the side, telling host (and future senior vice president at MTV) Tom Calderone that it "is all about Weezer now."

Sharp's indecisiveness about staying or leaving, however, was irking Pat Wilson, and in April the drummer came out in the press against the bassist. During a report on plans for Weezer album number three, Pat insisted Matt had his priorities out of whack. And Pat also announced that as far as he was concerned, Sharp was all but officially out of the band.

"Matt needs to concentrate on the Rentals, and we need to make our record," Patrick told music Web site *SonicNet* by phone from his home in Portland. "I think it is likely that we will make it without Matt." Meanwhile, Weezer had already begun accepting applications for a permanent replacement.

Sharp had repeatedly missed recent Weezer rehearsals, and was becoming increasingly estranged from the group since February '98. He was still undecided when it came to making his intentions known to Cuomo, Wilson, and Brian. "Matt just doesn't want to deal with it," Pat declared. "I think he's basically stringing us along. I don't have any problems saying that, because if someone is really doing that, they should be able to face it."

After two months of speculation, an anonymous source close to the band had finally made the news public on April 8: Sharp was indeed exiting the group to devote all of his energies to the Rentals. Having already recorded "My Head Is in the Sun" that same winter, the new collaboration with Cuomo that Matt had earmarked for his upcoming Rentals record ironically found the just parted bandmates sharing a co-writing credit for the first time.

"Rivers was out in L.A., actually trying to replace me at the time," Sharp laughed later. "I was in Boston, living in his house and mixing the end of [*Seven More Minutes*]. He came back to Boston, and I showed him the song I was working on. We sat around and sang a bunch of stuff together. He played me [the Homie] song, and I ended up producing it for him. So we still get along, probably actually artistically better than we ever did when we were in the same band together. Which is too bad, because I do believe we could have done some great songs, written them together. With me and him, it's just not meant to be that way, I think, in the end."

As for the song, Sharp had fleshed out most of it, but became uncertain of its direction until Cuomo helped hone the melody line. "I came to Rivers and said, 'I want you to listen to this and let me know how you feel about it,'" Matt remembered in late 2003. "The first thing he said was, 'You need to simplify this,' and we sat down at a piano in his basement and we both worked on the verses. His advice over and over again, which is usually my advice to people, was to keep simplifying it."

Sharp assured that his exit from Weezer was less about clashing egos or internal problems and more about the realization that after achieving success on his own, he just couldn't be happy playing bass on someone else's songs or singing someone else's words. While he hung in there for *Pinkerton*, Matt found his role in Cuomo's band increasingly suffocating.

So after hemming and hawing much like Patrick had alluded to, the bassist finally quit the band, and retreated to Barcelona, Spain — a place he had discovered in the three years of nearly nonstop touring that led up to his decision — to continue focusing on his solo initiative.

Explaining why he was leaving the band that yielded him fame and money, Sharp said soon after his departure, "As much as I love Weezer with all my heart, when your life is completely flipped out and explosions are going on and all these things are changing and you're having the best sex in your life, you want to express that. I had a hell of a time expressing that playing bass on somebody else's songs. I would have to be a much better bass player to pull that off."

"Matt obviously wasn't satisfied being in the band, and he ended up leaving, so that takes care of him," Cuomo eventually sniped about the bassist's departure. But Matt's division from the group was unclear. "It still wasn't technically a split," Wilson said later. "I think Matt's still technically in the band. It's a classic case of he said we fired him and we said he quit. Unless we want to litigate, we're going to have to settle, and no one wants to litigate. Although I think we'd win, we have more money. That's what it comes down to — hire a big-time litigator. Whatever. It's bullshit."

Cloudy circumstances aside, with Sharp out, Weezer had compiled a short list of potential replacements on bass. While Pat and Rivers' former housemate Justin Fisher was available after his own band Shufflepuck had dissolved, Fisher said that his old buddy Rivers never approached him. "A lot of people ask me if I would have entertained that notion, but I try not to think about it," said Fisher, who went on to front his own outfit Psoma and play bass for a short spell with Sharp and later join Nerf Herder. "I don't know if I'd want to go back into that kind of relationship again with those guys. It would be weird to try out for them. Obviously, I'd have a great time playing with them because they're all really cool dudes."

Among those that Weezer did audition were former Redd Kross member Steve McDonald, old friend Pat Finn — who was heavily considered for the role — and short-lived Rivers Cuomo Band member Mikey Welsh. "Steve is great and he's an awesome bass player," Wilson proclaimed at the time. "If we were going to be more into an instrumental focus, I think that Steve would be a nice fit because he's so creative. But I think with the current outlook and the way our ensemble works, I think we need more of a foundation-style player."

When contacted in spring 2003 to talk about this matter, Pat Finn was very friendly and appreciative of the offer. "Rivers doesn't own me or anything," he said, "but I still see him socially." He doesn't say anything further on the matter.

By the spring of 1998, Patrick Wilson revealed that he and the rest of the band were happiest with Welsh and he was soon selected as a permanent member.

Mikey Welsh

Born Michael Welsh in Syracuse, New York, on April 20, 1971, Mikey was raised in Brookline, Massachusetts. Welsh grew up in a house that prized art and music, and both had a major influence on the future Weezer bassist, who caught the Van Halen *Fair Warning* tour at age ten and first picked up a guitar in junior high school. "I was thirteen, but I was never really serious about it," said Welsh, who was weaned on The Who and The Doors. "And then I got a bass when I was seventeen and I started playing like twelve hours a day and got really into it."

Mikey formed his first band, Left Nut, in 1988 while he was still in high school. The group quickly rose to prominence in the Boston music scene. Alongside vocalist Steamy Latrine (born Norman Jabar), drummer Gary Gardiner, and guitarists Barry Edwards and Don Gardiner, Welsh found himself in the throes of the 1990 WBCN Rock & Roll Rumble when Left Nut placed in the semi-finals. The back jacket of the band's self-released *Bad Attitude, No Apologies* CD — which housed titles like "Hard Drugs," "Torch This Place," and "Long Time to Cum" — described the quintet's sound. "Left Nut always gave the audience their money's worth with hard driving duel [sic] guitars and a no wimps blend of Punk Rock and Beer Drinking Southern Slam."

By 1993, Mikey joined Boston scene veterans Heretix for what wound up being their final record, *The Adventures of Super Devil*, for local label Cherry Disc. Stripping away the acoustic guitars and U2-inspired sensitivity of their earlier work on major label Island Records, the band dumped their back catalog — which included the 1989 EP *A.D.* and the following year's *Gods and Gangsters* album — for a loud and attitudinal approach. The record, which opens with the number "Liquid California," wished death-by-flooding to that state.

"I thought Mikey embodied what was fun about rock 'n' roll when he first started out," says John Horton, Cherry Disc's founder. "He was young, cocky, had great clothes, and instantly made people take notice of him. Heretix was an established band who had managed to sign to Island and were more of a commercial thing. But after that failed, Mikey — who was pretty young compared to the others in the band — linked up with the singer, Ray Lemieux, and he gave the group a new lease on life."

Welsh, then a young opportunist, admits that he schemed his way into Lemieux's group. "For me, Heretix was a chance to get into a band that was doing well," he later remembered. "It kind of legitimized them because it wasn't all the same members; they'd gotten this punk kid in the band. Part of me liked playing big shows, but part of me wanted to revolt and do raunchier, nastier stuff."

When Heretix played their final show in June 1995, Mikey went on to form Jocobono with ex-Orangutan drummer Todd Perlmutter and former Seka frontman Billy O'Malley. Welsh described the band's testosterone-driven, alcohol-fueled sound as "cock rock."

Horton believed in Welsh enough to sign Jocobono to Cherry Disc before the band had even landed a weekend-headliner slot at the Middle East. Met with the immediate envy of those on the scene who scoffed that Jocobono hadn't paid their dues, Mikey responded to the jealousy. "We may all be pretty young, but we're not spring chickens," Welsh said. "We've all been hacking around here for awhile. So the first thing is that I think we deserve [the attention]. The other thing is that we didn't call John Horton. He called us. And we didn't call clubs who wanted us to headline, that was their trip. We want to lowbrow and go out and open for all our friends' bands, but if clubs want to pay us money, we're not going to argue with them."

If Welsh wasn't yet a rock star, he exuded a confidence that the locals reacted to. "Jocobono was this total cock rock thing he was doing, but by then everyone in the Boston music scene knew who Mikey was," Horton remembers. "The record they did for my label got a lot of local press in the *Boston Phoenix* and beyond." The highlight of the band's self-titled 1996 disc was "Last Call at Foley's," a homage to getting drunk in a townie bar and then pleading with the bartender for a six-pack for the road. Jocobono's live show was quite a spectacle as they smashed their instruments in blatant contrast to what Welsh called "PC college-radio crap." Mikey, an employee at a local hair salon, colored Jocobono's live gigs by regularly dressing up in women's clothes.

"Mikey certainly took a lot of shit, because a lot of times he would do the cross-dressing thing," said Horton. "They would dress as women and play their shows and your typical meat-and-potatoes rock fan at the time was a little disturbed by it. People would be booing them and throwing beer bottles at them and stuff. So he would take it a little further and he and Billy O'Malley would just, like, kiss each other on the mouth onstage during a show just to piss people off. He caught a lot of flack, and I know people have said otherwise, but the guy really could play the bass, and he played the rock star part to perfection well before Weezer."

Following Jocobono, Mikey hooked up with Chevy Heston, a band already in progress that featured his old friend Zephan Courtney on drums. "Mikey and Zephan were tight from way back," said Horton, who also released three Chevy Heston discs. "Zephan was one of the principals with this guy, Matt Martin, but they had this kind of revolving door of members. Chevy Heston was also on my label, so after Jocobono, Mikey sort of crossed over to playing with them."

His stint in that band was short lived, but by early fall 1997, and at the tail end of Welsh's tenure with the band, Rivers Cuomo took notice and tapped Welsh and Courtney for a pair of solo Boston shows. "One of my best friends, Nate [Albert], who I grew up with in Boston, was the guitarist for the Bosstones," Mikey remembered. "Me and the Bosstones guys used to play a lot when we were younger, so Rivers met Nate and Rivers was looking for a bass player, so that's how we met."

"The thing that always struck me about Mikey," says his former label boss Horton, "was that he just had this crazy personality, but like a true rock star, he was able to balance it by being a true professional. At the same time, if he saw an opportunity he'd take it. I, to this day, imagine that once he befriended Rivers for those solo shows he had it in the back of his mind that he might end up in Weezer. I'm sure that once he learned that there was friction with Matt Sharp, he kind of nudged his way in there. I mean, Mikey could party his ass off, so I'm sure he showed Rivers Cuomo a good time and things just sort of blossomed from there."

DANIEL COSTON

Mikey Likes It: Welsh joins forces with Cuomo

After flying to Los Angeles in the spring of 1998 for a series of tryouts, it was Mikey — by that time playing in Juliana Hatfield's band — who landed the coveted bassist spot in Weezer. Back home in Boston, the news spread rapidly throughout the music scene. "So many people thought it was weird that Rivers would fire him from his solo band and then hire him later to join Weezer," says ex-RCB'er Kevin Stevenson. "And you've got to admit it's pretty strange."

But strange was par for the course with Rivers, and with the matter of Matt Sharp's replacement resolved, Weezer were reportedly coming close to wrapping pre-production on album #3. Or at least that's what Wilson told *SonicNet*, adding that he had written four new tunes for the band and that Cuomo had brought forth several more. "It's going to rock," the drummer predicted of that album. "I think it will be more focused than the last record. If we can somehow put everyone's abilities together, it will be a bigger thing than it used to be."

Having holed up in a Culver City condominium near Sepulveda Boulevard underneath the Santa Monica and San Diego Freeway interchange by August 1998, Bell, Wilson, and Welsh would work in Cuomo's newly acquired digs, where Mikey, new to L.A. and already friendly with Rivers, also lived. Here they wrote and rehearsed in excess of fifty songs. Few titles are known from this era, but those that have surfaced include "Damn That Wine," "Ol' Backwater," "I Have to Kill You," "Turn It Off, Now," and "Everyone," with the majority of the material being put to tape at TK Rehearsals on the west side of Los Angeles.

"We're working hard and getting along well," Wilson said of the progress, disclosing that he and Bell had been permitted to submit four and three songs respectively to the band. "Each day is a happy event for us," Pat said of the new material that came closer to the experimental style of Spiritualized and Radiohead than the band's own patented sound.

"We're like water; we flow around obstacles and problems." Seeking a producer to help the group execute its third album and get back to the winning formula of *Weezer*, Wilson declared through the media, "We're not dickheads anymore. We're earnest, happy young gentlemen."

In homage to Cuomo's beloved Pixies, the band recorded a version of that outfit's 1990 single, "Velouria," at Mouse House Studios for a future tribute compilation, *Where Is My Mind?* In addition to the cover — which surfaced in early 1999 through L.A.'s Glue Factory Records and also featured artists like Superdrag, Local H, Nada Surf, Eve 6, and Reel Big Fish paying tribute to Black Francis and Company — Weezer laid down new tunes like "Every Man," "Trampoline," and "Sunshine." These three Cuomo originals were left incomplete, however.

"We were making a very concerted effort to get the band together to write songs, to rehearse and to make an album," Rivers remembered. "Every day I'd write a song and every day we'd go to rehearsal and try. But for whatever reason I just didn't feel good about what was going on." During the early fall of 1998, they plowed forward anyway, and more material was demoed. A second run through "Sunshine," plus new numbers like "Girls Soccer," "Average Town," and "Crazy One" were attempted. Non-Cuomo material like "Seventeen" and "Butterfly Collector," penned by Brian Bell, was also introduced around this time, and although Pat and Mikey were down with attempting to demo Brian's tunes for Weezer, Rivers decided against considering them as Weezer material. When their domineering leader was absent, the trio took a stab at them anyway.

"Something wasn't clicking for me," reflected Rivers. "It felt terrible. I just kept banging my head against the wall, and eventually the guys just said, 'Rivers, we can tell this isn't going anywhere. We're leaving.'" Cuomo had become withdrawn, as rehearsals whittled from three hours daily to one, and from three days a week to one. Tired of waiting around, Wilson

— who had known Cuomo the longest — elected to pack up his drumkit and head home to Portland.

"Things were going in circles and the band wasn't getting anywhere," Koch said later, "and [Patrick] finally needed some time away from the frustration." But not before he worked with the group to demo two additional Cuomo titles, "Do It Again," and "Everybody Wants to Get High."

Asking Rivers to call him back down to L.A. when things were in motion again, months went by without any contact. In early '99, Patrick would voice his frustration to the alt.music.weezer newsgroups, telling them that during the aborted sessions he learned that he and Cuomo "didn't have much in common, creatively or personally."

"I used to wonder why bands couldn't just shut up and play their damn music," Wilson wrote. "It seems so simple! What's the big deal?! You've got a sound, now will you please just rock?! Well, I wish it was that simple."

"Our heads were just so screwy at the time," Mikey said later. "We all had different ideas about what we should be doing. We were just struggling a bit with trying to get songs together, and what kind of sound we wanted."

With Pat now out of the mix and things barely progressing with the remaining L.A.–based members, Mikey Welsh's friend Todd Phillips sat in behind the drum set for sporadic song demos and rehearsals. An offshoot of these efforts was a side outfit dubbed Goat Punishment, which featured Rivers, Brian, Mikey, and Todd focusing strictly on covers by the likes of Slayer and Hank Williams. Designed to bring some of the fun back into playing, the ultimate goal was to inspire Cuomo creatively.

It was a bleak time for Rivers. He wasn't happy with the new material he was writing, and out of desperation he painted the walls of his condo black and covered his windows. It seemed that some of Cuomo's desperation was attributed to the loss of Matt Sharp. "When Matt was in the band," Rivers would later say, "he was always there to cheer me on. When he left, it became difficult to get things going on my own."

His apartment, located across from an ugly cement-mixing plant, did little to cheer him up. Here the eccentric rocker basked in loneliness for weeks on end. In addition to the black walls, Rivers said he eventually lived without television or music, and he "actually put fiberglass insulation all over the windows and then black sheets over the fiberglass so that no light could get through.

"I became depressed," Rivers divulged. "I was saying, 'I don't know what I want to do, I don't know who I want to be, I just want to be alone.'" Yet somehow, by November 1998, Weezer, minus Pat Wilson with the Goat Punishment line-up, actually played a pair of "secret" gigs in the Los Angeles area, beginning with a Nirvana tribute show in Hollywood at the Garage's Club Sucker. The first performance focused on the influential trio's early 1988–1991 output — including tunes like "Aneurysm," "Breed," and "Blew," among others — while a subsequent gig paid homage to Oasis' 1994 debut *Definitely Maybe*.

That second event, held in Santa Barbara, was a far less secretive affair, however, as word of the gig spread throughout the Southern California music scene. Sadly, the unexpectedly large crowd had to be dispersed by police, leaving only a few dozen lucky observers to witness the event. The big draw proved that rock music fans still wanted their Weezer, but the band was having trouble keeping it together, leaving Mikey to ponder whether ditching his position with Juliana Hatfield was such a smart idea after all. And although no one knew it at the time, the second Goat Punishment gig would be the last public performance by Rivers for a year and a half.

Cuomo himself blamed a failed songwriting experiment for the aborted Weezer efforts of 1998. "A lot of guys can write songs that have nothing to do with their lives, and they're great, but I don't seem to be able to do that," he said. "For a long time I was trying to write without relying on personal events — just writing, purely musically or purely structurally. The songs were kind of good, but they were kind of bad at the same time; they didn't have that much emotional life to them."

Cuomo, as he put it, was "accomplishing nothing," and Brian Bell agreed. "We had some moments where we were drifting in space," the guitarist admitted of the work that soon came to a halt. After the remainder of his bandmates "all left town to do their own thing," Cuomo, on his own in his apartment, was in deep trouble. "I didn't have the confidence to put anything together," he said. "By the end of any day, I'd start to have some of the darkest thoughts and fears and feelings."

Holed away, Rivers became completely anti-social, mourning the failure of both the recent sessions and the *Pinkerton* album. "When the second record didn't do so well, everyone wanted to blame someone, and the person to blame, obviously, was me," Rivers later observed. "Everyone formulated their own theories as to why I was an asshole, and one of the guys even left the band." Cuomo's lack of self-assurance "started a really dark period for us," Welsh recollected. Mikey, who lived with Rivers for a time, was concerned about his Weezer boss. "We really withdrew from each other and became pretty unsure of what was going to happen."

chapter twenty

somebody save me

After a false start in 1998, the members of Weezer had gone their separate ways by the beginning of 1999, with Pat resuming his efforts with The Special Goodness and Brian jumping feet-first into the Space Twins, having reunited with Tim and Glenn Maloof and drummer Mike Elliot. Mikey Welsh eventually reconnected with Juliana Hatfield back in Boston. But for Rivers, January 1, 1999, marked a day of new beginnings as a songwriter.

"There was no one there to pick me up," he remembered of the day he realized he needed to get his shit together. "It was up to me to learn how to do that for myself or forever go under. I realized that I had to accept responsibility for my life." During the year, Cuomo disconnected the phone and stayed in his apartment, which was in that same "crappy" area of West Los Angeles nicknamed "Palms." It was here, on Sepulveda, in the vicinity of Pico Boulevard and National Boulevard, that Cuomo crafted 121 songs, of which close to half became demos.

Writing songs in short bursts each morning, Rivers would devote "forty-five minutes or an hour a day" to his craft. "All your senses have to be very fresh so you can really be open to feel what the next note is supposed to be."

Some of the intriguing titles that made it to the demo stage in '99 included "O.G.'s," "Kitty Pettin'," "Movie Theatre," "Mergatroid," "Pisspot," "Turn Your Love Away," "The Black Rider," "Sumeria," "Sickboy," "Don't You Criticize," "Attack, Attack," "Midwife," "Alpha-Beta," "Labrador," "Genie,"

"Neto," "Fits in the Blood," "Cold and Damp," "Hospital Error," "Stand Up and Fight," "Robinson's May," "Destination Take Me Home," "Valley Forge," "Ayleen," "Down Down Diggity," "Suicide Plot," "Been Down to Jesus," "Roomate," "Kiliminjaro," "Weapons Expert," "Jimmy McFarlane," "Somebody Save Me," "Homeless," "Sixth Xmas," "My Brain," "Phlegm Man," "Stupendous," "Greyhound," "One More Time," "French Pop," "Always," "Jodi," "So You Sense It's a Sad Situation," "C'mon Siobhan," and "Island in the Sun."

According to Todd Sullivan, Cuomo hunkered down indoors, even giving up on playing his beloved soccer. Some suspect Cuomo curtailed the soccer activity after *Spin* ran a report speculating that Rivers was actually homeless when he was spotted showing up to a recording facility drenched in sweat from practice.

Now he was spending his time evaluating the catalogs and successes of bands he admired — from Nirvana to Oasis — with the hopes of jump-starting his own writing. Or was he? Word spread around Los Angeles that old R.C. not only had a screw loose but was really in bad shape, perhaps even suicidal. "When I'd hear things that other people were saying, I'd think, 'Man, maybe I'm never going to get out of this.'" But Rivers downplayed any notion that he was ever as deeply distressed as rumors suggested he was. "I mean . . . it's true that I would go for months without talking to another human being, which is a very intense experience," Cuomo conceded. "It was fucked up. And when you [finally] do speak to somebody, it's physically difficult, difficult to form words.

"I kept thinking that other people thought I was mentally unwell," he admitted. "Gradually I stopped talking to everybody. Though people would want to get in touch with me, I didn't want to see anybody. I just wanted to be alone. Casual social interaction just became very painful to me, but it honestly felt as if I were totally sane, just that I had some serious work to do, although I knew it appeared that I was going nuts, due to me being a personal failure or whatever. But I've always had faith in myself and my songs. I've always had faith in my potential."

"I'm not sure how you help someone out of that," Sullivan added. "You have to let them search through it for a while. It was very dark. But did I think he was suicidal? No. It wasn't that dark."

Meanwhile, Sullivan had woes of his own in early 1999 when he became a victim of the biggest corporate shakeup in music business history. Universal Music Group owners Seagram's — originally a beverage company — purchased Polygram Music Group and soon morphed Geffen Records (plus eight other record labels) into four divisions. In doing so, UMG drastically cut its staff, resulting in dozens of artists being released from their contracts. And Weezer's members were surprised when they learned they fared better than many peers.

"Everybody was being dropped," Brian Bell remembered. "People kept asking, 'So, you guys got dropped?' But no, we didn't. I felt kind of guilty. Two bands stayed — us and Beck — from the whole Geffen roster as far as alt-rock. That call could have come any day, but it never did."

The record company's apparent faith in Weezer gave Bell hope that things would rekindle again somewhere down the line. "I felt pretty secure," he added. "I knew we'd eventually do it because all the songs that Rivers was coming up with were great. I knew when he was ready, it would be great."

"I was just waiting till I felt excited again," Rivers said of his approach to songwriting in '99. "I was utterly confused. But then as I slowed down and let things happen naturally, all outside activities stopped, and I just ended up in my room by myself. I was writing and I was thinking and waiting and resting, just being patient.

"Every day I'd wake up feeling very positive, energized, and determined," he added. "But definitely toward the end of the day and into the night I would start to feel sad and discouraged. But I think one of the keys to my getting out of my depressed state was my ability not to romanticize the situation. I wasn't aware that I was turning into a freak or that I was becoming negative. In my mind I just felt that I needed to be alone. It wasn't a consistent mood either. I was probably withdrawing more and more, sort of midway through 1999."

"I stopped getting emotional about things," Cuomo later reflected. "I adopted a very scientific attitude. I told myself, 'Okay, here's how I'm going to figure out [how] to climb out of this, one step at a time.' I learned not to get so overly dramatic about having fallen, but instead every day [I would] try and get up and write a song and try to figure which parts of my life worked and which parts didn't work. I tried to make slow, gradual progress, and I allowed myself the time to do that."

Without a phone, and virtually no contact with friends, business associates, or even family members, Cuomo said the experience of being isolated was cathartic as opposed to negative. "Being by yourself when you know that only a short while ago you had thousands of girls screaming at you, and now you have nothing — that crash can make you tough," he said. "Really it was a chance to recharge and think, to do some emotional weightlifting. Over the months I gradually calmed down and started writing."

As Rivers eventually began to emerge back into society, Bell — the only other Weezer member still based in Los Angeles — would occasionally drop by his house to poke around and play some piano duets and Cuomo eventually came forward with some new material. "I was delicate in getting him to play me new things," Bell said. "I knew how he felt about them and that he was very insecure. I walked into his room and there were all these song titles written all over the walls and the first one I asked about was 'Island in the Sun,' and that is the first one he played for me."

As the spring of '99 sprung, original Weezer bassist Matt Sharp finally saw the release of the Rentals' second album, *Seven More Minutes*. Released on April 13 — three and a half years after its predecessor — the disc was delayed many times throughout 1998 because of Matt's obsessive remixing hands, and later because of Maverick Records' displeasure with the final product. According to Koch, the label "kept holding things up by requesting that Matt change things that Matt refused to change."

"This record is the most important thing I've ever done in my life," Sharp declared, gushing about the project that housed collaborations with Rivers, Petra Haden, Blur's Damon Albarn, Donna Matthews of Elastica, Lush vocalist Miki Berenyi, and Ash singer Tim Wheeler. "Everything has been altered through this process in a negative way and in a positive way," he said of the follow-up to *The Return of the Rentals*, which had earned a SoundScan tally of 96,000 copies in the three and a half years since its release. "I've lost friends, gained friends, made revelations, had celebrations. This record really did that for me."

Seven More Minutes was recorded with *Return of the Rentals* holdovers Rod Cervera and Jim Richards, plus touring drummer Kevin March. It chronicled Sharp's gypsy rock star life, bouncing between Barcelona (where it was written), London (where it was recorded), and Boston and Los Angeles (where it was mixed). The disc opens with the Moog-touched, Blur-inspired "Getting By," which bounces into the Pixies-like pop of "Barcelona" and meets up with Blur frontman Damon Albarn on "Big Daddy C," a tune that gives listeners a taste of what Albarn's future hip-hop inspired side project, Gorillaz, might sound like. Just prior to the subdued closer "Jumping Around," Weezer's core clientele is treated to "My Head Is in the Sun," Sharp and Cuomo's first and last-ever songwriting collaboration.

Speaking of the song in hindsight, Matt observed that "the thing with Rivers is the first thing we ever soloed together, after all the Weezer stuff.

It was a good thing for me, to know that we had such a positive impact on each others' lives, even after the fact.

"[It] was the last song that was completed for this record," Sharp said. "It was very important to me that it was on the record. It had gone through a hundred different forms, lyrically and melodically. I was still working on it when we were mixing the record in Boston. I was living in Rivers' house and he came back from L.A. with Weezer for a weekend. We sat around in his basement and played acoustic guitars and piano and sang songs. And that's one of the songs that came out of that, the completion of that song.

"There were highs, there were lows," Sharp revealed of making the record and exiting Rivers' band in one fell swoop. "There was a coming to grips with the ideas of 'this is what I do.' Weezer is a family to me. We started doing something together and I think all of us went through an incredibly beautiful and surreal experience together."

But for all that lovey-dovey stuff, Sharp was pleased to be free of the confines of the dictatorial Weezer arrangement. "I could never have made this record if I had been in a traditional band," he proclaimed at the time. "This record is a much more collaborative experience than anything I've ever done before.

"I'd say it's twice the scale of both Weezer records and the first Rentals record as far as the impact that it has had on my life," Sharp insisted, before conceding that the project was exhausting. "At this point in my life, I have no desire to go back into the recording studio," he said the week *Seven More Minutes* was released. "This record took a lot out of me. Making it was the most difficult thing I've ever had to do in my life, but in the most beautiful way."

The record was created over nearly three years with no solid plan, and Sharp said, "I wanted to let things evolve erratically. With most of the people that guested on the record, the day before they contributed I probably didn't envision it that way. Like, with Donna Matthews, it was a last-minute thing, her vocals on 'Say Goodbye Forever.' After she had done her part, I couldn't really imagine it being anything other than what it became.

"I've been pretty devoid of plans for the last few years, which I'm sure drives the record company crazy," Sharp confessed. Still, on the surface Maverick was committed to supporting the project. Postcard mailings to key retail, radio, and press outlets, plus notification of the record to members of the Weezer and Rentals fan mailing lists were some of the ways the label supported the set. Distributing cassette samplers with lead-off single "Getting By" and album cut "Hello, Hello" at concerts by "like-minded" outfits was another way to hype the sophomore set.

Guy Oseary, who signed the Rentals to Maverick and was head of A&R and a partner in the company with Madonna, even came out in support of the disc in the press. "This is a really great album, and it has so many great ideas," proclaimed Oseary. "My concern is taking nothing for granted and building up again from scratch."

Part of this build-up included alerting fans of the disc through classified ads that resembled real rental display ads in regional arts publications like the *L.A. Weekly*, the *Boston Phoenix*, New York's *Village Voice*, Seattle's *Rocket*, *San Francisco Weekly*, and the *Chicago Reader*. The ads contained the April 13 street date for *Seven More Minutes*, along with a number to call and hear snippets of music, get tour information, and receive the aforementioned two-song sampler.

Reviews were largely positive, and plentiful in the wake of the Internet's increased popularity. *Popmatters.com*, for instance, wrote: "Sharp's cheery, Moog-drenched new wave crossbred with Buzzcockian brash pop is still in fine form. There's the all-out synthesizer fest of 'The Cruise,' the Devo-esque 'Insomnia,' and the nod to Oasis on 'Hello, Hello.' All in all, *Seven More Minutes* proves Sharp has grown far beyond the confines of his former Weezer life."

Pitchforkmedia was less kind. "On a whole, the thing kind of falls flat," wrote Chip Chanko. "I want the keyboards, the hooked-on-phonics between verse oooh-ooohs, the overly simplistic love stories. Where is P? Do we have to estrange ourselves from Weezer, move to Spain, live it up big-time, get back in touch with Rivers, and return to America to see this thing through the right set of prescription sunglasses? I have enough real life in my real life, thanks. I don't know, Matt. It's just not the same any-more. Hmm . . . At least the booklet smells as good as the last one."

Meanwhile, more mainstream outlets like the *All Music Guide* also slammed the record. "*Seven More Minutes* proves that the Rentals are more than just a side project," wrote Stephen Thomas Erlewine, "but it finds them searching for a distinctive identity when, ironically, they had one when they were just a side project."

And over at *Rolling Stone*, Rob Sheffield mostly praised the disc. "While the liner notes proudly proclaim that the songs were composed in Barcelona and recorded in London, the shit sure sounds like L.A. Like Weezer's *Pinkerton*, *Seven More Minutes* is clever modern-rock fluff that buries the catchy tunes in concept-album filler, including the latest (last? please?) song about the millennium. But wade through the hour-long *Seven More Minutes* and you'll find a half-dozen keepers — especially 'The Cruise,' a Gary Numan clone that would've been the third-best song on *The Pleasure Principle*, and New Wave geeks like the Rentals know that's high praise indeed."

Although Sharp expressed a strong desire to tour behind *7MM* early into his press junket, he didn't manage to perform a U.S. date with the Rentals until October 1999, when the group — then consisting of some of his core studio band plus Justin Fisher on bass and a guitarist named Josh Hager — fleshed out its first live show since 1996.

Sharp said he spent the summer of 1999 tracking down guitarist Greg

Brown, who had worked on the *Meet the Deedles* soundtrack and was in alternative rock outfit Cake. "I was trying to get Greg to work with me on a third Rentals record," Sharp said. "We wound up talking about that but he was busy."

While that never came to be, Sharp linked up with Hager at the suggestion of Rivers. "I'm not exactly sure of the story," said Sharp, blaming his memory on a codeine and caffeine episode the night before. "I know he had played with Rivers for a millisecond when he was in Boston. I was looking for a guitar player to come with me to do a tour of Japan with the Rentals and Rivers had boasted about Josh. At the time I was a complete asshole to him, I guess, but after I went to see him play I was blown away."

With Fisher and Hager in tow, the Rentals rocked the Opium Den in Los Angeles on October 13. That gig served as a warm-up for the group's two-week tour of Japan — including two dates at Tokyo's On Air East on the 16th and 17th. But despite a solid, early buzz on *7MM*, it failed to repeat the success of the Rentals' debut. Devoid of U.S. touring — based on little, if no tour support from his stateside record company plus Sharp's own lack of strategy — the record that the ex-Weezer bassist obsessed over never really got off the ground. Summing up the record succinctly, Koch described it as being released "to a small, enthusiastic audience that failed to grow due to Maverick's mysterious, sudden lack of promotional muscle. An unfortunate, anti-climactic result to Matt's three years of work, but a fine album nonetheless."

Within the active Weezer line-up, band proceedings were on hold indefinitely as Cuomo focused on his songs and Pat took time out to help his old buddy Pat Finn by drumming on demos for Little Pat's upstart outfit Organic Mechanic. The Special Goodness demos also continued to pour out of the Weezer drummer as he demoed new numbers like "Bull Shit,"

M'LOU F. ELKINS

The Need For Speed: Rocker gearheads Pat Wilson and Atom Willard
unite in The Special Goodness

"It's Only Natural," "Each Other," "Somebody Else," "What You're On,"
"Reason to Worry," and "What You Can Forget." Meanwhile, TSG's self-
titled long-delayed debut had been put on indefinite hold by Geffen and
was ultimately scrapped during the Universal Music Group shakeup. The
decision left the album commercially unavailable outside of Japan.

Although there was no domestic release to support, TSG set out on a
small, six-date West Coast tour in the summer of '99, with Welsh on bass
and a drummer by the name of Lee Loretta. The first-ever Special
Goodness gig was held at 17 Nautical Miles in Portland on July 7. A second tour, consisting of twenty-three dates, ran from late October to late
November 1999 with the same band line-up, augmented by Koch in the
role of tour manager.

During the trek, Mikey exhibited questionable behavior in New York
City, standing on top of TSG's van outside of a venue in New York City's East
Village to serenade a homeless man with the Red Hot Chili Peppers' "Around

the World" before donating a quarter to the individual in need. Two weeks later in Minneapolis, Welsh nearly passed out onstage, overcome with an illness that forced the cancellation of the next night's gig in Milwaukee.

Existing on a diet of Taco Bell, Denny's, and T.G.I. Friday's in between nightly accommodations that varied from Motel 6's to the floors of friends, this touring style was undoubtedly a comedown from the heyday of *The Blue Album*, but Pat seemed happy to be playing music. Most funny perhaps was a Pittsburgh gig on November 2, which the promoter had billed as "The Special Goodness playing all the Weezer hits." A subsequent karaoke rendition of "Undone" and "Tired of Sex" was required to appease the misled attendees, although the performance was plagued with what Koch described in his tour diary as "forty insane frat guys" who surrounded the microphones and screamed out the lyrics.

"There was kind of a need to do something else," Wilson said later of his roadwork with Welsh and Koch. "At the same time, if we could have been doing Weezer, we would have been doing Weezer."

Outside of his roadwork with TSG, Mikey Welsh spent most of '99 home in Boston helping Juliana Hatfield write and record material for what would eventually become *Juliana's Pony: Total System Failure*. For his efforts, Welsh earned a co-writing credit on four Hatfield tunes — "Metal Fume Fever," "Houseboy," "Road Wrath," and "Breeders" — when the set saw release in May 2000 on Zoe/Rounder Records.

Elsewhere, Brian demoed Space Twins tunes throughout '99 with titles like "Rust Colored Sun," "There's Always Tomorrow," "Louder than Lies," "Rings of Saturn," "On the Other Side," "Butterfly Collector," and "Goddess of Love." Brief gigging around Los Angeles also followed, as the group aligned with The Special Goodness for a unique trio of dates at the Club Mesa in Costa Mesa, on November 23, the Viper Room in Hollywood the following night, and Club Cocodrie in San Francisco on November 25.

Meanwhile, Rivers used his time away from the band to focus on self-improvement. Aside from writing piles of songs, and as he said later, "watching *Friends*," he got braces on his teeth and corrective laser surgery for his eyes. The eye surgery reportedly left him with a slight prescription, retaining the need for the dark-rimmed glasses that helped define his public image.

"I've got the accelerate program with high-tension wires," Cuomo bragged a few months before the braces were due to come off. "It hurts twice as much, but it's worth it. But it makes it tough to sing. I can't get out certain words clearly, like 'free.' And who wants to be on MTV with braces?"

Still, the braces wreaked havoc with his already iffy self-esteem. "It's tough to buy something at the checkout line when you've got a mouthful of metal," he said of the experience. "You don't want to smile when you say thank you because the person will think you're a loser. So you don't smile and you don't say thank you and then they think you're an asshole."

Unbeknownst to Cuomo, the cult of Weezer was ballooning, due in large part to the expansion of the Internet as a way for fans to connect, dissect, and just plain geek out over the band's music. File-sharing services like Napster, which launched in mid-'99, quickly became the ideal place for Weezer geeks to abscond with bootleg MP3s and rarities.

The online Weezer community was launched as early as 1995 through the formation of the pioneering Rebel Weezer Alliance, and blossomed by 1999 as Weezer.net and endless numbers of fan sites sprung up. RWA's driving force, Karl Koch, was using the Weezer.net URL to make use of the "rotting boxes" of tour mementos he had from his days in the mid- to late-1990s on the road with the band. It started simply, with some pictures of the band. He soon added the band's videos and posted news when he had it for the few people he thought cared. The reality was that many people still did, and soon enough "Karl's Korner" became the authority for Weezer information.

During the band's long period of inactivity (both real and perceived), kids who actually 'got' the emotional thrust that steered *Pinkerton* were launching bands of their own, and Weezer's oft-mauled second album not only found redemption but became a cult phenomenon. Before too long, pop- and punk-influenced "emo" groups — some who also owed a debt to 1980s emo-core pioneers Rites of Spring and 1990s brooding, melodic Sub Pop outfit Sunny Day Real Estate — began cropping up, with names like The Promise Ring, The Get Up Kids, The Anniversary, Jimmy Eat World, and Ultimate Fakebook. They soon found success of their own on the underground.

As *Pinkerton* quietly shifted thousands of units each week, Koch was doing a service to his employers by putting them at an arm's reach of their fans, unintentionally helping to revive a band many had left for dead. "The response grew stronger and stronger," Karl acknowledged. "And we realized that most bands weren't really giving the amount of info, pics, and stuff that we were; the fans were becoming very loyal to the site, and of course their loyalty to the band was being reinforced, too."

"I can only speak for myself," said Matthew Pryor of Kansas City's The Get Up Kids, about the cult of *Pinkerton*. "I was a Weezer fan from the get-go, and when [the album] came out, I was just as excited. We'd get interviewed for fanzines, and the writers would ask us who we listened to and we'd mention Weezer and a couple other bands. Underground cult successes happen all the time; look at *The Rocky Horror Picture Show*."

Cuomo, alone with his thoughts, was evidently unaware of what was going on in both computerland and in the emo-rock underground. Sequestered in his apartment with no Internet access, no telephone, and no television, he had cut himself off from the outside world. Despite the resilience of these fans — who soon crowned Cuomo a geek god in the emo scene as they traded bootleg MP3s of his 1997 solo Boston shows —

the frontman humbly mused, "We certainly haven't given them much to stick around for."

But Pryor believed, "good music transcends all boundaries," and pointed out how the fickle indie rock community's disdain of major label product was overlooked because *Pinkerton* was a commercial bomb. "People tend to forget about their political convictions against the [music] industry if they really like a song. And that's all Weezer's about — liking the songs and having a good time. And there shouldn't be anything wrong with that."

Meanwhile, Cuomo was filling up notebooks and demo tapes, amassing hundreds of songs, and fixating on the future of Weezer. "Like anybody else, part of me was thinking, 'I think there will be a third record,'" the songwriter-guitarist said of the time. "And part of me was thinking, 'Well, clearly there's *not* going to be a third record.' Part of me was just thinking, 'Damn, I hope there's going to be a third record.' Probably all those thoughts and feelings are going through my head at the same time."

"It was kind of like, 'Well, what's gonna happen? Is this it or what?'" Koch said. "And for a while, Rivers was just hunkered down, writing, never really talking to people, and I just figured, 'Well, he's gonna eventually realize he doesn't want to do music 'cause it's driving him crazy, or he's gonna come out with a batch of songs.' And as it turns out, he came out with a batch of songs. He came out with tons of batches of songs. It was just kind of a necessary period. It just had to be like that."

Summing up the downtime, Cuomo would later acknowledge quite simply, "I had to go on a little journey. I just wasn't ready."

chapter twenty-one

gonna make my move

By January 2000, Rivers Cuomo had enough confidence in his newly penned songs to plunk down a wad of cash on a big house in the Hollywood Hills. Aside from its quiet and desirable location on Rodgerton Drive in Beachwood Canyon by Griffith Park, the home possessed an attached garage that the Weezer namesake was hoping to soundproof and eventually turn into a practice room/recording studio for his then-estranged group.

Inside his new abode, R.C. continued to nurture the songwriting streak that was reportedly brought on by a year spent in isolation. Away from live gigs and parties, the anti-social rocker adhered to a self-imposed ban on radio listening and record buying. In doing so, Rivers conjured up even more new tunes with titles like "Fanny Bone," "Sweet Talk," "Mr. Docksider," "Tremendously Awful," "Robot Man," "I Screwed It All Up," "Yer Fun to Play With," and "You Stupid Piece of Shit."

As February approached, a prolific Cuomo talked to *RollingStone.com*, breaking his self-imposed media silence and speaking to the press for the first time in two and half years to clarify the status of the group. Denying an online rumor that Mikey was now out as bassist and former Smashing Pumpkins member D'Arcy Wretzky was in, Rivers countered, "I have no idea how they got that idea. But I like to hear crazy rumors. Didn't I die in a car accident? My mom called me about that one — she was really concerned. And then there was the time I raped someone. My mom also called me about that: 'I'm so disappointed in you!' But she doesn't call me about them anymore. I banned her from the Internet."

Cuomo also took the opportunity to blame the Universal Music merger for the band's absence from the music scene. And while band's longtime Geffen A&R rep Todd Sullivan lost his position in the corporate restructuring, the excuse was only partially true.

"Once it became apparent that Weezer wasn't getting dropped, at that point it was, 'Okay, they want us, so I guess that means that they want us to do an album,'" Karl Koch remembered. "But we really didn't have a contact person because [Sully] got let go. So it was like, 'Who do we know here at this company that we're on?' Nobody. So it took a while to re-establish the lines of communication."

But the placement of the story was the first solid indication that there was indeed a real future for the band. As Rivers vaguely informed readers that his new batch of tunes sounded like "Weezer," *RollingStone.com* reporter Jennifer Vineyard probed for a better description. "Which Weezer?" she wondered, citing the debut's "undeniably catchy, irony-rich Weezer" and the "much more serious and bitter" incarnation that spawned *Pinkerton*. "A bit of both," Rivers confidently boasted, obviously pleased with his new songs. "It's pretty much the same old thing. It's good."

As Cuomo continued to write material between February and March 2000, Weezer's West Coast–based side bands kept busy by playing out. While the Space Twins rocked Yesteryear's in Pomona playing a one-off on March 24, The Special Goodness embarked on a second tour on March 8 at the Satyricon in Portland, with Koch again serving as tour manager for the month-long van tour.

Notable is a gig at Johnny Depp's Viper Room, which featured TSG and the Space Twins locking arms for another night of rock in Hollywood. The show found Rivers — now apparently over his superstitions about River Phoenix's death outside the venue — joining up with his Weezer mates for the first time in same room since the fall of 1998. After the gig, Koch and Wilson headed back to Cuomo's sprawling new crib, but for lack of a guest bed, they wound up sleeping on his living room floor.

Wrapping the tour on March 23 in Salt Lake City, Wilson, Welsh, and the others drove sixteen hours back to Portland to demo TSG tunes like "Life Goes By," "In the Sun," and "Let's Go Down." With the recording complete and sent out to twenty record company talent scouts, Pat and Mikey took off to L.A. to join up with Weezer for rehearsals. These April practices were hurriedly arranged when an extremely lucrative offer to have Weezer perform in Japan in August 2000 was presented to Cuomo, causing his ears to prick up. It resulted in renewed interaction between members, who, by late 1999, had been reduced to communicating only through management.

Sorting out their difficulties was not necessarily for the betterment of the band but for the betterment of their respective bank accounts. Despite the fact there was still an air of tension at times, the work was potentially lucrative and the group came to the realization that they really needed one another.

"I think that there were so many rumors about us breaking up after *Pinkerton* that, after a while, you just couldn't take it seriously," said Wilson. "If you talk about breaking up enough, you won't. And, you know, it's always the same thirty kids on whatever it is — a newsgroup or a chat-room or a message board — saying stuff. You've got to be careful what you read into those things."

Of the offer to play the Fuji Festival, Wilson acknowledged it "seemed to kind of kick Rivers' ass. I don't think we would have done anything if it wasn't for that show." Group practices and demos promptly ensued, moving sessions to Cole Rehearsals in Los Angeles beginning in May and running through July. While Cuomo was largely silent at the outset, after a few days getting reacquainted, things began to gel.

So, at 6 p.m. daily, the men of Weezer would gather for three-hour rehearsals at the Hollywood facility, initially jamming on Slayer songs like "Angel of Death" and "Black Magic" to work out any kinks (local zoning officials had curtailed plans for a studio to be built in Cuomo's garage). Future Weezer album cuts like "Hash Pipe," "Dope Nose," and "Slob" were among the eighteen tunes fleshed out soon after reconvening. Reinvigorated, the band was also talking about getting to work on a new studio album after the Japanese dates.

"Hash Pipe" immediately charged the group up in these rehearsals. Later referred to by Cuomo as "the strangest song ever," the songwriter explained how he first brought it down to their rehearsal room. "The guys were like, 'Holy cow! That's fun.'"

By mid-May, Weezer was plotting a handful of low-key June dates in and around Los Angeles to again get the feel for live performances. To be performed under the Goat Punishment alias, and communicated to their growing number of ardent fans via Koch's "Karl's Korner" on the band's then-official www.weezer.net URL, the shows were designed as warm-ups for not only the Japan trek, but for high-profile performances the band had secured — but not officially confirmed — on a run of eight Warped Tour dates. As May wound out, unspecific plans for future activities in the Weezer camp counted a full U.S. tour and the eventual recording of the long-awaited third album.

With Weezer's career on the apparent rebound, Matt Sharp was looking for a place to hide. Having exited the band to dedicate his attention to the Rentals and their second album, the previous-year's commercial bomb, *Seven More Minutes*, Matt had reportedly parted ways with Madonna's record company and moved to Tennessee to try his hand at an entirely acoustic album. Seeking more concrete details, one fan wrote a letter to Weezer.net webmaster Koch to try to get the skinny.

"I don't think he's on good terms with Maverick for a variety of reasons, most of which appear to be his fault at the core," wrote Koch, who was apparently on speaking terms with the bassist after having caught up with him at one of The Special Goodness gigs earlier in the year. Citing Sharp as appearing "chubby" and "acting weird" at the time of their interaction, Koch continued, "I think he's in the bad position of being on a major label that won't help him because he made them mad, but won't let him go either as they probably consider him capable of making them money at some point."

Such speculation aside, Sharp said he moved to a small country house an hour outside of Nashville, in Leiper's Fork, Tennessee, to work on a solo album with a completely different approach to music than anything he had done before in the Rentals or Weezer.

"I guess the biggest changes are sonic. This record doesn't have any electric guitars or bass or drums or synthesizers," Sharp said of the material he concocted there. Collaborating with guitarists Josh Hager and Greg Brown — both who had impressed him during his post-Weezer studio and touring initiatives — Matt said it was important to have the session marked by a different locale.

"I always try to have each record marked by a different environment, you know?" Sharp said of his decision to relocate. "Then you have an imprint on your memory. It's a stamp of a certain time. Like the first Weezer record, it was done in New York, and I hadn't ever really spent a lot of time in New York before that. And the last Rentals record was done mostly in London, and I still have a really vivid memory from both of those times, so it is similar in that way. A friend of mine knew I wanted to make a record in Nashville at some point, and talked about this place for a while.

"So anyway, this girl calls me and says, 'I have a little house. It's not in

Nashville, but it's like an hour away and it's deep in the country and it's more beautiful than Nashville.' So I call Josh. And he was the person who really pushed me through the door to try making music from this approach. And I'm like, 'Hey, dude, I found out about this house.' And he's like, 'Go.' He starts helping me get my stuff in the van before I had a chance to say yes or no, and we were on the road to Nashville.

"I didn't want to think about units or product, or any of those things while we were writing," Sharp said of the Leiper's Fork sessions, which took place at 4212 Old Hillsboro Road. "Especially because I didn't know what we wanted to make. If I had a really good grip on what I was trying to do, I might have been able to handle dealing with record company people, but the truth of the matter is I just wanted to get a little disconnected from everything and be left to my own devices."

Taking a tip from Rivers Sharp said he too, "had no radio or MTV or a television at all for that matter. I just wanted to be most drawn to making music without any of that outside influence. Besides I didn't really know what it was going to be, so I couldn't really tell any label people. I couldn't say, 'Okay, I'm going to make *this* kind of record.' I didn't tell Maverick what I was planning, because I didn't know if it would end up becoming anything.

"For me, my feeling about music has never changed creatively," Sharp continued. "I'm always trying to make the kind of music I'd like to hear from other people. Creatively, the same thing turns me on now that did when I was twenty-whatever and making those Weezer records. That was the exact kind of music that I was into at the time. That's what I was most inspired by and those were the kind of concerts that I would go see and the kind of records that I would have bought."

While he was away, it became apparent that many Weezer fans really missed Matt and weren't sure what he was up to. After all, it would take him until 2003 to put out a four-song EP from the Tennessee excursion.

But clearly his former bandmates weren't missing having him around, even if his ego had been deflated.

"Matt's probably pretty humbled by now, I would imagine," Brian chuckled, referring to the failure of the Rentals. "I love him to death. God bless him."

Sharp's replacement, Mikey Welsh, remembered encounters with the bassist. "We got along really well. I like Matt." However, Welsh — mirroring Westrich's assessment — conceded, "He's nice to people that he thinks he should be nice to. Which isn't most people, so I'd say that he probably isn't very nice to most people."

Comparing Welsh to Sharp, Brian Bell observed, "Mikey doesn't have the crazy inflated ego Matt had." Praising Welsh's role with the band, Koch concurred, "Mikey gets pretty wild at times, but is very gentle at heart. He rules on bass, he plays old Fenders, he isn't an asshole, and he only wants to [play] — nothing else."

"[Mikey] is really businesslike. It's like, show up, play, make sure you don't suck — not too much drama," Pat Wilson said, noting the differences between the two. "I think [Matt] may feel a little freaked out. Because, obviously, there's gotta be a part of him that's like, yeah, maybe I shouldn't have left Weezer."

One couldn't blame Sharp if he was eating crow, as Weezer's Goat Punishment shows throughout California went off tremendously well. Beginning at The Yucatan in Santa Barbara on June 16, 2000, and with Nerf Herder — now featuring Justin Fisher on bass in the wake of Marko 72's departure to form Sugarcult — Weezer not only delighted hardcore fans, but rocked their worlds. Mixing up material from their Geffen catalog, but focusing largely on the debut material, the band also brought forth a few songs of new material.

"Rivers called me to set up the first official Weezer show after their long hiatus," Nerf Herder's Parry Gripp remembered. "They wanted to play a show in Santa Barbara, and he told me that it wouldn't be a secret show, that they were going to use the Weezer name in advertising so that some people would come. [The Yucatan] had a capacity of about 300 at most. I told him, 'The place is going to be sold out really fast!' And he said, 'Ohhh, I don't know. We haven't played for a while. People may not remember us. . . .' Of course it sold out instantly and tons of people were standing outside during the show. It was crazy!"

The next night at Jerry's Pizza in Bakersfield the band not only tore through a killer set but served up autographs after outside the venue. Then, on June 20, the group went down to San Diego and, if you'll pardon the play on words, rocked The Casbah. Fans stood in line for admission as early as 6:30 a.m., and although it, too, was advertised as a Goat Punishment show, the marquee outside broadcasting "Weezer" spilled the beans. Long Beach's Lava Lounge — itself part of a Bowling Alley called Java Lanes — was the site of the GP gig on the following night and marked performances of new tunes like "My Brain Is Workin' Overtime," "Dope Nose," "Preacher's Son," and "O-Girl."

After the crowd dispersed at the Lava gig, Rivers sat down to talk with fans, revealing he was anxious to play the Warped Tour. "I was getting used to being a complete nobody again," he confided. "But I think I prefer to be somebody. I feel more in my natural element doing this stuff." *OC Weekly* reviewed the Wednesday night Lava gig, reporting that wealthy Japanese fan-kids flew in to L.A. just for the gig, with very loud screaming from all in attendance as the "geek-rock icons" took the stage. "One of the Japanese girls actually wept with ecstasy," read the review, which also noted the emergence of a mosh pit and a subsequent fight that broke out.

"Cult bands! What are you gonna do?" the piece continued, before

DANIEL COSTON

Weezer Reconvenes: Brian Bell rings up a smile

DANIEL COSTON

Rivers, Pat, and Mikey tear it up on stage

acknowledging that Weezer, as the "anti-Korn/Limp Bizkit," were "as much a vital alternative today as they were to whatever prevailed back in '94." For Rivers, Pat, Brian, and now, Mikey, rocking was just like riding a bicycle, and under the thin veil of Goat Punishment, they blasted their way into Spaceland, tearing up the L.A. venue on June 22 and bringing forth another new tune, "Slob," amid the chaotic, oldies-saturated set.

"I think the most important thing was getting back out there and playing shows again," Rivers said of the band's new life. "Put it all on the line. Get all the criticism and get all the praise. That's when you feel like the gun is at your head and you'd better get your act together. That was the catalyst that really made it all happen."

The next night, Weezer joined the Warped Tour with Green Day, The Mighty Mighty Bosstones, The Suicide Machines, and Papa Roach, among others at the Fresno State Amphitheatre for the first of eight planned dates on the West Coast. Added to the festival after their then-manager, Pat Magnarella at Third Rail, went to the tour organizers asking to sneak them on some West Coast dates of the bill, the double-platinum rockers had to concede that they wouldn't be paid for their appearances and they would need to travel in a van.

"We asked to get on [the Warped tour] because it seemed like the place to be at that point," Karl Koch later announced. "Green Day was headlining and we know them and that was cool."

"Believe me, it was torturous," Cuomo said of their Warped commitment, which they would fulfill on July 1 after a San Francisco date at Pier 30/32. "It was downright terrifying going out there the first few times, because our self-esteem was at an all-time low, combined with the fact that that's not really our crowd. That's a punk crowd and they're notorious for voicing their opinions if they're not into you. When we showed up that first day, the Lunachicks were on. The announcer said, 'Coming up later,

Weezer,' and the whole place went crazy. That's when we knew we were going to be safe."

In fact, through fan anticipation, Cuomo — complete with an overgrown bowl cut and braces — would have his revenge on Dicky Barrett for that embarrassing night in Boston back in 1997, as Rivers' delirious disciples began to chant "Weezer, Weezer" loudly, over and over during the end of the Mighty Mighty Bosstones set at the Anaheim Warped stop on June 29.

When Weezer took the stage minutes later, the punk rock audience went ballistic, and widespread crowd-surfing ensued instantly. For a generation of fans who picked up on the band during their early teens and elevated them to cult icons courtesy of *Pinkerton* in the late 1990s, the surprise of seeing Weezer live was something they never could have imagined. "You can't blame them if they thought that," Cuomo announced. "We were just as happy to see them."

"We went in there fully expecting to be booed and to have things thrown at us," Rivers said after that first gig. "But it was exactly the opposite, people were singing along to all the songs and just going crazy, giving us the best support. And I think that gave us the confidence we needed.

"I was practically in tears," Cuomo said. "After years of isolation and being 100% certain that no one cared about us anymore at all, then to step out in front of 20,000 people that are screaming their heads off because of us was really cool."

"I think people love songs they can sing along to and that was probably one of the reasons we got such a great reception," rationalized Mikey in regard to Weezer's stint on the punk-packed Warped Tour. "We were the only band that was so different, musically." By the second night on Warped, courtesy of Napster, there were fans in the crowd who knew the words to the new Cuomo originals.

"Stylistically, Mikey Welsh was like this punk misfit in the band," The

Reunion Show's Brian Diaz observed. "He kind of gave Weezer this bad boy image, which was funny. I have this picture that a friend of mine took of Mikey and Rivers together backstage at Warped Tour and Mikey is towering over Rivers. It looks like he's an ex-con who's part of the Big Brothers

CHRISTINA RADISH

Don't Call It A Comeback:
Ol' Nerdy gets Warped!

and Sisters program and he's about to take Rivers out for some ice cream."

Fans in high places like Billie Joe Armstrong of Warped headliners Green Day were quick to acknowledge Rivers, Pat, Brian, and Mikey were on the comeback trail. When an attendee at one of Green Day's London shows later in the summer looked to knock Cuomo's band as has-beens, Armstrong quickly rushed to the defense of his friends. "Let me tell you something about Weezer," he said. "They are better than ever, man. They have a new album that's going to be out next summer and, seriously, Weezer are coming back."

Enforcing the same notion were two legitimate headlining gigs that followed Weezer's Warped Tour obligations and took place at Pomona's Glass House on July 3 and 4. By this point, the group had real momentum, not only booking a two-week run of West Coast dates for mid- to late July, but announcing plans for a three-week club tour of the East Coast and Midwest for late August and early September.

"We played some kind of secret shows, some clubs in Bakersfield, and that turned into, 'Hey, you want to come do eight shows on the Warped Tour?'" Wilson simplified. "And that turned into, 'Why don't we just keep going?'"

"It was weird," Koch added, "because, as of last spring there was a big question as to whether anything was gonna happen or not. They started to rehearse again and Rivers was kinda happy with his songs after a long period of writing songs and not being sure of them or really knowing if he liked them. So somehow, out of the blue, we got this great offer from Japan, for later in the summer that was good shows, good money, everything is good about this, you are a fool not to do this. Like, 'Wow, Japan. Let's do it.' And to warm up for that we should play some shows in the States, right? And that turned into all of a sudden finding out that all of these cities were offering really good shows. It's like, 'Wow, they really have confidence in the band that they can sell some tickets here.'"

The ten-date West Coast jaunt launched on July 17 at Cane's Bar & Grill in San Diego and wrapped up at The Whiskey back in Los Angeles on July 29. On July 20, the group was reunited in Salt Lake City with Mykel and Carli Allan's parents for the first time in nearly three years. Wayne and Claudia Allan came to the show with their sons, and brought the band cookies and milk to honor their daughters' devotion to the

Weezer camp. Continuing to premiere new tunes like "Superstar," "Modern Dukes," "Too Late to Try," "Mad Kow," "Your Sister," "Ev'ry Nite," "Hash Pipe," and "Slob" along the way, the band's 23 gig in Portland and the following day in Seattle were unique in that both were opened by Pat Finn's band, Organic Mechanic.

Meanwhile, through an Internet poll on Weezer.net, fans selected their Top 10 picks for producer to oversee album #3. In order of preference, the results were as follows: Ric Ocasek, Nigel Godrich, Butch Vig, Mark Trombino, J. Robbins, Jon Brion, Sean Slade and Paul Kolderie, Brendan O'Brien, Jay Baumgartner, and Jerry Harrison.

The band was also using the Weezer.net site to interact with fans about their new material. After recording the songs in a live setting, the group was asking loyalists to vote on the material to help them narrow down tracks to a suitable four that could be used for a demo CD to send to potential producers. Through an onslaught of e-mails, fans ultimately chose "Slob," "Preacher's Son," "Hash Pipe," and "O-Girl."

"I'm sure they think we totally screwed up our second record," Cuomo said, speaking about the suits at Geffen Records, which by the year 2000 had become little more than an imprint for the Universal-owned giant label Interscope Records. "I feel like it came out exactly like I wanted it to." Maybe so, but the label — now a much different beast than it was back in 1996 — did indeed deem *Pinkerton* a failure and insisted the group hunt for someone to man the boards.

But with Weezer on the rise again after his years of woodshedding, Rivers Cuomo wasn't dwelling on the past. He had emerged a new, confident man. "I feel as if I've made some huge steps forward now. I don't feel like I need the emotional support of those around me and that's very liberating. I think this time around it would be a lot harder to take success away from me."

With Weezer's rebirth, Cuomo's schedule quickly became hurried, and following the Whiskey show, he, Wilson, Bell, and Welsh had two days to recharge their respective batteries and pack before heading out to Japan on August 2 to support Green Day. The tour was off to a rocky start when Weezer's flight was canceled after a broken part on their airplane was discovered and a replacement wasn't in supply. Delayed a day, the band and crew spent twelve hours in the sky before performing their first gig at the Osaka Summersonic Festival with a serious case of jet lag. Simultaneously, news of the band's demo for potential producers — plus the full itinerary for Weezer's three-week club tour, set to embark at New York's Irving Plaza on August 23 — reached the online music sites.

The Osaka Summersonic show found Weezer rocking a crowd of 20,000, bringing forth two new numbers ("Too Late to Try" and "Superstar") in the span of their fifty-minute set. Filmed for Japanese television, the performance saw Rivers addressing the audience in their native Japanese, saying thanks ("Okini") and asking, "How are you?" ("Genki?"). Rivers no doubt impressed the crowd by serving up more than just the requisite arigato. The next night, a second Summersonic concert in Mt. Fuji — roughly an hour outside of Tokyo — took place at a large amusement park located in the Fujikyu Conifer Forest Grounds.

California punk outfit NOFX was also in Mt. Fuji for the gig, and that band's bassist, Fat Mike, who also doubles in punk cover band Me First and the Gimme Gimmes, recollected an amusing illicit experience with Mikey Welsh during the trip. "I had been friends with Mikey since he joined Weezer," Mike said, chuckling. "We were in Japan together at Summersonic, but we played on opposite days. I wrote a little note to him in the dressing room. And after that, we all got together and did a bunch of mushrooms in Japan. Maybe that's when Mikey started to go crazy, I don't know. He ate a whole bunch of mushrooms."

Recreational psychedelics aside, plans for a performance in Okinawa on August 8 were shelved by a typhoon that thwarted air travel and left the band with a day off in Tokyo. Two days later, Weezer rocked Tokyo's Club Quattro in what Koch later described as an "intense" tour closer. For one, the group dusted off "No Other One" for the first time since '97, and, as Koch explained, "the show ended with a freaky combination of Rivers stage-diving — the first time that has happened in many years — Mikey shoving his bass into the rafters and then stage diving, Brian exploring some feedback techniques, and Pat jumping down from the drums to add a spastic guitar solo to the mix." During his jump from the stage, Rivers lost his trademark eyeglasses. Fearing they had been trampled in the madness, the Weezer leader surveyed the crowd and discovered them held high above the head of an attendee who kindly returned the spectacles intact.

With the upcoming East Coast dates looming, the band was — through Koch — continuing to interact with the swelling Weezer fanbase through the Web site. Polling Weezer.net visitors (having yet to acquire the Weezer.com URL from an existing fan site), the band queried loyalists to see which old songs they would like to see eliminated from its live set. However, when the number one song voted by fans to be dropped from the upcoming shows wound up being "Buddy Holly," Cuomo decided to defy his fans orders. "On the Internet, the fans unanimously voted down 'Buddy Holly' as the song they wanted us never to play again," Rivers said. "But actually, I love playing that song so we're gonna keep playing it."

Back in Los Angeles after the tour of Japan and days before the commencement of an East Coast club tour, Cuomo and Koch elected to defy local inspection officials and took to the power tools, building a home studio in the Weezer frontman's garage in a matter of days. With the drum riser, entrance ramp, and sound-proofing finished, an electrician and carpet installer finished off the basement-level room. With Weezer's new demo and rehearsal space complete, the band broke in the facility amid meetings with possible producers. The group also selected Dynamite Hack, purveyors of a catchy radio favorite "Boyz in the Hood," itself a reworking of the 1988 Eazy E gangsta rap classic, as their support act for the looming tour.

As far as the producer situation went, Pearl Jam and Stone Temple Pilots veteran boardman Brendan O'Brien had a prior commitment, as did Garbage drummer Butch Vig, who oversaw Nirvana's seminal 1991 disc, *Nevermind*. Meetings with former Talking Head Jerry Harrison, known for work with Live and Creeper Lagoon; Barkmarket brainchild Dave Sardy, who had worked with Nine Inch Nails, Helmet, and the Red Hot Chili Peppers; plus Jerry Finn, who was hot off Blink-182's *Enema of the State*, all ended in uncertainty with the band. Sadly, Rivers' hopes of securing a producer for album #3 by the outset of the late summer tour were dashed. Despite being plagued with worry over the producer situation and how it might delay the long-anticipated *Pinkerton* follow-up, the group still managed to accept it as fact and rallied together for a barbecue at Cuomo's house on the eve of the trip.

The New York tour opener at Irving Plaza was a rousing success, prompting *Rolling Stone* to proclaim the show a "triumphant return to the stage." Reporter Jennifer Vineyard — an early champion of Weezer Mach II — described Rivers' appearance as "resembling a younger Rick Moranis with his thick, clunky Clark Kent glasses and a buttoned-up-to-the-collar shirt. [Cuomo] didn't exactly yell 'rock star.' But that's part of Weezer's daily dose of irony — you never know, nor are you supposed to — if it's entirely an act or not." Rocking out before Weezer's flashing giant "W" sign — itself an homage to Van Halen's seasoned logo — Rivers, Pat, Brian, and Mikey informed New York City that they were indeed "still making noise." Alongside staples like "In the Garage" and "Why Bother," new material like "Your Sister" and "Too Late to Try" proved this was a band with a future.

Backstage after the gig, former Weezer producer Ric Ocasek — who had since manned the boards for alternative outfits like Guided By Voices and Nada Surf — came by the dressing room to celebrate the future of the group and express interest in offering his production services. Soon enough Ocasek would be in talks to produce the forthcoming disc, provided he could alter his personal and professional itinerary. Ric's visit put Cuomo's production fears at bay somewhat, but if things went off without a hitch in New York, the following night's show at the Stone Pony in Asbury Park, New Jersey, would more than make up for it in terms of hassles.

Despite selling out the venue in a record seven minutes, the August 24 gig was bogged down in problems. First, the New Jersey Department of the Treasury threatened to stop the show because the band didn't have a state tax identification number (despite the fact the group's federal number superceded any state-issued number). Then the local police hassled the group about its tour bus registration, almost resulting in it being impounded. Later, just minutes before sound check, Koch took his skateboard to one of the venue's outdoor skate ramps and subsequently broke off one of his teeth, requiring emergency dental surgery. The Weezer camp clearly couldn't catch a break in the Garden State.

Aside from such pitfalls, the show itself was tremendous as Weezer took the stage to the theme music from CBS Sports blaring beneath them. Still, the gig *was* oversold as some patrons were forced to watch the show from outside in the muggy August air. (This writer wound up standing on a card table chair in order to see the event.) Despite a large, drunken crowd surfer who attempted to ruin the show — who was eventually met with loud audience cheers upon being ejected — the gig was great fun and marked the return of "Only in Dreams" to the live set. To cap off the night, Brian Bell's guitar was nearly stolen after the gig, until fans and Stone Pony security intervened and recaptured the axe.

"The Asbury Park show will live on in my heart as one of my all-time favorite concerts," said The Reunion Show's Brian Diaz. "The feeling was just right. No one had seen them in forever. Everyone was singing along almost louder than the band. They played *Blue Album* stuff and *Pinkerton* songs, some new stuff . . . It was truly amazing. And they hadn't at all lost it. They were the same band I remembered from back in the day."

Gigs at Boston's Axis and Lupo's Heartbreak Hotel in Providence later in the week were big successes, with the latter finding Weezer rocking out 1,800 stoked attendees. In Philadelphia, following the band's TLA (Theatre of the Living Arts) gig, Rivers met with fans and signed autographs until the Philly cops told him he was creating a disturbance. Cuomo persisted in signing autographs, and his defiance nearly got him arrested.

Jim McGuinn, program director at Y100, Philadelphia's modern rock outlet, was at the sold-out TLA gig. "For years, I'd talk to Pat Magnarella, their manager at Third Rail, and I'd be like, 'What's going on with Weezer? We want 'em in Philly.' So I wasn't surprised by their ability to come back, although I think a lot of people had written them off. But I always felt that there was something there, and from talking to young bands you knew that they were having a tremendous impact. A lot of people who got *Pinkerton* really got it profoundly and went out and started a band. Some people say that *Pinkerton* is to Weezer's career what *Paul's Boutique* was to the Beastie Boys. *Paul's Boutique* was a real heavy, intricate record that followed the light, party aesthetic of *Licensed to Ill*. And it wasn't very well received at the time. But the people that got it, totally got it. If they had put out *Licensed to Ill Part II*, that would have come out and their career would have been over. It's similar to Weezer, where the lack of platinum success has sort of left *Pinkerton* for them to have this resurgence."

Comeback or not, the Weezer frontman was still struggling daily when it came to compiling each evening's setlist. At times, relying on the audience to help him decide what songs to play was a way of getting around this process. "Making the setlist is the most stressful part of the day for me," he said on the tour. "There are so many opinions out there on what we should play and it's really hard to make everybody happy. Every night after we get offstage, it never fails, somebody comes up to me and says, 'why didn't you play such and such a song,' and I always feel bad."

As the tour progressed, the audiences swelled, with 2,400 fans packing in to see the Weez at Runwayz in Cheektowaga, New York, for what drummer Wilson's hometown paper, the *Buffalo News*, later described as a "new spirited and confident Weezer." To promote the show, Pat talked to the daily about why he opted out of his ten-year Clarence High School reunion. "It wouldn't have been personally fulfilling for me to come back and have some bragging rights over people. 'Hey, you were cool in twelfth grade, and I'm cool now and you're lame.' I would feel terrible doing that." He also commented on the local hockey team: "The Sabres? All I have to say about that is: no goal."

Simplifying the band's three-year absence, Wilson said, "We just took a break. Matt went and did the Rentals. That turned into Matt leaving the band. There was an adjustment to make there creatively. That seems to have settled down now. We have a new bass player. So, we decided to do some new shows. Next thing we know, it's like, 'Okay! We're going out on tour.' And we're making a record this fall."

"The band is heavier now," Pat added. "It's just more powerful and tighter. The emphasis on songs and melodies is also there." But this was no mere print-savvy band, as they'd prove by making an evening news broadcast — unintentionally — a few days later. Lounging in a Milwaukee park on a day off from touring, Pat and Rivers were approached by a reporter from ABC affiliate WIJN Channel 12, who asked Wilson his views on the impending presidential race between George W. Bush and Al Gore. Later, back at the hotel, the band had quite a chuckle watching the story.

Positive press out of Chicago found the *Sun-Times* giving the thumbs up to the group's September 3 performance at The Metro: "A student of rock history, Cuomo has merged the melodic hooks of Cheap Trick, the punk fury of the Buzzcocks, and the harmony singing of '6os girl groups into his own garage rock gems. The new tunes 'Too Late to Try' and 'Superstar' were encouraging signs that the forthcoming disc could be a keeper." Complete with stagediving from Mr. Welsh, clichéd one-liners from Cuomo like "You people ready? All right, let's rock," and a crowd so loud during sing-alongs that Rivers had to struggle to be heard, the gig (which saw fans outside offering $100 or more for a $14.50 ticket) was called plain "exhilarating" by the *Chicago Tribune*, which equated Weezer's songs to "manna from heaven."

With the same fans that supported Weezer-inspired outfits like Weston, The Promise Ring, The Get Up Kids, Jimmy Eat World, and Death Cab for Cutie now clamoring to get inside Weezer's shows, and with all the gigs selling out in just minutes, Cuomo explained the band's resurgence. "I guess because we've been relying on word of mouth for such a long time instead of mass media exposure. So it just takes a long time for people to tell their friends that, 'Hey, Weezer is actually pretty good, you should check them out.' And now the word has finally spread, I guess."

"It's just bananas," Karl told the *Dallas Observer*, after surveying the frenzied fan response up close all summer long. "It's like mini-Beatlemania every day."

"It seems like they're a little more . . . crazy now. Like, literally crazy," Rivers laughed in agreement. "Kinda frightening. Like some of them might actually be dangerous — people following our bus and stuff. It's been unbelievable. Every show has been sold out, and everywhere we go, we've broken the record for merchandise sold in whatever venue we happen to be in. Just incredible audience response. It's pretty exciting. I like hanging out at home and doing nothing too. But this . . . it's pretty okay."

In the midst of such an ego-boosting comeback, the post-Cobain, pre-Creed stylists in Weezer bravely plotted an extensive U.S. tour for February 2001. The group had also penciled in a possible album release date of April 1, 2001, having already booked studio time in Los Angeles for the coming months of October and November, despite having no officially confirmed producer. But the band was leaning toward Ocasek and Pat let the cat out of the bag that same week. "I think Ric is going to produce it," he told a student reporter from the University of Michigan.

If the plan was to utilize the same producer, little else had remained the same in the seven years since Weezer first hit the studio with Ocasek. "I think we're just more focused now — Matt and Rivers had their own creative thing," said an upbeat Wilson before the Detroit show at St. Andrews Hall. "I think Rivers had to kind of figure out how to write the songs he was happy with without anybody else's help and think of the band as players that would come in and flesh the shit out, instead of 'this is how I want it to be.' You know, it was never really like that, but it was more like that with Matt. And plus, Matt really wasn't into playing the bass . . . he didn't love it. Mikey, it's his only thing. He just likes to play the bass.

"I think it works good when we're in this band," Pat enthused, and as the tour continued to unfold, the rhythm section of Wilson and Welsh bought BMX bicycles to keep themselves entertained during the downtime between gigs in Lawrence, Kansas; Tulsa; and Houston. In Dallas, Cuomo first learned of Weener, a Weezer tribute band. "I'm dying to hear them," he admitted. "That's a great name. I hope they're not better than us; that would suck."

On September 10, the mighty Weezer rocked 101X Fest, sponsored by

Austin's commercial alternative radio outlet and held at Audiotrium Shores, appearing alongside hip-hop–influenced outfits like Everlast, the Kottonmouth Kings, and Cypress Hill. After their set, Rivers, Pat, Brian, and Mikey signed autographs for three hours to more than 1500 devoted fans there to see the band. "I wouldn't deny that our fans look nerdy," Pat said proudly of Weezer's loyalists. "I think they're totally nerdy. In a good way, I think. Good for us."

Not so good, however, were the operational headaches surrounding the band's gig at The El Rey Theatre in Albuquerque, which possibly usurped the Stone Pony show in terms of mayhem — and this time it impacted the fans. Power issues gave way to the club's sound system failing midway through the band's live set. An extensive Rush-inspired drum solo from Patrick couldn't help keep the electricity from cutting in and out several times, eventually fostering an hour-long interruption as a new mixing board was brought in.

While that audience hung in there and got the rock they were craving, they not only had to work for it but witness Welsh playing in his underpants. And if the next gig at Denver's Ogden Theatre was far less traumatic, the tour closing gig in Clovis, California, itself a late-addition festival appearance date, was addled with bad food, a bad sound system, and police with a bad attitude. Still, Cuomo and his rock 'n' roll posse elated a roaring crowd that was 5,000 members strong. Just after Mr. Welsh took lighter fluid and a match to his bass during an encore of "Surf Wax America," the men of Weezer walked off the stage on a high not felt since some time back in 1995.

Looking back on Weezer's amazing resurgence, Wilson simply commented, "It's perplexing. It's amazing." A stunned Bell bragged in agreement, "We did nothing. And somehow we're more popular than ever."

"It's definitely given us the confidence that we can actually make another record," Rivers said of the ecstatic response from fans. "I think if we had never come out of our garage, and we had just kept rehearsing and playing to ourselves, we never would have gotten anywhere."

chapter twenty-two

don't let go

The Internet continued to play a prominent role among Weezer's fans as the group's 2000 touring activities wound down. In the wake of the band's summer trek, tour demos captured live on the band's mobile unit during sound checks and concerts soon surfaced on file-sharing services like Napster, often as group-sanctioned MP3s. Most often referred to as "Summer Songs 2K," this material landed efficiently into the hands of Weezer fanatics who just couldn't wait for new Rivers Cuomo–penned numbers to arrive on a new album.

When fans weren't downloading "My Brain," "O-Girl," "Dope Nose," "Ev'ry Nite," "Hash Pipe," "Mad Kow," "Modern Dukes," "Preacher's Son," "Slob," "Superstar," "Too Late to Try," "Your Sister," and "Peace and Quiet," they were participating in a Karl Koch–orchestrated poll via Weezer.net to select opening acts for the band's already-in-the-works February 2001 tour.

Without question, the band's presence online, as much as anything else, was responsible for both the rebirth of *Pinkerton* as a classic and influential album and the band's newly iconic stature. "I think it has to be," Rivers agreed, adding, "We'd still be doing Weezer if the Internet crashed, or whatever. This is our fate."

Cuomo was again a firm believer in himself and his band, and took to morale-boosting his crew in the press, calling Wilson and Welsh "the best rhythm section in the world right now.

"I have a really good feeling about the songs to come," an optimistic Rivers declared, expressing a desire to get off the road and focus on songwriting. Back in Los Angeles, the band members went their separate ways for a few weeks. The frontman finally had his braces removed in late September, while word spread to KROQ radio listeners that Weezer's first new song in four years would be recorded for contribution to the 2000 *Kevin and Bean Xmas Album*.

But Interscope/Geffen Records' level of dedication was already in question, as the powers that be at the company prevented Weezer from officially starting work on their third album. Out of frustration over their producer dilemma, Cuomo announced that the group would start recording on October 23 as planned "with or without" a producer. The record company quickly put that plot on ice.

Undaunted, pre-production on the project got underway that month despite such label woes, as the band regrouped and began rehearsing and arranging both the Summer Songs and newer material that Rivers Cuomo had continued to craft in the weeks after the tour. Down in Rivers' garage, Weezer worked with independent Los Angeles engineer Chad Bamford to decide which tunes would survive and which would be canned. It was an arduous task, but a critical move in terms of efficiency, considering the expense involved in renting a state-of-the-art recording studio.

"They're a very interesting group of guys," said Bamford, who had previously worked on *Ladies and Gentlemen We Are Floating in Space*, the acclaimed disc by U.K.–based experimental rockers Spiritualized. "And they work in a fairly unconventional way, which I actually love, though I think it would drive a lot of people crazy."

Koch would put the fruits of the band's work onto CD-Rs every few days and send them off to Ocasek, who had been on board for months despite the group's hesitancy to officially announce it to fans. Mostly the reluctance was due to an ongoing debate over where to record — in Weezer's L.A. hometown or Ocasek's New York base of operations.

"Rivers started sending me a lot of demos that summer," Ocasek remembered. "We had our pick of, like, sixty songs. Rivers always writes a lot of songs, an obscene amount. There was a little debate over doing it in L.A. or New York. Of course, I always want to do it in New York, because I live here. But eventually I did come to L.A. I know [Interscope President] Jordan Schur kind of wanted them to use me."

As the production got sorted, Weezer began working on a new number, "Move It On," which Cuomo, Wilson, Bell, and Welsh intended to lend to the aforementioned KROQ compilation. Yet, soon after they started it, the song was aborted and supplanted by the more apropos, seasonal number "The Christmas Song."

As plans for the upcoming February–March 2001 tour began to surface, it was revealed that Internet company and search engine Yahoo! would be corporate sponsors for the jaunt, officially titled "The Yahoo! Outloud Tour." But, as word spread, some fans cried foul about the decision to align with the sponsor, who had hosted a similar tour featuring Smash Mouth and Luscious Jackson the year before. Meanwhile, others pondered how Weezer — a band that had once sold two million records — could actually be knocked by loyalists as sell-outs?

By early November, the group told fans that they were still having trouble with the suits at Interscope/Geffen. The "higher-ups" still hadn't given their official approval. In an effort to sway them, a five-song demo was worked on meticulously. "If the bigwigs can't hear the awesome-ness of these new songs with this tape," posted Koch, "then they simply aren't listening."

The Interscope/Geffen demo consisted of five numbers, "No More Confusin'," "Sugar Booger," "Don't Let Go," "Ayleen," and "Cryin' and Lonely." The same week the demo was sent to Interscope A&R bosses, the group — having learned of a last-minute cancellation — went to check out Cello Studios, which was once part of Western Studios. In addition to being the facility where the Beach Boys had cut the landmark *Pet Sounds* album back in 1967, the studio, located at 6000 Sunset Boulevard, had been used by modern rockers like R.E.M., Stone Temple Pilots, Matthew Sweet, Green Day, and Blink-182. With that in mind, and understanding what an influence Brian Wilson and the Beach Boys had over Cuomo's songwriting through the years, the band couldn't help but jump at the opportunity and booked the studio.

In tandem with that decision, Weezer finally confirmed to the media that they were indeed working with Ric Ocasek and had plans to start sessions in early December in Los Angeles, where Rivers, Pat, Brian, and Mikey strongly believed they would be the most comfortable and fecund. With six weeks of demos in hand, Ocasek provided constructive feedback by telephone, and soon said, "We really have a great connection and work well together. This is going to be an amazing record."

Interscope's final approval was still needed for the project to move forward, and the label finally "green lighted" the project on November 15, after Schur — who had previously signed multi-platinum angst-addled rap metal merchants Limp Bizkit and helped launch a successful campaign behind their *Chocolate Starfish and the Hot Dog Flavored Water* album — visited Weezer at Rivers' home studio and liked what he heard.

Giving full approval to start studio work in early December, Schur also commissioned an audible Christmas card to be targeted at key radio people. In an effort to get the word out to programmers and listeners of the modern rock format that Weezer and Interscope were finally on the same page, the lads quickly readied another holiday song. Known as "Christmas Celebration," they coupled it with a remixed version of the KROQ compilation contribution, "The Christmas Song," and put a photo of the boys in

Santa Suits for the cover of the promotional single that Geffen sent to hundreds of instrumental radio people.

To promote their seasonal numbers, Weezer had agreed to play a few high-profile holiday gigs in Los Angeles and San Diego, as well as some low-key warm-up dates around Los Angeles, again under the guise of Goat Punishment. Meanwhile the official details on the Yahoo! Outloud trek revealed plans to initially sell the tickets exclusively through the Internet. Tickets for shows in strong Weezer markets like Philadelphia and Chicago sold out effortlessly.

"We're confident that this year's tour will give Weezer fans a truly unique online and offline music experience," Yahoo! Music's brand manager Tiffany Hein said in a news release announcing the nationwide tour, which was slated to hit twenty cities that surrounded more than sixty college campuses. Webcasts, Web chats with Weezer members, and an exclusive Web site for the tour were also planned.

"We are really looking forward to headlining this year's Yahoo! Outloud tour," Rivers said in a ridiculously canned statement. "We're well aware of how important the Internet has been to the band and our music. By making the tickets available early to our fanbase, Yahoo! is helping Weezer send a big thank you to all of our fans."

Back in the garage, the boys continued to demo new music daily with increased enthusiasm thanks to Schur's approval to move forward. Weezer started weeding through more than seventy-five demos, honing in on twenty-five potential album inclusions in anticipation of Ric's arrival. Rivers continued writing nearly a song a day, with titles like "Break-Up," "Tough Guy Hat," "Drink in the Water," "Mr. Taxman," and "Castles in the Sand" emerging.

Meanwhile, mid-December appearances at both of KROQ's Christmas concerts — designed to benefit local youth charities — plus a New Year's

Eve gig supporting punk/poppers Blink-182 in San Diego were announced, despite being scheduled smack-dab in the middle of proper studio work.

When word of the Blink-182 show and the whole Yahoo!-sponsored tour reached the die-hard fans, shit immediately started flying on Weezer's message board, with allegations of a sell-out. Saddened by the way the band was marketing itself, calling the Yahoo! tour unnecessary and accusing Weezer of only caring about popularity and making money at the expense of true fans who had supported and defended the group in its absence, a large sector of the band's online community was irate.

Cuomo defended the New Year's Eve appearance, explaining through Koch that he was a fan of their tunes and was looking forward to playing a big arena gig. As for sailing under the Yahoo! corporate flag, the group was claiming "complete control over the tour" and "dictating how the shows are going down."

Combating cries of "sell-out," the band's Goat Punishment gigs — designed as warm-up performances for the KROQ and Blink shows — were a way of redeeming themselves to the diehards. Weezer hinted to fans in the know that "this really neat band that we think are worth checking out" had just booked area gigs at Spaceland, the Troubadour, and the Knitting Factory.

Meanwhile, Cuomo was genuinely bothered that so many fans were pissed off at the Yahoo! affiliation and observed it to be no different than a Coca-Cola sponsorship. As shows in Los Angeles, Detroit, New York, and Lowell, Massachusetts all went on sale and sold out in one day, the band used Weezer.net to try to diffuse the situation.

"Weezer fans come in many, many styles," the band — through Koch — wrote diplomatically on December 4. "The great things that unite them are their passion about good music and love of rocking out. The differences between fans can be subtle, such as the difference between someone who just listens to the CDs every day and loves them, to someone who might not constantly listen, but who will drive 500 miles to catch a show. Both of these types, and the hundreds of other types of fans, are fantastic, and Weezer is acutely aware of how lucky they are to have gained any of them."

The group was worried about alienating loyal fans, but not to the point of containing its ever-increasing profile. Following the rapidly sold-out club tour the previous summer, bigger shows were a necessity. By hooking up with a sponsor for the February trek, ticket prices remained inexpensive. As for the Blink-182 show, it was merely looked at as a diversion from recording and fun way to rock in the New Year.

Weezer wasn't just unique for using the Internet as direct line to their rabidly loyal and frequently critical fanbase, it was the first band in rock to ask fans to help pick the support acts for a tour. Kansas-based emo rockers The Get Up Kids and Los Angeles–area quintet Ozma, who had yet to play outside of their home state, were selected in the opening acts poll at #1 and #2 respectively, and both accepted. Weezer also became industry trend-setters by being one of the first high-profile groups to post an official MP3 — "Christmas Celebration" — to their Web site.

Out of Cuomo's garage and into a rehearsal facility in Hollywood, the band settled on twenty or so songs by the time Ocasek pulled up in his rental car in the second week of December to check on the quartet's pre-production progress, as well as to observe and critique arrangements.

As things were getting exciting in pre-production, Weezer finally claimed their rights to Weezer.com — previously home to a fan site — bolstering their presence on the World Wide Web. With Weezer.net and Weezer.com now pointing Internet surfers to the same destination, the group remained focused with Ocasek, trimming the list of contenders down to a realistic eighteen tracks. They were: "If You Want It," "Sugar Booger,"

"Island in the Sun," "Crab," "Childhood Ties," "Don't Let Go," "Inside a Smile," "Hash Pipe," "O Girlfriend," "I Wish You Luck," "Gimmie Some Love," "Starlight," "Teenage Victory Song," "Knock-down Drag-out," "O Lisa," "Break-Up," "Homely," and "Always."

Of these songs, one in particular, "Island in the Sun," would have probably been left behind without Ocasek pushing it back into the band's consciousness. "He had an old demo of it and we'd completely forgotten about it. But he said, 'That's a good song, you should do it,'" Pat remembered.

Five days after his arrival, Ocasek went back east for the Christmas holiday, with plans to on return December 26 to commence work in the recording studio. Despite a week of time off planned prior to the Goat Punishment shows, the Weezer boys decided to ditch the break in favor of continued rehearsals. Rivers, Pat, Brian, and Mikey were each determined to be ready when recording kicked off two days after Christmas.

By all observations, the Goat Punishment club shows and the KROQ Christmas gigs — which saw Weezer perform alongside modern rock luminaries like No Doubt, Moby, Deftones, Incubus, Papa Roach, Coldplay, Moby, and At the Drive-In — were rock extravaganzas. Of the =w= live spectacle, *Los Angeles Times* critic Steve Hochman wrote, "Weezer has picked up where it left off, with leader Rivers Cuomo's brand of power-pop balancing bright melodies with brooding lyrics, refreshed and renewed after the hiatus."

When Ocasek came back to Los Angeles on the 27th, the group embarked on what would be close to six weeks of studio work by playing tunes like "Don't Let Go" and "Knock-down Drag-out" repetitively in order to track bass and drum parts. They also captured "scratch takes" of the vocals and guitar, designed to get accurate rhythm tracks before being redone to perfection later in the album-making process.

"He just says, 'Do it again,'" laughed Wilson, a Ludwig Vistalite enthusiast, while thinking about Ric's production approach. "He's a good presence to have around in the studio, a swell guy."

Midway through basic tracking on the fourth day of recording, the band left to do the month's third Goat Punishment show at the Knitting Factory. The following night's gig down in San Diego with Blink-182, New Found Glory, and Lefty meant that the band wouldn't be back at Cello Studios until New Year's Day. The band — along with manager Pat Magnarella and booking agent Jenna Adler — donated proceeds from the Goat Punishment event to the medical bill fund of Petra Haden, who had been the victim of a hit and run earlier in the year but was lacking insurance to cover her enormous medical bills.

Picking up studio work where they left off late on New Year's Day, Weezer and Ocasek persisted in perfecting the rhythm tracks. The band was pleased with its progress until, on the tenth day at Cello, the Interscope henchman dropped by to rain on Weezer's parade. Startling the band, the label higher-ups announced their dissatisfaction with several tracks. Concerns over how this might impact their already tight schedule — with the Yahoo! tour looming — sparked a lengthy caucus. Eventually the meeting forced the band to discard a few of the album contenders, but a new song, "Gonna Make My Move," bubbled up.

That week, Wilson — always lucky when it came to getting on television — wound up on NBC's *The Tonight Show with Jay Leno* when the show's star and crew knocked on the door of his Los Angeles apartment, as part of a bit he does from time to time. Filming an impromptu segment with Leno, which aired on January 9, the drummer informed a national television audience that he played in Weezer and once almost appeared on the show with the band. He then broke into versions of a few Elvis classics, belting out "Love Me Tender," while standing adjacent to the host and a

Presley impersonator. For Patrick's unexpected performance, Weezer scored a nice plug when the show's producers ran a brief snippet of the "Buddy Holly" video during the bit.

Back at Cello after the Interscope buzz kill, the group relocated into a smaller studio in a different part of the facility where Rivers and Brian got to work on guitar takes, while the whole band put down vocals. Mikey — mostly a novice when it came to recording in a state-of-the-art facility — corrected his bass lines under Cuomo's strict direction. "Rivers can be extremely particular when working in the studio," Ocasek observed. "He can get hung up on something that's extremely small. And until he thinks it's right, he'll persist on that one little thing. I've seen him find fault with bass parts that virtually sound perfect on tape. And he'll make them be done over and over again until he felt that the moment clicked."

Ridiculously picky or tremendously focused, Team Weezer was determined to kick some studio ass, as the band's guitarists put basic rhythm guitar tracks on twelve songs in one day. During another session, upon discovering the studio's air conditioning system was causing their guitars to go out of tune, Cuomo and Bell played for ten hours in an uncomfortable, sauna-like atmosphere to keep to their recording timeline.

"[Rivers] always does his guitar parts in one take," said Ocasek. "With guitar stuff, Rivers barely ever fixes anything, which is very cool. He doesn't like loud volume; when he recorded his guitar tracks for that album, he turned the volume down way low. You could almost hear the strings being hit in the studio without the amp. And then you'd push it up and it would be perfect. Or you'd run through a take, and he'd hear something and he'd say, I've got to fix something in the third verse. But it would be something I hadn't even heard yet. We'd go right to that spot. He'd fix it. And then he'd get up and go away. He kind of left a lot of the sound up to me, like he didn't want to be bothered with it."

Two weeks into the process, Koch — witnessing everything firsthand — informed Karl's Korner readers that things were really shaping up. Taking a swipe at Weezer's label heads, he wrote, "I really can't believe the criticism we've encountered on this project so far. I, for one, believe that the naysayers will be proven utterly wrong."

Three weeks into the sessions, guitar work had all but wrapped up and Rivers was hard at work on his lead vocals, testing out different microphones and alternate keys. After several days cutting multiple takes for each song, Ocasek and the project's engineer, Ken Allardyce, spent time "comping" Cuomo's efforts. Allardyce had engineered Green Day's 2000 album *Warning* and the Goo Goo Dolls' 1998 smash *Dizzy Up the Girl*. Ken had been recommended to Weezer by Magnarella who, at the time, also managed Green Day.

"I think we all knew we had good songs," Allardyce remembers of the hiatus-breaking third album. "There was a lot of uncertainty on behalf of the band members, not so much with Rivers — or perhaps his was manifested in his seriousness. The band members' uncertainties lay in other areas; Rivers played his cards close to his chest and kept them guessing a lot."

Allardyce says the group exhibited some worry about how the record might be perceived. "Of course they were concerned," he said. "All bands are. Rivers' work ethic and attention to detail is indicative of this. I don't think that the hiatus made them any more concerned, although they were certainly aware that their fans were waiting and anticipating the record.

"Band decisions were for the most part Rivers'," the project's engineer continued, "and the band was very much his mouthpiece, which undoubtedly caused some tension on occasion. I found the band guys pleasant and easy to work with and Rivers was easy to work with. He knew what he wanted and is such a good player that we didn't spend much time screwing around."

Again, Cuomo was making it clear that Weezer was his band and, for the most part, he had a vision in the studio. "To a degree he was receptive to ideas from Ric, less so from the band as he pretty much knew the parts he wanted," Allardyce recollected. "As far as the sound, both Ric and Rivers let me get on with it."

"It's a weird thing because you're basically hiring someone else to disagree with you," Cuomo said of Ocasek. "If he wasn't around I would have done things exactly my way. He was right on a lot of counts."

With the ever-important mixing phase of the disc fast approaching, Cuomo decided to take the results of Weezer's work at Cello and put it in the hands of Miami-based studio wiz Tom Lord-Alge. With that process slated to begin on January 31 in Southern Florida, Rivers continued obsessing over his comeback album. Ocasek, however, returned home to New York before flying in to join Cuomo in Miami. Leaving the band to wrap up work in Los Angeles, Allardyce says that Ocasek's exit from that piece of the project left the Weezer frontman to his own devices. "[Rivers] did what he wanted after that."

Still, the facility began to resemble an infirmary when Welsh got food poisoning, followed by Cuomo contracting a sore throat. A doctor's prescription numbed Cuomo's voice long enough to tweak some vocal lines, and by the following day, the band's thirtieth in the studio, Cuomo's pipes were on the mend. The final hours in Los Angeles were spent putting background vocals on "Starlight" and perfecting "Island in the Sun."

"Working with Weezer was a fairly joyless affair," says Allardyce, summing up his involvement with the group. "This was not a happy band having a fun time. However the music was good and this is how I generally characterize a project. I would say it was fulfilling and creatively rewarding, but without some of the fun that usually accompanies working with bands."

Wilson was absent from the bulk of the session and completely out of the mixing process, getting his drumkit duties out of the way early, in order to return home to Portland for a few weeks of home studio recording as The Special Goodness. "I [recorded] while the rest of the guys were finishing up the new Weezer record," Wilson admitted later. "I kind of hesitate to tell people that because I don't want people to think, you know [we're breaking up]. We're not going to, obviously, but people say that all the time."

Guitarist Brian Bell was also absent from the mixing process, leaving the rest of the Weezer posse — obviously still a much frailer collective than the outside world knew — to touch down in Miami on the last day of January 2001. Rivers, along with companions Mikey and Karl, went straight to Lord-Alge's South Beach Studios facility, where they found him already at work behind the mixing console; the tapes from Cello had been sent by Federal Express in advance of Weezer's arrival. Lord-Alge, who already had a long resumé of mixing credits with Sarah McLachlan, Oasis, U2, the Rolling Stones, Peter Gabriel, Marilyn Manson, *and* Hanson, believed in pumping out the mixes in rapid succession, averaging a song or more per day.

"At the beginning of a project I like to sit with the band and talk with them, and just get to know each other and shoot ideas," said Lord-Alge, shortly after the Weezer sessions. "Sometimes the record company or the producer is also there, and my job is to digest all the different things they may be saying and come up with something that makes everyone happy. Then I like to be left alone with the tape, because I feel that the music speaks for itself. When I'm nearing completion of a song, usually in the afternoon or early evening, I'll call the band or producer in, and I have no problems if they don't like a mix and want to make changes. I bring objectivity, and part of that is being able to say, 'this part isn't working,' and then being able to make it work. I try to get everything to work in the service of the song."

So while Lord-Alge was hard at work on the completed track "Gimmie Some Love," the members of the Weezer camp that had made the trip to Florida reunited with Ocasek for the first of an eleven-day stay. As Tom mixed, Rivers touched up various vocal and guitar lines.

"He's extremely, extremely talented," Ocasek stressed of the Weezer leader after the sessions. "Even instrumentally, he's way beyond what he plays. He pulls it way back. He does some amazing things in the studio that would really shock people. He does all his guitars in one take. He can do the most intricate things in one take and then say, 'Let me just fix the second bar in the third verse.' He's amazing."

Largely there to oversee matters and tweak parts of tracks, Cuomo — with Welsh and Koch along for the ride — caught movies, took golf lessons, and even took in a soccer match at the Orange Bowl between the U.S. and Colombian national teams. But the kings of nerd rock were no doubt out of place among all of the Armani-clad, Cristal-sippers in South Beach.

Cuomo and Koch addressed Weezer's business affairs, scheduled photo shoots, honed in on album art ideas, and considered merchandise designs. And Cuomo took Weezer's third album down to the wire by fixating on "Crab," a tune that had yet to be mixed. Demonstrative of his perfectionism, Rivers cut close to two dozen vocal takes in a row before he would hand "Crab" off to Lord-Alge — who was just a few days away from honoring his commitment — for a final mix.

"It was Rivers' idea to use a big-time mixer like Tom Lord-Alge, and I didn't know how that was going to be when we went down to Florida," Ric Ocasek says. "But Tom nailed it right away. And you know, when I saw Rivers smile — he walked into the studio, heard it, smiled, and walked out — it was great. And it sounded phenomenal the way he mixed it. Tom works really quickly. He just does a couple a day. The first song might take a day, but once he's locked into it he's doing two a day. Which is kind of cool. You don't need to wait too long. I'd take them up to the hotel room at night and think, 'He nailed it. He nailed them all.'"

Toward the end, Rivers was the only member of the band left in Miami, as Mikey took a short break from his scrutinizing boss. Even in the eleventh hour, Cuomo was still at it, perfecting two songs for the project that showed the softer side of Weezer. Obsessed with getting things right on the ballad "Always" for his comeback attempt, the geek-rock icon decided — in the absence of his band — that one of the tunes (known at the time as "New Song") couldn't be finished in time to give to Lord-Alge, so he'd have to bring it back to Los Angeles for completion and mixing.

When fans learned that Cuomo was holed up at South Beach Studios, they showed up only to be sent away. "Please do not take this sort of thing personally," Koch wrote to fans of his friend and employer. "It's sometimes just not the best time for Rivers, who is known for his bouts of shyness and intense concentration on the work at hand." While he wasn't up for autographs that week, Rivers was able to pull himself away from the studio to head to a midnight beach party celebrating the arrival of a full moon.

"Rivers does have a nice, strange personality, which I like," Ocasek opined. "He can be very communicative, depending on what he wants to talk about. He's definitely in his own world, but he's logical about stuff. He knows what he wants to do, and he'll go after it. When he needs to be verbal, he certainly can be."

The final two days found Cuomo again working intently, polishing everything he could in the presence of Lord-Alge. After revisiting several tunes, final mix-downs on five songs — "Gonna Make My Move," "Teenage Victory Song," "O Lisa," "Hash Pipe," and "Gimmie Some Love" (again) — occurred during Rivers' final day at South Beach Studios.

After delaying his flight home by a day in order to wrap work on "Always," an understandably exhausted Cuomo left the song in Lord-Alge's hands as tour and promotional responsibilities loomed in Los Angeles.

The full Weezer line-up reconvened in L.A. a few days later for press responsibilities, band rehearsals, and the recording of "New Song." In the short period between the Miami trip and preceding the Yahoo! Tour, Cuomo was still fiddling with the record, editing songs at Music Grinder Studios as he handled interviews. "There's a lot of girl songs," Cuomo told *Rolling Stone* point blank. "After all these years of pop music, why are there so many girl songs? What else is there to write about?"

It might have seemed simple to readers, but Cuomo was still uptight, obsessing over the supposedly finished record, making last-minute changes, and working Koch to the bone on the eve of the tour. "I'm sitting there and Rivers is like, "I wanna hear what this sounds like with an extra bridge,'" Koch recounted later. "So I'm on my computer making a kind of a rough remix. It doesn't even sound that good because it's not a quality dub. I'm sitting there cutting and pasting stuff, saying, 'Alright, if the bridge was here,' and then, fooling around for a little while. I gotta burn a CD and get it to him and he's got to listen to it, and he's got to think if he likes that or not. So all these last-minute things: 'Is this right, is this right, should it be these chords,' and I just wanted it to be done. Every night I'd be up burning these practice discs to see what the stuff sounded like and I'd be up 'til four or five delivering the CD to him and collapsing."

"He went right to the edge on that one," Ocasek said. "You know sometimes when you're making a record you just don't want to leave it alone. I think with record making, especially for a songwriter like Rivers, is that once it's finished the thrill is gone. It's not about putting out the record and seeing if it sells. That's really boring shit. The part that's great is making the record and going from nothing to something. As soon as it's born, then you might as well go to the next one. Sure there's the touring and playing live, but you know, fuck that stuff. That's not the fun part for a songwriter. It was never the fun part for me. I just wanted to make the next fucking record. Touring always kept me from writing. And I think the same goes for him."

JAY BLAKESBERG

Shred 'Til You're Dead: Rivers has an out-of-body moment while Mikey keeps on keepin' on

Cuomo's perfectionism resulted in the forthcoming album being remastered several times, even after the Outloud Tour had gotten under-way. Yet even at this late stage, right before the tour was to begin, Weezer's scheduled meeting with the often critical and at times downright negative record company executives had them all a bundle of nerves. After all of Cuomo's attention to detail the most important question was, Would the Interscope suits like the final product? Schur and the Interscope suits would have to be insane not to run with the record. Not a note had been played yet on the Yahoo! Outloud Tour, but it was a sold-out success. Web traffic on Weezer.com was so heavy that the site had become "gridlocked" and modern rock radio stations were inundated with requests for Weezer hits of yore.

Upon meeting with the label the day after Valentine's Day (and Weezer's ninth anniversary as a band), all of Cuomo's fears were assuaged when Interscope execs said they loved the disc. "They had nothing but supportive and excited things to say about it," Koch immediately informed fans in a somewhat sugar-coated post. "All the comments and talk being spoken tonight were positive and definitely the kind of things we were hoping they would say. And these were thoughtful and insightful comments, not just empty enthusiasm. It seems that all the late night recording and mixing and countless hours of detail work to the point of total exhaustion have paid off. While it is of course YOUR opinions that matter most to Weezer, getting the record company on Weezer's side is simply essential to the process . . . so, right on!"

That said, both fans and the band were bummed to learn that a penciled-in release date of April 17 had been erased with no date in mind to supplant it. The Interscope suits were so elated that they wouldn't commit to a release date at all. The problem lay in "Hash Pipe," Rivers' controversial choice for a lead single, which lyrically focuses on a transvestite prostitute and has been described by the man himself as a combination of Aldo Nova's "Fantasy" and the riff from "The Spyhunter Theme."

"I get so irritated by the pressure and that sense of responsibility to one's audience that I just want to put out an insane song to scare everybody away," Cuomo ranted. "And that's what all the stress was about today, because the president of our record company, the president of MTV, and our manager all called me — everyone's haranguing me about switching the single."

Calling the lyrics to the song "totally gay," Rivers — aside from unveiling an apparent homophobia — explained, "When I wrote 'Hash Pipe' I was completely oblivious to the words. I was very drunk and ended up writing a very 'homo' song. I only realized six months later when I was transcribing it. I was like, 'Wait a minute.'

"I put myself through an experiment as a songwriter," Cuomo continued. "I set my alarm really early and I got up at, like, six in the morning. And I took a bunch of Ritalin and had like three shots of tequila. And then I just went into my backyard and started pacing frantically, and I wrote the song in my head, wired. It's pretty funny."

As for the pressure to get him to change his mind and go with the probable album-opener "Don't Let Go" as first single, Rivers said, "They wanted something more straight up. Man, it was a huge fight."

In a meeting with Weezer's longtime manager Pat Magnarella and executives from Interscope and MTV, Cuomo started screaming in frustration. If they were all out to prove the Weezer chief wrong, he said, the move would cost Magnarella dearly in terms of his commissions in the coming months. Not to be swayed, Rivers stuck to his instinct that day in mid-February, when he declared, "As of right now, 'Hash Pipe' it is."

If anything, the brisk sales for Weezer's Yahoo! Outloud Tour — underwritten by the search engine and sponsored by Pepsi and Hewlett-Packard — affirmed that the future of the group was bright. For instance, the 4,500 tickets for the March 9 Chicago show at the Aragon Ballroom sold out in a single day three months in advance of the gig. In fact, fifteen of the twenty dates, totaling 90% of the trek, sold out before any advertising was announced beyond the World Wide Web.

Talking about the successful presale, Ticketmaster.com President Tom Stockham called Weezer's ticket strategy "the wave of the future." Yahoo! Entertainment made no secret that the group was handpicked to headline the tour due to its extremely "wired" fanbase. "We looked and said to ourselves, 'Who is the largest wired demographic online? College students," Yahoo! representative Tiffany Hein said in a junket to promote the tour.

"Promoting exclusively online wasn't without effort, but it was without the costs of television advertising and radio advertising and so on," Stockham said at the time. "It was a perfect way to target Weezer's audience." The low advance ticket price — a mere $15 — and The Get Up Kids, also served as motivators for buyers of the nearly 87,000 tickets.

"We've always had a loyal fanbase," Cuomo soon boasted of the sold-out tour. "We've always sold out shows."

"I've heard they took a poll on their Web page for the bands Weezer fans would like to see touring with Weezer," said Get Up Kids drummer Ryan Pope days before the tour started. "I guess it's a good thing we share a lot of the same fans. When you break it down it's all pop rock for the kids to bob their heads to. I think Weezer puts on a really good show, and I think most people that are into them, that aren't familiar with us, can dig our songs."

With 99% of the studio work on the disc behind them, Mikey — now free of his hideous cop moustache — and Pat re-joined Rivers and Brian in Los Angeles a week before the tour's scheduled February 21 launch in Austin, Texas. In between practices to prep for the road, the band shot the album cover photo for the forthcoming disc, which consisted of the band against a lime green backdrop in a manner resembling 1994's *Blue Album*, paying homage to working with Ocasek again. The identifiable concept would also let record buyers know that Weezer were again back to basics, and getting a copy of the new disc meant exposure to a catchy melodic sound akin to "Undone" and "Buddy Holly."

"I set out to design the package exactly how I would want it, and it just turns out that it's very similar to the first album," Cuomo would later admit. "I'm the same person as I was then, pretty much. I have the same taste so I don't see why it should be different."

The color not only signified the label's "green light" on the project, but the "green" money that was nearly guaranteed to come the group's way as attendees of their upcoming tour were a given to plunk down $16.99 for a copy of the new CD. Like the band's debut, 2001's Weezer offering would also be self-titled, but would nearly immediately be known by fans as *The Green Album*.

With the album release date up in the air, the Outloud Tour got underway in late February at the Austin Music Hall. A step up from the previous summer's club trek, this tour found Weezer playing against a backdrop decorated like a high-school dance — complete with colored streamers and basketball hoops. Still apprehensive about the corporate endorsement, Cuomo dictated that the sponsors could not put their booths too close to the stage. However, little things — like the poster Yahoo! put together — irked the band.

Despite the aversion to corporate sponsorship, it was hard to argue with the dirt-cheap ticket prices. "There's no way to do a concert, a concert like this, at the prices that we're charging," Koch explained. "It's like, if it's gonna be all this stuff and it's gonna be forty bucks, what's the point? But because it's cheap, it's like, if you don't like the displays and the stuff they're bringing in, don't look at them. You're only paying fifteen bucks."

Early on in the tour, Cuomo found himself with a few days off in the Fort Lauderdale area and booked studio time at Loconto Productions' Sunrise Studio. Over the course of two days, he managed to cut three new, experimental demos at the facility. Describing the arrangements on "Listen Up," "Keep Fishin'," and "High Up Above," Koch called the material "very hokey," "down home," and "not rockin'."

With these demos, Rivers was already focusing on the future of the band. Describing the new material for album number four, he said, "I've been writing songs every day. I'm just so excited about these new songs. I can't wait to do them. It used to piss me off, like, 'Why can't we make records like regular people?' But now we're making up for it. We have, like, 100 songs that are of the same quality as the [third] record. We're gonna keep pumping 'em out."

If fans were ecstatic about the tour, Doug Levy — who reviewed the band's New York show at Roseland for *Dotmusic.com* — had mixed opinions of Weezer circa 2001. Calling "Island in the Sun" a "major let-down," Levy said that the new material was "no major departure from what the band was doing half a decade ago" while criticizing the new tunes for lacking "those magic hooks" of yore. If Weezer was "a long way away from becoming dinosaurs," in this critic's eyes, these slightly older dogs had no new tricks.

Later on in the trek, with a day off between shows, Cuomo was again eyeing Weezer's fourth album by booking time in an area studio. Akin to the Sunrise demos, Rivers — whom associates described at the time as "inspiring," "extremely guarded," "incredibly bright," and "functionally nuts" — came away with two more album four contenders, "Saturday Night" and "Happy Grunge."

Backstage at Detroit's State Theatre, the somewhat socially inept Cuomo displayed his nightly routine in front of a reporter for *Blender*. "Want to see what I do every night?" he asked the scribe as he stopped in front of an open door to a room full of female fans with backstage access. Spotted by one of the smitten disciples, Rivers began faking terrible internal pains, bowed over, and backed away. Apologizing, he ran away, up a flight of stairs to a secure area in a fit of laughter, and yelling over his shoulder, "How awkward was that?"

If it was awkward for him, it was undoubtedly upsetting and disappointing to his fans. Again, Cuomo — who confessed on the tour that he often just went from the bus to the venue and back to the bus again — was still

JASON NELSON/BLISTERING.COM

Hit That Kit: Camouflage or not, Patrick can't disguise his need for rock

having trouble living up to the expectations of full disclosure that usually accompany being a rock star. Not that it meant he was heading back into seclusion. In fact, Rivers was finally easing into adulthood in his own unique way, had more confidence than ever, and had every intention of kicking ass.

As they played to 9,000 fans in San Francisco near the end of the tour, Weezer's future album and single plans became official. Their third studio album — and first since 1996 — would be released on May 15, 2001. And the disc's lead-off single would officially hit radio several weeks in advance of the long player.

From a business standpoint, the results of the innovative, month-long Outloud Tour were extremely positive. "Weezer is smart," Marc Geiger, CEO of Artistdirect.com, said after the San Diego finale. "They know where the world is going and know they do not have or cannot count on airplay, so they leverage the Web. The only issue is that one out of 1,000 artists are doing this effectively today. I absolutely believe that any artist who has a fanbase and reaches out to them, programs to them, offers them special access, will grow their base, their sales and find a more loyal audience that will stick with them longer. Artists who learn how to build a community will find what the hippie bands already know: It is all about word of mouth."

"When you're dealing with a niche audience, a sense of community is extremely important," said Ari Sass, co-founder of online indie-rock retailer Insound. Weezer let people feel "like they [were] part of something special that speaks to them as an individual."

The band defied all conventional wisdom on how to stay popular, and Perry Lavoisne of concert and radio conglomerate Clear Channel explained the fans' frenzied reaction. "It was pretty much the same as when these classic rock bands go back out for the first time," he said. "The fans just come out."

And even though the tour was a complete success, Rivers Cuomo was concerned about the impact it had on his core audience. He listened when followers expressed anger over the corporate sponsor and cried "sell-out." Empathizing with the skepticism of his loyal fans, Rivers recognized the affiliation with Yahoo! was a big mistake. "I understand why they would be bummed out," he said midway through the jaunt. "We're not going to do [a tour like this] again. It's just kind of creepy: 'Yahoo! Outloud featuring Weezer.' It just kind of creeps me out."

chapter twenty-three

golden *green*

After wrapping up the Yahoo! Outloud commitment, the men of Weezer scheduled a few weeks off in late March 2001 to recharge their batteries. Patrick went home to Portland to again focus on The Special Goodness, Brian and Mikey got some rest and relaxation, and even Cuomo — these days a workaholic — took a sorely needed, albeit brief, vacation to Puerta Vallarta with a lady friend named Kelley.

As April began, the foursome regrouped in Los Angeles to prep for an imminent tour of Japan, finalize B-sides for "Hash Pipe," and lens a video for that song with "it" director of the moment, Marcos Siega. In the meantime, Rivers continued to work on tracks, overnighting mixes back and forth with Tom Lord-Alge right up to the time the group boarded their plane for the Far East. In the final hours before heading to LAX, Cuomo finally decided on the official track listing for the disc. The running order of the album would be: "Don't Let Go," "Photograph" (previously known as "If You Want It"), "Hash Pipe," "Island in the Sun," "Crab," "Knock-down Drag-out," "Smile" (trimmed down from the aforementioned "Inside a Smile"), "Simple Pages" (which at the last minute replaced "Teenage Victory Song"), "Glorious Day" (previously known as "Gonna Make My Move"), and "O Girlfriend." Bumped altogether was "O Lisa," a contender to the end. The U.K. edition of the record would also house a bonus tune, "I Do," while the Japanese version also featured that song and "The Christmas Song."

Shortly after the album was shipped off to New York for mastering by Vlado Meller at Sony Music Studios that month, someone at the mastering studio stole an unfinished copy of the disc and leaked MP3s of the incomplete, out-of-sequence material to file-sharing services like Morpheus and Napster. Cuomo, himself a Napster advocate known for a time to download "lots of '80s songs," had become a victim of the piracy, and was understandably upset by the theft of his new record.

Aside from this irritation, tensions within the band began to crop up again, as evidenced by a *CMJ New Music Monthly* feature that ran the same month. In a magazine piece designed to represent the new and improved Weezer, poor Brian was asked in front of Cuomo about his side band, the Space Twins. Replying to the inquiry, Bell started talking. "It was a whole different thing . . ."

Evidently, this was a big no-no with the boss.

"It's a *Weezer* interview," Cuomo interjected, cutting off bandmate. "We don't need to talk about the other shit." When reporter Jon Regardie interpreted the domineering frontman's move as a joke, laughing along, Rivers tossed him a blank stare to show him he meant serious business. "We don't need to talk about it," he informed the *CMJ* scribe. What Cuomo would talk about, however, was his fear of getting too popular "in a crossover way that pisses off fans."

The Weezer Army — arguably the strongest Internet-using fanbase in rock — was his bread and butter and he knew it. After all, fans had little trouble letting him know about their dissatisfaction with moves like playing alongside commercial punks like Blink-182 or tying in with a sponsor for their U.S. tour. Those very same fans had logged one million hits to *Weezer.com* by this stage, and as a way of saying thanks, loyalists were rewarded with some free, old-school Goat Punishment MP3s from the 1998 Nirvana tribute show. Meanwhile, "Hash Pipe" had already begun getting airplay on critical radio outlets like WHFS in D.C., Y100 in Philly and, thankfully, by the ever-influential KROQ in L.A., where it became the top requested song on the station.

Within days, the Weezer camp was denying published reports they would be joining the 2001 Warped caravan. Despite announcements early in the year via both Karl's Korner and the official Warped Web site that indicated Weezer would be playing some dates on the annual punk rock caravan, it was not to be. Festival promoters insisted Weezer dropped out of the line-up, but Weezer disagreed, saying that while Weezer had been offered the tour, Cuomo never signed a contract or formally accepted the offer.

Elsewhere, it seemed as if Interscope executives were trying to derail the incredible momentum that *The Green Album* was gaining by attempting to bump back the planned May release. "It is true that the record label had tried to further push it back 'til June," Koch reported at the time. "But this did NOT go over well with the band. In a heated, behind-the-scenes debate with some label higher-ups, the exasperated guys got their way, and May 15 stuck."

Dave Richards, program director at Chicago's Q101, wasn't surprised that Cuomo got his way. Calling the upcoming disc a "sleeping giant," he marveled at how this band with minimal if any sex appeal managed to sell out a tour online some seven years after its first hit. "You can usually tell when a band still has 'it,' when six years after a hit they are causing commotion, selling out shows. You know something is going on."

And something was indeed going on at Universal Studios' backlot on April 10, as Marcos Siega directed the "Hash Pipe" clip. On a set designed to look like a sumo wrestling ring, the band spent a full day on performance footage, with Siega later incorporating shots of several real, 500-pound sumo wrestlers. "They look especially large standing next to me, because I'm very small," Cuomo said after the shoot. "They have huge tits. We heard T&A videos were big, so this is our version of a T&A video. There's some serious ass shots that you won't believe."

By the time the band hopped a plane to the country where sumo wrestling originated, the internal stresses on public display in the CMJ piece were gone — temporarily at least. During the tour, Weezer's live sets were peppered with surprises. One night, at Tokyo's Blitz venue, the band unearthed "Butterfly," which it hadn't played live since 1997. Another night, in Sendai, as the band learned of Joey Ramone's passing, Welsh dedicated "Only in Dreams" to the late punk icon. And following an Osaka gig, Cuomo informed the crowd he was off to a specific Shinsaibashi nightclub. At the stroke of midnight, Rivers flowed into Club Stomp, gave out autographs, and spoke with fans.

When the band rocked Hiroshima on Welsh's thirtieth birthday, drum tech Atom Willard brought a cake onstage and the audience sang "The Birthday Song" to him. After blowing out the candles, the cake was dumped on Mikey's head and he wound up playing an encore with cake frosting covering his bass guitar and upper torso. It wouldn't be the last time Mikey would be publicly ridiculed by his bandmates.

Back in the States, promotion for *The Green Album* was underway. MTV2 sponsored record-listening parties, and the band played a high profile performance at California's Coachella Arts and Music Festival. Appearing alongside techno-specialist Fatboy Slim and recently reformed headliners Jane's Addiction, Weezer set off brand new rock 'n' roll dynamite like "Photograph" and "Hash Pipe" with Schur there to show his support in the pre-album build-up.

The show was a rousing success by all counts, although Cuomo would later criticize the event for its lack of illicit substances. "I fully expected that to be the totally decadent event, and it was really lame, older Dave Matthews Band–style fans. And no drugs at all! It's insane," he said half seriously. "I mean, it's a Jane's Addiction show! You'd expect somebody to be smoking some pot or something, but everyone was drinking bottled water."

Following Coachella, the members of Weezer went back down to Los Angeles to take care of more press duties and ready themselves for the looming Hooptie Tour, a month-long promo outing slated to launch in San Diego on May 8. In the wake of the new album, a surprising follow-up article appeared in the May 2001 *Alternative Press*. Despite his controversial January 1997 *AP* feature, writer David Daley was given a second crack at the band. Daley had been the target of much criticism, specifically by Cuomo and Bell, in the months after the first piece ran.

Portraying Weezer as nerd rockers coping with a second run of success and self-confidence, Daley marveled at how Cuomo's return to the spotlight once seemed as unlikely as 1991 one-hit wonders EMF topping the U.S. charts a second time. And as the article unfolds, Rivers is clearly in defense mode over what went down when they first encountered each other in a Sydney, Australia, hotel back in late 1996. Cuomo was careful not to repeat the same mistake twice, sitting down with the writer in the presence of his bandmates this time out. Perhaps in an effort to prevent the type of responses that fueled Weezer's 1997 implosion, the five-foot-six Cuomo sat silent for the first fifteen minutes of the interview, letting Bell — who delivered mostly clichés and short responses — do nearly all of the talking. And Brian's words were about as revelatory as Rivers' lyrics for the *The Green Album* would pan out to be.

By the time Cuomo opened up, it was to look back on *Pinkerton*, but he didn't give Daley anything Weezer fans didn't already know, talking about how he was surprised that it wasn't a success right off the bat. "I was truly excited," he said. "I thought we had come up with a great new sound. It seemed important and meaningful and I thought people were going to like it. Instead, it seemed like everybody hated it. So I was totally disappointed."

When asked about lyrical themes, Cuomo shrugged blankly, proving that his new, predominantly vague lyrics yielded pretty mundane interview responses. "I guess I'm still writing about the same stuff." In fact, the only real interesting bit in Daley's second Weezer feature is elicited when Rivers comes clean about his new single. "'Hash Pipe' is about being a transvestite prostitute, which is something I've never written about before," he admitted. "That's the first time I ever wrote a song telling a story from a fictional point of view instead of a real life experience.

"I mean, yeah, [the record's] definitely less personal," Cuomo affirmed.

"*Except* 'Hash Pipe,'" an also present Koch interjected rather comically, in the presence of Daley. Cuomo's guard was completely thrown off.

"Fucker," retorted Rivers. And then a rare glimpse of the real Cuomo, complete with a sense of humor, shines through. "Maybe that was what I did in 1999. Yeah, now I remember. . . ."

Wrapping up his second, noticeably tame encounter with Daley, Rivers had emerged victorious, retaining control of the interview. Cuomo explained that he was optimistic about the future of the band and revealed plans for a fourth album, now that he was back in the creative groove.

Weezer's fans were reassured of that sentiment as they downloaded MP3s of the leaked mixes. Meanwhile, the hard rocking, metal-laced "Hash Pipe" continued picking up steam at radio. The video for the song surfaced on Canadian video outlet MuchMusic in early May, beating MTV to the punch and debuting the song's video intact. Oddly, MTV viewers were forced to endure an edited version of the clip when it premiered a few days later. Titled "H*** Pipe," the tune was inexplicably censored; however, the same powers-that-be at the leading music video network deemed that close shots of sumo wrestlers' ass cheeks were suitable for those tuning in.

Censoring the word was hypocritical. After all, MTV repeatedly aired Tom Petty's pot-endorsing "Last Dance with Mary Jane" eight years earlier and has had little worry over objectifying women in its twenty-plus–year history. As for MuchMusic leaving the clip as is, Sarah Crawford, a representative for that network said, "We didn't see 'Hash Pipe' as any sort of glamorization of illegal drug use."

The song wasn't about doing drugs, it was merely a hook-injected rocker about a stoned transsexual prostitute looking for work on Santa Monica Boulevard. The fact that the song title and content were censored by MTV — from the very start — couldn't keep the song off *Total Request Live*, its daily countdown show.

Calling MTV "such a vulgar channel," a half-serious Rivers was nonetheless pleased but surprised to be on *TRL*. "We're way too weird to have mainstream success," he said, evidently blocking out the first Weezer frenzy of '94 and '95. Apparently KROQ disagreed with him, delving into "Photograph," a second track from the record.

By the eve of the Hooptie tour, Cuomo had become displeased enough with manager Pat Magnarella that he was looking to dump him and began seeking advice. Taking lunches with various power players, including his record company's namesake, David Geffen, and independent, punk-minded successes like Fat Wreck Chords founder "Fat Mike" Burkett, Rivers was weighing his options.

After a photo shoot for *Entertainment Weekly* one morning in the first week of May, Cuomo hopped a plane to San Francisco. As he described the events of his post-shoot day, R.C. was careful not to let anything specific out yet about his decision. "I went to the airport and had a meeting at the gate with my business manager," he said the following day. "We had some very important business to discuss. There's some crazy things happening right now and I'm not at liberty to discuss them, but there's some serious stress happening and I had to talk to him."

Soon after, Rivers was sitting in first class aboard a San Francisco–

bound plane to meet with Fat Mike for dinner. "He filled me in on what it's like to run a record company," Rivers said of the meeting, hesitant to reveal the truth yet. "I don't have a desire to do that, but I'm just interested in learning more about that side of it. Then we went to a very strange club and saw a man dressed up as Hitler spanking a girl with sausage links. Then I went back to my hotel room and went to sleep."

Fat Mike recalled the incident. "We took him to a club called Stinky's Peep Show," he laughed at the memory. "It's sick — it's a punk rock strip club, sort of. But it's a club for fat girls. All the strippers are fat chicks. Some of us have a preference or fetish for fat girls. It's always a different show; you never know what's going to happen. I've seen pizza-eating contests and tubs of pudding — weird stuff. So that night there happened to be 'Hitler the Butcher' and a woman who looked like the St. Pauli Girl or a Swiss Miss maid. And she ended up strangling Hitler to death with the sausages. It was weird."

When it was suggested that it was an unorthodox place to have a business meeting, Fat Mike said, laughing louder, "I felt really weird because I'm a Jewish vegetarian. I was kind of freaked out. I have pictures of it, but I don't want those getting out.

"[Rivers] just called me up and said, 'Do you want to have dinner tomorrow night? I'll fly up.' I said 'sure.' We weren't that close, at the time I was probably closer with Mikey than Rivers.

"It was a funny dinner," Burkett continued of the meal preceding the sausage incident. "I remember, because first we were eating at a really nice restaurant and the first thing Rivers does is put his laptop on the table. I was like, 'That's weird.'"

Getting to the crux of the meeting, Fat Mike said, "He actually asked more about self-management. My band, NOFX, has always been self-managed. So he just wanted to do what we do. We don't do press, so it's a lot easier for us. So I said, 'Rivers, you're in a big band and you do MTV and you do press, so, you have to have someone take care of you. But that person doesn't necessarily need to make ten or fifteen percent. You know, pay a bro' a hundred grand a year and have them take care of shit. Don't give someone a percentage. You have a huge fan base, you made a great album, and everyone is going to cover you.'

"And I guess he kind of took it to heart," Mike concluded.

Indeed he did, as Cuomo — along with the other members of the Weezer partnership — promptly fired Magnarella when he refused to reduce Atlas/Third Rail's commission rate as they insisted. Weezer attorney Peter Paterno — also representing Metallica, Silverchair, and the Goo Goo Dolls — was next to be sacked, when the group retained Michael Jackson's attorney at the time, John Branca, to replace him.

Magnarella responded by filing a superior court action seeking writs of attachment against Weezer. The band in turn filed a petition with the California Labor Commission two months later — on July 20 — seeking an order claiming its personal management contract with Third Rail was void on the ground that Magnarella's company was performing the functions of a talent agency without a license. As a result, Weezer — through its attorneys Stanton L. Stein and Yakub Hazzard — were seeking reimbursement of all amounts paid to Third Rail pursuant to the personal management contract in the year preceding the filing of the petition, as well as reimbursement of incurred attorney's fees relating to the proceeding.

In self-management mode, Rivers' world had become very stressful. "My life has become so intense at every moment that it's difficult to remember everything," he said in the hours before the Hooptie Tour. "For a while there, I was trying to avoid all stimuli, and I pretty much succeeded at that. I just rested for a long time. Then I started to follow my impulses more. The more I followed my impulses, the more active I seemed to become, to the point where it seems like I'm doing a billion things all at once."

Drastic changes in Rivers' behavior accompanied Weezer's successful return and Cuomo's increased management tasks. "I've only just started smoking for the first time in my life," the thirty-year-old explained that spring, as he learned to roll a cigarette with the help of a reporter from the NME. "I started to eat meat recently, too, and I've never done that before either. I was raised a vegetarian."

Excited by the virgin experience of using tobacco, Cuomo couldn't explain why he had been undergoing such drastic changes in behavior. When asked if he was going through a mid-life crisis, Rivers — possibly thinking about his youth on the ashram and the absence of his father — replied, "Since the day I was born."

The Hooptie tour took Weezer to radio-sponsored performances and autograph sessions in unique venues like barbecue pits, bowling alleys, record stores, clam shacks, and skate parks. And in conjunction with their third album's release, they played at a handful of radio festivals that spring.

In the wake of the band's full schedule, including just-revealed plans to appear on the 2000–2001 season finale of NBC's long-running series *Saturday Night Live*, Rivers was worried about how Weezer's new disc would be received. "I don't expect it to succeed commercially, unlike everyone at the record company," he said. "They're all gonna be incredibly disappointed in a few weeks."

Concerned that his fans would hate his new lyrics and missing *Pinkerton*'s extremely emotional content, Cuomo acknowledged he was singing the new songs with less feeling, but contended that the new studio set was a stronger overall recording. The apprehensive rocker also started rallying for support from his loyalists.

"I would like to say one thing, and that's that I hope people stick with us," he pleaded. "All these records are just phases I go through, and when you're younger and kind of inexperienced, you go through more extreme phases, and *Pinkerton* is maybe on the emotionally extreme side. This record is on the anti-emotional extreme side. And I hope people stick with us, because in the future I'll be going back and forth and probably finding some middle ground that makes us all happy."

Rivers told the media it was his aim to write timeless standards from this point forward, aiming for mediocrity. While he contended he had no desire to leave behind an abstract body of work, the lyrical and musical uniqueness of his comeback single, "Hash Pipe," flew in the face of his conventional aspirations.

On Tuesday, May 15, 2001, Weezer fans nationwide flocked to their favorite record retailers to get their hands on Cuomo's first collection of new songs in fifty-six months. Upon cracking the cellophane on *Weezer* zealots were met with the quote "Torniamo all antico e sara un progresso," which loosely translated from Italian means "Let us return to old times and that will be progress."

And what they discovered was an instantly alluring record, starting with the perky and contagious, Kinks-circa-1965 strains of "Don't Let Go" — complete with "ooh whoa whoa" background vocals and a dated, kitschy synth line. Next up was "Photograph," a pop nugget of the highest order. Containing large guitar chords, candy-coated melodies, and bitchin' hand-claps, the song instantly invaded one's consciousness. If the aforementioned riff-roaring "Hash Pipe" was well received on the radio dial, "Island in the Sun" was a brilliant, minor-key tune — and future single — if ever there was one. Talking about the tropical flavor of the latter, Bell said at the time, "It's kind of a Caribbean sound. Then the chorus kicks in with distorted guitars. It's my favorite one because it takes you someplace else."

By design, *The Green Album* was a collection of ten virtual modern rock

singles. For instance, "Crab" was a memorable rocker with a soaring guitar line and innovative, layered vocals. Meanwhile, the perky-punk of
"Knock-down Drag-out" was a forceful homage to Green Day, offset by
the near-ballad drag of "Smile," arguably the most innocuous of a remarkable collection. The irresistible "Simple Pages" was propelled by a clean,
forceful guitar line, but it was the expertly crafted "Glorious Day," with its
slow build, that had a melodic brilliance few, if any, bands in rock could
rival. Wrapping the record was "O Girlfriend," the disc's most vulnerable
and heartfelt moment. Too fast to be deemed a ballad, but confessional in
a way the other nine were not, the song easily stood among the finest
Rivers Cuomo had ever written. The simplicity of heartbreak conveyed
with Cuomo's poignant delivery gave it a leg up on the others. Less revelatory lyrical themes ruled the record, but R.C. came close to redeeming
himself to the emo rock *Pinkerton* loyalists with this one moving number.

"Weezer fans are rabid and patient," observed Dave Leto of Rye Coalition.
"They all stood by them and just waited. When they came back it was like they
never left. All of the rumors about Rivers and all the stories about him on his
off time kept everyone wanting more. When they came back with the *Green*
album, it seemed as though they were more popular than ever."

Early reviews recognized the power of the comeback disc. *Flak
Magazine* called Weezer's second self-titled release, "a 29-minute pop/rock
bonanza." Elsewhere, *Kerrang!* awarded the succinct disc (which was actually only twenty-eight minutes long) 5 K's — the publication's highest
honor. "The chances of there being a better album than *The Green Album*
released this year are slim," the magazine professed. *Entertainment Weekly*
called it "a return to their winning formula of sugary power pop and smart-
assed rants," and bestowed it with a solid B+.

An essential four-star review in *Rolling Stone* was accompanied by these
words from Rob Sheffield: "They actually took the time to make a totally

crunk geek-punk record, buzzing through ten excellent tunes in less than half an hour with zero filler and enough psychosexual contortions to buy Cuomo's shrink another hot tub." Across the world in the land down under, Sydney's *The Daily Telegraph* also awarded it four stars, saying, "It's easy to criticize the instantly hummable 'Photograph' or 'Island in the Sun' as shallow and throwaway, but the fact is, no one does 'simple' guitar pop this well. No one's even close. Cuomo stands alone as the best pop melody writer around today, and *Weezer* is yet another exquisite collection that will bring out the obsessive in all of us. Don't believe me? Just try and turn it off."

The album lacked a lyric sheet because Cuomo branded the words to his songs as "terrible," but critics disagreed with his assessment en masse. Mixed critiques came from Isaac Guzman of the *New York Daily News*, who still gave a mostly positive assessment, calling the first half of the disc "nearly perfect." Dismissing *Pinkerton* as "a critical and commercial misstep," Guzman championed Rivers for reviving the group's "quirky, crunchy guitar riffs, blending influences as disparate as Black Sabbath, Kiss, the Beach Boys and the Pixies" on Weezer's third album.

Speaking of the Pixies, in talking to the just-launched rock magazine *Blender* for its premiere issue, Patrick noted that Weezer shared the unique intra-band dynamics of that seminal alternative band, citing dynamic frontman Black Francis, who was also emotionally distant and reluctant to share songwriting duties with bassist Kim Deal (who left to form the Breeders). Wilson was sad because, after reading an article about the personality struggles within that band, he saw a frightening number of similarities.

"Rivers wants to be a benevolent dictator," the drummer added, publicizing his on-again, off-again frustration with his supporting role in Weezer. "We're fortunate to be able to play [his music] and dig it. But at the same time, I feel like if things had gone differently, we would be a much bigger band than we are."

Perhaps, but Cuomo's composition pen yielded even further praise. Roger Catlin of the *Hartford Courant* noted the short running time of *The Green Album*, but wrote, "what's here, though, is choice." While there were few negative reviews to speak of, the smartass *Pinkerton* worshippers at *Pitchfork Media* called the disc stale, polished, and emotionless, brandishing it with a score of 4 out of a possible 10.

Responding to this type of reaction, Rivers — more interested in being compared to influential albums by Nirvana and The Beatles than his own back catalog — defended his move away from poignant lyrics. "People expect me to be extremely sensitive and emotional, insecure, conflicted," he said at the time. "Whatever I feel, I don't feel like showing it. I don't want to wear my heart on my sleeve."

Looking back to look forward in 2001, Cuomo talked about the history of the group. "When you start out, there's the excitement of being a new band, of coming up from the underground, of having people rooting for you and of having those people wanting you to win," he reflected. Calling *Pinkerton* "embarrassing," Rivers said, "we were coming off this tremendous success and I put my neck on the line and said 'Alright guys, I have to make this really personal statement — trust me, it's going to work.' And everyone hated it." Even his bandmates. "I remember we were having so many fights at the time, but they defiantly brought up that subject."

When Weezer finally got their shit together enough to give it another try, Cuomo says the spark came from the band's devout following. "I think the catalyst to our comeback was getting out onstage in front of an audience again and playing — putting it all on the line and saying, 'Okay, folks, here's what we have. I know it's not quite ready yet and it's not great, but it's the best we can do.' The fans went so crazy and showed us so much support that it gave me the confidence to write songs, improve what we were doing, and make a record."

Back from the dead, Weezer's high-octane pop transcended boundaries to catch the ears of geeks, freaks, preppies, punks, stoners, and beyond. Transcending social classes and target demographics, their sound and non-image appealed to anyone who ever felt the awkwardness of adolescence. "Either you or someone very close to you has experienced something that makes Weezer a familiar sanctuary in the world you live in," wrote John Santos, supporting this notion in the May 2001 issue of *Meltdown*. "Their audiences are filled with an absolute melting of social acceptance. There is almost its own demographic for these fans. You have 12–24, 25–32, and Weezer fans — try to swing that in the marketplace. Weezer has crossed lines as no band could."

"Fans feel a lot of empathy for these guys," Koch concurred. "[Fans] think, 'They're just like me. They're depressed about girl problems or this thing or that.' They come across as vulnerable, yet they get up on stage and they make these rocking albums. They don't have the rock-star aura."

"How great is it that enormous amounts of people are spending tons of resources trying the make the band I'm in successful?" mused Patrick on the junket for *The Green Album*. "It's fantastic." Weezer's appearance on the cover of *Request*, donning gold and white tuxedos and Elvis Presley–inspired pompadours, nice coverage by the likes of *Spin* and *Rolling Stone*, and countless Web outlets and fanzines worldwide only helped up the group's profile.

Wilson, speaking of Weezer's variety of rock, added, "[It's] the kind of thing that's not a fad or a trend but is very basic and pure and something that I don't think ever goes away." Still, some of the fans that rallied around *Pinkerton* during Cuomo's darkest hour and had helped give Weezer their second life on the road in 2000 just weren't buying into the new, slicker-sounding material that easily. "It's tough," Cuomo confessed. "The fans have given us this miraculous career, and it's all because of *Pinkerton*. That's all they want, that's all they care about. It's so frustrating, because I don't want to turn my back on them, but I sure as hell don't want to do *Pinkerton*.

"It was a hideous record," Rivers attested, discounting the biggest cult rock album of the 1990s, one that initially failed but after a slow build revived the group and gave them more credibility than ever, even if it was unwanted. "It was such a hugely painful mistake that happened in front of

HOPE NORTH/CORBIS OUTLINE/MAGMA

Need A Date? The lads in Weezer prep for KROQ's "Punk Rock Prom"

hundreds of thousands of people and continues to happen on a grander and grander scale and just won't go away. It's like getting really drunk at a party and spilling your guts in front of everyone and feeling incredibly great and cathartic about it, and then waking up the next morning and realizing what a complete fool you made of yourself."

Not that his famous fans or bandmates agreed. For instance, NOFX's Fat Mike is a huge fan of the band and counts *Pinkerton* among his favorite albums. Not to mention endorsements by The Deftones, Chino Moreno, Green Day, Dashboard Confessional's Chris Carraba, and punk upstarts The Ataris to name a few. And Welsh — who doesn't play on the record — said at the time, "I think it's a brilliant record. But the way it was received was really hard on Rivers. He'll say he doesn't want to play any of it, but I think he was just so hurt by the way people responded to it."

So after a year spent working to balance that credibility with commercial success, Cuomo appeared ready to come to terms with the notion that he might be angering and alienating the fans who stuck with him through the lean years. It was a bold but wise career move.

As the buzz around *The Green Album* hit a fever pitch, Weezer soldiered forward. The band spent May 15 ushering in their new disc with a KROQ-sponsored appearance at Hollywood's Tower Records. Los Angeles–area members of the Weezer Army camped out the night before in order to buy the new disc when the retailer opened the following morning in order to obtain one of just 325 special passes to the in-store performance. In doing so, they were also treated to a special surprise when Cuomo, Welsh, and Koch strolled around the parking lot outside the store, hanging with them and taking pictures.

The spectacular event at the same Sunset Boulevard store that Rivers worked in a decade earlier came complete with an additional sound system and a Jumbotron screen for attendees who came by for the performance but would not fit inside the store. Syndicated entertainment program *Access Hollywood* covered the gig, which found the band interviewed by Pat O'Brien.

Later that week, Weezer played alongside the Offspring at another KROQ appearance, called The Punk Rock Prom. The contest gig — performed for two area high schools at Six Flags Magic Mountain — found Mikey returning to his cross-dressing ways of yore, rocking through the gig in a prom dress. KROQ, in turn, kept plugging "Hash Pipe," which had become the top-played song on the station and would soon peak at #2 on *Billboard*'s Modern Rock Chart.

After a redeye flight to New York for SNL rehearsals the next day, Weezer befriended Will Ferrell, who lent his maraca skills to the band's second nationally televised number, "Island in the Sun." With barely time for a breath, Weezer hopped a flight Sunday morning to St. Louis to appear at KPNT's "Pointfest" alongside acts like Staind, Run DMC, Our Lady Peace, and Alien Ant Farm. But unlike their normal, first-class air-travel methods, the band's tour manager, Gus Brandt, summoned a private jet to get them there. If that move didn't say "rock star," then Weezer's #4 debut on *Billboard*'s Top 200 Album survey surely did. And the first-week success put an end to Cuomo's worries that all of the *Pinkerton* fans had left the band in the lurch. Perhaps the chart placement is what gave the band the courage to crank out five new songs during its St. Louis set.

"We knew that, if we made a good album, then we could be huge all over again," Rivers said, with all of his confidence suddenly back in tow. But if it turned out to be shitty, then we'd have been dead . . . [we're] still living."

In Canada, *The Green Album* did even better than in the Lower 48, placing at #2 behind *Lateralus*, the new disc from cult rockers Tool. Reacting to the album's immediate success, Patrick said, "I think [Rivers] is psyched. I think he was worried that people weren't gonna like it, because it's not as heart-on-your-sleeve emotional, but I don't think it's that different. I really don't."

Late in the month, with a two-day break from ongoing promotional duties in Washington, D.C., the band hit the city's Monster Island Studios to lay down twelve all-new songs, ten of which were completed. The full list of tunes attempted were: "I Can't Tell You," "Happy Grunge," "December," "High Up Above," "Burndt Jamb," "Listen Up," "American Gigolo," "Keep Fishin'," "Take Control," "Not in Love with You" (which later became known as "Zep Song" and "Zep Jamb"), "Puerto Vajarta," and "Saturday Night."

Designed to solicit producers for their next album, the band soon posted eight of these twelve songs in MP3 form on the Audio/Video page of *Weezer.com*. Excited about the new material, Weezer was readying itself for the opportunity to make another album. Rather than endure another lengthy demo process, the boys got themselves in ready mode. As Koch put it in a post during the Hooptie jaunt, "They want to rock and they want to rock now."

When probed about the ten-hour D.C. demo session, Welsh said, "We're just really excited about all our new songs." To which Bell added, "The songs are great. These songs that are on the new record we've been living with for over a year now."

And when he wasn't publicly tagging newscasters like Connie Chung and CNBC's Maria Bartolomo as "hot," Rivers, too, was excited about the developing material. "The new songs are better. They rock harder. They're more fun to play on the guitar."

"I think the next record will be a little different. I think it will be more like 'Hash Pipe,' really," Wilson predicted at the time. "'Hash Pipe' is the one song on the record that I think everybody feels really great about as far as how we play and what's going on in it compositionally. It's just fun as hell to play. It's just a big rip, you know?

"We could make [another record] right now," boasted Wilson, "and we sort of feel in a way, like, let's just get on with it so we can do the new stuff. We've got a whole record that we could just put together right now if we wanted."

But *The Green Album* had just been released and it was selling impressively. In two weeks it had sold 215,000 copies in the U.S. according to SoundScan. Things showed little sign of slowing down as the lads flew over to Los Angeles in the midst of their East Coast obligations to make a rehearsal and tape a subsequent performance of "Hash Pipe" at the Shrine Auditorium for the *MTV Movie Awards* on the first day of June. As the band wrapped their promo tour of North America with stops in New York and Toronto, fans were finally apprised of the Magnarella firing.

"Weezer has parted ways with their management company and are currently doing a good deal of extra work on the road because of it," Koch posted. "So if you see a Weezer member with a far-off look in his eye, it's probably because he's got a lot on his mind these days. I'm not sure if this situation is permanent or temporary, but so far we are doing okay."

While in New York, Rivers met with entertainment management outfit The Firm — who represents Stone Temple Pilots, Linkin Park, and Audioslave — among others. And in an odd move, Cuomo — never one to pass on a creative challenge — rushed into a New York City recording studio hours before flying off to Toronto in order to concoct a demo for Enrique Iglesias. But Cuomo was never happy with the hastily recorded song, "A Dio," and wasn't surprised when it was ultimately passed on by the Latin superstar.

The last North American promotional appearances were planned for Toronto before the band moved on to the United Kingdom and an ensuing tour of Western Europe. In the Ontario metropolis, radio station CFNY, otherwise known as Edge 102.1, gave away 2,000 tickets to Weezer's first planned performance. As "Hash Pipe" topped the station's Top 30, the band returned the love by blasting through a full set — augmented by five new songs — for its loyal followers in the area at the Molson Amphitheatre.

The following morning, Pat and Rivers went to MuchMusic to film two interview segments, one before fans and another behind closed doors. Originally planned as an interview and in-studio performance, intentions for the latter were scrapped over a contractual dispute between Cuomo —

wearing his manager's hat — and the music video network.

As the Hooptie tour gave way to the Euro Freak Out Tour 2001 during an Air Canada overnight flight to London, Weezer found themselves part of a late-night television monologue, as CBS show host Craig Kilborn laid down the following, guffaw-prompting joke: *"Weezer* played their new song 'Hash Pipe' last night to many screaming fans at the *MTV Movie Awards*. This sets a new record, as it marks the first time in four years that MTV has played real music."

Touching down at Heathrow Airport, Weezer hauled ass over to the set of *T4* to tape their "Hash Pipe" segment of the Sunday night Channel 4 variety show. Next, the group went to their hotel and crashed in order to wake up fresh for the following day's print, radio, and television interviews, plus photo shoots for both a *Kerrang!* cover story and an *NME* feature.

Rivers and Pat were interviewed for London's XFM on June 12 and participated in a subsequent "XFM Hijacking," where they selected and introduced a variety of tracks, running the gamut between "Walk On By" by Dionne Warwick to Slayer's "Angel of Death." Another TV appearance was taped that afternoon, this time with the quartet lip-synching "Pipe" for *Pepsi Chart*, a cheesy *Top of the Pops*–styled program.

On his thirty-first birthday, Cuomo took Weezer into BBC Studios to record material for a Radio One Evening Session. Hosted by Steve Lamacq, the opportunity called for the band to record four songs, including a cover and re-recordings of "Island" and "Hash Pipe." However, Cuomo insisted that they do only new material and the Beeb acquiesced. Having rehearsed the songs live and during sound checks over the past month, the band was able to work efficiently enough to record eight songs.

"Burndt Jamb," "High Up Above," "Take Control," and "Listen Up" were prepped for BBC listeners, with the program airing one a week over the next four weeks. Meanwhile, the remaining four ("Keep Fishin',"

"American Gigolo," "December," and "Saturday Night") were shelved for the time being, when they were deemed too rough around the edges for the airwaves.

The tour stopped at the ProvinssiRock Festival, in Seinajoki, Finland, plus locales like Stockholm (for the Hultsfred Festival) and Oslo. But perhaps of all the cities on the "Euro Freak Out" trek, Copenhagen was most notable, as it marked the introduction of foosball to the band following their sound check at the Pumpehuset club. Before long, the table sport would become a backstage addiction for both the band and crew, usurping even Pat and Karl's beloved hacky sack.

Meanwhile, the band's U.S. tour plans for late summer were thrown into doubt, after heavy rumors of a support slot for Jane's Addiction's forthcoming "Jubilee" tour were quashed. Weezer also altered its U.K. tour plans for early July, and ended the tour prematurely to fly home to Los Angeles in order to shoot the video for "Island in the Sun" with Marcos Siega. With just a little more than a week's notice and after much internal debate, shows at Manchester Academy and Scotland's T in the Park Festival with emo-rock openers Jimmy Eat World were sacked and postponed to the fall. Yet the camaraderie in the band seemed as warmly dysfunctional as ever during the European jaunt, as evidenced by an exchange between Rivers and Mikey following one of their best shows of the tour.

"It wasn't good, but it wasn't a disaster," said Rivers, half-jokingly after a Barcelona gig at Razzamatazz. "Let's just say we survived. Mikey was fucking up through the set, and intruding on my emotional space."

"I fucked up nothing," Mikey grinned, giving it back to Cuomo. "I wasn't the problem, it was him. He wasn't concentrating and, consequently, he ruined things for everyone else."

Cuomo and Welsh frequently paired up for interviews on this tour, and while Rivers was traditionally informative and educated in his answers to the press, Mikey was clearly there to offset Rivers with some comic color along the lines of sex, drugs, and rock 'n' roll. When asked what places in the world the band would like to tour, Mikey's reply was: "Places like Argentina where there are hot chicks and free drugs."

Three consecutive shows at the Shepherd's Bush Empire in London on July 3, 4, and 5 with Jimmy Eat World wrapped the European tour, with the band making time on the final day for a *Top of the Pops* performance. Playing "Hash Pipe" as "Half Pipe" right before the shortened Euro Freak Out trek closer, Weezer changed the title and lyrics to pass the BBC censors. The last gig was bogged down with what Koch describes as an "axe-clash," finding Mikey — sporting a Blue Öyster Cult T-shirt — and Rivers knocking into each other. Welsh, caught up in the moment, tossed his bass into the audience, where two fans wrestled for it for close to a half hour.

Out of these dates, a rumor started to circulate that Rivers had forbidden the guys in Jimmy Eat World from making eye contact with him, which Cuomo would later adamantly deny. "I didn't tell 'em that. I talked to them everyday! Someone [in London] told them not to look me in the eye, I think, but it wasn't me and it wasn't anyone associated with my crew. I think it's a wonderful idea, but I hadn't come up with it at that point."

In support of these dates, Rivers spoke extensively to the *NME*. Aside from plugging *The Green Album*, he professed his extremely strong interest in soccer. Seeming to forget the corrected leg injury that plagued him for much of his life, the Weezer boss told the weekly music paper that he still took a soccer ball with him everywhere he went and bragged that he was an excellent left-sided midfielder who could've turned professional in any other country. Although it seems to be a pretty arrogant declaration, the sport clearly runs through the Cuomos' blood, as his half-brother Gabriel, some fourteen years his junior, was also known to be an impressive soccer player in his late teens while an American abroad residing in Germany,

CHRISTINA RADISH

On The Way Out: Mikey gets left behind

according to *Soccernova.com*.

Meanwhile, back in the States, rumors were circulating that the band had canceled summer tour plans to make a new album. But while Weezer was looking to record a new disc before the end of the year, its break from the road was designed for time off and songwriting after a very busy six months.

Back to their respective homes and hotels in Los Angeles with a few days' preparation prior to the "Island in the Sun" video shoot, the members of Weezer gathered on an Eagle Rock, California, side street with director Marcos Siega. The concept for the clip — which was selected because it *didn't* have the same 'island' themes that other directors had been pitching — found the group performing and partying on the set of a Mexican wedding on July 11 and 12. Curious fans somehow found their way to the set, but were kept at a distance by security, as time was of the essence. With the song picking up steam at radio, the clip — which saw the band perform on a residential front lawn — was wrapped and quickly edited that week for MTV and VH1.

Saved by Ric Ocasek from a pile of Cuomo solo demos, the album's second single had a "loose feeling" in its initial form, the album's producer explained. Mikey recalled that "Rivers had recorded 'Island' all by himself, doing all of the instruments in his house. He made this really beautiful little version of it — it was really scrappy sounding and really pretty and kind of melancholy. I really love that one — it seems like a nice summer song."

A day after lensing the clip, Cuomo was visited at home for a *Rolling Stone* photo shoot that would accompany an upcoming feature by Chris Mundy. Already hard at work on a new song, Cuomo asked the photographer to sit tight until he finished work on the tune. The next evening, Saturday, July 14, Mundy trailed Cuomo around Los Angeles. Ever the eccentric, Rivers sported khaki pants, a long-underwear shirt, and a soccer windbreaker in the summer heat, as he made his way around his home city.

Stopping for a hot chocolate in a French bistro near his crib, briefly making the scene to catch indie rockers Ivy at a small area venue, and then on to a dance party at the Palace in Hollywood, an extremely wealthy Rivers is documented using his fame to avoid paying a twelve-dollar cover at the first club and working his magic to get the VIP treatment at the second, despite defying the venue's dress code. Mundy chronicled Cuomo in action, as a line of beautiful people around the block looks on.

Discreetly informing the Palace bouncer he was Weezer, Rivers is ignored by the club employee until he reveals a laminated backstage pass with his picture on it. After pulling a few strings, he gets inside, where he lasts roughly five minutes amid the gyrating bodies and thumping techno and is soon back out on the sidewalk.

Responding to allegations by his own bandmates that he's "the weirdest person you've ever met," Rivers responded, "I don't have any friends." When probed by the reporter, who wondered if former Avant Garde members like Nerf Herder bassist Justin Fisher or AM Radio frontman Kevin Ridel counted as friends of his, Cuomo asked to turn the music off in the car they were riding in and went silent. "Game Over," wrote Mundy.

Later, discussion turned to Leaves, a professor of sociology at the University of Washington, known professionally as James A. Kitts. Describing Leaves as highly intelligent, Rivers sadly admitted he is mostly estranged from his brother, just too caught up in his own dream to take the short plane trip to Seattle. He did, however, confess to being pleased with how his baby brother turned out.

"I'm so proud of him," Cuomo confided. "And he's married. That totally blew my mind. We've both always been very anti-relationship, especially anti-marriage. And then one day he just sent me an e-mail that said, 'I got married.'"

Elsewhere, Rivers proclaimed his pleasure with being back in L.A. after a very busy few months hyping *The Green Album*. Speaking about his then-current songwriting methods, Cuomo explained how he discovered that he could write effectively only in short bursts of forty-five minutes to an hour a day. And finally, as he and the scribe parted, Rivers alluded to an interesting practice of unwinding, telling Mundy of plans to treat himself to cough syrup with codeine upon his return home.

A taste for cough syrup didn't affect Cuomo's management of the band. By mid-July Weezer had been confirmed for the KROQ "Inland Invasion" concert, slated for August 25 and also featuring the Offspring, Incubus, Social Distortion, Pennywise, Cold, and others at the G.H. Blockbuster Pavillion in Devore, California.

Even sooner was the group's one-off show at Y100's Feztival, held in Camden, New Jersey, on the outskirts of Philly on July 25, followed by plans two days later for an appearance back in L.A. on NBC's *Tonight Show with Jay Leno*. "First, I'm dealing largely with Third Rail," Y100's McGuinn said of setting up the 2001 Feztival show. "And then all of a sudden Magnarella's not in the picture anymore and I'm dealing directly with Rivers. Which is something that is very unique. When you need a phoner, you send the singer an e-mail. That's really special, at least for me. I don't know, maybe he doesn't answer other people's e-mails, but he answers mine. And I'm like, 'Holy shit! That's Rivers.'"

While "Hash Pipe" kept resurfacing on TRL, "Island in the Sun," the new Weezer clip, premiered on MTV in late July. A day before the Philly show, the group performed a secret gig at New York's Irving Plaza. Passes to the show — which also included openers Guided By Voices and high-profile attendees like Tenacious D's Jack Black and Kyle Gass — were given away by the network, New York CD retailer FYE, plus local radio outlets like K-Rock and Z100.

The hype around the new Weezer video clip found it debuting in the TRL Top 10 a day later, as the band rocked the Tweeter Center in Camden. As MP3 savvy fans downloaded free demos like "Keep Fishin'," "Saturday Night," and "Zep Song," a Thursday flight to Los Angeles put the band back on the West Coast for their visit to NBC Studios, where they dined at the network commissary and took viewers and fellow *Leno* guests Antonio Banderas and comedienne Wanda Sykes to their own special "Island." Little did fans know that the show would mark bassist Mikey Welsh's last appearance with Weezer.

chapter twenty-four

i wish you luck

Soon after their *Leno* appearance and in the weeks leading up to their "Inland Invasion" gig and a tentative fall tour, the members of Weezer regrouped in their practice space. However, bassist Mikey Welsh was conspicuously absent. Intent on demoing sixteen all-new Cuomo songs, Rivers wanted to couple these demos with those from the Washington, D.C., and BBC sessions. As August progressed, Rivers was still writing close to a song a day, giving the band several dozen tunes to consider for album #4.

As word broke of the band's former management company suing them, Koch explained on *Weezer.com* — now approaching three million hits in just a year and half — how the news caused the organization's "stress level" to reach "new heights."

Citing breach of contract, Magnarella's company was suing the band for more than $2 million through the L.A. County branch of the Superior Court of California in Santa Monica. Atlas/Third Rail Management, Inc. was seeking damages from three separate defendants: The Weezer partnership (with Cuomo and Wilson the only active founding participants left), longtime guitarist Brian Bell, and Matt Sharp's replacement on bass, Mikey Welsh. The suit, filed on July 6, claimed Weezer failed to honor the terms of its seven-year-old agreement.

The filing alleged that Weezer, in the events leading up to *The Green Album*, "without any contractual basis for doing so, attempted to renegotiate the agreement to reduce the amount of the commission to be paid to [Atlas/

Third Rail], simply because [Weezer was] about to release a new album."

Then, the suit claimed, "On or about May 18, 2001, when [Atlas/Third Rail] declined to gratuitously reduce the commission to be paid by [Weezer] to [Atlas/Third Rail] under the agreement, [Weezer] purported to terminate the agreement in direct violation of the provisions of the agreement."

The contract called for the plaintiff to receive 15% of Weezer's gross earnings, and according to the suit, the band owed the firm $1 million for income generated since the breach of contract. Included among the commissions that Third Rail were staking claim to included $15,000 of the band's $100,000 fee to perform at Coachella, $75,000 from the $500,000 advance payment received by Interscope for Weezer's third album, $67,500 from the $450,000 it earned on personal appearances from the eleven-day April tour of Japan, plus $30,000 from the $200,000 the band earned in merchandising during the Japanese trek.

In spite of the stress surrounding the suit, Koch wrote of the band getting along like never before and looking forward to future endeavors, including touring and record making. But strangely, it was just three-fourths of the band working together like never before. Mikey, who was rumored to have a dalliance with drugs, had yet to surface for rehearsals by the middle of August. And when the news broke that Welsh was absent, some speculated on the Weezer boards as to whether he was even invited to participate. Others, meanwhile, defended the band's position that he was a no-show.

The band made a casual mention of Welsh's absence in one of Koch's regular updates, releasing news of their bass player's absence *after* an announcement of plans to shoot a *second* "Island in the Sun" video with original Weezer video master Spike Jonze. It was certainly odd that the mysterious absence of a group member didn't get top billing in what was arguably Koch's most informative post, ever.

The decision to redo the video stemmed from an incident in which

Rivers had reportedly learned from Jordan Schur — when he dropped in on the band's July Irving Plaza show — that Tom Calderone, MTV's vice president of programming, wasn't a fan of the original Marcos Siega–orchestrated "Island" clip. So, together, Schur and Cuomo orchestrated a plan to get Jonze behind the camera to create a new video at a cost of several hundred thousand dollars. Although the first clip of "Island" was being played twice a day, Interscope had hoped to get "Island" into heavy rotation, knowing what such a score might mean to album sales. Weezer's first collaboration with Jonze in seven years was arranged in a hurry.

Regarding Welsh's absence in an August 11 post, the band minimized the subject through its webmaster as if the whole thing was a planned departure. "Meanwhile, not everything is so rosy. I've learned that Mikey has not come to rehearsals in L.A. yet, due to some sort of private medical problem," Koch announced in his second news bullet. "No, not a cliché rock-star drug problem; he has been holed up in Boston near his family."

If the remaining members of Weezer were waiting for word about Mikey, they decided to try out some bass players in case Welsh was unable to meet their upcoming performance and recording commitments. In between learning new songs in rehearsal, Brian, Pat, and Rivers began auditioning different bass players. "In case Mikey can't make it," read a key line in Karl's post, as if Cuomo had already made up his mind. And in fact, fans would later learn that Welsh was out of the group.

Why would the band downplay his disappearance and speculate on his whereabouts, fans wondered. Was this all just some kind of charade? If Welsh had some kind of drug addiction or psychiatric woes, and they really were concerned, why wouldn't they give him a few weeks to get himself on the right path?

Now running through bassists the way Spinal Tap went through drummers, Weezer allegedly held private, invitation-only auditions with musicians that included former Ben Folds Five member Robert Sledge. As the days crept by, and *Weezer.com* MP3 aficionados scored more freebies like "Puerto Vajarta" and "Listen Up," speculation that Mikey was fired persisted. Next, the Weezer partnership announced that the Brookline-reared bassist had checked into a psychiatric hospital in the Boston area.

As the Weezer organization planned a lengthy fall tour with hard rocking Interscope labelmates Cold as openers, they informed fans through their Web site that they were concerned that they hadn't received any more news about Mikey. In the meantime, with the tour itinerary taking shape, tryouts continued. Touting Welsh's disappearance as a leave of absence, the band added additional mystery by insisting that he had inexplicably missed a scheduled flight from Boston to Los Angeles to join the group on the set of "Island" video #2.

Through Koch, the group wrote, "At this point, we're wondering if either . . . Mikey is in worse shape than we thought (but we still don't know the nature of what could be troubling him, and no one close to him is passing along any such info) or . . . Mikey has chosen not to come on purpose. Without any word from anyone close to the matter, we are about as much in the dark as the fans are on this one, and are forced to speculate."

When probed at the time, Weezer's record label declined to comment on Welsh.

So, with strong encouragement from Schur, the remaining members of Weezer got to work on their third music video of 2003. The reshoot was ironic, since Cuomo and company were first attracted to Siega's treatment due to its simplicity and lack of an island theme. But like *RollingStone.com* stringer Greg Heller wrote on the eve of the shoot, "What's good for the goose isn't always good for the Interscope."

The clip was shot as scheduled when it was filmed on Wednesday, August 15, at a private ranch at the top of Browns Canyon, in the hills of

Chatsworth, California. Jonze's treatment called for the remaining members of Weezer to hang out with a bevy of wild animals, including a 500-pound bear, a black panther, a chimpanzee, a giraffe, and a trio of wild squirrels.

By August 19, after a series of rehearsals, the group had chosen the relatively unknown bassist Scott Shriner to replace Welsh. First announced as a "fill-in" member to cover the following week's KROQ show, Shriner was also likely for any U.S. and European tour dates on the horizon for September and October.

Slated to launch on September 11 in San Jose with opening acts The Start and Cold — whom Cuomo handpicked — the tour was being booked and arranged by Don Muller. Rivers hired Muller, a former Lollapalooza organizer, to plot out the dates and road particulars so that he had time to focus on the new demos.

Culled largely from a two-week July 2001 writing binge, the new material Weezer was grooving on included eighteen new compositions: "Your Room," "Broken Arrows," "Song from Yesterday," "We Go Together," "Anything but Love," "Take Back the Love," "Death and Destruction," "Through Other's Eyes," "Take a Listen," "Stupid Feelings," "I Wanna Know," "The Dawn," "Farmer John," "Don't Pick on Me," "How Long," "On Holiday," "Don't Bring Me Down," and "Everybody Depends on a Friend." An additional dozen or so new songs had also come to fruition in recent weeks, bringing the total number to more than thirty songs — not counting the BBC and D.C. demos.

Although lacking specifics about Mikey, the band informed fans that contact had been made with the bassist, learning ten days after Welsh had gone missing that he was stable and in no danger. "The guys have gotten no definite indication of when or even if he can return," the news read. "In the meantime, they wish him well, await further word, and extend their invitation. It must be noted that there remains considerable confusion over what exactly is going on with Mikey, as very little info has filtered in, and it remains extremely difficult to get a hold of him or those who are close to him."

Some suggest that Welsh's departure was curt, Cuomo-initiated, and planned for after the *Leno* appearance, while others maintain that Weezer merely acted swiftly to keep its comeback momentum going. Speaking about how he was removed from his position, Welsh later said, "I took some time off to get help for something and they basically took off on me, abandoned me. The way it went down was pretty lame. Being in a band with guys that long and being as good friends as we were, having them just kind of split was definitely cold."

No doubt, Welsh had to be rethinking his assessment of Rivers as a "sweetheart" just two months earlier. Describing activities of the time like playing on *Saturday Night Live* and the jets, parties, movie stars, and models that followed, Welsh said in hindsight that all this was accompanied by *Behind the Music*–like tensions. "It's been like this gaping wound with Rivers," Welsh said in late 2002, describing how his close friendship with Cuomo eroded into a clash of egos, band politics, and money. "It's been a very difficult year for me. It's been traumatic in a lot of ways."

Welsh confessed to having a substance abuse problem and later informed *Rolling Stone* that he was a "recovering addict." Despite attempts by this author to get an elaboration from the discarded bassist on what happened through requests to his management and publicist on a number of occasions in 2002 and 2003, Welsh eventually declined to comment for this book at the advice of his lawyers. After Weezer, Welsh went on to a brief stint in The Kickovers with Nate Albert, formerly of the Mighty Mighty Bosstones, before quitting music in late 2002, moving to Vermont, getting married, getting a puppy, and focusing on a new career in art.

Mikey — like Jason Cropper before him — was bound to the confidentiality agreement that accompanied the amicable settlement he reached with Weezer sometime in mid-2003. Oddly, Welsh did speak to *Devil in the Woods*, a West Coast independent music magazine, about his situation with the band. Taking an opportunity to plug his budding new career, Mikey did, in fact, reveal he was at McLean Psychiatric Hospital in Belmont, Massachusetts, in the summer of 2001, and had since gone on to study painters like Jackson Pollock and Willem de Kooning. Looking back on his time in Weezer two years after his departure, Welsh spoke of the year 1998, when he resided with Cuomo. "[Rivers] and I lived together for about a year out in L.A. And at the time I was messing around with painting because we had a lot of downtime," explained Welsh, who hopes to be taken seriously as an artist and not some rock star painter. "But when I left [Weezer], I was in the hospital for a while and I decided that [being in a band] was something I didn't want to do anymore. I was really burnt out and sick of everything involved with the music industry."

After isolating himself and taking his creativity in a new direction, Welsh was now painting full time, happy not to have to deal with Cuomo's swollen ego, and finding solace and satisfaction in his art. If the merit of his creative contributions in Weezer were debatable by fans of the group, Mikey *was* instrumental in reviving the band, having lived with Rivers during his songwriting drought.

Welsh remembered repeatedly watching the Metallica *Behind the Music* episode with Cuomo in their shared digs. As they high-fived each other in the midst of Rivers' writer's block, the world outside assumed Weezer as washed up. "I was like, 'Man, I totally believe in you. I'm your brother. I'm right here and I'm not going to leave,'" Mikey said. "I mean, I was in that band for fucking two and a half years before we even played a show. And I believed in him."

After Welsh escorted Cuomo back to the top of the charts, he says he had a "massive nervous breakdown." At the height of the group's resurgence, in the face of drugs and pressure, he sought help. In doing so, Welsh was abandoned by his friends.

Cuomo, so wrapped up in his own agenda, failed to extend Mikey the same courtesy he himself had received in '98 and '99. Welsh contended Rivers refused to give him the time to get his head right.

One day Welsh was a bona fide rock star, the next he was in McLean, trying to rebuild his life. If his relationship with Cuomo was complicated by a lot of emotional baggage, plagued by dictatorial band control, psychological mind games, and humiliation, Mikey spoke of having no regrets, a lot of pride, and plenty of fond memories from his time in the band.

"I think that things happen the way they're supposed to, honestly," concluded Mikey, before taking his parting shot at Rivers. "All I can really say about that guy is that he doesn't do well with big success. He and I were very, very close; we were like brothers, and I don't know — he's able to completely shut down, like a block of ice. All I can say really is that if I told you exactly what happened with me and how I left the band, and you printed it, he'd probably try to sue me. Because if our fans knew the truth of what happened, I don't think they'd like him very much."

Addressing Welsh's departure months after the bassist's exit/firing, Cuomo — who hadn't spoken to Welsh since the day of the *Leno* appearance — made it seem as if Mikey's exit was indeed his own doing. "Mikey has his ups and downs like everybody else, but overall he's an amazing guy. None of us knows the details surrounding his departure and I'm sure it's not as depraved as some people think. I have nothing but great memories of the guy and I'm sure we'll be back in each other's lives some day."

And they were, if only with shared signatures on the legal document that finalized Welsh's settlement.

Scott Shriner

As for Scott Shriner, the Toledo, Ohio, native was a ten-year Los Angeles punk and metal scene veteran on loan from the aggro rock outfit Broken. Born on July 11, 1965, Scott started his musical career by learning the trumpet in the fourth grade. "My dad is a saxophone player and a very good one at that," Shriner explained. "He encouraged me to play whatever instrument I wanted, so when I was getting ready to go to high school I feared that trumpet playing would not be very cool and I was having a hard enough time fitting in as it was, so I decided to try guitar lessons. One month later, I asked my dad, 'what is that instrument that makes that low bump-bump, Pop?' The rest is my destiny, to rock the bass."

Shriner says he was weaned on various genres, "from Motown to punk fucking rock to rockabilly to funk and just plain heavy metal. I have been a fan of Elvis Costello, The Beatles, Led Zeppelin, and Black Sabbath since I was a wee small guy."

At Toledo's Start High School, Scott admitted to being a "a messed-up kid" with "too much going on in my head like a lot of young people.

"I had no idea how to fit in," he revealed. "I sucked at sports and kept trying anyway. I was a small guy and not too sporty. The only way I could deal was [to] saturate myself in music. It was the one thing that I loved. I smoked a lot of weed and hid out behind buildings with my couple of friends trying to get someone to buy us beer. I followed girls around at malls . . . and got high. I found another misfit who played drums and we would jam every day after school. Learning Rush, Police, and other songs we could figure out. So I spent a lot of time in basements and hiding behind buildings. I was what was considered at that time a stoner."

In the summer of 1983, right after high school, Shriner joined the U.S. Marine Corps for a two-year stint. "It was perfect because I wasn't really sure what I wanted to do," he professed. "I was just kind of a smoked-up kid through high school and I didn't have a lot of direction or self-confidence. The Marines showed me what I was capable of, and by taking all of my freedom away it showed me what it was that I love the most and what I wanted to do. That's what really gave me my whole direction to focus on playing bass. That's when I realized that that was what my heart wanted."

Before exiting Toledo at the age of twenty-five, Scott did time in an R&B band called The Movers, a punk and alternative-inspired group known as the Exciters, another known as Loved By Millions, and, finally, The Great Barbecue Gods.

"My goals were to achieve great rock stardom," the bassist admitted. "I felt that I had played with all the people in Toledo that I wanted to play with, and I could either move on and keep growing, or I could stay there and make a decent living and have fun. I always thought that I wanted more out of life."

Shriner joined Weezer on a provisional basis, when it was uncertain whether Mikey Welsh was temporarily or permanently out of the band. "Rivers got my number through a mutual contact," Shriner explained, "but I didn't know about it. So when he called me I thought it was a practical joke. 'Yeah right, you're Rivers Cuomo, uh huh.' But it sort of dawned on me; this guy's being too serious to be making a joke.

"I just froze for five minutes by the phone," Shriner added, referring to the moment he recognized Cuomo's voice. "Moments like that are worth savoring. My crappy phone service only saves messages for so long, but I'll always have it in my head. I'll always remember that moment."

It seemed as if Rivers was looking for a certain type of bassist to supplant Welsh all along. "I just called this guy in L.A. that knows a lot of musicians and I said, 'Send the baddest, meanest, most evil guy you got,'" he said. "And he sent Scott. And I said, 'Okay, cool. You're in.' That easy. He's got a gold tooth. There's no requirements. It's like, 'Come on in. Let's see what you can do, and I'll give you plenty of support and just give you plenty of space to be yourself, and encouragement. Let's see what happens.' That's what it was like. It's not like there was a predetermined role that I was trying to fit him into."

At the same time, the blond-haired, bespectacled, and tattooed Shriner — whom folks in the Weezer camp often refer to as Shrinedog — was becoming restless with the limited musical scope of Broken and his other band, the AC/DC-inspired, female-fronted Bomber. So he began looking for another musical outlet right around the time his phone rang.

Scott said that his first impression of Cuomo, Wilson, and Bell was that "they seemed like guys who weren't trying to come across one way or another. They were just being themselves. I guess that's why people are into it. There's nothing worse than something that's posed, unless it's overly posed to the point of being funny."

And although Shriner, a self-professed Slipknot fan and a Camel smoker, said he was a little surprised when Cuomo asked him into the fold, he imagined he'd be a perfect fit. "The thing is, I've always thought of them as kind of a heavy band," Shrinedog explained. "Maybe not heavy in the sense of tuned-down guitars and screaming their heads off all the time, but the songwriting has always been very heavy. 'Say It Ain't So' is probably the first Weezer song that really hooked me on them, and that song is heavy as hell."

Still, Shriner — who once auditioned to play in both Ozzy Osbourne's and Lenny Kravitz's bands and played for a spell in Vanilla Ice's rap metal group — conceded he was worried about how things would work out. "I never thought in a million years that I would fit in with those guys. I was just being myself and that was the sound they were looking for."

Shriner walked into the band right after the Welsh incident, but if Mikey's departure was a setback at all, Weezer quickly rebounded. "It took about a minute to get used to working with each other," said Shriner. "We hit it off really well and started working harder than they've ever worked before." Added Cuomo, "he played with us once and I immediately knew he was the right guy."

Shriner gelled with the band so well he was asked to stay on for the "Inland Invasion" gig and new demo sessions. While some in the camp, including Karl Koch, had initial concerns that he might have been a "square peg in a round hole," Shriner's capable playing and professional outlook soon put fears to rest. Once it was publicly revealed that Mikey Welsh was not coming back, Shriner accepted a permanent role.

"It wasn't really discussed what was going to be the plan next month or next year or the next day," Shriner said of his first days with the band. "That's how I operate in life in general. There's no philosophy or strategy behind it." And perhaps Shriner's outlook explains his good fit with the group. "I feel that my sole mission in life is to bring the rock to the people. And I really mean that. People need to have rock brought to them. The rock saved my life as a kid, and I'll do anything for the rock, bro."

Shriner's live initiation came during the high-profile KROQ "Inland Invasion" gig, when an attendee jumped on him and put him in a headlock during Weezer's set (it turned out to be a recent bandmate of his upset that he bailed on Broken to join Weezer). While it took two security guys to pull him off, the fact that Shriner kept playing said a lot to the remaining members of the band about his tenacity.

"Welcome to Weezer," Cuomo told Shriner in front of the stadium crowd.

"That was a challenge," the former Marine recollected of the massive debut gig. "It was the biggest show I have ever done and my first with Weezer. I am glad that my friend jumped on my back because it broke me out of my trance . . . It was wild."

TODD WOJTOWICZ/MUSICHEAD.ORG

Introducing . . . Shrinedog. Weezer's third bassist — complete with tattoos, muscles, and a gold tooth!

The gig was also unique as it marked the debut of a bald Patrick Wilson, who had decided to shave his head, and two brand new tunes, "Get Me on the Line" and "So Low." Social Distortion's Mike Ness also gave props to the group during the gig, taking the stage and telling the audience that Weezer was a great band.

As August came to a close, news of an "Island" CD single was confirmed for the U.K. designed to coincide with the planned October dates. Three officially unreleased B-sides for the disc included "O Lisa," which had been floating around on the Internet since it was leaked in April, the string-laden ballad "Always," and "Brightening Day," previously known as "My Best Friends Are Gone."

Around this time, as Weezer posted yet another MP3 — this time the "December" BBC demo from early July — the band learned that MTV had nominated the "Hash Pipe" clip for a Video Music Award, which was odd, considering the fact the cable channel had run a heavily edited version of the song all summer long. When asked about the edit, which took his every utterance of the word "hash" out of the song, in conjunction with the nomination, Cuomo said, "We don't really care. We were not really activists. The point of the song was not to promote hash-smoking, but it does seem ridiculous, MTV censoring hash, considering what MTV does allow, in more violent and sexual-related material."

Revealing that he never even smoked hash, Cuomo noted, "I ate it once, though, in Amsterdam. I got sick from it and went to sleep. I woke up half an hour later, and it was like I was on the moon."

With two weeks to go before another round of U.S. dates, Weezer tracked twenty-four demos at Sage & Sound Studios in Los Angeles in three days with engineer Joe Barresi. Along with aforementioned titles like "Death and Destruction," "Don't Bring Me Down," "Don't Pick on Me," "Farmer John," "How Long," "I Wanna Know," "On Holiday," "Song from Yesterday," "Stupid Feelings," "The Dawn," "Through Other's Eyes," "Your Room," "Broken Arrows," and "We Go Together," were a host of new songs.

Among them were "Beg and Cry," "Change the World," "Diamond Rings," "Do You Want Me to Stay?" "Fall Together," "Get Me on the Line," "Gone to Stay," "How Long," "Living without You," "Sandwiches Time," "So Low," "Somewhere," and "We Go Together." Meanwhile "Anything but Love," "Take Back the Love," "Take a Listen," and "Everybody Depends on a Friend" were put on ice.

"[With] the new stuff," Cuomo observed, "I'm trying to be dynamic. Now we have some real metal songs, and some pretty instrumental songs, pop songs." Touting the new material, he said, "It's heavier, it's funkier, it's poppier, it's stronger. I think it's going to be one of the best records ever. I think it's going to be our 'breakout' record."

On September 2 — as word was received that "Hash Pipe" was in the running for "Pot Song of the Year" by marijuana advocacy publication *High Times* — the members of Weezer took a meeting with the suits at Interscope and were given the go-ahead to ready a fourth album for May 2002.

Speaking of the short lag between albums three and four, Cuomo later observed, "I write maybe one song a week. That adds up to fifty-two songs over a year. People think I'm some kind of freak, but it feels like I'm slacking. Why should I wait two years for a typical album cycle to end so we can put out another one? We're just kind of doing what we want to do."

The same day they met with the label, the group confirmed what most by now suspected — that they would indeed launch their imminent tour with Shriner on bass. With a week before the tour launch, Rivers seemed glad to be rid of Welsh. Anticipating the upcoming tour and future album plans, he said, "I'll tell you, rehearsals are really fun right now. We're just totally rocking out." Cuomo was promising that the upcoming material would have a harder vibe than anything they'd released to date, and couldn't wait to "punish" tour attendees with the new songs.

Pat, too, was stoked to have Shriner in the group. "Suddenly I felt like I had a partner in the rhythm section that was committed to being really, really good and it has definitely raised my level," Wilson would later say of Scott's abilities. "He was the first guy to come in and not have a fuzzed-out bass sound, which is a shock because for years that's all we heard was really over-driven bass. It's super fresh to have a bass sound like a bass."

Although he had an Ivy League education, Cuomo made no bones about his devotion to the simple cause of rock 'n' roll. "'I think I'm an extremely cynical person in a way, and it would suck if my music sounded [too deep]," he said on the eve of the tour. "I like music to be pure and innocent. It shouldn't have to carry the burdens of philosophy and scientific thesis. It's just pop music.

"It's an injustice when musicians make music carry their philosophies," Cuomo explained. "It's Bob Dylan's fault. I've never listened to him, but a lot of musicians I like have gotten worse when they listened to Dylan. [Like] The Beatles. The later Beatles [music] is unlistenable. The end of the '60s was an embarrassment."

Continuing to lay into folk rock's most famous bard, Cuomo opined, "I think Bob Dylan is one of the most influential musicians. For the most part it's been a bad influence. Music was a lot better before he screwed it up. He got people thinking that music should be something more than music; it should have some literal meaning."

Rivers obviously took an opposite stance and validated it by simultaneously touting techno-pop, admitting that he listened to acts like Vengaboys or LSDJ to pump himself up. And in a startling disclosure to Weezer fans, Cuomo admitted a genuine fondness for Fred Durst's band. "I love Limp Bizkit, because they rock," he said point blank, and no doubt swayed by the now-regular companionship of Jordan Schur. "I like 'My Way' and 'Nookie' and 'Break Stuff' and 'Mission Impossible' . . . I don't know if [Fred Durst] writes those songs, but if he does I think it's great."

That declaration went over like a fart in church with Weezer disciples.

chapter twenty-five

broken arrows

On September 10, 2001 — as SoundScan numbers found Weezer's third album approaching platinum after achieving sales in excess of 909,000 copies in the U.S. — the band took a Southwest Airlines flight out of Burbank Airport up to San Jose. The next morning, as the band awoke with plans to head off to the Events Center to rock the masses on the first night of their U.S. tour, they learned of the terrorist attacks on both of the World Trade Center buildings and the Pentagon.

While the nation mourned the senseless loss of thousands of Americans at the hands of Osama bin Laden's hijackers, the city of San Jose and the state of California canceled Weezer's September 11 show. Out of respect for those who were killed and considering the fact that the band and the bulk of its fans were still too fragile to play or attend a rock concert, the move was a wise one.

Extending thoughts and sympathies to the victims and their families as all of the United States went on high alert for terrorism the next day, the group was unsure what its next move should be and began looking for feedback from fans about the tour. "Like you, we've all been following the story of these horrifying acts of terrorism, and we are all just as stunned and shocked as you," read a collective Weezer post. "Normal life stuff, including the very act of being in a touring rock band, seems incredibly strange. Everyone feels terrible for the victims of this, and a sense of frustrating anger over an inability to do anything about it."

With permission to do their show the next day in Oakland, the band was still uncertain of how to act. With a large collective of fans flooding Koch's inbox with support, matched by a still substantial number suggesting the group cancel a second night in a row out of respect for lives lost and those deeply in mourning, Cuomo went ahead with the difficult decision. "I want to do something about all this, but the only thing I can do is play music," Rivers explained to fans. For some ticket holders it was just too early, too painful, or too scary to make it to the show in the midst of all the chaos back east, but Weezer got down to the business of rock music just the same that night.

Looking back on the events of September 11, 2001, with nearly two years of hindsight, guitarist Brian Bell commented in the summer of 2003, "You know I think it initially changed my perception about being safe around that time. I became hypersensitive of things American. I was kind of taken aback that people were so pro-American and into waving the flag. Like, why weren't they before? Why does it take this to show love for your country? So I had mixed emotions at the time. I don't think about it much now. It never comes up in conversation. The only tragedies we have out here in California are earthquakes. So, I think it made people value life more."

Despite the ongoing chaos and threats to national security, thousands of fans at the Henry J. Kaiser Arena in Oakland were undaunted and went about their lives. In return, these attendees were treated to a unique medley of Weezer songs delivered by the University of California, Berkeley, Marching Band, who followed Cold's less-than-appreciatively received set, but preceded Cuomo, Wilson, Bell, and Shriner's spirit-lifting one.

Two nights later, the quartet's next scheduled show, planned for San Diego, was postponed due to the Cox Arena's concerns over security. Instead, the band traveled on to Las Vegas on the National Day of Mourning, uncertain if the show at that city's Cox Pavilion the following night would go off as planned. When it did, with Ozma guesting as openers instead of Cold (who had another commitment), the Weezer camp, like much of America, started to regain some normalcy.

While the band had hoped that one of the two postponed shows could be made up on September 16, a scheduled day off on the original itinerary, it was not to be, as the business arrangements couldn't be made on such short notice and the venues had already been contracted for other purposes. The next night in Salt Lake City, hard rockers Cold were catching more abuse than ever from attendees. Clearly mismatched with Weezer's audience, Rivers' choice to have them open the trek was a puzzling one, and fans were vocal with their disdain in cities like Denver and St. Paul.

Onstage the following night at Chicago's 13,000-capacity sold-out United Center, Cold couldn't handle the crowd's insults and obscene gestures. With fans on the floor of the venue giving the group the middle finger and yelling, "You suck," singer Scooter Ward flipped off the audience in return and then dropped his microphone, abruptly exiting the stage prior to completing his band's set.

"No one believed it at first, but sure enough Cold packed up and went their own way after the show was over," Koch reported. "I've never really seen anything like this before, and it's a bummer. It's no fun for a tour to lose a band like that, but if that's their decision, we have to respect it."

"It got pretty violent before Cold quit the tour," Rivers would later acknowledge, despite being a fan of the group. "The audience hated them... [they were] like throwing projectile missiles at the band." With newcomers The Start now sliding into Cold's lead support slot in time for the next night's gig in Detroit, the band resuscitated the hard rocking Summer 2K song "Dope Nose."

Weezer also made its final public comment on Mikey Welsh two months after his disappearance. When Mikey's attorney allegedly contacted the band to resolve his public claims of wrongful termination, it prompted the following announcement to fans, still wondering about the bassist's status with the group. "What's going on between Mikey and Weezer is a private matter," read the post. "There will be no further announcements, news, or speculation unless and until everyone involved is ready to make any statements on the matter."

While the band never actually said that he was fired, it appears that Weezer basically deemed Welsh's absence as job abandonment and ran him out the door. The move was timed perfectly with Rivers' aim to take the band in a harder direction. And as Welsh got to work in the studio around Boston with his new band, the Plastics (later to be called the Brakes and finally the Kickovers) with Nate Albert from the Mighty Mighty Bosstones, Weezer's tour rolled on without a hitch. On their way to the 9,000 capacity D.C.–area Patriot Center, in Fairfax, Virginia, late that September, the band drove right past the badly damaged Pentagon building, just two and a half weeks after the terrorist attacks.

On September 29, the band was up in the New York area, but many miles away from Ground Zero, where emergency personnel worked day and night for many months to clean up debris from the attacks. Over at the Jones Beach Amphitheatre on Long Island, the last show of the tour was a cold one for most in attendance. Unfazed, Weezer played hard and closed out another successful run of live dates.

As the trek wrapped, Pat Wilson was asked by a reporter to explain the group's reinstatement as leaders of the geek-rock charge, but in typical fashion, the drummer quipped, "We're just so good." To which Cuomo countered, "Who else would they form a cult around? Who else was popular in the mid-'90s and dropped out in the late '90s who could have a cult around them?"

"Tool," Patrick replied.

"Tool," Rivers nodded. "Tool has a cult. Their cult's bigger than our cult."

If the cult of Weezer was bigger than ever, it must have been especially disconcerting for the popular rockers to learn from their Interscope publicist that they had been bumped from playing CBS's *The Late Show with David Letterman*. Believing they were overlooked in favor of former Clash mouthpiece and punk icon Joe Strummer — who was in town to play Irving Plaza — the truth was later learned that the publicity department at Weezer's record label had actually declined the offer from Letterman's staff to appear. Shut down by an apparent directive from the suits at Interscope, the group was outraged and fans knew it.

Cuomo also became steamed when he learned that Weezer's October tour of Europe was going to be postponed, but not because of fears over travel in the wake of the recent of events on September 11 and ongoing terrorist threats to airlines. Oddly, despite a million U.S. sales of their third album in just four and a half months, Interscope decided at the last minute that Weezer wasn't enough of a priority and withdrew funding for the trip. In markets outside of Japan and North America, where Weezer was not yet touring at a profitable level, support from the record company was critical.

So irked by these Interscope directives, Cuomo reportedly stopped talking to Schur for months. Left with no choice but to bump Weezer's European travel plans to 2002, Weezer continued to rehearse extensively in Los Angeles. The goal for the final quarter of 2001 was to work out the new material in a live setting under the Goat Punishment moniker, plot an Extended Midget Tour of the United States for November and December, and track their fourth album into the new year.

At the outset of October, the band posted MP3 demos of the prior month's "Death and Destruction" and "Your Room" recordings to the audio/video page of its official Web site. As fans continued to download new music with delight, details of the Extended Midget Tour began to take shape, with a makeup of the 9/11 cancellations set for San Jose and San Diego on November 19 and 20, respectively.

After the Cold fiasco, better-suited opening bands like Tenacious D and Jimmy Eat World were an important factor in designing the tour. With the band regrouped at Swinghouse Studios to work out six new Cuomo numbers — "Smiths Jamb," "Space Rock," "As the Day Goes By," "It's Nothing At All," "High and Dry," and "Slave" — Rivers' assistant Sheeny Bang reported the events to be "really tight" and added, "It's all coming together as a monster rocking sound and it's pretty amazing to see it."

Meanwhile, Weezer merchandise (including a lunch box and a 2002 calendar) hit the marketplace as Cuomo began taking a vested interest in AM Radio, consulting for the band fronted by his old friend Kevin Ridel. In addition to handling Weezer's affairs, the coming months would see Rivers begin to manage Ridel's group and help raise its profile.

AM Radio was tapped to open Weezer's first Goat Punishment gig of 2001, planned for the Knitting Factory on October 24 and set for taping by HBO for their *Reverb* program. The show sold out immediately, just five days before it took place, when tickets were advertised in advance by the *L.A. Weekly* and given a mention on KROQ. Just prior to that GP club gig, Weezer started recording a new set of pre-production demos at Swinghouse Studios, but later moved to the Cello facility where *The Green Album* was tracked. The self-funded studio activity proceeded without Interscope's knowledge.

Around this time, Cuomo met with attorneys Yakub Hazzard and Stanton L. Stein in preparation for Weezer's petition with the California Labor Commissioner against both Atlas/Third Rail as a corporation, and Pat Magnarella as an individual. The seriousness of the meetings and the repercussions at stake put the camp on edge and made it difficult to focus on creativity.

In a hearing to determine controversy on October 31, 2001, a summary of the findings of fact were as follows:

Weezer, also performing on certain occasions as Goat Punishment, were formed in 1992. Between 1998 and 2000, Weezer performed under its alternate moniker on seven or eight separate occasions, generally when they wanted to play before a relatively small audience of knowledgeable fans, without the pressure of performing under their more-widely known name.

In late 1993, Weezer hired Roven Cavallo Entertainment, Inc., to provide "personal management" services. A written contract was formalized around January 1, 1994, specifying that in return for its services, Weezer would pay its personal manager 15% of its gross earnings. The contract specified that Roven Cavallo was not a licensed talent agency, and was not licensed, permitted, or authorized to attempt, offer, or promise to procure employment for Weezer. At some point between 1994 and 2001 Roven Cavallo's corporate name was changed to Atlas/Third Rail Management, Inc., of which respondent Pat Magnarella was a partner, although neither party had ever been licensed as a talent agent.

Weezer's first point of contention surrounded the release of Weezer's first record in May 1994. Rivers Cuomo testified that he expressed his frustration to Magnarella that no record release party had been scheduled, but Magnarella said that he'd get a show booked at Club Lingerie. Magnarella testified that he had no role in obtaining the May 9 engagement, and that he believed that it had been booked by William Morris Agency, Weezer's booking/talent agency at the time. According to the Labor Commission, Weezer, as petitioners, failed to present any evidence to rebut Magnarella's testimony on this issue.

The group's second complaint was around an October or November

2000 incident where Magnarella asked Rivers Cuomo if the band would be interested in acting in the movie *Scooby Doo*, which was scheduled to be filmed in early 2001. Magnarella testified during the hearing that the film was being produced by Atlas, and that along with managing musicians the corporation also produced movies. Magnarella sent the band copies of the movie script but Rivers ultimately advised his personal manager that the band was not interested in the offer. The California Labor Commission deemed this matter invalid, because Magnarella's offer to appear in the movie — a role that later went to pop rockers Sugar Ray — did not constitute procurement in the state's labor code.

In November 2000, Weezer agreed to perform at KROQ's Acoustic Christmas shows on December 16 and 17, 2000. In preparation, petitioners wanted to do some live warm-up performances prior to these shows under the name Goat Punishment. Rather than contact their booking agents at Creative Artists Agency, Weezer contacted Christopher Donahoe, an Atlas employee who had been an assistant to Magnarella since December 1998, to arrange for these performances. Donahoe's regular duties included scheduling rehearsals for musicians and previously he had set up rehearsals, both without any audience and with non-paying private audiences of record company executives, but Magnarella's assistant was not licensed as a talent agent, and prior to November 2000, he had never sought to procure live public engagements for Weezer.

On or about December 1, Donahoe made phone calls to talent bookers at Los Angeles clubs, seeking to procure engagements for Weezer to play live before paying audiences under the name Goat Punishment in the days immediately prior to the KROQ Christmas shows. As a result of Donahoe's calls, Goat Punishment was confirmed to perform at Spaceland on December 14 and The Troubadour on the 15. Donahoe negotiated the financial terms of Weezer's Spaceland appearance, agreeing to a $500 guarantee plus a percentage of the gate. Patrons were charged an admission fee for that show, and the band received $900. Although Donahoe did not negotiate any terms of compensation for The Troubadour appearance, Weezer — one of four bands on the bill — was paid $250 for that appearance. Atlas received no compensation for itself as a result of either of Weezer's Goat Punishment shows.

Magnarella testified it was not until the month of the hearing that he learned of Donahoe obtaining the December 2000 Goat Punishment engagements. However, there was no indication from the testimony presented that Magnarella had ever instructed Donahoe that he could not procure live public engagements for Weezer.

The Labor Commissioner's legal analysis called the instances of procurement at Spaceland and The Troubadour in December 2000 "troubling." "These were musical performances before a live paying audience that were advertised and open to the public. The fact that petitioners performed these engagements under the name 'Goat Punishment' rather than the name 'Weezer' is irrelevant, as is the fact that Atlas did not collect or seek to collect any commissions for these shows."

Citing the Talent Agencies Act of California, which stipulates a license is required to engage in procurement activities even if no commission is received for the service, the contract between the band and Atlas was deemed to be illegal and unenforceable under the act.

And although Atlas contended it had no liability for the actions of Christopher Donahoe — who was not authorized by his employers to procure the Spaceland and Troubadour gigs — it was ruled that "a corporation cannot escape liability for the misdeeds of any of its employees" and that Atlas was indeed liable for the consequences of Donahoe's actions.

In Weezer's filing to determine controversy with the Labor Commissioner the previous July, the group sought an order declaring the original contract between the band and Atlas void *ab initio* on the ground that respondents performed functions of a talent agency without a license. Weezer also sought reimbursement of all amounts paid to Atlas pursuant to the personal management contract in the one-year period preceding the filing of the petition (totaling $134,011.13) plus reimbursement of attorney's fees.

While Pat Magnarella was listed as a respondent, Weezer's contract was with the corporate predecessor to Atlas and not Magnarella himself. This put all liability on Atlas. Cuomo was victorious when the original contract was concluded to be void as soon as the personal management outfit acted unlawfully as a talent agency in December 2000. As a result, Atlas was ordered to disgorge all commissions (totaling $78,355.54) paid by Weezer after December 1, 2000. But while Weezer prevailed before the Labor Commissioner, the fact that the case was heard in an administrative proceeding rather than in a court of law meant they were not entitled to attorney's fees.

Now rid of Magnarella and Atlas/Third Rail, Cuomo, Wilson, Bell, and Shriner could focus on pre-production of album #4. Able to "work freely and independently of unnecessary baggage that only serves to slow bands down and keep them unsure of themselves and overly dependent on others," as a Koch post put it, Weezer's plan was to forgo a producer and oversee the disc on its own. The group cranked out new material at a record pace in the two weeks left before the Extended Midget Tour launch at Portland's Rose Garden Arena.

Meanwhile, a third radio single, "Photograph," was being officially serviced to North American modern rock radio in early November to coincide with the trek. Dropping hints to knowledgeable fans, the group made a subtle announcement about three upcoming Goat Punishment shows at the Viper Room, slated to take place at "Johnny Depp's House of

Botany on Sunset Boulevard" on November 6–8. Few were surprised when AM Radio were tapped to support again, but the inclusion of The Special Goodness as openers came as a surprise to many who never thought they'd see the day when Rivers would allow it. For the performance, TSG — in need of a bassist since Mikey's Weezer vacancy also left him out of his duties in Pat's band — found a fill-in player for these shows by the name of Murphy Karges, himself of platinum popsters Sugar Ray.

Three days before the GP shows, Weezer returned to Cello Studios on their own dime and tracked twelve tunes. They left six more open to be completed after the Extended Midget trek working under Cuomo's edict: "Record until you fall over."

Onstage during the November 2001 Goat Punishment shows, Weezer exuded more confidence than ever playing all new material to enthusiastic fans and celebrities like *Jackass* star Johnny Knoxville. But Cuomo, Wilson, Bell, and Shriner weren't just acting like a team onstage at the Viper Room or in sessions at Cello Studios — they were, for the first time, making the team theme part of their public image. In an amusing nod to Rivers' all-time favorite sport, Weezer even donned soccer garb for an infamous publicity photo.

modern dukes

Following the Cold fiasco on the Midget Tour, the Extended Midget Tour's Portland, Oregon, to Portland, Maine, month-long itinerary with Tenacious D and Jimmy Eat World was what many fans to this day consider the best Weezer tour ever.

The ill-fitting vibes of Cold were supplanted with Tenacious D, a metal parody act steered by actors/comedians Jack Black and Kyle Gass that audiences loved immediately. With crass satirical numbers like "Fuck Her Gently," "Kielbasa," and "Cock Pushups" — each culled from the D's self-titled 2001 Epic album — plus a hysterical stage presence, the duo won over crowds in mere minutes.

In contrast to Tenacious D, but still befitting the same Weezer audience, Jimmy Eat World was a serious-minded emo rock outfit finally getting the praise it deserved after a number of years, thanks to a new disc on DreamWorks that was bolstered by fabulously melodic anthems like "A Praise Chorus" and "Sweetness." And because of the high profile opening slot on the Extended Midget jaunt, the band's single "The Middle" began an ascent at modern rock radio that would eventually land the song at #1. Interestingly enough, former That Dog member and old Weezer accomplice Rachel Haden joined the other Jimmies — singer/guitarist Jim Adkins, bassist Rick Burch, drummer Zach Lind, and guitarist Tom Linton — adding backing vocals on the trek.

Up to Seattle on November 14, Weezer recorded all new material in a

KNDD-endorsed studio session. Glenn Sound demos for "Spacerock," "Slave," and "Cygnus X-1" (the latter previously known as "Smiths Jamb") were put to tape. While they never aired on the station, Karl Koch posted them as MP3s, and downloaders snatched them up from *Weezer.com*. As the next night's concert at the Key Arena played out, portions of Weezer's October 24 Goat Punishment gig were seen by Weezer fans with HBO subscriptions around the world, amid footage of singer/songwriter Pete Yorn and indie rock icons Guided By Voices.

CHRISTINA RADISH

It's in the Photograph: A photogenic Bell earns his paycheck

The tour had its mishaps, like when Brian fell off the ramp after taking a bad step on his way back to the stage in St. Louis for an encore, but things generally ran smoothly as the journey progressed into hubs like Normal, Illinois; Columbus; Kalamazoo; and Cleveland. While Weezer fans took to the Internet and phones trying to hype "Photograph" to radio, the band soon discovered that the song lacked the staying power of "Hash Pipe." Considering this, the group passed on a big-name director for a planned "Photograph" video in favor of having Koch shoot and edit an on-the-road clip on the cheap.

By the last week of the tour, Weezer's regular rehearsals of the new material at sound check meant that Cuomo could compile the first of what would be several tentative song listings for album #4. The titles, accompanied by the numeric designation applied to all songs written sequentially by Rivers since New Year's Day 1999 included #284 "Acapulco," #319 "Ain't Got Much Time," #305 "Death and Destruction," #320 "Fall Together," #296 "How Long?," #190 "Modern Dukes," #186 "Preacher's Son," #317 "Sandwiches Time," #344 "Space Rock," and #354 "Slave."

As fans downloaded a demo version of "Sandwiches Time" as well as the seasonal, non-album track "The Christmas Song," the final tour dates of 2001 found Weezer, Jimmy Eat World, and Tenacious D bouncing from Cleveland to Baltimore and finally on to Portland, Maine. Preceding the last show of the tour, Cuomo spent a day off on the afternoon of November 10 watching soccer before heading out to a Portland club known as The Skinny, which Weezer had rented out for an end-of-tour party. In celebration of the successful jaunt, which saw the tour rock approximately 125,000 fans in thirty days, the shindig yielded an unplanned, alcohol-fueled jam session.

Dually known as "Portland, What?" and "The Power Station II," the impromptu supergroup consisted of Rivers on drums, Pat on bass, Tenacious D's Kyle Gass on guitar, and Jack Black on vocals. Attempting eighteen classic rock staples, including The Cars' "Just What I Needed," AC/DC's "Highway to Hell," and Blue Öyster Cult's "Don't Fear the Reaper," this one-night-only outfit capped off what was one of Weezer's most enjoyable tours to date. The next night, just prior to exiting the stage during the "Surf Wax America" encore, Gass and Black took matters to the next level as they ran onstage in their underwear to provide an "interpretive dance," much to the amusement of the band and the elated crowd.

If most assumed Weezer's live commitments were fulfilled for 2001, two nights later the quartet performed an unannounced corporate gig for Molson Inc. at Toronto's Kool Haus. Highly compensated for this private performance (which some fans would later complain embodied the term "sell out"), Rivers, Pat, Brian, and Scott played Toronto's Molson Canadian Blind Date Concert before 200 contest winners, flown in from all over Canada for the event.

Meanwhile, down in the Lower 48, year-end accolades began piling in for *The Green Album*. *Spin* placed it at #9 among 2001's ten best albums and the disc also landed in the *Boston Globe*'s year-end Top 10, with the newspaper calling it, "bracing punk-pop with a mess of hooks." Far away in the land down under, Australia's *Herald Sun* listed it as the top set of the year, describing it as "lean, loud, and hungry power pop. Exquisite."

"Shorter than an episode of *Facts of Life* and catchier than smallpox, *Weezer* was the best traditional power pop of 2001," wrote future *Spin* staffer Chuck Klosterman in the *Akron Beacon Journal*. And after the album was proven by a platinum certification, Cuomo himself firmly believed in his own product. "I pose the question to myself this way: If I could only leave one of the three albums for posterity, which would it be? And all things considered, I would definitely say *The Green Album*," Rivers said. "I think of the three albums, it's the one that will be listenable to the most people across cultures and across the ages."

In the *New Times* Los Angeles music awards, Weezer snagged best local rock/pop artist, local artist of the year, and major label album of the year honors. Speaking to Weezer's comeback single, the *Toronto Sun*'s Jane Stevenson called "Hash Pipe" "one of the year's best" songs, and Brad Kava of the *San Jose Mercury News* called it "the best single of the year, just for sheer catchiness." Elsewhere, the *Atlanta Journal Constitution* wrote, "Despite the MTV censorship, which called it simply 'Pipe,' that grinding guitar riff was undeniable, making for the year's most unlikely hit."

With the post-9/11 sentiment, *Rolling Stone* spoke appreciatively of Weezer's successful, million-selling return in its year in rock and roll 2001 issue. "And if any America worth living in is worth laughing in, we consider it our patriotic duty to pay our respects to the risible, the pathetic, the fool-hardy, and the just plain dumb. Plus that indomitable human spirit, which reached its purest expression this year in the fact that Weezer are still around."

But perhaps it was weighty praise from the *L.A. Weekly* that best explained Weezer's return so eloquently: "Cuomo's weakest song on his worst day would be the masterpiece of a lifetime for mortal musicians."

As year-end accolades continued to pour in for album #3, the lads in Weezer flew home to Los Angeles from Toronto to focus on their future. After a day of rest on Saturday, December 15, the making of their fourth studio disc was officially underway the following day when they were joined by one-time Rental Rod Cervera in an engineering capacity. Tracking Scott's bass and Pat's drum tracks (while performing them as a whole), the band immediately began using their Web site as a forum for instant fan feedback.

Through a series of question-and-answer e-mails with Weezer fans in late 2001, Rivers became interested in his hardcore fans' points of view, because in many instances their comments were noticeably similar to observations a producer or executive might make, except the advice came from people who had no financial interest in the outcome.

A fan writing as "Asschun," also known as "DJ," was the first to tap into Rivers' psyche, criticizing how Cuomo sang the post-*Pinkerton* material in a letter to Koch. Accusing the Weezer frontman of delivering the recent material less emotively, in what he describes as a "gay" manner, Asschun's comments — relayed to Rivers — surprisingly prompted more requests for feedback. When the word spread on the Rebel Weezer Board, Cuomo got just what he wanted.

Calling Rivers' vocals on the pre–*Blue Album* demo, the subsequent debut disc, and *Pinkerton* "awesome," Asschun disliked the singer's "new voice" and criticized him for singing songs like "O Girlfriend" and "I Do" less energetically and with "excessive quivering."

"I associate that with cheesy," the fan wrote. "If only Rivers sang like he used to." Taking a new song to task, Asschun critiqued the "Slave" MP3 that had recently been posted to *Weezer.com*. "It sounds like he is singing slightly off key, which hurts my ears. It happens when his voice sounds like it breaks on purpose . . . do you understand?"

Cuomo, using Koch's e-mail account, wrote back to DJ. "I'm not hearing what you're hearing on 'Slave.' Can you explain your view a little more? I'm sorry for all these questions but I can't resist the urge to ask. I'm a little obsessive sometimes.

"I don't necessarily agree with all of your views but they've certainly helped me to see things that I want to fix.

"One other thought: I went through a massive Oasis phase in '97–'99. I bet Liam [Gallagher] rubbed off on me. He's a very non-dynamic singer. Perhaps his influence wasn't a good thing."

Replying to Cuomo, DJ called *The Green Album* "a disappointment." Insisting he didn't hate it, he took the same position as many longtime fans. "It's not a bad album, it was just nothing special," DJ wrote. "I can't even compare it to *Blue/Pinkerton*, for obvious reasons."

Rivers responded appreciatively, writing, "Thanks for the help. I honestly prefer talking to people like yourself, rather than a producer, a manager, or a record executive. You make suggestions motivated by artistic concerns, you possess greater knowledge of Weezer music, and you notice the tiny details those other hired-hands miss.

"I wish I could grasp the rock entirely on my own, but the truth is, I, and most other musicians, need some sort of advising — whether it be from a manager, a girlfriend, or in my case, an ex-fan, so as long as you're willing to give the criticism, I'm willing to take it."

Similar fan criticism — acknowledged by one participant as "nitpicking" — continued and Cuomo continued to be largely receptive to the feedback about his vocals. In fact, he asked open questions like, "Do you think the difference is really in my vocal approach or is it in the melodies themselves? 'Paperface' is kind of a screamer melody; *Blue* and *Pink* are broad, almost instrumental-style melodies; *Green* are much smaller, more manageable, vocal-style melodies (à la Oasis). Do you think the simpler melodies are what's turning people off? I tell you one thing: they're a lot funner to sing."

When another fan knocked Rivers' newer songs' lyrics as "empty words hastily contrived together," the rocker wrote back to explain that his spontaneous approach to songs had been a tentative procedure.

"It's clear to me that many listeners would prefer if I actually sat down to write 'about something,'" Cuomo acknowledged to the Rebel Weezer Board. "I hope my experiments over the past few years haven't been a complete waste of time, but please don't spare my feelings if that's the case."

A fan posting as Gogokain took the bait, speaking to the differences in musical quality between the in-progress "Slave" and *The Blue Album*'s "No One Else." "It's like comparing Britney Spears or Slipknot to Billy Joel," contended the fan. "You simply can't say it's a matter of opinion. Seriously, the quality is obvious. Maybe you like Britney Spears better, but Billy Joel writes higher quality music, and no one in their right mind would argue against that."

Writing back to Gogokain, Rivers asked, "Do you like The Beatles? How do you think they were able to get away with writing songs with wholesale repetition of verses and bridges without development? Each verse is essentially the same as the last. How about Nirvana? How about nearly every song ever written before acid hit rock music? That's what I'm trying to do. I'll admit I haven't pulled it off yet but I haven't given up either. (Maybe I should?) The difference between songs like 'No One Else' and songs like 'Slave' is that the former is composed of different ideas tacked onto each other in an ad hoc fashion whereas the latter flowed out naturally from one germ of an idea. I have to believe the latter is a more sound way to compose music."

Cuomo — in truly unique form for a rock star of his popularity — continued to reply to more letters of criticisms and suggestions by fans. One fan, writing in as "Matt" about Rivers' use of repetition, noted that the earliest example of this was on the Homie tune, "American Girls."

Rivers wrote back to explain that, "'round about the time I wrote 'American Girls,' I started getting interested in what one of my [Harvard] professors calls 'Strophic' composition: where one verse is essentially the same as the last. I think this form produces less 'emotional' music, but the masters of the form, including The Beatles and Nirvana, don't seem to let their listeners down with it. I'll admit I haven't found a way to pull it off yet."

This sort of fan interaction was so inspiring to Rivers that beginning on December 17, in an unprecedented move for a band of Weezer's stature, the first in a series of many MP3s chronicling Weezer's progress in the studio began appearing on the Audio/Video page of the Web site. As soon as the blueprints for "Mr. Taxman" and "American Gigolo" (262 and 281 respectively) were tracked, the incomplete songs (housing rough guitars and vocals) were posted on the site. Within hours the Weezer-related message boards were flowing with observations about the songs, and Cuomo was lurking. Rivers was so juiced by the process of letting his fans steer his progress that he even wrote a song that week called "Message Board."

Rivers also admitted to using a few of the message boards "to pick up girls," and says he turned to the Web for fan interactions when face-to-face meet and greets yielded the same conversations night in and night out. But mostly, it was about his own craft. "Sometimes a person will say, 'This solo is gay,'" he explained. "And they all gang up on me and so I go, 'Okay, I guess I can do better.'"

In mid- to late December, a number of MP3s surfaced for feedback. They included "December," "High Up Above," "Listen Up," "Better Off Alone," "American Gigolo," "Spend Some Time," "How Long?," "Saturday Night," "Keep Fishin'," "Your Room," "Possibilities," "Slave," "Serendipitous Time," and the left-for-dead 2000 composition "Dope Nose." Each appeared in various stages of completion, with some appearing on multiple days as Weezer tweaked or changed things with insight from fans.

Midway through studio work, Weezer splintered for a five-day break from studio endeavors on December 23. Rivers entertained his mother, Beverly, in his Hollywood Hills home during Christmas week, but his mind was largely on his work. Remarkably, despite the stress of the holiday, he managed to pump out four new songs ("Motion to Me," "Untenable," "Private Message," and "This Bulging River") as she visited.

"My mom came out and stayed with me," Cuomo told a Philadelphia radio audience soon after, calling in to Y100 disc jockey Ben Harvey to thank listeners for voting "Hash Pipe" the #1 song of the year. "She didn't get me anything," he jokingly complained. "You know, I told my family that I don't want to deal with presents anymore. A couple of years ago, we had a big celebration at my grandparents and I showed up and said, 'You know what guys, I didn't get anybody anything and I'm proud of it.' I don't want to have to go to the mall and get them the same lame ass thing that everyone else gets. It's just a big hassle."

If Cuomo's Christmas message to fans on the Weezer Web site was mixed ("Thanks for a killer '01. Too bad we couldn't please everyone"), the group showed no signs of slowing down. Back in the studio on December 28, the band resumed its recording and posting initiative, continuing to allow fans access to material as it progressed. Aside from the aforementioned titles, the next week found songs like "Sandwiches Time," "Space Rock," "Take Control," "Acapulco," "Seafaring Jamb," "Porcupine," "Broken Arrows," "Don't Pick on Me," and "Death and Destruction" downloaded by enthusiastic and involved Weezer loyalists.

By January, *RollingStone.com*, *Billboard.com*, *NME.com*, and Canada's *Jam! Showbiz* hopped on the MP3 posts as news items, helping to spread the word on Weezer's latest studio initiative. The latter heavily endorsed the song "Slave" and proclaimed, "Now *this* is how smart bands use the Net: not just to tell their fans they're working on a new album, but to let them hear the demos for it."

"1 like the instant gratification of people hearing my new songs. Sometimes you don't get a good response. But a lot of times you do, and it feels good," Cuomo said at the time. "We want to get praised immediately. The irony, of course, is that we put the things up and we're immediately criticized. That just makes us want to work again the next day and try to get praise again."

In an online chat with the since-disabled fan site *Weezon.com*, Cuomo asked participants which new songs should be used to expand the upcoming disc to thirteen songs. Among the tunes suggested was an old forgotten Weezer number known as "Slob." Disciples urged Rivers to give the raw, attitudinal song another try, and the frontman, confessing he didn't have a track listing confirmed for the record yet despite the fact it was "crunch time," expressed a desire to improve it while retaining the "'tude" of the original version. And when the old *Songs from the Black Hole* track "Blast Off" came up in the same discussion, Cuomo rewarded fans worldwide by having Koch put the song up on Weezer's A/V page.

"Everyone's shredding. It's hard rock, cramming all the bombast of a three-part Yes song into two minutes," Cuomo said excitedly, assessing the band's sonic goals for 2002.

"We never consciously set out to go in a particular direction," he also revealed. "With each new record, we make up for the mistakes we made on the previous one. We were kind of disappointed with the lack of rock on *The Green Album*. The fourth record is going to bring back the rock — let me clarify that — we're going to bring back the heavy metal. We're substantially more Judas Priest–like now. I think we were more like Stryper before."

But simultaneously, through the Web site, Rivers was polling old and new fans alike about the new material, continuing to "incorporate his fanbase into his psyche" like no other artist before him. Cuomo even began posting directly to the Weezer message boards. Posting secretly at first under the pseudonym "Ace," Rivers soon enough confirmed his true identity.

With the necessary feedback gathered through Rivers' various online fan interactions, Cuomo was able to complete recording in a manner that pleased both the band, and hopefully, his devout followers. Or was he? Cuomo later admitted that he delegated longtime A&R man Todd Sullivan to pick most of the songs for the disc. "I don't trust their taste — they have terrible taste," he said of his fans, taking their critical observations with a grain of salt. "They would pick all the wrong songs. I do mean it; we asked them what songs they liked and they picked the wackest songs."

Working with Rod Cervera and engineer Chad Bamford, the notable difference between the sessions for *The Green Album* and the fourth disc was the healthier, more natural interactions between members. "When people are breathing down your neck and watching every move like, 'Oh no. I hope they don't do anything weird,' you're very restricted," Brian said in defense of Rivers. "You're concentrating on playing robotically, almost. When you leave a musician to his own devices, you feel a lot more inspired and willing to take risks."

One of those risks, according to Bamford, was Weezer's approach to the creation of the new disc, which was different from the ways most groups work. "It was definitely not 'Okay, we're going to go in for these four days and cut the drums on all the songs, and then we're going to take two days and do bass on all the songs,'" he said. "It's really a constantly evolving process. It involves *everything*. We were literally still cutting drum tracks up to about twelve hours before they had to leave to go to the mix. So, basically, everything's always on the table and always up and always ready to go, depending on how they feel and what we feel we need to do. I guess they're just trying to stay flexible."

Putting their trust in Bamford and Cervera, the duo manning the studio consoles let the group know when they had cut a good and inspired take. "I think we're all realizing now that we don't want to make canned music like everybody else," Pat said. "At least 50 to 75% of what people see in Weezer is that they're actual people playing actual music and they can do it in front of you. It's so simple.

"You can make a case that the most successful song on [*The Green Album*] is probably 'Hash Pipe,' and that's the least stiff and most creative song on there. That's the direction we want to go now," Wilson continued. "I think [this new album] took a step toward *Pinkerton* in that it's more bombastic. What we're honing in on now is the perfect combination of creativity and togetherness."

Weezer set about overdubbing vocals and guitar as necessary prior to Rivers, Brian, and Scott's mid-January flight to Lord Alge's Miami-area facility. As with the previous year's mixing journey, Wilson would again sit out the trip, this time in favor of a series of L.A.-area gigs with The Special Goodness. A few thousand miles away, the rest of the band again worked to tweak, mix, and sequence the new record over a two-week span.

Although Wilson didn't make the trek to Southern Florida, he disclosed afterward that the band and Lord-Alge did have their share of disagreements. "We would fight with him. We'd be like, 'C'mon dude, there's good stuff on here,'" said the drummer, who — in his absence — had Todd Sullivan defend his studio efforts. "Scott especially was fighting with him because he was a tone monster. I mean, he plays a vintage P-Bass through an SVT and he takes a lot of pride in his sound, and here comes Lord-Alge who's like, 'Okay! We're not going to use the amp sound. Let's plug it right into the SansAmp.' Scott was bombed. He was like, 'Ggg-uhhh.'"

But Rivers tried not to criticize Lord-Alge on the first listen of his mixes. "I like to sit with the mix first, rather than go with my knee-jerk reaction," he explained. "For example, the first tune he mixed was 'Take Control,' and it was so radically different than what we had envisioned that we all panicked. I told him, 'Step aside, dude. I'm mixing this one.' Then I listened to both mixes twenty-four hours later and I realized my mix was horrible and his was amazing."

There was no time for suntans and piña coladas as the group holed up in Lord-Alge's recording compound. "We couldn't leave until we got certain things worked out," Shriner said of being sequestered at Lord-Alge's studio. "It felt like a year and a half, but it was really six days."

"I think if we didn't fight for stuff, it would sound like Creed. And I don't think any of us want that," Pat continued. But Wilson conceded that the mixer has the magic touch. "He does the best radio mixes; that's all there is to it. I mean, a program director sees 'Tom Lord-Alge' and they're like, 'Done!' He does a good job at making it sound exciting."

With the mixing behind them, Weezer would head back to Los Angeles and hand the tapes over to Stephen Marcussen, a man whose album mastering credits include prominent artists like Stone Temple Pilots, Tom Petty, R.E.M., the Red Hot Chili Peppers, and Incubus, to name a few.

And for the second consecutive year, Cuomo would back Weezer into a tight scheduling corner, planning a February tour of the United States directly on the heels of the disc's completion. Known as the Hyper-Extended

Midget Tour and featuring rising emo-rockers Saves the Day in the support slot plus show openers Ozma, the three-week trek was geared to start at Charlotte's Independence Arena just four days after finishing the mastering process. Speaking of his decision to again employ Ozma as openers, Cuomo said, "I think [they're] going to be legendary at some point."

In tandem with Weezer's efforts, the Grand Rapids–based independent record label Dead Droid Records put together *Rock Music*, a tribute album featuring Weezer-weaned bands like Piebald, Grade, Further Seems Forever, Midtown, Dashboard Confessional, The Stereo, Impossibles, Mock Orange, and The Ataris covering cuts from *The Blue Album* and *Pinkerton*. When asked about the tribute record, Rivers denied having listened to it at the time, but took time to comment on being an influence on other acts.

"Nine out of ten times, I don't like it," he declared about the bands spawned in the wake of Weezer. "I feel like people just take one superficial aspect of what we're about and copy it. They just take the lyrical persona or something but they won't take any of the hard rock. It just becomes all wussified."

chapter twenty-seven

dope nose

As January 2002 wrapped up, Rivers announced the title of Weezer's fourth album. And disciples ran immediately to their dictionaries, wondering just what the hell "maladroit" meant. Doing away with the self-titled move of discs one and three, the title — translated as "clumsy" or "awkward" — was suggested through the *Weezer.com* message boards by a boardie known as "Lethe," who received an official credit for the idea. "I just thought it sounded cool and metal," Cuomo said later about choosing the title. "It sounded evil to me."

As word broke of U.K. dates to accompany a March trip to Portugal and Spain, Cuomo continued to speak of the harder direction Weezer was taking on *Maladroit*. "It's higher voltage," he confessed. "All those Kiss riffs that have been repressed in my subconscious are finally bursting to the surface. I tried for a long time to hide them because they sound really stupid. But I wanna rock."

And U.S. radio stations wanted to play Cuomo's rock compositions. Commercial radio outlets and college stations alike were all jumping on the new MP3s, giving airplay to "Take Control," "Keep Fishin'," "Dope Nose," and "Mr. Taxman," to name a few.

Through all of the sessions, mixing and mastering, Cuomo and Interscope boss Schur had remained estranged, and Weezer was paying for the new record out of its own pockets. Referring to the group's existing state of operations as "chaos," Rivers revealed to the press that the group was "making a record right now, but we are no longer speaking to our label."

Making comments like, "We have no idea what is going to happen, but the record will come out one way or another," this was no mere public threat — Cuomo was developing a plan of action. In an effort to solicit opinions about the material from radio insiders, Rivers began to circumvent traditional record label promotion maneuvers and take matters into his own hands, sending completed tracks to outlets like KNDD in Seattle and WPLY Y100 in Philadelphia.

"Interscope was sort of unaware," says Y100 program director Jim McGuinn, putting it mildly. "All of a sudden this package shows up with two Weezer songs on a CD-R inside of it. And then the next day, Rivers called me. He was in Florida mixing the record. And he's like, 'Did you get the package?' And I'm like, 'Yeah. What's up?' And he's like, 'Well what do you think?' And it was 'Dope Nose' and 'Keep Fishin',' so I begin to tell him what I liked about them and didn't like about them, and as we're talking I could tell he really wanted the feedback, and wanted to know if they were going in the right direction and if it was what the listeners would like. He wanted to know which one I liked better. So I said, 'Hey, we could pit them against each other in this nightly feature we have called "Cage Match,"' and he says, 'You can do that?' And I said — laughing — 'The only person who can stop me from doing it is you.' And he's like 'Wow.' So we did it, and the results were 900 votes for one song and 850 for another."

"When I sent it out to all the radio stations, I asked them, 'What song do you think should be our first single?'" Cuomo said. "And a lot of them said, 'Dope Nose.'"

Back in Los Angeles in late January, Weezer readied for the third round of Midget dates and continued making some minor tweaks to *Maladroit* tracks like "Living without You" and "Slob," in the days preceding the Hyper-Extended Midget dates. When the tour did kick off, Cuomo heeded his fans' correspondence and Weezer reverted back to amplifiers after several tours using ear monitors, which, according to Koch "gave the sound a crunchy extra flavor and seemed to fuel the overall stoke factor."

To promote a tour stop two nights later at the 7,000-capacity sold-out Tsongas Arena in Lowell, Massachusetts, Cuomo spoke fondly of his days in nearby Cambridge, even hinting that returning to Harvard wasn't something he was completely ruling out. "If I go back to Harvard, I'm sure I'll play out a lot," he speculated. "I love Boston musicians. They're not all trying to be the singer-songwriter in the band — unlike in Los Angeles, where everyone wants to be the frontman, not the bass player."

Comparing Boston with L.A., Rivers revealed he liked his hometown, even though he didn't feel like he fit in there. "I try to get out and hang with cool people. But I'll go to a cool party and just kind of sit there by myself," he said. "But even though L.A. is superficial and freakish, there is a lot of talent there."

With eyes on an April 30 release of *Maladroit*, but no official Interscope confirmation, Rivers also revealed that he was considering an extension of the No Doubt/Offspring show set for February 26 and designed to raise money for the Recording Artists Coalition. "There's talk of a tour with them. We booked one show at the Long Beach Arena and it sold out very quickly, so that got us to thinking that it might be worth looking into."

But that tour would only happen on the condition that Weezer headline the jaunt, despite being relegated to openers for the Long Beach benefit gig. The move stood in direct conflict with Cuomo's claim that the only band he'd ever open for would be Metallica.

Commenting on the large venues of the ongoing tour, Cuomo was thrilled to be rocking large crowds. "I way prefer to play huge arenas. Small clubs are a bummer, because it's not epic," Rivers said. "Being famous rules. I don't think I really thought about being famous too much.

I thought about being on stage and having thousands of people screaming at me. I think everyone has those fantasies."

As the Hyper-Extended Midget Tour progressed into arenas in locales like Rochester, New York; Wilkes Barre, Pennsylvania; East Rutherford, New Jersey; and State College, Pennsylvania, the band reached its tenth anniversary on February 14 when the trek touched down in Hamilton, Ontario.

Midway through the busy tour, the group learned that the fully mixed version of "Dope Nose" that Rivers had circulated to a handful of radio outlets had been officially added to key playlists at KROQ and 94.7 The Zone in Chicago. In response to this news, plus strong albeit unofficial play at WXRK in New York, 91X in San Diego, WHFS in Washington, D.C., and Atlanta's 99X, Interscope intervened. The label shut down Weezer's Audio/Video page, putting an end to further downloading of finished versions of "Keep

M'LOU F. ELKINS

Rockers For Literacy: Cuomo flashes a rare smile as he shares
a couch with Shriner, Wilson, and Bell

Fishin'" and "Dope Nose" by fans and radio station personnel alike.

"It's a shame," said Rivers, reacting to the record company's strategic silencing of the MP3 section of *Weezer.com*. "Because the most important thing in the world to me is getting our songs out there. And we have a ton of them and I wish we could just constantly put new songs up for people to hear."

An equally disturbing but much scarier incident took place while en route from Columbus, Ohio, to Nashville. As members of the band slept in their respective tour bus bunks in the early morning hours of February 20, the vehicle's front tire suffered a blow-out. Luckily, Weezer's driver managed to keep the bus under control, bringing the vehicle to a safe halt on a Kentucky roadside. Frightened and unscathed but stranded and waiting for repairs, Cuomo, Wilson, Bell, and Shriner caught a lucky break when their road crew's bus came along the same route about an hour later and took the members on to their hotel.

Prior to the following night's Music City show, Cuomo and Wilson found themselves plagued with flu-like symptoms. Despite the illnesses, which included Patrick logging in a 103° fever, the band's founders made it through the sold-out gig. The next day in Raleigh, after much rest and fluids, the bug was waning, but still interfering with the group's work. Closing out the Hyper-Extended Midget Tour with a pair of Florida shows at the Tampa Ice Palace on February 24 and Miami's MARS Amphitheatre the following day, Weezer's illnesses continued to plague the energy quotient of the gigs. The *Palm Beach Post* dubbed the tour finale "lackluster" and cited Cuomo's vocals as worn. "Weezer ended its national tour with an alternative rock whimper Monday night. The originators of geek rock played a tired and sloppy show," read the review.

Despite being run down, Weezer was up and at it after just a couple hours of rest, catching a five-hour 5 a.m. flight on February 26 in order to make its 45-minute opening slot at the Recording Artists Coalition in Long Beach. Considering the ongoing tensions between Cuomo and his record label, the quartet's presence at the show was remarkably well timed.

Meanwhile, the popularity of "Dope Nose" continued to soar at radio stations, despite Interscope's odd demand that Rivers write a letter of apology to the stations to which he had sent *Maladroit* advances. "I felt that he had jumped the gun and I wasn't quite sure how it would figure into our agenda," Jordan Schur said later, defending his position.

"I just got the feeling from the label that they didn't want us to make *Maladroit*," Cuomo said. "I just got the sense that they wanted us to spend three years in the studio with a top producer and painstakingly craft the ultimate alternative rock album."

Four months of silence between the label and the band was sparked by a philosophical difference over how often the group should record. Interscope was opposed to the idea of a new disc hitting the marketplace so soon after *The Green Album*. Additionally, early versions of the songs for album #4 were met with resistance by the suits, who likened the material to the classic rock of Lynyrd Skynyrd. No longer seeing eye-to-eye and with no executives leaning over its shoulders, the musical collective became more independent than ever.

Making recordings was one thing, but servicing them independently to key radio and press folks was another issue altogether. Interscope's heads were deeply disturbed when they learned of the radio activity. "We went and funded this record entirely on our own without consulting the label or getting their approval on any of the songs or the recording process in general," said Rivers later, laughing at the thought. "The first they heard of it was when they started hearing it on the radio. So they were very surprised and . . . concerned. And I wasn't surprised by that."

Schur wanted Cuomo to put an end to the airplay, and asked him to write a letter to the radio stations asking them stop playing the new songs. After thinking it over, Cuomo felt that the letter was a good idea, but he wanted it to come from Interscope's radio department. Schur put his foot down, not wanting to appear like the bad guy. "Our radio department didn't want to be portrayed as the big bad record company telling the radio station they can't have their Weezer," said Schur.

The irked record company was now forcing one of its largest money-makers in 2001 to ask radio to hold off on playing the tune — plus others like "Take Control" and "Fall Together" — until a proper, label-sanctioned promo single could be generated. Cuomo relented, acknowledging the frightening amount of power Interscope had over his life. The executives were angry, and Rivers, fearing they might try to ruin his career and make it virtually impossible to release music, had little choice.

If the group was concerned that the label-insisted move would kill the song's momentum, the gesture had the opposite effect, with stations either adding the song or digging deeper into *Maladroit* to acquiesce fan requests. "We certainly want to work with labels, but part of our obligation as a radio station is to provide new music to consumers," said Bill Gamble, program director at Chicago's wzzn, The Zone. "If fans of Weezer are hearing three or four-tracks online and the station is saying, 'well, we'll have it in a month,' all of a sudden, we are not relevant. If the music is out there, then we better put it out on the radio."

Cuomo's personally signed, apologetic letter specifically spoke of how he wasn't supposed to have sent the album in the first place, how his do-it-yourself promotion landed him in big trouble with Interscope and how — to curtail further repercussions — radio stations should cease playing the disc. Explaining that he "was overeager for you all to hear it and . . .

jumped the gun," he also included a second advance copy of the disc with the letter, making his nudge-nudge wink-wink insincerity pretty evident.

"I didn't expect that we would get in so much trouble," Cuomo rationalized, acting naive. "I think the record company is just surprised because they're not used to a band being able to achieve any kind of success on their own without the record company's help. They were uninvolved with the whole process, and only vaguely aware that we were even in the studio. Next thing they know, they're hearing our song on the radio and [they] kind of freaked out."

Weezer's rabid online followers took action in response to Interscope's gag order, with the Unreleased Weezer for the Masses (UWFTM) Web page leading the charge. Through a UWFTM sub-site dubbed "Free Maladroit," where all of the demoed and allegedly final versions of album cuts and B-sides were available for download, the Weezer community rallied behind their band to "make Interscope see their wrong-doing and encourage them to promote *Maladroit* and release this album ASAP."

Reacting to the move by Weezer followers, Rivers said, "Our fans are incredible. But, at the same time, that rabid quality can be used against us. If we make a song that they don't like, they attack us with the same rabid quality." But judging by the UWFTM-driven initiative, that didn't seem likely. Posting radio and label contact information, plus a guest book and downloadable flyer to print and post, Cuomo's disciples deeply criticized the parent company of Geffen with comments like "Interscope must die; I hope the whole label goes to hell." While suits like Schur weren't specifically named, the fans' sign of solidarity took straight aim at high-profile Interscope VP/Limp Bizkit frontman Fred Durst.

With radio showing no sign of relenting, "Dope Nose" scored 410 defiant spins from thirty-five of the eighty-two Modern Rock outlets under watch by Airplay Monitor. When the tune pulled down a #25 debut at the radio format, Interscope got wise and officially serviced the single to all of the Modern Rock on March 4.

But the song's continued success hardly put an end to Cuomo's power struggle with the label. First, an article in *Spin* surfaced claiming that Geffen had never asked Rivers to recall the CD. The frontman flipped out after reading a quote by an Interscope source saying that he had recalled the album on his own because he felt it wasn't ready. "I was shocked at [these] lies," he said. "At that point, it just became clear that there was a conflict of interest there if our publicist is actually employed by our record company — the very group we are having a problem with."

Next, they did battle over who actually owned the forthcoming *Maladroit*. With "Dope Nose" taking over the airwaves, the record company finally decided to show an interest in the album. But instead of mending fences, Interscope's move to claim ownership and take possession of the *Maladroit* master tapes — which Weezer created, produced, and paid for themselves — caused further strain between the two parties.

While Cuomo was hesitant to fork over the masters, he knew that the label had the right to claim ownership of the tapes. "It's crazy," he balked. "It's totally unfair. I mean, that's us on the tape. That's me singing. Those are our songs. That's us rocking out. How come they can just walk in and pick up the tapes and say, they're ours? They didn't even pay for 'em."

An Interscope rep's only response was, "When Rivers is ready to put out his record, Geffen is ready to put it out." Clearly the label had changed its tune after Cuomo forced their hand by sending the song to radio. By the time his retraction letter had reached programmers, it was too late. "Dope Nose" was a hit.

"They realized that the single already had so much momentum that to stop it would basically be to kill the song, kill the album, and there wouldn't be a second chance," said Rivers in hindsight.

"They would have made us use a top producer and spend years in the studio crafting the perfect pop album," he theorized. "And that just seemed very counter to our rate of artistic development. We want to produce as much as we can and keep moving and learning and growing rather than trying to force out the perfect album every time."

chapter twenty-eight

maladroit

At the time Cuomo was duking it out with his record company, he still had a lot of management responsibilities on his plate. Conveniently, Rivers had again arranged to raise AM Radio's profile by taking Kevin Ridel's band to Japan as Weezer's support on nine upcoming shows in May 2002. Another U.S. tour — dubbed the "Dusty West '02" — was also shaping up to kick off on April 23 in Edmonton, Alberta with AM as openers and singer/songwriter Pete Yorn in the middle slot.

When he wasn't sipping on Mountain Dew, instant messaging his cybergirlfriend, or extolling the virtues of bands like Limp Bizkit and Drowning Pool, Cuomo continued posting as "Ace" on the Weezer board, responding to a fan inquiry as to whether he still listened to his first two records and speaking directly to *The Blue Album* tune "Only in Dreams." "No I don't," Cuomo wrote back. "And I can't imagine that anyone here actually sits down and listens to that eight-minute piece of shit."

Saying that new material like "December," "Slob," and "D+D" (a.k.a. "Death and Destruction") killed "Only in Dreams," he wrote, "Is anyone here man enough to admit that ["Only in Dreams"] is boring? That the vocals are contrived? That the lyrics are GAY as hell? . . . GAY! GAY! GAY! DISNEYGAY! My brother almost disowned me when he first heard the chorus . . . That the bass line is an exact ripoff of 'Have You Seen Her'? None of you agrees with me. Play it for any sane person and they'd fall asleep before they had a chance to give you their verdict . . . Worst song on a bad album . . . I can't tell you the courage it takes to sing these lines every night."

Once he sensed he'd gone too far, pissing off and alienating his fans, Cuomo wrote, "Just having fun," before riling them up again with the post, "Would you guys mind if I dropped the Blue songs from the live set?"

Aside from such message board activities (which were often addled with his politically incorrect use of the term "gay") and woes with Interscope, Cuomo took his energy into the recording studio in the days prior to an imminent European tour launch, set for Lisbon, Portugal, on March 11. With a tentative *Maladroit* release date of April 30 in doubt, Weezer's fourth record was at least eight weeks away from hitting record store shelves. But that didn't stop the group from using the first week of March in pre-production on album #5, approaching the all-new material by feel and playing with a newfound looseness.

Working through Cuomo compositions like "Private Message," "Sugar Cookie," "Prodigy Lover," "Wool Cap," "Misstep," "The Victor," "Untenable," "She Who Is Militant," and "Garbage Can," plus Summer 2K holdovers "Mad Kow," "Superstar," and "Modern Dukes," the group made the best of its time in early March. Perhaps the session also marked Brian Bell's first official Weezer entry as a singer/songwriter, when the group rocked through "Yellow Camaro."

"The fifth record should really come out in November," Rivers said idealistically at the time. "I don't see why we can't release two records in one year, but the industry still wants you to wait between them, the bastards." Two days before Weezer embarked on its fifth trip to Europe, most of the basic tracks on the aforementioned songs were finished, leaving Scott, Brian, and Rivers to work on vocal parts.

During dates in Lisbon and Oporto — two cities new to the band — the quartet began sound-checking its first-ever cover song. At the request of director Spike Jonze, Weezer worked through the Turtles' 1966 chart topper "Happy Together," for a possible soundtrack inclusion.

The Portugal shows also marked the first time Rivers and Brian switched roles for the live debut of Brian's track, "Yellow Camaro." "We were both nervous as hell because of the role reversal," Bell said of the move to allow Rivers to concentrate solely on guitar. "We hadn't felt that way in years."

Opening for the Cranberries on these dates, Cuomo was sporting a strange look comprised of an unruly beard, woolly hat (which spawned the aforementioned "Wool Cap"), and always-present headphones. Rivers' unorthodox image had one member of that outfit's entourage publicly commenting on him. "It's like he's trying to shut out everything. The bloke is crackers." It would be on this same trek, with the band en route to their Barcelona venue — after having stayed out until nine in the morning wandering around the city's center in search of trance clubs — that Cuomo would eject his U.K. publicist from the bus before he would agree to an interview with *Kerrang!* Observing the matter, Patrick responded to the interviewer, "Great. He's in one of those moods. We'll probably have an interesting day, too."

Backstage, Cuomo was unaffectionately referred to as Elvis, but aside from his detractors, Brian Bell was quick to come to Cuomo's defense. If Rivers seemed weird to outsiders looking in, Bell contended his boss always had the group's best interests in mind. "He doesn't like to go along with the norm of what's easy," Brian explained.

Rivers was indeed a strange kind of platinum-seller, admitting he had a high school–aged cybergirlfriend that he met on *Weezer.com*. The frontman also dismissed celebrity disciples like Chino Moreno of the Deftones before confessing that he'd tried cocaine only once in order to dispel rumors he was addicted to the drug.

When queried about his "little rock star trip," Cuomo revealed it was nothing new and contended that anyone in his shoes would act the same way. Conceding to being "selfish [and] immature" Rivers disclosed he was comfortable with having "everyone hating" him. "I've tried all different kinds of ways of living and I've discovered that this is the most conducive to creativity, acting on whim regardless of consequences," he explained. "Occasionally, I'll have pangs of conscience but I try to overcome them. To me that's a small price to pay."

A few days later, in Manchester, England, Cuomo used a two-day break to pen a new song called "Booby Trap," his second of three tunes written on the journey. If his songwriting wasn't as fluid as it was in the comforts of his own home, Rivers was finally finding a way to write new tunes like "Mo' Beats" and "Buttafuoco" in hotel rooms.

As the band rocked the U.K., U.S. radio was continuing to play the hell out of "Dope Nose." Now the "official" first single from *Maladroit* courtesy of Interscope's delayed blessing, the song was unstoppable. Canada's *Jam!* put the song at the top of its "Anti-Hit List," and wrote, "clocking in at a brutally efficient two minutes and fifteen seconds, this [song] is so insanely catchy, it makes 'Hash Pipe' sound tuneless by comparison. Hell, they even shoehorn in a guitar solo."

The final European gig, at London's Brixton Academy, was a star-studded affair attended by members of Ash, Muse, and Travis, as well as 4,000 other Weezer aficionados. Cuomo — previously referring to fans as "just a sea of faces" — appeared pleased to be picking up new record and ticket buyers, even if it meant that some of his old *Pinkerton* worshipers were dropping off.

"I prefer young fans," he said at the time. "Their tastes are purer, they are excited to rock out, they like catchy tunes, and music doesn't have to take on too much social significance for them. It's just music and that's how I hear things too. I really relate to twelve-year-olds in that sense."

Perhaps it was the twelve-year-olds in France that helped earn Weezer their first ever #1 pop single with "Island in the Sun." The success of the song no doubt prompted the group to take the lightning-fast Eurostar train through the English Channel down to Paris for two days of exhaustive television appearances and press. Appearing on the Top 40 program *Hit Machine*, Weezer happily lip-synched its way through its very own mainstream smash.

Back in Los Angeles in late March in time for some promotional interviews and photo sessions with the likes of *Alternative Press* and *Spin*, Weezer proudly hyped *Maladroit*. Over the next three weeks, the band hunkered down in the studio, continuing work on its "fifth album" in between press obligations with everyone from *Playboy* and *Guitar Player* to small, power-pop magazine *Amplifier*.

Sunday, March 31, marked an important day for the band, as Weezer's determined frontman reportedly smoothed over matters with Jordan Schur, securing the health of Weezer's forthcoming disc. It was from this meeting that Cuomo got an official May 14 release date for *Maladroit*, as well as the permission to restore the band's fan-cherished Audio/Video page.

"It's not only smoothed over," Cuomo said of the resolved situation with Interscope, "it's basically become the ideal label/artist relationship in my opinion. They've seen the wisdom in what we're trying to do with our development and our philosophy of continuing to produce and move forward. I think they trust us now and want us to lead the charge and do whatever we need to do. They said that now they'll basically just help us do that, so I really don't anticipate any more battles."

Ironically, the dispute that could have ended the Weezer–Geffen affiliation had actually strengthened the relationship. "Ultimately, it's a good thing because I firmly believe that Weezer's fans need to know Weezer is running the show," Schur concurred. "That's what I want. I want it to look like Geffen

Records works for Weezer, because that's how we sell the most records."

While "Dope Nose" continued its ascent in the Modern Rock format, rising to #14 on that *Billboard* specialty chart, Cuomo began to describe the forthcoming disc to those who hadn't been privy to advance copies of it. "[It has] that live quality of *Pinkerton* but with a little more clarity," the Weezer leader bragged. "That's exactly what we were going for [on *Maladroit*]. The record says we produced it, but we didn't do anything. We just went in and played our songs, so it's kind of unproduced. It's really simple.

"If anything, it should say, 'Produced by the message-board fans,'" Rivers acknowledged. "They were listening to the demos every night and posting their criticisms. We would take those into the studio the next day. Most of [the feedback was] really mean and unjustified, but even that is good. That's what producers do sometimes. They just say really mean things to get you all pissed off. I really think it [helped]."

As for the disc's runaway radio hit, Cuomo wrote the infectious song in a method identical to "Hash Pipe." "[It was] six in the morning," he said. "I had three shots of tequila, and I forget how many milligrams of Ritalin, and I just went in my backyard and sat down. In like half an hour I was just like foaming at the mouth, and I just wrote it in one manic burst of about three minutes. Sitting there in the chair, composing in my head. Not even with a guitar. Just all in my mind. Bam. There's 'Dope Nose.' It's not about anything. It's just a bunch of garbage lyrics."

Explaining the need for intoxication, be it chemical or emotional, Rivers acknowledged waiting for such feelings to arise. He'd then seize the moment and fuel his songs. With Weezer taping nearly every practice since it got back to work some twenty-four months prior, drawing on its enormous backlog of songs was a snap. But Cuomo wrote at such a rapid speed the group was always most likely to record his most recent material. This was the case when the fellas again went into Cello Studios for an eighteen-day run in early April. Laying down Cuomo tunes like "Mo' Beats," "Booby Trap," "Steamroller Action," and the ballad-like "Queen of Earth" — all of which were penned in the months of February and March 2002 — the group also continued to focus on the Bell-fronted, hard-rocking "Yellow Camaro" and the Wilson-sung "It's Not So Bad."

"I feel like I was designed and built to do exactly what I'm doing on the very deepest level," said Cuomo, attempting to define his intense drive to create and perform. "Like I'm a machine designed by evolution to rock, to be in a band, to travel around the world playing music, to write songs, to sing onstage, be in front of people."

When the time came to take a break from the stage and studio, the foosball table was there to soothe them from their hard work. "I don't know how it happened," Wilson explained. "Somehow foosball has just become immensely important to our day." Patrick was even considering pitching a show to MTV. "It's gonna be Weezer against the Foo Fighters, and it's gonna be like a seven-show miniseries about how a grueling foosball season is gonna make us better friends."

"We spend hours on the foosball table every day, and we just totally mellow out," Rivers added. "We play it very seriously, but there's no, like, negative sense of competition. We just bond over the foosball table."

In between the weeks of studio recording and foosball action, Weezer again aligned with video director Marcos Siega in early April to shoot the high action "Dope Nose" video. The clip was notable, not only for Brian and Scott's hard rocking moves, but Pat's electronic drum kit, and riff-blastin' Rivers' bushy beard, which had, by this point, been a staple of the rocker's image for months. Amid the nighttime, parking-lot rock 'n' roll setting, rival Asian motorcycle gangs challenged one another with their wheelie-popping skills. If the presence of hot Oriental cycle chicks seemed apropos based on Cuomo's female preference, the apex of the "Dope

M'LOU F. ELKINS

Foosball Frenzy: Rivers in full, Brian Wilson–styled
beard, kicks it on the foosball table, as
Rod Cervera looks on in awe

Nose" video came when one of the motorbike daredevils jumped the band's giant flashing =w= stage prop.

With the "Dope Nose" video shoot finished, preliminary work on album #5 continued well into April 2002, even though Weezer's fourth disc, *Maladroit*, was still a month from release. The band — no stranger to legal entanglements, settlements, and non-disclosure agreements — was slapped with a five-count federal lawsuit by founding bassist Matthew

Sharp on April 19. In a suit against his former bandmates — filed in U.S. District Court for the Central District of California — Sharp alleged that he was owed money for songs he co-wrote, including Weezer's first hit, "Undone — The Sweater Song." Sharp contended that he co-authored the song with Rivers Cuomo and Patrick Wilson and adduced that he owned one-third interest in the song. According to the suit, "Cuomo represented to plaintiff that he would receive compensation for his contribution to writing 'Undone' . . . on or about March 20, 1996, however, Cuomo claimed complete ownership in the copyright in and to 'Undone.'"

Additionally, Sharp argued that he owned a 25% interest in the first nine tracks on *Pinkerton*, although the songs had been credited solely to Rivers. The suit acknowledged that the dispute over song credit had been a long-standing debate between Sharp and Cuomo. Citing an April 24, 2001, e-mail from Cuomo to Sharp, the suit quotes Rivers as writing, "it's [sic] looks like we're gonna start making money again so we (you and I) had better get this thing squared away sooner rather than later so the money flows to all the right places without getting hitched up."

Interestingly enough, the suit goes on to add that Cuomo and Sharp had continued speaking in spite of this issue, revealing that the bassist continued to participate in the "Weezer partnership" after his exit from the band. It even states that Matt had intended to appear in the music video for the song "Island in the Sun" after it became clear that drug problems suffered by Sharp's replacement, Mikey Welsh, would force him from the band.

Listing Rivers and Patrick, the group's only remaining founders, as defendants, the suit also claimed Sharp's contributions to the band in its earliest stages were more than musical. Matt contended that he handled most of the business affairs, including hiring attorneys and accountants. He also claimed to have helped land Weezer their record deal and locate a director for the band's first music videos.

Stating that Sharp stopped performing with Weezer in February 1998 after differences arose among the members, the suit alleged Rivers Cuomo still asked Sharp to listen to compositions being considered for *The Green Album*. It also stated that Sharp and Cuomo allegedly co-produced "American Girls" for the soundtrack to the Disney movie *Meet the Deedles*, and that the band had borrowed Sharp's equipment.

In addition to seeking co-writing credit for ten songs, as well as royalties he claimed to be owed, Matt charged his former musical mates with breach of fiduciary duty, legal malpractice, dissolution of partnership, and declaratory relief. Seeking damages to be determined at trial, as well as a full accounting record of his alliance with the band, Sharp went on to say in an interview, "The songwriting stuff is a very small part [of the suit]. Legal speak is not human speak, and it's real easy not to get a good idea of what it's really about.

"All I can tell you is I found out some things recently about their actions that really changed the whole thing and, all in all, really broke my heart," Matt added, claiming he was led to believe he'd be rejoining the band when Mikey exited. "They left me with no choice than to have to deal with it this way."

"The allegations brought against Weezer by Matt Sharp are completely without merit," the band collectively commented when the news broke. "Rather than address this at length in the press, we will use the proper venue, a court of law."

Matt continued to talk to the media, however, saying there were many misconceptions about his relationship with Weezer. The biggest, he informed, was that he voluntarily quit the band. "It's simply not true," Sharp asserted. "In no way did I ever walk away from those guys, quit, or leave Weezer."

"If I could tell you everything," Sharp told fans in an online interview to promote a series of mid-2002 solo concerts, "I'm sure you would understand completely, and would realize it was absolutely necessary, and that it was an absolute last resort. All you really need to know is that while I was in Weezer, my belief, love, and devotion to the music and to all of you was pure."

Going back on his word, Cuomo also spoke of it publicly. "In the cases where we have been sued, it's always been complete bullshit. The suits themselves have served to defame me, so of course I'm going to stand up for myself and do everything I can to clear my name."

In late April, "Dope Nose" premiered on MTV and landed adjacent exposure on Canada's MuchMusic. Although *Maladroit* was still out of reach for record buyers, Weezer fans were able to look beyond that disc when Cuomo had Koch post newly recorded MP3s of "Private Message," "Prodigy Lover," and "Yellow Camaro," plus the "Dope Nose" B-side "Living without You" on the official site's no longer restricted A/V page.

When the Dusty West '02 trek launched at Edmonton's 3,200-capacity packed AgriCom Arena on April 23, Weezer's unique tact with rock music was not lost on critics. "These unlikely superstars from Los Angeles delivered a straight-ahead rock show of the highest order," praised Mike Ross of the *Edmonton Sun*, calling the band's presentation "a glorious display of pop-rock perfection loaded with jangly goodness and hit after hit after hit."

"It's such a special feeling when you're playing a Weezer show and people are singing the songs so loudly you barely can hear what you're doing," Bell agreed. Meanwhile the Canadian Weezer connection hit its stride when the band got a unique mention on ESPN2 during a wrap-up of National Hockey League highlights two nights later. Speaking of the Toronto Maple Leafs' left wing, announcer John Buccigross said, "His name is Jonas, he's carrying the wheel. Jonas Hoglund with the goal for the Leafs."

While Rivers would have probably preferred the nod during World

Cup soccer action, he had to be pleased that "Dope Nose" was up to #10 on Modern Rock charts. Reviewing the single, *Entertainment Weekly* wrote, "With its crunchy guitar riffs, grabby 'oh-oh-oh' vocal hook, and no-frills production, the first single from Weezer's upcoming album has all the right moves. Except one: a killer chorus. It's half of a great single, lacking only that all-important payoff."

If the song's hook touted the olfactory delights of cheese on burnt lamb, it didn't slow Dusty West ticket sales, as the band rocked cities like Calgary, Vancouver, Washington, and university towns like Pullman, Washington; and Missoula, Montana. Perhaps touring through so many college locales over the last year and a half had again given Rivers an urge to learn, as he hinted again that he wanted to resume his Harvard studies in early 2003. Of course he faced one conundrum: would they let him back in?

For the time being, though, Cuomo's datebook was full with touring obligations. But Rivers' hesitation in playing songs from Weezer's fan-cherished second album recurred during the tour. While some ticket buyers were angered and felt betrayed at his unwillingness to bust out the *Pinkerton* songs, the frontman had little interest in that part of his past. As a result, Weezer usually (and only begrudgingly) performed just one song per gig from their sophomore disc.

Sometimes the flack from the audience was intense. "There have been some really scary shows, where I thought violence might break out. Like, me against 10,000 people. I'll fuck with them sometimes. I'll start to play one of those *Pinkerton* songs and they start to cheer and then I'll bust into one of my gay pop songs."

As supporting act Pete Yorn saw his star continue to rise with hits like "Life on a Chain," "Strange Condition," and "For Nancy ('Cos It Already Is)" from his 2001 debut *musicforthemorningafter*, Rivers was hoping to get AM Radio similar exposure. Hatching a plan to start his own imprint,

Cuomo shopped the idea around to various major labels as a tie-in with his clients AM Radio, whom he was planning to executive produce. Rivers was reportedly taking in meetings with major label executives before, during, and after the Dusty West trek with folks like Interscope CEO Jimmy Iovine, Maverick boss Guy Oseary, and Capitol president Andy Slater. Cuomo also apparently took in meetings on behalf of Ridel's band with producers like Don Gilmore, who had worked with Linkin Park, and Howard Benson, who had worked with P.O.D. and was in A&R at Elektra. It was presumably Benson who helped Rivers link up with Sylvia Rhone, head of Elektra. Not only did Cuomo get the lads in AM Radio a deal with the label, he got Benson — who was also producing *Year of the Spider* for his friends in Cold — to oversee Ridel's group's studio progress.

Despite his busy work schedule, Cuomo had admitted to doubting himself less at this point than in any other time in his career. When it came to songwriting, he was trusting the muse and letting his long-suppressed love of 1980s heavy metal infiltrate both *Maladroit* and the as-yet-untitled album #5 material.

"Rivers has just unleashed the shredding beast in himself," Bell observed at the time.

"It's been there all along, and I've had to consciously repress it on our first three records," laughed Cuomo. "I had to force myself not to bust out with Scorpions riffs. And, at this point in my life, I just wanna let it all hang out. So, on *Maladroit*, it all just came pouring out."

If *The Green Album* was about reaffirming Weezer's identity, *Maladroit* was about moving forward while respecting the past. "I learned how to play the guitar by playing metal, and I was always in metal bands as a kid," Rivers added. "So, really the aberration was the first two Weezer records. I was very consciously repressing my actual self. Unfortunately, millions of people then came to identify that style with the quote 'real Weezer' or the 'real Rivers,' which is not the case at all. I think now that I have more confidence and more experience, and I've just been doing this so long, I can't force something that's not natural anymore. I have to let my instincts come out. I think over time you just learn to be more natural and to not force things and accept who you are."

Indeed the circumstances between the albums were far different. "During the making of the *Green* CD, we had to have a hit album or we would be in danger of being dropped by our record label," Bell explained. "[Producer] Ricky O really had a lot to do with the success of that album. I feel he is responsible for 'Island's' sound. He really pushed us on making that feel right. Although I remember he wasn't too crazy about 'Hash Pipe.' *Maladroit* is produced by us so instead of having somebody else worry about all the boring stuff, we had to. Scott and I were left pretty much with free reign to do whatever we wanted to Rivers' songs, and we tried many different things. *Maladroit* is more 'hands on.'"

Busting loose on the guitar was a natural response to the tightly structured pop that ruled Weezer's third disc. "I would never want to play something that is difficult for me or that doesn't come naturally to me," Cuomo explained. "Every note I play, every note I sing, is effortless. I don't want to have to practice scales every day before I go onstage. I mean, I did all that stuff when I was a teenager, but I don't need to do that now to feel like I'm expressing myself on my instrument. I don't dumb down, but my point in playing lead is not to show the extremes of my technique, it's to try to say something melodically. But if you put a gun to my head and said, 'Shred!' I could blow some motherfuckers away. It would probably be shocking."

"American Gigolo," the tense, infectious riff-a-thon that opens *Maladroit* sets the pace for Weezer's powerful, skilled fourth album. With its bold guitar power, flashy solos, and bone-crunching rhythms, *Maladroit*

— complete with its peculiar cover depiction of a bachelor lounging on 1950s *Leave It to Beaver*–styled living room furniture — was indeed taking the band into all-new terrain. According to Rivers, "Gigolo" was "one of the most hated songs by the Weezer Internet Community. They hounded me for a month to take it off the album, but I love it, so they have to deal with it. Why did they hate it? They thought it was gay."

The bite-sized anthem "Dope Nose," clocking in at a mere two minutes and fourteen seconds, again incorporated hip-hop lyrics into a Weezer hit, as R.C. sung of busting rhymes. "'Dope Nose' has no meaning whatsoever," Rivers revealed, saying the song came from "just kind of writing random lyrics. It's kind of weird that we're singing a song about drugs all the time, 'cause we're not really a druggie band, and we don't have any political stance about it. It's just kind of random drug references that we don't really mean."

Not that Cuomo was a stranger to mind-altering substances, but he attributed their use to approaching songwriting in a different light. Experimenting with illicit and prescription substances in what he dubbed "a very scientific manner," Rivers took notes on how each drug impacted his songwriting. "I almost always find that the best songs come about in a chemically sober state, but perhaps in an emotionally toxic state," he said.

It's unknown what state he was in when he came up with the contagious "Keep Fishin'," but it's superb shuffle, descending into an irresistible pop chorus that would later prove incredibly airwave-worthy. Perhaps some of the tune's appeal was fostered by the creative shift in Weezer's modus operandi when it came to fleshing out new tunes.

Speaking to the differences between *Maladroit*'s affable nuggets and past recordings, Bell explained, "[Rivers] leaves it up to us to find the hooks. That definitely wasn't the case before. He's not gonna take 100% of my ideas, but Rivers is definitely listening to them."

The Eddie Van Halen–inspired solo on "Take Control" embodies the drastic evolution in sound the band experienced since the entrance of hard rock enthusiast Scott Shriner. In contrast, Cuomo's heartbreak is felt on the painful ballad "Death and Destruction," where he gets ditched by a lover.

While the somber mood continues on the album, the bluesy guitar fills don't last long as the metallic blast of "Slob" takes over to find a concerned mother (perhaps Rivers' own?) trying to motivate her son into marriage and responsibility. "Maybe once a week or something I'll get overwhelmed by a situation in my life and write a song about it," he explained of the song, crafted in one of his "emotionally extreme" moments. "If I were to put all those songs on an album you'd think I have a really bleak life, or I'm an emotional wreck or something. But really, I only feel that way for an hour or two. Most of the time I'm a pretty cool character."

Elsewhere, the funky strut of "Burndt Jamb," a longtime instrumental, began with Rivers "singing about potato chips, just to dust off whatever it is in your brain that comes up with lyrics," Bell commented. "He was reading off a package of Pringles or something. I still remember that the line, '1.5 grams of carbohydrates' was in it.'"

Cuomo's falsetto vocals are matched by a smashing, blink-and-you'll-miss-it "Space Rock" roar that he says was inspired by Spacemen 3. The track gives way to the much-ballyhooed "Slave," but Rivers' own belief in the song — as argued about with fans on the Weezer boards — is upheld, as the single-worthy tune is as sugary and sorrowfully blissful as R.C. creations get.

The punishing crunch and blistering soloing of "Fall Together" found Cuomo reliving his adolescent rock star fantasies at the expense of his melodic tendencies. By comparison, the punky charge of "Possibilities" was effortless, if fairly anonymous (according to boardies it, too, was "gay"). "Love Explosion," about being smitten with a young girl who thinks her family wants to kill her in her sleep, was a memorable rocker.

Bowing with the doo-wop inspired love lament, "December," Cuomo sings appropriately, "We give our best away." And critics agreed with Rivers' words when reviews of the group's fourth album began to surface in May 2002 issues of music magazines. Giving *Maladroit* the disc a four out of five rating, *Q* said the set housed "some of the finest songs of Weezer's career," while *Billboard* wrote, "We all knew Weezer rocked, but who knew the band could kick this much ass?"

Touting "Dope Nose" as one of Weezer's "all-time greatest songs," *All Music Guide* said, "the band is tighter than ever, the record crackles with energy — nothing new, per se, but still vibrant, catchy, and satisfying." *Amazon.com* hailed *Maladroit* as "blissfully thunderous" and the *Austin American-Statesman* said, "Cuomo's power pop skills and pop metal pleasures still hang out like old pals."

Ann Powers of *Rolling Stone* blessed it with a four-star review, citing Cuomo as a "nasty little fella" who "has ascended to the throne previously held by improbables such as Joey Ramone, Elvis Costello, and old Buddy Holly himself: He's this era's model of a most unlikely rock star." Citing Patrick Wilson as "a monster behind the [drum] kit," the lead review describes *Maladroit* displaying "the band just absolutely in love with rock and dedicated to upholding its form and spirit."

As overwhelmingly positive reviews were in ample supply, shouts of mediocrity were hard to find, but they existed. The *Village Voice* had high expectations, writing, "Hey, it beats Nickelback. But, as welcome a respite from radio's sprawling angst as the coupling is for some, Weezer's tight song construction (13 tracks in 34 minutes) and vague, clichéd lyrics don't add up to an exceptional pop record, memorably catchy or not." Elsewhere, *Pitchforkmedia* accused it of being "the slightest effort yet from the Weez, marking a continuation of their distressing downward trajectory and a perpetuation of their post-comeback complacence."

"I'm always trying to be upbeat," Cuomo said, responding to the criticism. "I'm always shocked at how I misperceived myself because everyone always writes about how negative and pessimistic and misanthropic I am. So I think I have to take a look at my writing process because something is going wrong because I'm really not that kind of a person. I don't feel like that when I'm writing. I mean yeah, well, sometimes things don't work out, but I'm not a bitter person. I'm not an angry person. I always try to look on the bright side, and that's what I feel when I'm writing music. It's weird that it just comes out so pessimistic."

Like many artists, Rivers has been known to filter out the praise and focus on the criticism. Other nasty reviews included Dallas/Fort Worth's *Star Telegram*, which said, "the group's fourth record is the worst thing it's done. Gone are the pleasantly familiar guitar-rock gems. In their place are messy, unfocused songs that give you an idea of how capricious band leader Rivers Cuomo can be." And *TimeOut New York* dissed *Maladroit* as "possibly the band's most determinedly dumb album yet."

Such negativity failed to permeate the Weezer camp as the band's new album hit store shelves. In a unique move, harking back to something not seen since The Beatles' *White Album*, the quartet arranged for the packaging of each of the first 600,000 copies of *Maladroit* to include individual numbering, running from 000001 to 600000. If the unique marketing approach signified that previously strained matters between Rivers and Interscope were well in the past, the subject was hardly taboo for R.C.

"I give 'em shit all the time," he said in the days leading up to the disc's release, despite having hammered out an agreement with the company giving the band more control. "They have no idea how to deal with me. I don't want to be difficult; I just have to protect my band and our creative selves. The industry is geared toward exploiting our creative resources and laying them to waste, and I have to protect them. So I get a reputation as being difficult. But if you're willing to help us and nurture us, I'm not difficult at all."

With "Dope Nose" now at #8 on the Modern Rock survey, and a television commercial for *Maladroit* running during MTV's highly rated show, *The Osbournes*, Rivers gave the impression he was in full control, but was he really?

"These are really crazy times," Rivers told *Billboard*. "No one knows what the hell's going on in the industry or what's around the corner. So I think Weezer's like a little experiment for [Interscope]. Like, 'Let's see if this guy can figure out what's going on.' I end up trusting them even more — because I know that, at the end of the day, I have the power to make the decision either way. So I'm more likely to listen to what they have to say. And they are very smart guys, and I totally respect them."

If it seemed like ass kissing of the highest order to make a statement like that in a music industry magazine, it was more apparent than ever that Cuomo knew what strings to pull and what buttons to push. Whether there was an ounce of sincerity behind the comments above, only Rivers himself knew. But one thing was indeed certain by this point in his career: Come hell or high water, Rivers Cuomo would somehow always get what he wanted.

chapter twenty-nine

take control

A year after firing Pat Magnarella, Rivers Cuomo was becoming a music industry power player. Although he had started his own label imprint and was managing both AM Radio and Weezer, he said that things had gotten far simpler.

"I mean here's somebody that doesn't really . . . he's not in the band," said Cuomo about the disadvantages of having a business manager in the picture. "He doesn't play music, and yet he's kind of hanging around, trying to tell us what to do. We don't really need that. I don't see why anyone would want that."

With the professionals who had instructed Weezer how to play the game now fired, the band was free to play music as they wanted. There were some inevitable mistakes, but the emphasis was on fun. Steering Weezer through the release of their new album, Rivers revealed that the group was tentatively eyeing a February 2003 release for album #5.

He was having little difficulty making up for the lost years of his career. When asked for his advice on life and how to live it as a rock 'n' roll power player, he suggested, "cut out the business and promotional side of being a musician and focus more on just playing. What we've found is, if left to our own devices, we kind of stop doing a lot of things that bands are supposed to do [these days].

"Managers and record companies and the industry as a whole — they just want to sell as much product as they can," he said. "They don't want to allow you the space to develop. I just realized that I don't want those sort of people telling me what to do or trying to influence me. Their motives are all wrong."

Approaching music the way Fury had back in 1983, Weezer had come to think of itself as more than just a tool to market an album for the greedy record label. Cuomo wasn't cranking out the Kiss covers anymore, but his band's approach was far more natural without the day-to-day meddling of a manager. "We've cut a lot of the bullshit out of our operation," Rivers said with pride.

"When I want to do something, I do it, and when I don't, I don't," he said simply. "I don't have to deal with somebody whispering in my ear, 'You ought to do this because the record company will be happy.' I don't have anyone telling me what to do. I don't feel like I have to do deal with anything I don't want to do now and I don't really do anything I don't want to do. I don't even really feel comfortable saying I manage the band. Basically we're unmanaged. What I've done is just cut the industry off from access to us. We're in our own little bubble here. That's my management philosophy: 'Leave us alone!'"

"One thing that has changed within the band is that because we feel more mature and more responsible of what the future holds for us, it's kind of reassuring," Brian added. "Who would have better interest in us than Rivers? No one."

After all, Weezer was still Cuomo's band in that anyone but he could leave and it would survive. Rivers insisted, though, that such a hierarchy no longer caused friction in the band but instead let everyone know their place, which kept things running smoothly.

Such proclamations portrayed Shriner, Bell, and Wilson as Cuomo's employees rather than members of a popular rock "band." But the other members of the group did little to argue the suggestion. In fact, Shriner —

upon being informed of Rivers' assessment — proudly defended his boss's description of the group's organizational structure.

If Wilson, the band's only other remaining co-founder, at first seemed surprised at Rivers' proclamation, he soon conceded, "That's probably true. It *is* his band, man. I don't think that's a strange comment."

Bell, too, admitted he had long accepted — and was comfortable with — his position in Weezer. "Before I even joined the band I knew that Rivers had the final say, and I was fine with that. I'm glad somebody does, and why not the songwriter? I try to [find a balance with Rivers] but he has final say on everything. Sometimes I go, 'Is this worth the fight? No.' But other times, if I feel strongly enough I will fight and usually I will win . . . or at least I'll be heard."

"I think probably the best thing that Weezer ever did was have Rivers be more responsible for his band," Patrick opined. "I mean, it's our band but he's the guy. It's cool to see him more involved and I think he had this epiphany that, 'Nobody is going to devote more energy and care and time to this band than I am.'"

Now, instead of just ruminating over his songs, Cuomo had taken on unforeseen, but not unwelcome, duties and tensions in the role of manager. Just being the singer and the songwriter had been so boring to Rivers that he went to college as a diversion, but with Magnarella out of the organization life was regularly a challenge. "I'm pretty much constantly obsessed with the world of Weezer and whatever problems are going on," he declared. "So it can be a bit stressful, but I have a very high tolerance for stress. It's the kind of life I like. If everything was all peaceful and happy, I'd probably freak out. I wouldn't know what to do."

The material slated for album #5 was an amalgam of Cuomo's favorite styles, including pop, metal, alternative, rap, goth, and emo. "We're gonna have the mother of all styles," he predicted.

"[It's] kind of a shift back toward a little more melody," said Chad Bamford, who was involved in the spring 2002 sessions. "[It's] a little less riff-oriented, and more song- and melody-oriented."

In creating recordings for album #5 that embodied those elements while marking a shift back to "personally expressive songs," Weezer was to the point where it had no interest in outside help unless the record label was forcing the issue. "We don't feel like, 'Oh, we're going to make an album now. Let's go bring in this totally different person out of our normal routine,'" said Rivers. "That just doesn't make sense to us. This is what we do. Just press record. That's how we make an album."

Defying the conventions of major label rock music, the band was on a roll creatively and showed no sign of coming to a halt any time soon. And the truth was the group had no reason to halt its insanely productive run. "If I have any advice to give to any band it would be to always work. Waiting around for a record company to make you huge is about the dumbest thing you can do," Pat said of the D.I.Y. Weezer.

"I feel like I've reached a certain level of craftsmanship, and I don't see any reason to hold back," Rivers added. "Look at The Beatles — they were just cranking it out. They weren't over-thinking what direction they wanted to go in; they just got on a roll and went for it. They did two albums a year, at least. I think the only way classic albums will get made is by cranking them out."

"What we want [to make are] exciting recordings that sound like people who were having a good time, and I don't hear that in a lot of music today," Wilson continued. "I think it's because a lot of bands get talked into making these 'perfect-sounding' records because shareholders are demanding it from executives. But it creates these fake acts that can't go out and play, and that's a drag. I mean, God bless 'em if they can go out and make money doing that. But it's just not solid. It's just not a solid scene."

Bringing the magic of *Maladroit* to Japan concert stages that May, playing gigs in cities like Sendai, Tokyo, Fukuoka, Hiroshima, Osaka, and Nagoya over the course of two weeks, Rivers observed how the scene there had changed in the six years since Weezer first rocked the country.

When the group first played Japan in 1996, it was the recipient of extreme hero worship, but by 2002, the fans resembled "jaded American rock kids." If the energy in the audiences was significantly different, the vibes within Weezer were greatly changing as well. Cuomo wasn't only allowing Scott, Pat, and Brian to work out their individual musical parts to his songs by this point, but he had relinquished control of the stage in order to give Bell and Wilson a crack at the microphone during the Far East shows.

If the guys weren't actually what Cuomo would call friends by this point, things were continuing to evolve relationship-wise as the group arguably reached its healthiest arrangement in a decade. "I guess we all consider ourselves friends," Rivers said. "It's just I'm not like a friend kind of guy. I'm so focused and so into working, I don't just watch football games with the guys. I was always super-focused from as far back as I can remember. Even being five years old — very focused, and I've just gotten more so as I get older."

Often withdrawn and short on personal relationships, it seemed peculiar that Rivers could be so vocal in the presence of a journalist's tape recorder but so reclusive with family and "friends." But in his own self-assessment, Cuomo felt "extremely normal and bland," and blamed the media for dubbing him "crazy or cracked or weird." He complained about being portrayed as an isolated, insulated Brian Wilson type of oddball talent. "I feel like nobody has any idea of what I'm actually like, judging by the articles I've read."

And opting not to leave his New York City hotel room — despite the valiant efforts of his assistant Sheeny — to attend a *Guitar World* photo shoot to promote *Maladroit* did little to correct this portrayal.

Unwilling to blame his behavior on an illness or touring fatigue, as some other rock stars might, Rivers — after agreeing to do the cover shoot in his hotel, not at a photo studio — defended his actions. "Too many musicians kiss the industry's ass and are led around by their managers or record companies, which I think will kill a band," he contended, donning a vintage Yngwie Malmsteen T-shirt and clutching a genuine Van Halen–styled guitar for the camera. "We focus on what we do: playing Weezer shows and making Weezer albums. Everything else is just kind of an annoyance."

In the same piece, Cuomo turned on his diehard fans, calling the same group that helped him shape the sound and contents of *Maladroit* "little bitches." Pledging to avoid fans at all costs, Rivers called *Pinkerton* "worthless" and labeled emo — the subgenre he helped define — "bad music." He also claimed that if he was growing up in 2002, he'd be into bands with odd time signatures like System of a Down.

"I would think Weezer were a bunch of fags," Cuomo chuckled, showing that his political incorrectness hadn't changed at all.

The group's latest hire and resident System fan, Scott Shriner, was clearly rubbing off on the rest of Weezer. "He comes from a different background, where shredding is okay," Cuomo acknowledged. "He just gets up there every night and puffs his chest up and just shreds, and I think we all get excited and follow his lead." Because of Scott, Cuomo not only became increasingly open to input from other members, but largely did away with any preconceived ideas and encouraged creativity from Shriner, Wilson, and Bell.

"He really made us man up," Pat explained of Shrinedog's place in the band. "I'm so excited to play with a guy who's into all the classic rock stuff.

Now we're just out of our minds playing music and having fun."

Rivers still kept a three-ring binder that he called "The Encyclopedia of Pop," which featured analyses of different artists like Oasis, Green Day, and Nirvana. And while he dissected the works of Noel Gallagher, Billie Joe Armstrong, and Kurt Cobain, Rivers was proudest of his enduring affection toward angst rockers and Interscope labelmates Limp Bizkit. Fans couldn't help wonder what the fuck that was all about: Was it the result of some kind of Jordan Schur–sponsored brainwashing session? Was Cuomo just completely full of shit?

In reality, Rivers was just a fan of Fred Durst.

"I love how Limp Bizkit manage to combine metal and rap and pop so seamlessly," he said. "I really see us as moving in that direction. I have no interest in emo. I'm all about rap metal."

MIKE GUASTELLA/WIREIMAGE.COM

"Seriously, Rivers, I Did It All For The Nookie!" R.C. gets chummy with ol' Red Cap himself, Fred Durst

Thankfully Brian Bell put Weezer's frightened followers at ease. "We're not going to sound like Limp Bizkit," he assured. "What Rivers might be talking about is the intensity we want to exude when we play."

In any event, before too long the Weezer frontman had moved on to a revived trend called goth. Inspired by 1980s bands like The Cure, Siouxie & the Banshees, and Sisters of Mercy, the ghoulish scene had taken on a new life. Propelled by darker punk bands like A.F.I. and Alkaline Trio, the '00s version of goth briefly captivated Cuomo, who had gone so far as to show off black fingernail polish, silver rings, and leather wrist cuffs in the presence of *Rolling Stone* scribe Jenny Eliscu. It seems Rivers had become fascinated with a certain female who embraced the style. Cuomo's goth look, like his "Grizzly Adams" unkempt beard appearance before it, was a short-lived phase, soon supplanted by a love of business suits he would develop during Japan World Cup '02 tour.

Smartly, the soccer-loving Cuomo plotted the Japanese dates around the World Cup, with a planned vacation in the Orient to follow the tour in the early weeks of June. But before the fun could begin, work obligations had his group launching the trek at Sendai's Club Zepp. During the gig Weezer dusted off "Holiday," playing it for the first time since Shriner joined the group. It was just the start of the live show curve balls Cuomo was tossing on the jaunt.

Two nights later, at Tokyo's Zepp facility, the band debuted Wilson's "The Story Is Wrong" amid a classic mix of seasoned ("No One Else") and new ("Smile") tunes. Reacting to his opportunity out in front, Pat was admittedly shocked and thrilled. "If anyone knows our history, it's less than smooth," he said. "So it was super cool, playing a song, and no one's like, 'you're not playing it right.'" As the tour progressed some 900 miles southward into Fukuoka, Bell was next to get a turn out in front, as his high-energy number, "Yellow Camaro," made the live scene.

The next day, word was received from the United States that *Maladroit* had debuted at #3 in the *Billboard* album survey, achieving its highest chart position in the Top 200 ever. With the successful chart entry of Weezer's new album, the argument that downloading music online was hurting an artist's record sales was weakening. In fact, some would argue that the accessibility of the material actually helped spread the word on what the band was up to, keep its profile high, and in turn assist with record sales.

In Canada, the disc did even better, pulling down a solid #2 debut, with impressive entries in the U.K. (#16), Ireland (#15), Australia (#11), and Germany (#29), despite the fact that no commercial single was available internationally to boost sales. And after four months on the airwaves, "Dope Nose" was losing steam and Cuomo and Schur were working to an agreement on a *Maladroit* excerpt to supplant it.

Back in Osaka, "Getchoo" was unearthed for only the second time in five years. If the appearance of the song in the set list left many Weezer fans in attendance open-jawed, Koch must have had a similar reaction when his Karl's Korner page exceeded 10 million total hits around the same time. Wrapping up the Japan World Cup Tour with a pair of Tokyo gigs, the group unearthed "Falling for You" after five years in hiding and was sound checking a full, electric version of "Butterfly." The live focus on *Pinkerton* tunes — songs Cuomo openly disdained — was unusual. It left fans to speculate over whether Rivers had decided to revisit the tunes in an effort to tap into his personal side that he had avoided on *The Green Album* and, to a lesser extent, *Maladroit*. After all, wasn't *Pinkerton* the disc he was so embarrassed by that he had vowed to one day get full ownership of it and take it out of print?

Around this time, the group also made an upcoming six-week tour of North American amphitheaters official, announcing opening act

JASON NELSON/BLISTERING.COM

Rivers, looking every bit the godfather of emo rock

Dashboard Confessional, plus additional support by the hotly hyped Strokes for a couple of dates. The Enlightenment Tour '02, as it was being dubbed, was designed to take advantage of the summer weather, and also made room for show openers Sparta, which featured former members of the recently splintered and sorely missed At the Drive-In. Set to start in Salt Lake City in early July, the trek was slated to wrap up in San Diego in mid-August.

"It's gonna be awesome," Pat Wilson said of the summer shed tour. "The sound just goes. In an arena, it sounds stupid, but when we hear stuff and it goes out and then comes back, it has a certain feeling to it, but in these places, it just feels like the sound you make goes forever. So we'll probably be more like, I don't know, Phish."

Dashboard principal Chris Carrabba was thrilled to open for his heroes in Weezer. "The day that their first record was released, I bought it and was blown away. I've loved every record they've made, some more than others," he declared. "Right down to collecting B-sides. To me, it is a huge deal. Plus, they're massive. Everybody has been asking me, 'How does it feel to have gotten where you've gotten?' and I keep thinking, 'Where have I gotten?' But I guess if I'm in that same league as Weezer, albeit on a smaller team, then I must've gotten somewhere. Plus, it's 20,000 people a night."

In tandem with Carrabba's discussion of the trek, an announcement for additional opening acts on the Enlightenment Tour, to appear on special side stages or neighboring venue, was also made, with groups like Loudermilk, Hometown Hero, Rooney, Wilson's The Special Goodness, and — surprise — AM Radio to appear on some or all dates.

Reacting to The Special Goodness getting the opportunity to play on certain dates, Brian Bell later said, "When Rivers asked me how I felt about The Special Goodness opening I said, 'I think that's great but in the future I would like to have the same opportunity.' So I hope it's possible."

When Weezer's road crew went back to Los Angeles after the World Cup dates, the band remained in Tokyo to prep its next single. In an effort to not terribly impact his well-plotted FIFA (Fédération Internationale de Football Association) World Cup vacation itinerary of Japan and Korea that June, Cuomo kept Pat, Scott, and Brian behind and flew in the *Maladroit* production and engineering team of Chad Bamford and Rod Cervera for a three-and-a-half day session. The end result was a complete reworking of "Keep Fishin'" that the Interscope suits could really get behind.

"We were in Japan, and we knew that [the original version of "Keep Fishin'"] was meeting resistance from radio because they thought it was kind of 'indie sounding,'" Pat Wilson explained. "Which is so stupid, because, listen to The White Stripes. What could be more indie than that? But what they are talking about, and I have to partially agree with them, is that even The White Stripes album is done to a click track. It sounds all lo-fi but it's very even. So we just went back and recorded it with a click. It does sound more together, in a commercial way, though I think it lost some of its charm."

Still, programmers didn't think so, and within mere days of the song's completion on May 31, Schur ordered his radio department to quickly press and rush the new single version of the tune to modern rock outlets. On June 4, the new version of "Keep Fishin'" premiered on KROQ, where it quickly became a hotly requested and heavily rotated item on the station.

With Bell, Shriner, and Wilson on their way back to the States for a two-and-a-half week break from Weezer activities, word spread of the group's return to Japan for August's Summersonic '02, where they would appear just beneath headliners Guns N' Roses on the Outdoor Stage, but atop heavy hitters like No Doubt, the Offspring, NOFX, and Sum 41.

Rivers — after going on a business suit-purchasing spree in Seoul — was soon joined on his trip by some of his soccer enthusiast friends, including Justin Fisher, to attend the World Cup games. Simultaneously, new, free MP3s of album #5 demos like "Peace and Quiet," "367," "The Victor," and "Private Message" began to trickle out.

"I think Weezer is kind of the most punk band in some ways," Pat Wilson said, referring to Weezer's active MP3 page. "We just full-on make songs and show 'em to our fans for free. It's like the punk ethic. And I can't tell you how many levels of irony are wrapped up in that. When we were coming up, all of us had a severe self-image problem. We knew that Fugazi was the shit, and we thought, 'We can never do that.' But at the same time, we didn't really examine their methods. Now, *Maximum Rock 'n' Roll* will put us on the cover, saying 'Weezer is superpunk!'"

However, Weezer's "test marketing" wasn't something guitarist Bell was extremely jazzed about, as he was somewhat uncomfortable with letting people hear "music that isn't finished." It was just another example of how life in Cuomo's band left little room for democracy.

The same month the band landed on the cover of *Spin* in a picture notable for featuring a shoeless Pat in a classic air guitar pose and sporting a vintage Iron Maiden T-shirt. While the photo depicts Brian and Scott in tough-as-nails poses, the cover shot is perhaps the last high-profile shot of Cuomo wearing his bushy, Brian Wilson–gone–bonkers beard.

Defending his decision to grow facial hair, Rivers said at the time, "It's just a beard. Why does it have to mean Brian Wilson? Millions of guys have beards, not just me and him." Just the same, Cuomo smartened up and shaved the awful thing in time to lens the video for "Keep Fishin'" when he returned to Los Angeles in mid-June.

In the *Spin* story, Cuomo reflected on being the product of 1970s commune-style hippie parenting. The irony was that it made Rivers and his little brother straight arrows in their teen years — an extremely rare distinction for American kids. In fact, he never tried drugs or even smoked a Marlboro until he was in his twenties. When asked about the future of the band, Cuomo professed a love of hip-hop, touting Jay-Z and the art of "dis songs." But by the time the group had reconvened for more studio work on June 20 at Sunset Sound, the new dimension in the group's sound was the keyboard.

In a move designed to augment the Weezer sound, Cuomo hired multi-instrumentalist Ryan Maynes to man the keyboards. Best known as Shmedley, the bassist in Los Angeles Sub Pop–signed rock outfit Arlo, the Huntington Beach–reared Maynes learned the piano when he was three years old, and had long been a fan of the group. "They have been very welcoming to me, making me feel at home," Shmedley said of his involvement with the band. And while Maynes spoke of expanding his musical creativity with Weezer, his involvement with the band was a short-lived experiment.

Upon his return to U.S. soil, Rivers Cuomo learned that *Maladroit* had been awarded a gold disc by the Recording Industry Association of America a mere month after its release. Soon after his arrival, he met with future AM Radio producer Howard Benson, agreeing to lend a guitar solo to Benson's current project, the in-progress record by rap/metal merchants Crazy Town.

But first, it was time for the freshly shaved Cuomo to join his Weezer bandmates, director Marcos Siega, and their Muppet co-stars to shoot the "Keep Fishin'" video on a Manhattan Beach soundstage. Based on Siega's idea, the group shows up for an appearance on *The Muppet Show* and encounters Kermit the Frog backstage. Except there's one problem: drummer Pat Wilson is missing. The band starts the song without its drummer, with Animal in his place. A subsequent scene finds a smitten Miss Piggy holding Wilson hostage.

With Rivers out in front wearing a new gray business suit with a dark red tie, Kermit — sporting a =w= on his shirt — supplies Cuomo with harmony vocals. The surprise move prompts Weezer's frontman to flash his often sequestered but telling smile. Backstage, Pat manages to lock Piggy in the closet and cut himself free from the chair he had been tied to with the aid of the Swedish Chef's meat cleaver.

"I'd forgotten how much they meant to me as a kid," Rivers said of the Muppets from the set, as the television show *Access Hollywood* caught behind-the-scenes footage. "They're just really likable characters that I really identified with. Something that I thought was very cool was that they didn't play down to kids. I used to play along to the soundtrack album from *The Muppet Movie*. I would set up pillows as a drum set and play along to Animal's parts."

"It was really fun," Shriner said of the shoot. "Being around a bunch of puppets has a way of making you happy. You can't help it. Marcos did a great job. Besides our shitty acting, I think it turned out fantastic."

Siega, who called Weezer his "favorite band," has said he considers himself fortunate to have worked frequently with the group. "I really admire Rivers Cuomo," the director explained. "At the fear of sounding like I am blowing smoke up his ass, I think he's a genius. I find him interesting and a fascinating guy to talk to."

As for the idea of merging the infamous Muppets with rock and roll, Siega revealed, "I came up with the idea years ago and had pitched it to Blink-182, Ozzy, and even Weezer for 'Hash Pipe.' It was never the right song or attitude. Then 'Keep Fishin'' came down and Rivers said, 'I think that could work.' Everyone knew it would work, despite the fear it might be too kitschy."

In late June, Weezer had moved pre-production for album five into Sunset Sound Studios. But Cuomo's business schmoozing, managerial responsibilities, press duties, and continuing fixation on the ongoing World Cup had drastically cut into his once prolific songwriting. From early April to early July, Rivers had only written seven songs, with titles like "Running Man," "Fontana," "Lullaby," "The Organ Player," "Egg Beaters," "Fourth of July," and "Perfect Situation." Still, since January 1999, the man had penned a remarkable 384 songs.

"I'm gonna be slowing down," he said at the time. "I'm already slowing down, really, and taking more time on my lyrics. So whereas before I'd gotten into the habit of writing a song every morning without fail, now I feel like my default mode is to do nothing but lounge around, and if a song comes along, I'll go with it. Before I wanted to keep moving, whereas now I feel I've arrived."

With Shmedley guesting on the session, the Weezer boys also reworked previous demos like "The Victor," "Mo Beats," and "Private Message," plus the aforementioned "Lullaby" and "Running Man." Brian's new entries, "Birthday Booty" and "Louder than Lies," plus Pat's composition, "Reason to Worry," were also attempted.

The highly productive two-week sessions also saw the group tear through older and newer items like "Mad Kow," "Sacrifice," "367," "Steamroller," "Misstep," "Hey Domingo (a.k.a. The World Cup Song)," "Sugar Cookie," "Acapulco," "Private Message," "Booby Trap," "Prodigy Lover," "Mr. Taxman," "Mansion of Cardboard," "Saturday Night," "Queen of Earth," "Superstar," "We Go Together," "Listen Up," "Modern Dukes," "Misstep," "She Who Is Militant," and "Buttafuoco."

As "Keep Fishin'" picked up steam at radio, news of the video spread when Weezer issued a press release to the media. "Being a guest on *The Muppet Show* was a childhood dream we all shared, so we were ecstatic when the Muppets agreed to be in our video," said the band collectively. "The Muppets can really rock."

Supporting this position, Kermit the Frog reported, "Weezer fit right in. They're rock stars, they're used to being around animals, bears, and egotistical pigs." The band was now among such musical celebrities as Alice Cooper, John Denver, and Debbie Harry, all of whom had worked with the Muppets. News of the collaboration even made the CNN Headline News ticker.

Elsewhere, "Island in the Sun" was licensed with its author's approval for a Snickers candy commercial in Australia just as an upcoming July 25 appearance on *Late Night with David Letterman* was announced. As work wound down on pre-production for album #5, Cuomo showed up at the Crazy Town session on the night of July 3 to lay down his guitar parts as promised. Apparently, Cuomo *was* serious about his love of the heavy metal/rap hybrid.

If the pairing seemed odd, it was Cuomo who first professed his love for the nu-metalists after meeting Crazy Town guitarist Craig Tyler at a Fresno rock festival. Later, "Craig happened to see Rivers out at a nightclub and Rivers starts calling his name," explained Bret Mazur, one of Crazy Town's vocalists. "Craig couldn't believe he remembered his name."

Showing up in yet another suit, this time a sophisticated green outfit complete with a lighter green shirt and a blue tie, Rivers might have looked out of place at the studio, but his licks on the tentatively titled "Hurt" (later to be known as "Hurt You So Bad" when the album *Darkhorse* was released in late '02) said otherwise. As for the fashion shift to snazzy threads, which he planned to continue wearing onstage throughout the summer, Rivers explained what prompted the move. "I was really cold in an air-conditioned restaurant, so I went across the street to the department store to get a jacket. Before I knew it, ten salesladies were throwing all these clothes on me. I walked out a half-hour later with a suit on, and I've been wearing suits ever since."

The group headed off to West Valley, Utah, to begin the Enlightenment Tour, Weezer's biggest concert trek ever. Keeping a diary from the road for Cuomo's own official, password-protected Web site (the since-disabled riverscuomo.com), Sheeny Bang began writing to fans on July 4, 2002, and telling of how assisting the Weezer frontman was "always interesting" despite the ups and downs of her job. "There's always something going on — so much so that at times it's hard to keep up! Another reason could be that he lives a lifestyle that is mysterious and intriguing to most, especially since he is in the public radar to a certain extent — but without the spotlight I think he'd be just as fascinating.

"Well, whatever the case, helping him out means that I get to go where he goes and see what he sees and at times vicariously experience the things he does. I guess here I'll try and pass that on in yet one more incarnation. — SB"

A Strong Suitor: Cuomo morphs from bearded freak
to fashionably chic, July 2002

The following day, Sheeny explained that Cuomo had been in great spirits, punching the air ecstatically after learning that veteran producer Rick Rubin had agreed to produce Weezer's next album. While Rivers kept this news from the media for many months, the move surely meant that the album #5 songs the group had been posting in recent months wouldn't make it to store shelves by February 2003. It also meant that the whole self-production concept the group was ardently embracing so recently was now out the window.

Rivers obviously changed his mind in the days following his chat with *Rolling Stone*'s Steve Knopper, who reported that the best out of the forty new songs the group cut in the preceding two and a half weeks would be released by early 2003. And who could blame Cuomo for being thrilled about working with Rubin, who had manned the boards for career-defining albums by the Red Hot Chili Peppers, the Beastie Boys, System of a Down, and Johnny Cash.

With the tour in motion, the *Salt Lake Tribune* ran an amusing piece asking "Are You Emo?" to plug the opening night's gig. Explaining that "emo" was more a look than a sound, the article asked, "Is your hair dyed black and sporting bangs? Are thick, black frames for your glasses and clunky black shoes must-haves for your look? Is *Pinkerton* your favorite Weezer album? Did you sit down and sing along with every lyric during the Dashboard Confessional shows this winter? If you can answer 'yes' to more than one of these questions, you are tuned in to the latest pop-music trend — emo."

Speaking on the subject in a similar piece two days later in the *Los Angeles Times*, Jimmy Eat World's Jim Adkins explained, "Emo is whatever you want it to be. My band plays guitar-based, melodic rock. I mean, Weezer has just been written up as an emo band. That boggles my mind. They were a very successful band in 1996, and no journalist was writing about emo-core then! Emo is just what people have been calling the up-and-coming bands that haven't quite broken into the mainstream."

"Weezer frontman Rivers Cuomo's well-publicized search for valida-
tion and social acceptance has made him a poster boy for the Emo
Nation," the *Times* piece proclaimed.

But Cuomo failed to find much of a correlation between the whine of
Saves the Day and the frequent roar of Weezer. "I guess there *is* some con-
nection," he admitted. "We play electric guitars. We're white. We're male.
And we don't rap."

As the band trucked onto Red Rocks Amphitheatre in Morrison, Colorado,
Weezer kept tunes from its recently wrapped pre-production efforts out of
the group's live show. "We've been playing those songs every day, so I'm
happy to go back and play material from our released albums," he said.

When the subject turned to enthusiastic fans, throwing up the "W"
hand gesture and raising cigarette lighters in appreciation, Cuomo commented, "If people are expressing the stoke factor, I'm all for it. Sometimes
it comes out in dorky ways. And I'm certainly guilty of that myself — I bust
out metal poses all the time. But I'm not out there thinking, 'Am I being
ironic? Am I being serious?' I'm just stoked."

If recent tours found him sucking down a glass of wine or taking a few
hits off a joint before shows, as Bang explained in her online diary, for this
trek Rivers was approaching the shows sober. Sobriety left lots of time for
foosball, but that wasn't the only change, as the Weezer leader took time
to meet with some message board contest winners during the show, putting faces to the screen names he liked to chat with.

"The [fans] were very gracious and well behaved," Sheeny reported,
"and Rivers seemed to enjoy the meeting. They may have set the precedent for the rest of the tour and his obliging attitude towards meeting fans
again." The "little bitches," it seemed, were back in Cuomo's good graces
for the moment.

As the tour buses rolled toward the Midwest, Shriner (who celebrated his thirty-seventh birthday at the Windy City gig) and Bell managed to alternate regional press duties. "It's really incredible that anyone cares and wants to talk to you," said Bell acknowledging his celebrity status. "But, then again, I feel like, 'I'm not an actor' and I really don't want people to know that much about me. So a lot of times we're sarcastic and people think that we're being serious and we're actually lying. They're just games that you have to play to keep yourself sane."

Explaining the move toward flash pots and other pyro for Weezer's biggest caravan ever, Bell continued, "We're upping the ante on the stage antics. We're gonna have fire and explosions and stuff like that. Somehow this band is able to border on being ironic. We're not actually serious with our 'macho rock,' but then again, we are — so it's hard to tell. We'll see if we can keep that, or if people think we've totally cheesed-out."

With MTV, MTV2, and VH1 beginning to play "Keep Fishin'" regularly, word came in that the Strokes would be forced to drop off of their scheduled Cleveland, Indianapolis, and Columbus commitments with Weezer due to doctor's orders surrounding an unspecified illness that singer Julian Casablancas had contracted.

With a day off on July 16, Brian and Rivers hit the studio in Indianapolis for guitar and vocal overdubs on some in-progress recordings after flying production and engineering help in from Los Angeles. When asked at the time if he and Cuomo had creative struggles, Bell replied cautiously, "That is a dangerous question. But you know, I usually have to come back with I'm difficult sometimes, too. Everyone involved is difficult at one time or another. I think Rivers has set up this empire of his in a certain way where he has the final say on things and that's it. You either accept it or you don't. I'm not saying I could do any better. And if something goes wrong, then the blame is on him."

With roughly thirty demos up on the *Weezer.com* A/V page simultaneously after the group fought for its return, Rivers could do little wrong in the eyes of most fans. Still, Weezer loyalists weren't appreciative of the way Rivers — when spotted by autograph seekers — would run like hell. "It's a very intense love-hate relationship we all have with each other," Cuomo admitted, saying he would still prefer that the love (and the hate) come to his attention only by the Internet, for the most part.

"It's a real point of friction between me and the fans right now," he continued, talking about his stand-offishness and disdain for being approached on the street for his signature. "Even if I'm just walking around somewhere, in my mind I'll be working on some songs or working on some business problem and if somebody comes up to me and says, 'Hey can I have an autograph?' it completely destroys my train of thought and I get so angry."

By dropping $15–$20 on Weezer's latest CD, some fans argued that they were hardly off base in asking for an autograph. Yet, it was Rivers' position that he'd much rather forgo the signatures and meet-and-greets that accompany stardom. It was more important for him to be a productive artist than a commercial success obliged to interact with his audience.

"It's hard to describe something about Rivers with any real conviction 'cause he is such a mercurial character," Sheeny Bang wrote of her fickle boss in a diary post later that summer. "What may be true now may not be in a month's time. In some cases, change is gradual and at other times it's literally overnight. Even after over a year of doing this job, I still couldn't really say that I know him well. I know plenty about him — likes and dislikes, history, etc., but I can never say I really understand him 'cause he's always changing the goal posts."

As the tour pulled into outdoor sheds along the East Coast, news surfaced of *another* Weezer disc being prepared for 2002. A six-song EP, baptized *The Lion and the Witch*, would be made available in a limited press-ing of just 25,000 copies beginning on September 17, and only at select independent retail outlets. The special Geffen promotion would consist of live tracks from Weezer's recently completed Japanese trek. In reaction to Interscope artists like Sheryl Crow and U2 doing EPs with retailers like Best Buy and Target, groups of unified independent retailers approached the label to request the same treatment. These retailers specifically asked for Weezer, who in turn decided that they would create something new. Originally the revamped take of "Keep Fishin'" plus a hidden, unreleased tune called "Polynesia" were slated for the project, but when it surfaced it housed only live takes of "Dope Nose," "Island in the Sun," "Falling for You," "Death And Destruction," "El Scorcho," and "Holiday."

Despite the popularity of the tour, by late July *Maladroit* had rather alarmingly dropped to #89 in the *Billboard* Top 200, a considerable fall in the seven weeks since its #3 chart debut. But that same week, "Keep Fishin'" had jumped from #17 to #8 on the MTV2 Rock Countdown, and the allure of the single put the band in the company of David Letterman for the first time in seven years. The song also pumped some new life into the album as it snuck back into the hearts of college radio programmers, bumping it up into the *CMJ* top five again. Interestingly enough, the lads found themselves sand-wiched between acts like Arlo, the primary band of Weezer's hired keyboardist Shmedley, and former tour openers The Get Up Kids.

A day after the Letterman appearance, the group rolled down to the Tweeter Center in Camden, New Jersey, to rock the house. While in the area, Weezer took over the Philadelphia airwaves, spinning records during a four-hour, pre-recorded post-gig broadcast.

"I thought of the idea of letting Weezer take over the radio station," said the station's programmer Jim McGuinn. "But it wasn't exactly logisti-cally feasible to have them do it in the middle of the tour. So we went to them a few days beforehand. They each picked out, like, ten songs. Then I selected the ones that seemed like the most fun to put into a radio show and made the logs, and then I went to visit them with our midday guy, Brett Hamilton, and we sort of taught Pat and Scott how to be DJs. So they played Mötley Crüe and Pixies and Black Sabbath and Van Halen and it was really great.

The songs played during the July 27 broadcast of "Weezer Radio on Y100" — which also featured taped intros with Brian and Rivers, were:

"Keep Fishin'"
"Say It Ain't So"
"Immigrant Song" (Led Zeppelin)
"Summertime Rolls" (Jane's Addiction)
"Come As You Are" (Nirvana)
"Everything's Not Lost" (Coldplay)
"Machine Gun" (Jimi Hendrix)
"D'ya Know What I Mean?" (Oasis)
"Pink Triangle"
"A Quick One" (The Who)
"Last Night" (The Strokes)
"Beetlebum" (Blur)
"Breaking the Girl" (Red Hot Chili Peppers)
"Live and Let Die" (Paul McCartney and Wings)
"Hash Pipe"
"Should I Stay or Should I Go" (The Clash)
"National Anthem" (Radiohead)
"Hella Good" (No Doubt)
"Break Stuff" (Limp Bizkit)
"Loser" (Beck)
"Once in a Lifetime" (Talking Heads)
"Redemption Song" (Bob Marley & The Wailers)
"Buddy Holly"
"Hey Good Lookin'" (Hank Williams)
"Amber" (311)

"Fight for Your Right (To Party)" (Beastie Boys)

"Geek Stink Breath" (Green Day)

"Schism" (Tool)

"Ashes to Ashes" (David Bowie)

"She Blinded Me with Science" (Thomas Dolby)

"Supersonic" (Oasis)

"El Scorcho"

"Looks That Kill" (Mötley Crüe)

"Rain When I Die" (Alice in Chains)

"This Is a Call" (Foo Fighters)

"Where Is Your Mind?" (Pixies)

"Dope Nose"

"The Wizard" (Black Sabbath)

"Drain You" (Nirvana)

"Mean Streets" (Van Halen)

"Blister in the Sun" (Violent Femmes)

"Undone — The Sweater Song"

"The Middle" (Jimmy Eat World)

"We Are the Champions" (Queen)

For all of McGuinn's support for Weezer through the years, Weezer returned the favor. Aside from programming the only Modern Rock station in the country's fourth largest market, Jim also played in a local band, Cordalene. When it was discovered that one of the support acts would be unable to open for Weezer, Cuomo tapped one of his best radio contacts to warm up the Philadelphia area audience.

"For some reason, Sparta couldn't do the Camden show, so the promoter called and somehow I ended up Fed Ex'ing the CD of my band to Columbus, Ohio, for the band to review," said McGuinn. "And the promoter's like, 'If they like you, you're gonna open.' So it was really fun. And afterward, Brian and Pat said, 'I can't believe that was you opening for us.' And Rivers is like, 'I really like your CD, man.'"

It was just one example of how Cuomo, despite his erratic behavior, was always open to trying new things. Sheeny Bang enforced this notion in another post. "He used to drink loads of Mountain Dew, now his drink of choice is non-caffeinated tea," read her entry. "'Wilson,' as his soccer ball was nicknamed, no longer makes the journey on the road with us. Little as these things may seem, I think they indicate changes on a bigger scale within him. He's definitely entered into a new stage I would say, gradually this time, since the recording sessions at Sunset Sound. It should be interesting to see how the fall rehearsing and recording sessions will go if it keeps up as I'm almost certain it will have an effect on him musically — just as everything does in his life."

Over on the official message board, Cuomo — in a thread known as "Storrs, anyone" — had learned that one of his own fans was actually residing in the house where he lived in the 1980s. Speaking of Cuomo's mother, the message board member wrote, "She came over one day and said, 'I'm Buddhist and when I sold this house, I promised myself that the person who bought it would receive $3,000 off the price. And so all these years, I've been meaning to come back and give you this money. Here is a check.' And she asked, 'Do you know my son?' And we said, 'Yea.' Her name was Beverly.

"We found guitar picks in the closet in the room that's off of the kitchen on your right when you first enter the kitchen door," the resident "Owire" continued.

Minutes later, from Atlanta — where the group was just an hour from hitting the stage at the Hi Fi Buys Amphitheatre — "Ace" wrote back, "You live in my old house?"

"Yea," Owire continued. "We bought the house from [your] mom. I'm [sic] lived there since I was in elementary school, went to MMS [Mansfield Middle School] and everything . . ."

"It's creepy that you live in the house I grew up in," Rivers wrote back after the show. "I hate to reverse stalk you, but could I visit the house sometime?"

"If you want to come over, you can come on over," Owire replied. "I don't think that the house is much different . . . but we remodeled the kitchen."

"Thank you, Owire!" Cuomo replied. "Please PM me and send me your email address. Is it ok if my brother comes too?"

Packing up his laptop, "Ace" and his Weezer mates continued to swing through the South, bringing the rock to receptive audiences in Nashville, Houston, Dallas, and San Antonio before it was on to Irvine and the tour closer in Concord, California, just outside of San Francisco. If onstage banter like "You've been a great audience, we've been a great band" or "Damn, I'm sexy" was telling, Cuomo had a reason to be in up spirits. Team Weezer's foosball posse, which often featured pairings of Rivers and Pat, Rivers and Brian, Pat and Scott, depending on who was available, was regularly kicking ass during pre-show radio station–sponsored games with fans. Not to mention the fact that the band had rocked close to 200,000 ticket holders on the Enlightenment Tour.

To celebrate the success of the tour, Weezer held a private party at a Phoenix supper club for all of the bands (and their respective crew members) on the large summer caravan. Arizona rock legends Alice Cooper and Marty Friedman of Megadeth attended. Friedman — one of Rivers' teenage guitar heroes — wound up picking up an axe to riff away the night while Pat and Scott worked the rhythm section. As the party progressed, various members of groups on the trek took to the stage for covers by the likes of the Thompson Twins and Ratt.

In the final days of the U.S. tour, Cuomo began writing again, coming up with the first of nine new tunes during the month of August. Titles like "Turn Me 'Round," "Don't You Let My Heart Down," and "Everybody

Let's Rock" were written on the road. When the journey ended, the Weezer line-up returned to L.A. for three days to take care of some personal and business affairs and readied themselves for the festival appearances in Japan and England that would round out the summer. In between staff meetings, radio and magazine phoners, and his first stab at the game of poker, Rivers wrote another tune, "Hyde-King of Earth."

Arriving in Japan on August 15, Weezer was set to play a pair of Summersonic dates the coming weekend. The first Summersonic gig was held before more than 30,000 at the Tokyo Chiba Marine Stadium, with Weezer easily proving that they could command such a sprawling venue.

Cuomo's stage banter late in the set paid homage to headliner Axl Rose, one of his hard rock heroes in the late 1990s. "I just got one thing to say: Guns N' Roses!" he proclaimed, unknowing that Rose was enjoying Weezer's set from the side of the stage. Axl, in turn, reportedly revealed to folks around him that he counted Weezer as one of his favorite bands of the moment.

Later, Axl — the only original member left in GNR — gave props to Rivers and the band. According to a post by Koch, "At one point, Axl said to the crowd something like, '. . . [Well here we are] playing with Weezer . . . I never thought I'd [have the opportunity to do] a show with Weezer, after [all I went through] for the last eight years. . . .'"

In England the following weekend news broke that the band would support Guns N' Roses again, this time at the London Docklands Arena on August 26 at the special request of Axl Rose.

During the taping of an appearance for the U.K. television show *Popworld* earlier that week, Cuomo's peculiar behavior stunned those in attendance. In her online diary, Sheeny reported, "Rivers donned a long, blonde rock wig from a box of props and kept it on while the cameras rolled. It was funny to see the reaction of local crew as they laughed thinking it was a great joke and then when he remained straight-faced and kept it on, their laughter quickly turned quiet and hushed. After all this time it still cracks me up to see him freak people out and I don't mean that in a perverse way, it's just that when people don't know him and expect conventional, typical behavior and he doesn't supply [it], it's amusing. Okay, maybe it is a little perverse."

If the long blonde wig made him look frighteningly like Megadeth's Dave Mustaine in a suit, Cuomo had ditched the wig and the suits for casual clothes when Weezer appeared alongside groups like the Moldy Peaches, The Soundtrack of Our Lives, The Dandy Warhols, The White Stripes, the Strokes, Pulp, and Jane's Addiction at the Reading Festival. In front of 50,000 beer-swilling campers who attended the three-day outdoor festival, Weezer brought the hard rock, and by the end of their set, Wilson — in a rarely seen, Keith Moon–inspired move — kicked apart his drum set in a fit of reckless glee.

It was at Reading that Cuomo first encountered one of the newer bands on the bill, the Los Angeles–based outfit The Icarus Line. Travis Keller, who oversees that band's record label Buddyhead, is probably best known for the online rock gossip outlet of the same name, and talked about meeting Rivers.

"It was funny because we always sort of talked shit on Weezer and especially Rivers," Keller remembers. "You know, taking the piss on him for a while about his Asian fetish." Calling *The Green Album* by far the worst album of 2001, *Buddyhead* mauled it, writing, "this record is completely contrived and manufactured to pander toward self-professed 'geeks' everywhere, while these guys snort every line and bone every last underage Asian groupie in sight. Who fuckin' cares."

"Then, when The Icarus Line was playing the Reading Festival in 2002, we were running around backstage with our video camera, kind of fucking with everybody," Keller continues. "So, first we were talking with the kids from The Vines, and we're like, 'Dude, are you high on pot?' Because those guys are always talking about being stoned. We're like, 'Dude, you're crazy.' And then we ran into Rivers and he was with this big dude and we didn't know who it was. So, we're like, 'Hey Rivers, tell us about all of the Asian chicks you bang on tour.' And he was totally playing up to it, 'I don't know anything about this,' with kind of a giggle. But he was letting us fuck with him. And the dude next to him starts getting mad. He was like, 'Who the fuck are you guys?' So we told him, and he's like, 'I'm Jordan Schur and I'm gonna kick your ass.' So we, like, flipped the camera around on him. So, we have all this on film, of him flipping off. And I'm sure that the only reason he didn't kick our asses was that we had the camera on him, that saved us. He wouldn't pound us on camera. Then we were like, 'Dude, chill out.' And Rivers was kinda laughing, and then we got in this huge argument with Jordan about how he was ruining music.

"You know, we went over to Interscope for a meeting once," says Keller, "and we broke into Fred Durst's office at Interscope, and he has a closet full of red hats. So we put them on and took pictures in front of his gold records, and then we auctioned off these hats on eBay and got like $700 bucks a hat, and donated the money to a rape charity. So I think Jordan knew who we were and he was mad at us for several reasons. But Rivers was just standing there like he couldn't believe it."

Despite the fact that the *Buddyhead* Web site's gossip page — notorious for posting the home phone numbers of rockers like Fred Durst and Ozzy Osbourne — broadcast Cuomo's personal e-mail address to all of cyber-space, and regularly alluded to Cuomo's fondness for Asian teenage girls, Cuomo went so far as to e-mail Keller after Reading.

"I got an e-mail from him a couple weeks later. And he said, 'You guys were really funny,'" Keller continued. As far as the gossip goes, Travis said,

"He never really brought it up. I think that he was just really intrigued by the fact that we fucked him up, you know? I think he was really curious about us, because he really didn't know what we were. Later, and after he hung out with us a little bit, he kind of figured it out. Then he was totally nonchalant. 'Oh, I get it.'"

The next day in Leeds, word came in after meetings with Jordan that all post-GNR appearances — including a German TV spot and a *Top of the Pops* shoot — had been canceled. Just the same, Rivers was in a social mood, partying with Schur.

"Lord knows what they get up to, but whatever it was it kept them out 'til the wee hours of the morning," Bang wrote in her post. "He also went to [the] Reading Festival on the Sunday to see Puddle of Mudd and Slipknot play. It's funny 'cause like with all things that he does, there seems to be a game plan for hanging out and socializing. It's not just to have fun and hang out, there's a purpose and strategy to it and essentially it is all for the greater good (i.e. Weezer) and its progress. The only time that he seems not to be doing this is when he talks to chicks, but that's a whole different can of worms."

The Guns N' Roses show itself saw the debut of "Turn Me 'Round," but if Axl was digging Weezer, it wasn't translating to the hostile metal hooligans at the London Arena. Attendees let their plastic beer bottles fly towards Rivers, who was back to wearing a suit. Still, by the end of the group's set, the audience — including Schur and Puddle of Mudd's Wes Scanlin — was warming up to the band.

In his daily post, Koch wrote, "Rivers made the astute comment mid-set that this was just like the old days in L.A., when Weezer would play support to Guns N' Roses rip-off bands to crowds who were simply not having the non-big-hair-rock. And now, ten years later, they were getting a very similar effect, only supporting the real thing."

chapter thirty

turn me 'round

Upon returning to Los Angeles on August 27, Weezer canceled plans to resume work on their fifth album sometime in September. Having played to roughly 400,000 concertgoers throughout the world in 2002, the group needed a break. Having pulled down serious coin from all of Weezer's roadwork, merchandizing, and other endeavors, Rivers shopped for a new house. Meanwhile, rehearsals for the upcoming, Rick Rubin–produced disc got underway. However, "Climbing Clean Riff," "I Don't Want You," "Cloudy Day," "Baby Come Back," and "Another Lover" were the only new song ideas the once-prolific Rivers had to show for himself.

Perhaps it was Cuomo's "girl crazy" ways and fascination with women of "all types, kinds, and ages" that were cause for his reduction in output. According to Sheeny Bang, her eligible bachelor boss was "utterly amused and intrigued by them and vice versa.

"When Weezer were in Japan back in May, after one of the shows Rivers went outside the venue where there was a group of waiting fans, mostly girls," Sheeny continued. "As he came out everyone crowded around him hurriedly, but bizarrely no one said a word. Huddled around him they just stared in awe and he was still as a statue. After a few moments they started to slowly pet him on his head like a dog and then he broke the stillness by blinking and they all giggled with excitement. I'm told it was all very surreal but it doesn't surprise me, I've seen him have that effect on people."

Bang wrote of seeing a letter by a girl from Rivers' days back in Connecticut voicing her disappointments over "injustices inflicted by Cuomo" that indicated his behavior toward women was longstanding and not just a recent "rock star thing."

"I don't think he strings [women] along or tells them lies to make them feel this way, in fact I don't think he even thinks about it, he's just him and this is what happens," Sheeny posted. "I mean girls he meets and hangs out with seem to lose all common sense and logic and it happens quickly, letters and e-mails stating love and deep emotion after knowing him a mere couple of weeks." It seemed peculiar that Rivers' assistant would make such observations of her famous boss and then publish them with his authorization for certain fans to see, but it was fascinating just the same.

While Cuomo continued writing into October, the future of titles like "Pull on the Trigger," "Frozen Tears," "Take Me Home," "History's Child," "Everybody Wants a Chance to Feel All Alone," and "The Ruler's Back" were cast into doubt when the group unexpectedly took a break from rehearsals and recording after months of work. Although Rick Rubin was still on board, the band had been working nearly nonstop for two and a half years and a break from the grind was hardly unreasonable. With the downtime, Pat Wilson and Weezer's drum tech Atom Willard got busy, working on a Special Goodness studio album, while Brian Bell reconvened efforts with the Space Twins.

Reports came in that Cuomo was lending vocals to the forthcoming Limp Bizkit album when he wasn't plugging away at AM Radio business. Rivers also showed an interest in what was going on in the Los Angeles underground scene, so he again made contact with Travis Keller at Buddyhead Records, and went out on a Friday night that October to check out the action. "He came to see The Icarus Line when we played at the Roxy and he was right in front."

Rivers apparently liked what he saw and he became relatively friendly with Keller. The Buddyhead founder says, "Next, Rivers came over to my house, and he got driven over by his personal assistant. He's in the backseat of this huge suv, and she pulls up and he makes her wait in the driveway for two hours. So, we hung out and I played him all these records by bands he hadn't heard. I gave him a bunch of records. And then he came over and we played him a video of The Icarus Line tearing shit up and he's like, [affecting a nerdy voice] 'These guys are crazy. I've never seen stuff like this.'"

While Cuomo was checking out the sounds of the Los Angeles underground, his group's estranged founding bassist was also exploring a new musical terrain. Matt Sharp was back on the road in fall 2002 with an ambient, acoustic approach to music that was miles away from the Weezer and Blur-inspired Rentals records in his past. At the time eyeing a March 2003 release for his first-ever solo album — comprised of the drastically different 2000 Leiper's Fork recordings — Matt was still without a label deal and considering his record company options.

Insisting at the time that he was indeed "booted out" of Weezer, Matt had yet to resolve his lawsuit with Cuomo and company and did little to expound his alleged "ejection." "The only thing I can tell you about the whole Weezer thing is that, when I was doing it, and when I made those records and went through what we went through together, my head and my heart and my soul were completely invested in the band," Matt said. "So for me to say anything about it now, I just don't want to soil any of those memories. We met so many beautiful people on the road and those records meant a hell of a lot to me making them. And the more I think about it, the more I really get to think about the not-so-good part of those times. If I speak about it, it's just going to soil those memories for people, including me. I just prefer to keep those memories and that time in a really pure place, because at the time it really was a beautiful thing for me.

"I mean, there have been some weird times. Times where I've run into Mikey [Welsh] and he'd almost be like, 'Help me.' And I'd say, 'Good luck, man. You're on your own,'" Sharp continued. "I actually like Mikey a lot. I think he's pretty great. God bless him. I always hear shit about him and I'm like, 'Oh man, I hope he makes it through.' I mean *Rolling Stone* fucking put Mikey in their magazine. I got that and I was like, 'Check that out. Heroin, there's an original one.'

"People have fed me some hysterical information," Sharp insisted. "Fucking ridiculous stuff. I can't elaborate, really, but there are people who — for some reason — want to tell me about what absurd things [Rivers] has been doing. But I'm usually not into hearing about it."

Speaking to the changes in his own sound, which were now a far cry from the spectacle that steered Rentals rockers like "Friends of P" and "Getting By," Sharp said, "I guess the biggest recognizable difference is sonic — there are no electric guitars or bass or drums or synthesizers," he said. "It's somewhere between the solo records of [Talk Talk's] Mark Hollis and [Mazzy Star's] Hope Sandoval. I'm always trying to make the kind of music I'd like to hear from other people.

"When you take three years to make a record, that's no fun, sometimes," Sharp laughed, revealing he was without a manager or a lawyer much of the time. "By the time I had made the entire thing, I had sort of severed all my ties to the music business. So coming out of it, I think I've burned nearly as many bridges as I could, and cut as many ties as I could. I mean, it's been years since I've been playing nonstop, and now, when I've finally got back on the road, I have to ask myself, 'What the hell have you been doing all this time?'"

His agenda after almost four years out of the limelight was to promote a low-profile, acoustic tour of the U.S. that he threw together to road test new material. "The one thing that has changed most in my life is that I don't want to stay off the road," he said from his Omaha hotel room. "From the beginning of the first Weezer record to the end of that run of juggling that and juggling the Rentals stuff, I was pretty much on the road for four years straight. And I didn't get burned out by it. Touring is a comfortable place for me to be. It's the only place where I find that I can get some decent sleep. It's something about being on the road and having a schedule and being in a routine."

Talking about the tour, Sharp said, "After being away for so long, I had no idea what to expect and I was a little bit terrified. With a week's notice I told my booking agent I want to go out on tour next week starting in San Diego. So she just started booking it, kind of playing catch-up along the way. I've never toured under my name before, and it's been so long since I've done it, and this acoustic approach is much different. But people have been patient. We weren't sure what kind of crowds I might draw, but from the peak of my time with Weezer until now, all sorts of people have gotten into my stuff. Thankfully it's not just people looking to relive 1994.

"I think the thing that I discovered the most while making this record is that my peers and people that I grew up with making music in the '90s were totally infuriated and angered by me making a record like this. That fucking knocked me out," Matt observed. "They kind of look at it as giving up on life a little bit, like I'm being put out to pasture. It's true, by recording it in rural Tennessee, that I made the record out in the pastures, but they kind of feel like this is kind of giving up on the whole thing. The fact that I'm not out there, 'We will rock you!' and all this kind of shit must mean that I'm not relevant. People got all puffed and red-faced like, 'What do you mean you're not gonna rock it?' So that really terrified me going out on the road, thinking that if the audience is like this, I'm going to get killed."

Playing in mostly filled, small venues, Matt said, "The response has been just been insane to me. And thankfully, nobody's shouting out for fucking 'ooo wee ooo' [alluding to "Buddy Holly"] or some shit, so it's nice. I have a better understanding of where I belong now and I don't see these songs being affiliated with Taco Bell and out-of-the-park home-run smash hits. There's nothing wrong with Taco Bell, but it's not a suitable place for this music."

Confessing to having been in a cave for several years, Sharp — who again called L.A. home and professed a liking to "getting drunk on cheap wine and putting on his kimono" — was looking to land a deal with an indie label.

"I wasn't sure after the whole Rentals experience and Weezer experience, which were both with those big corporate monsters, if that's where this music belonged," Matt admitted. In the spring of 2003, Sharp worked out a deal with Portland independent label In Music We Trust, and released an EP titled *Puckett versus the Country Boy*. The disc featured the tracks "Goodbye West Coast" "Some Come Running Through," "Visions of Anna," and "Hey, What You Gonna Do?"

Looking toward the future, Sharp said he didn't have any concrete plans outside of wanting to be more prolific. "All I know is I just plan to make records a hell of a lot more regularly with a steady stream of music, be it albums or EPs or whatever. In my head the Rentals are not a dead concept — there's no reason to shut the door — but as far as the majority of my time, it'll be spent on making records like the one I've just completed. Greg Brown and I have actually just gone through all the song ideas for the next record after this one. The record after my first one will be an easier experience for people to digest. It will be shorter and catchier."

A few months earlier, Sharp had settled his suit with former bandmates out of court, but no details — despite inquiries to his representatives — could be obtained. Continuing to tour throughout 2003, Matt still planned to release the full album of Leiper's Fork material in the fall and was featured in an hour-long retrospective on influential KCRW in late August.

Still tight with Ash's Tim Wheeler — who guest-starred on *Seven More Minutes* — six years after they first became friends on a Weezer tour, Sharp confessed, "Those guys got me plastered and threw me into a movie they're making. I play God, but it's done kind of as if God was a flamboyant, gay Australian wardrobe stylist. I may be a mess, but they showed me some of the scenes starring Chris [Martin] from Coldplay and he's friggin' hilarious."

Summing up his post-Weezer life, Sharp noted, "Years have passed like days. You blink and the years have disappeared. I've had a few years in the last six that have vanished for me. I'm sure I did something in those years, but all of a sudden I'm turning around and I'm like, 'Wait a minute.' You're hearing the year-end wrap-up shows on talk radio and you're wondering where the hell it all went."

In fall 2002, when *Rolling Stone* readers were polled for their Top 100 albums of all time, every Weezer LP was ranked. Just four months old, *Maladroit* was the group's lowest placer, pulling down a still respectable #91. Calling "Keep Fishin'" a "hard-rock valentine" and the disc's "essential track," one reader assessed it, writing in, "It is a complete mixture of rock and melody! Weezer never compromise their infectious harmonies and yet they continue to rock out harder than ever!"

Ranking both self-titled discs at #21 because there was no way of distinguishing them on readers' ballots, the mag counted "My Name Is Jonas" and "Hash Pipe" as the albums' essentials, with a fan praising the "generational anthems, sparkling musicianship, wild emotional swings, and instrumental build-ups that would make Brian Wilson jealous."

And finally, *Pinkerton* — Weezer's worst seller — placed the highest, positioned at #16. The magazine dubbed "The Good Life" the disc's critical number, calling it the "template for dozens of emo bands." Accompanying the ranking was an amusing quote from Rivers on how he was inspired to write the emotional record. "I saw *Madame Butterfly*, and I've never cried so hard in my life. My face was caked with snot and tears and my chest was heaving." One reader's ballot simply said, "It's the most honest album I've ever heard."

By November 2002, the cult of Weezer had carried over into an online survey by Harvard student Jeff Rosenfeld, who wanted to analyze what kind of carbons and other particles Weezer fans are made of for his social-studies thesis. After all, it was hard to find a group of fans more loyal than Weezer fans. When filled out, the anonymous online survey entered participants to win either a $50 or $30 cash prize or autographed Weezer merchandise. The survey included questions like "How did you discover the band?" "How often do you visit their official Web site?" and "What are your top three tunes?"

The Harvard senior wanted to know why Weezer's popularity with teenagers soared during 1997–2000, when the band was on hiatus. Twenty thousand fans responded, and his research showed that the Internet's increased popularity directly correlated with the unification of Weezer fans. According to Rosenfeld, 25% of the people buying *Pinkerton* in 2002 did so mainly as the result of an online recommendation; the figure was less than 2% in 1996, the year the album came out.

According to Rosenfeld, that meant that Internet chatter wasn't just talk anymore — it was money. He also observed that illegal MP3 downloading hurt sales of Weezer's 2001 comeback disc more than it did *Maladroit*. And while most would surmise the downloading epidemic would hurt sales, the Harvard senior said, "fans feel like they owe them. That vaccinates the band."

Speaking of Harvard, in January 2003, Cuomo's genuine University ID — complete with his signature on the back — went up on the popular eBay

Internet auction site. Starting at a minimum bid of one thousand U.S. dollars, the piece of identification was available to be purchased outright for three thousand clams. So, how did the seller get hold of the rare collectible? He evidently found Cuomo's wallet at a Weezer show and when it was returned, Rivers offered him the ID as a reward.

Cuomo also rewarded his devout fan base in late 2002 by posting MP3s of Weezer's full set from the Reading Festival for download. And he was featured on a VH1 *All Access* episode that was dubbed "Rock's Most Eligible Bachelors," appearing alongside the likes of Trent Reznor, No Doubt's Tony Kanal, P. Diddy, Usher, Mark McGrath, Jay Z, and Jack White of The White Stripes, among others.

In the meantime, Pat had finally wrapped up work on The Special Goodness' North American debut. Featuring himself on guitar and vocals with ex–Rocket from the Crypt and future Offspring member Atom Willard on drums, the disc was slated for a March 2003 release on N.O.S., the pair's own Van Nuys–based independent label.

Recorded at Sage and Sound in what Pat calls a "relaxed style," with Chad Bamford producing, *Land, Air, Sea* was realized using the same approach that Weezer had perfected in the past year. "We've all figured out that it's the best way," Wilson explained, corresponding in December 2002 with this writer by e-mail. "We used to say, 'We have 'X' amount of days in a studio so let's work fifteen hours a day.' Now we just track if it's good.

"We're trying for as little hype as possible," Wilson wrote of his and Willard's self-released disc. "Lots of modern records have that full-on maximum sound and it's unlistenable after the first listen. We have a very musical sound that wears well over time — very smooth and full."

As 2002 wound down, Rivers, Pat, Brian, and Scott might have been on a break from Weezer, but it didn't keep *Maladroit* from cropping up on a number of year-end 'best of' lists. *Spin*, for instance, ranked the record the sixth best of 2002, writing, "At war with the demons in his head, Rivers Cuomo seems determined to transform his once-cuddly band into metal maniacs. But look behind the beard: if Weezer = metal now, then the touching, hook-packed *Maladroit* is their *Master of Puppets*. Cuomo may be desperate to rock, but nobody's better at rocking desperately."

And the *Orlando Sentinel* wrote, "If only for writing songs at a pace of one a week and relentlessly guarding the autonomy of his band against corporate interference, Rivers Cuomo deserves his reputation as this era's reigning rock hero. *Maladroit* is a reminder that he also happens to make brilliant music, a joyous combination of fuzzed-out guitars and irrepressibly hooky melodies."

With love like that from the national and regional music press on the heels of such a busy year, the four-man music machine known as Weezer had finally found internal peace and relative happiness with one another. Although the sessions for album five had begun with such passion in the spring and summer of 2002 only to come to a sharp halt, the disc's false start had had a positive, unifying effect on the band.

Bell — who had been putting together the long-awaited Space Twins album — and Wilson would utilize their free time in the first half of 2003 to focus on individual creative pursuits while Shriner became acclimated to his newfound wealth. As Rivers' post-1998 songwriting tally passed the 400 mark — meaning he was averaging one hundred songs each calendar year since January of 1999 — word had it that he was again looking inward. With the encouragement of Rubin, arguably the most important producer in popular music, Cuomo was back to writing lyrics from a personal place and putting quality over quantity with his songwriting.

In early January 2003, Karl Koch informed fans about Weezer's first trip into space. Promoting Space Shuttle Mission STS-107, which was scheduled to begin a sixteen-day trip into orbit, the band's webmaster explained how the pilot for the journey was United States Navy Commander William McCool, a proud fan of the band. So much so that McCool planned to include a copy of *The Blue Album* among the small amount of personal items that he was permitted to take with him on the Columbia flight, and vowed to take a photograph of the album floating in space.

Willie, a native of Lubbock, Texas, even visited the band with his three children during a stop on the Enlightenment Tour, presenting an auto-graphed picture to the group that read: "To Weezer with gratitude, thank you for your awesome music! Keep reaching for the stars." Willie McCool even invited the members of Weezer to the shuttle's January 16 launch, but unfortunately they could not attend the ceremony in Florida.

In tandem with the Columbia Space Shuttle announcement, Koch noti-fied Weezer fans that the extensive DVD he had been hard at work on over the months since the Enlightenment Tour wrapped, was being delayed largely because of issues surrounding legal clearance. And when he wasn't working on Weezer material, Rivers was out in the L.A. clubs that month showing support for 2002 tour openers (and Geffen roster-mates) Rooney, even working the DJ booth in between sets at an AM Radio club date.

With packaging for The Special Goodness' CD *Land, Air, Sea* coming together, Patrick was thrilled to learn that a song from the yet-to-be-released disc, "Life Goes By," graced the Los Angeles airwaves. Featured as KROQ DJ Jed the Fish's "Catch of the Day" on Friday, January 31 — one day shy of Wilson's thirty-fourth birthday — it was a first for TSG. But cel-ebrating didn't last long, as the Weezer camp heard about the peril of those aboard the Space Shuttle Columbia that Saturday.

When the Columbia broke up over Texas on its return to earth on the morning of February 1, 2003, all seven astronauts on board were tragically killed. "The Weezer community feels the particular loss of Commander

Willie McCool," the band said in a statement. "Willie was a huge music and Weezer fan, and brought his trusty *Blue Album* on the flight not only to listen to, but in hopes of getting a neat picture to contribute to *Weezer.com* upon his return . . . [We] feel so badly for his kids, who were so obviously proud of their dad and stoked on the rock . . . [We] extend [our] deepest condolences to all the families of the crew of STS-107, and trust that those seven brave souls are now at peace."

Matt Sharp, who attended Yorktown High in Arlington, Virginia — the same high school as Mission Specialist David Brown, one of the other six astronauts on board — was equally affected by the loss. "In the face of a tragedy of this magnitude to realize that someone with so much courage took any interest at all in something that once meant so much to me, is a truly humbling experience," Sharp wrote by e-mail to this writer after the disaster.

"Since recording the first Weezer album I've met so many beautiful people through making music," Matt continued. "I'm sad to say that I've lost more than a few of them along the way. It is never easy. In those times I've tried to reflect on all the positive things they have brought to our lives, realize how lucky we've been to have had any time with them at all and that every day is a gift. My thoughts are with the families of these brave men and women."

"There's nothing better than listening to a good album," McCool told *National Public Radio* from space on January 29, "and looking out the windows and watching the world go by."

The day after the Columbia tragedy, Rivers Cuomo was in the news, plugging AM Radio to Steve Hochman of the *Los Angeles Times*. He admitted that he'd "ripped off many a catchy tune" from the group's frontman Kevin Ridel during their seventeen-year friendship. Paying back a favor, Rivers spoke of managing the band and guiding them to a deal with Elektra Records.

As AM Radio readied to hit the road with Ben Kweller in late February, Rivers spoke of his commitment to managing Ridel's band, saying, "I had been fulfilling most of those managerial duties for a while and just kind of made it official." Still, outside of Weezer or AM Radio, Cuomo revealed no interest in adding further clients. "I don't have any interest in working with anybody else. Just them," he said.

Why, you might wonder? Well, Cuomo called his relatively unknown buddy Ridel a major influence in the direction of his music over the years, and admitted it was Kevin who directed Rivers toward the art of writing pop songs with melody and lyrical meaning. Rivers gradually moved away from noodling on his Charvel and established his own songwriting approach with Kevin's encouragement.

And Ridel was appreciative of Cuomo's support. "We used to just trade demos back and forth between the time Avant Garde broke up and Weezer took off," said Kevin, who had moved back to Connecticut at the time. "Rivers called me up and told me that he got a deal with Geffen. He said that the indie rock scene was really good in L.A. He got me back out, and he helped me. He drummed in my band, Lunchbox, and got me a few shows around town. He's always been that one guy who has always looked out for me . . . He just enables me with the financial support and the connections."

Speaking to MTV to hype AM Radio's Elektra debut, *Radioactive* — which was on that label's release schedule for July and drawing early comparisons to Britpop bands like Blur and influential U.S. groups like Redd Kross, Cheap Trick, and the Knack — Ridel told a recent tale of how he and Rivers got together with some other friends to play Risk. Taking the game a little too far, Ridel stopped and picked up an outfit at a costume shop consisting of a dictator's hat, a monocle, and an oversized cigar. "Rivers tried to dress up as some sort of French dictator," Ridel revealed. "But the hat was kind of nondescript, so he looked more like Fidel Castro."

Ridel also commented on the history of Cuomo's multi-platinum band. "I remember when he was first talking about Weezer," Kevin remembered. "I was giving him shit. I was like, 'Dude, that's the worst band name ever.'" But in the years since, AM Radio's frontman had learned better than to doubt his pal.

As Weezer's eleventh anniversary rolled around, Cuomo also took the opportunity to explain the group's sudden, post–Enlightenment Tour disappearance, saying that the group — at producer Rick Rubin's suggestion — decided to let the new material settle rather than rush into recording. "I feel a thousand times more patient and calm now, and I feel it's a direct result of having Rick on my team," Rivers said. "So I'm sitting on those songs and stepping away from the writing process and taking my time.

"I guess I should just reassure people that Weezer are still hanging out and making music together," Cuomo continued, insisting the group was still going strong and planning to record cover versions and previously released Weezer tracks in an entirely new manner.

"We might do them acoustically or with an orchestra," he predicted. "I'm thinking about something like 'Slave' or 'December' from *Maladroit* and maybe some old songs. I see us doing heavy versions of emotional songs." And although Rivers was lending his musical skills to records by hard rockers such as Limp Bizkit and Cold, his potential cover choices were downright peculiar. Cuomo had been considering emotional ballads like "The End of the World," by underground '60s pop-country songwriter Skeeter Davis, and Nilsson's '70s pop classic, "Without You."

Despite the focus on emotional, soft rock, Rivers kept his metal chops in order by co-penning Cold's 2003 rock radio hit "Stupid Girl" with the group's singer, Scooter Ward. Touting the track as a natural fusion of Cold and Weezer, Cuomo had planned to sing the first verse of the track, but decided against it after hearing Ward's vocal part, insisting Ward's voice was far better than his own.

"When we wrote that, it was kind of funny; we all went, 'Dude, that sounds like a Weezer song,'" Cold guitarist Kelley Hayes said. "We were hanging out with Rivers one night and said, 'Dude, you've got to come and do something on this song. It's perfect for you.' He ended up coming out and singing the verses, Scooter did the choruses, and they finished it together. It's awesome."

And the collaborations kept coming when R.C. wrote lyrics and sang on a track called "I Suck" for *Here Comes the Fuzz*, the 2003 debut record by Elektra recording artist Mark Ronson. "I wasn't familiar with him," said Cuomo, who appeared alongside hip-hop guests like Sean Paul, Nate Dogg, Q-Tip, Tweet, and Mos Def. "They just asked me, and the label sent me the track. I listened to it and immediately the tune popped into my head. It's about a girl at a club who didn't want anything to do with me."

As Bell was finishing the Space Twins' debut CD and heading off to the South By Southwest Music Conference to promote his band, Cuomo — perhaps for the first time in history — spoke enthusiastically of his mates' side projects. "I guess I should just reassure people that Weezer are still hanging out and making music together," Rivers said. "People want to do things different all the time, which freaks some people out, but we're all pretty chill."

February also found Weezer lending a previously unreleased, live version of "Why Bother" to a double 7" single designed to benefit one-time That Dog violinist Petra Haden after her accident. Appropriately dubbed, *A Benefit for Petra Haden*, the project — slated for a summer 2003 release — also featured tracks from the likes of Ben Kweller, Phantom Planet, and at Rivers' offering, a tune by AM Radio. The proceeds helped pay her steadily mounting medical bills.

Shortly after its March 4 release, The Special Goodness scored praise for *Land, Air, Sea* as the *Orlando Sentinel* wrote, "Wilson handles all the guitars and vocals, showing that Dave Grohl isn't the only rock drummer capable of fronting a band."

Still, *Pitchforkmedia* trashed the disc, with reviewer Rob Mitchum writing, "Wow, I've heard some third-rate Weezer knockoffs in my day, but this Special Goodness band takes the angel food. Seriously, I'd recommend Cuomo Inc. have General Geffen find them a good lawyer immediately, I think there's grounds for a lawsuit here. This shit makes Nerf Herder and Harvey Danger — monsters of the late-nineties alterna-dial — seem like veritable founts of originality and pep."

The band fared better in a *CMJ New Music Monthly* review that read, "Chock full of chunky riffs, arresting hooks and the straight-shooting beats of former Rocket from the Crypt drummer Atom Willard, *Land, Air, Sea* is a pleasant surprise with no hype and plenty of heart."

Meanwhile, online 'zine *Ink 19* joined *Pitchforkmedia* in the TSG mauling, writing, "Must . . . turn . . . this . . . off . . . now . . . before I lose any more respect for *Pinkerton* and *The Blue Album*. Please, Pat, we know you're capable of so much better than this." But despite the mixed reviews, the fans seemed to like it when the group opened for the Foo Fighters. And on dates with the Foos and the Transplants — the Epitaph Records–inked off-shoot band of Rancid's Tim Armstrong and Blink-182's Travis Barker — the sounds of *Land, Air, Sea* were alluring enough to the Epitaph staff to get picked up by the company for a January 2004 release date.

Prior to making this announcement official, TSG frontman Wilson continued promoting his side band. Many fans unfamiliar with the group until now were surprised to learn he could sing and wondered why he never sang in Weezer. Although Pat admitted that if it were up to him Weezer would be more like the Beastie Boys, "where people were picking up instruments and putting them down and changing shit up, having freakouts and having a good time," he was nonetheless accepting of the fact that in Cuomo's group, that would probably never happen.

Still, Patrick conceded that Cuomo was a lot more approving of the side projects lately than he had been in the past. When Rivers' behavior in the 2001 *CMJ* piece is cited — where he interrupted Brian mid-sentence — Wilson quickly points out that it was it was merely an isolated incident.

"I just think it's a maturing process, really, for everybody involved," acknowledged Wilson. "We were like twenty-three years old when we got popular, and we have been through a lot of crazy shit since then. We've all just kind of grown up. So I would say that if you have preconceptions about members of Weezer, maybe it's wise to think, *People grow*."

Perhaps Rivers *was* maturing, as he took the time to reflect on his thirty-two-plus years when he posted an online archive consisting of the significant events in his life. The day-by-day timeline was briefly available on the Internet for Weezer scholars at www.riverscuomo.com. The URL for Cuomo's personal Web page went above ground when it was featured in *Spin*. According to Mike Zaic, who runs the fan site *Mike's World of Weezer* and mirrored Cuomo's archives when he closed them to the public, the original site was reportedly created with the help of a computer savvy loyalist. Zaic told the magazine in May 2003 that the rocker apparently "brought [the fan] a big box of stuff — even report cards."

Chronicling the routines of life like haircuts, dentist appointments, band rehearsals, and lawyer meetings, as well as milestones like his high school graduation (complete with his full four-year transcript) and first Weezer gigs, the exhaustive spreadsheet lists every song Cuomo ever wrote between September of 1984 and October of 2002 in chronological order. Listing over 700 songs, among the hundreds of titles Rivers claimed to have written were "There's a Bomb in the Air," "Down Down Diggity," and "I Can't Stop, I'm 0 for the Day."

By May, news broke of Weezer's participation in *Gimme Skelter*, a compilation album put together by Buddyhead's Travis Keller and Aaron North that also featured unreleased material by the likes of Iggy Pop, Sonic Youth, Mudhoney, and the Yeah Yeah Yeahs. Keller wryly described the Nettwerk Records–distributed project as "a benefit compilation — benefiting the state of music," consisting of all new material, "with the exception of the Weezer rarity." Travis described the song as "a B-side recorded around the time of *Pinkerton* that's never been put out."

According to Keller, Cuomo "brought a CD over, and he's like, 'Alright. Pick out what you want.' At first we had picked 'Superfriend' but after a while I went with 'You Won't Get with Me Tonight.'

"Anyway, Rivers was kind of funny, because he's like, 'Jordan's gonna hate me for being on your comp,'" Keller said, referring to the altercation between Keller and Geffen boss Jordan Schur, "but that's what makes him pretty cool. He certainly doesn't have to do any of that shit anymore."

In the liner notes, Keller wrote about his interactions with the likes of Schur. "Have you forgotten about THE ART? Most of you who control this 'musical industry' should be selling stocks not music. What you really love is money and how filthy it makes you feel. Suck on this, swine."

Speaking to Weezer's submission, "You Won't Get with Me Tonight," Keller added, "Why is Weezer on here you ask? Cuz Rivers paid me off with a 4-track recorder and a real nice pair of shoes, that's why. Just joking. But not really. This song is slamming. It's a B-side from the *Pinkerton* sessions, which happens to be my favorite Weezer album to date. Try to not sing along, I double dog dare you.

"Another funny thing," Keller said of his Weezer interactions, "was that we ran into Brian Bell when we were mastering the compilation, and we're like, 'Hey, Brian, you're on our comp.' He didn't even seem to care that Weezer was on it. I guess he was all caught up in his other group. He's like, 'What band?' I said, 'You know that band you're in — Weezer?' He's like, 'Oh, yeah. Whatever.' I get the feeling he doesn't know shit about what's going on with them. He probably doesn't really give a fuck at this point, he's rich."

Part of Brian's confusion was due to the fact he was focusing on getting the Space Twins record out after a six-year wait. The band had been conceived ten years earlier and managed to release a few singles here and there, but Bell had to get approval from Rivers to release an album. And with no competing Weezer records in the summer of 2003, Cuomo gave Bell permission to release his Space Twins LP.

Explaining how the Space Twins — featuring Bell out in front on vocals and guitar along with old high-school friends Tim (on bass) and Glenn Maloof (on guitar), plus drummer Mike Elliott — finally managed to drop the debut CD *The End of Imagining*, Bell contends the band took the necessary time to craft a solid album.

"It's something that hasn't been rushed," he said. "And it took as much time thinking about the sequence as anything. I wanted the album to be able to be put on and listened to from beginning to end in a flowing manner and somehow gather some sort of ending synopsis or summary of 'Wow. That just took me for a complete ride.'"

Six years after he started, Brian spoke about the completion of the Space Twins album as being due to maturity, not only in his own music, but in Cuomo's willingness to realize that solo projects outside of his band aren't a threat to the future of Weezer. "It's only good and it really is just expression and art. It's not a competition," said Bell. Explaining that Matt Sharp's departure reduced Weezer's morale and fostered a bit of innerband paranoia, causing Cuomo to view subsequent side ventures as threats, Bell counted immature communication skills and the "underlying jealousy and backstabbing" that once plagued the band as some of the reasons for the delay in getting his own album out.

"We've actually been working on the album for about three years or so," Brian elaborated by phone in July 2003. "Years go by so fast now. The problem with living in L.A. is that the seasons never change, so three years have gone by and it feels like one. But sometime after *Pinkerton*, I think, the Maloofs moved back to L.A. Actually, I don't remember it exactly — Weezer has had so many of those lulls. I had been keeping in touch with Tim and Glenn the whole time after I left home when I was eighteen, and I would go back and see them at Christmas. Tim moved out first, and then we convinced Glenn to come out. Then, Mike Elliott — a guy who I had known when we worked together in a record store before I joined Weezer — came on board. What an interesting guy. When I was thinking of people for the Space Twins, I kind of wanted people who were sort of space cadets in the first place. I, too, consider myself to be one. And Mike is definitely a unique person that way. We were always jamming on and off and when we played things flowed easily."

Fast-forwarding to *The End of Imagining*, Bell says, "Anyone expecting it to sound like Weezer will probably be surprised. 'Rust Colored Sun,' for instance, is so unlike Weezer. We don't want my Weezer affiliation to have any bearing on whether someone likes us or not. We'll probably have to always deal with that to some extent but it's an entirely different thing. The Space Twins have our own chemistry."

As for "Yellow Camaro," the song Bell demoed with Weezer and played live in 2002 but then repossessed for his own band, Brian said, "It was a last-minute decision. And I don't even know if it was the right decision, but we needed an upbeat song for live shows. It was very close to being on *Maladroit*, or maybe it was the stuff we did last year. There have been so many false starts on Weezer recordings that I can't remember. Actually, it was after *Maladroit* when we were about to do another record, but didn't. Everyone seemed excited about it and I thought, well, I'm going to save it for the Weezer record. And then when there didn't end up being a fifth Weezer album right away, I took it back. I needed a song like that. I actually wrote it for Weezer, thinking that Weezer would do it justice, but when the guys in the Space Twins took it over, it became more syncopated and less straightforward. But in all fairness, both bands helped shape the song.

"We recorded the song 'Rings of Saturn' seven times," said Brian, who hoped to compete with Weezer in terms of quality. "It was the last song we recorded. When we finally got to the final version, we wound up simplifying it so much. The last lyric written for the bridge was 'it's the end of imagining.' And I was like, that's it. It's done. It's the end of imagining what this fucking record is going to sound like."

Featuring collaborations with former Jellyfish member Jason Falkner ("we caught Jason at a time in his life a few years ago where he had three days free") and the aforementioned Shmedley, Brian said he took the opportunity to utilize Shmed when it became apparent his services wouldn't be needed in future Weezer collaborations. "I met him through Weezer and we got along really well," Brian acknowledged. "That whole thing with Weezer trying out keyboard players was just an experiment. He was a great keyboard player, and I was like, 'Fuck, if Weezer's not going to use him, I'll use him someday.'"

When Interscope Records passed on its option rights altogether, Bell decided to release the disc on his own label, Raga Drop, named for a line in The Clash song, "Rock the Casbah." "When I was trying to think of a name for my label, it was right when Joe Strummer passed away," Brian remembered. "I was a huge Clash fan, so it was in homage to him. I never actually met Joe, but I met Mick Jones at the first Weezer show in London. I was so star-struck I could barely talk. I was kind of embarrassed. He came up to me and said, [fakes British accent] 'I really enjoyed your show.' I was stuttering, I was so in awe.' As far as Joe, he was relevant right to the end. I love that *Global a Go-Go* record."

Turning to future recording projects with the Space Twins, Bell said, "I already have a lot of songs, but I'm letting Weezer have first shot at them. I know I'll be lucky if Rivers picks one of them. But the way things are going it's looking like people are liking them.

"We have so many songs to choose from," Bell revealed of Weezer's long-plotted fifth album. "It shouldn't be too much longer before we actually start making it. But you never know, things could go in a completely different direction, but I think I have a lot of good songs for our next record.

"We're still in pre-production," Brian said at the time. "We're not in a recording studio yet but we should be soon. Rick Rubin is producing. But it's hard to say how it will sound. Right now we're just playing acoustically. I doubt it will be an acoustic album, but there might be more textures to this record.

"It should be all new stuff," Bell continued, indicating that most of the 2002 Weezer demos were out the window. "We are open to suggestions on the old songs, especially if Rick Rubin says, I want you to have a second look at this song you did last year. Nothing's out of bounds at this point."

As for the controlling, egocentric Cuomo, Bell defended his bandmate's sometimes unorthodox behavior during *The End of Imagining* junket. "I think I understand Rivers as well as anyone, and I think he's misrepresented a lot," said Brian. "I think it's unfortunate for him that people think that he's so difficult. He's a unique person. I like to use the word 'unique' over 'difficult.' I feel he is a close friend and also a colleague."

While Weezer readied to hit the recording studio in late 2003, fans of the group had already begun to celebrate the future of their beloved band, when the quartet lent a cover version of Green Day's "Worry Rock" to the Skunk Ape Records Green Day tribute album, *A Different Shade of Green*. Released on July 22, the disc housed Weezer's lush, shimmering acoustic version of the *Nimrod* number — complete with violin and cello accompaniment by Petra Haden and her sister Tanya.

If Rivers' heartfelt vocals on the Rod Cervera–produced track, cut in February 2003, filled in a lot of the blanks surrounding the promise and the future of the group, the song's presence was coupled with pictures on *Weezer.com* of Rivers, Pat, Brian, and Scott gathered around in a circle on office couches with smiles and acoustic guitars.

Meanwhile, plans for an expanded, special edition reissue of Weezer's self-titled Geffen debut, designed to commemorate the tenth anniversary of the landmark disc in 2004, were underway. With Koch's extensive work on a three-hour long DVD — tentatively titled *Video Capture Device* — nearly wrapped, the group's cultural impact was again ready to be tested.

Brian Bell's word that Weezer were finally reconvening in the studio after months of on-again, off-again pre-production were met with observations by Rick Rubin, who suggested that the upcoming disc might include some of the most introspective and revelatory songs Rivers had written to date. Rubin claimed that potential songs for the record found Cuomo "really getting to a very personal place with writing and it's, I think, deeper than he's ever gone.

"Lyrically, I would say that since *Pinkerton*, he's never really gone in that [darker] direction," Rubin concluded on the eve of formal recording. "And I know that from the beginning of this project, he was open to all those places that he hasn't gone since. And that was something he brought up."

Again, it looked as if Cuomo was willing to pull from within, even at the risk of embarrassment he faced in the wake of Weezer's long-dismissed and then finally understood second album. The dumbed-down lyrics, rock poses, and glossy radio mixes were a result of Weezer's comeback, not the cause of it. The "good vibes" Koch reported the band had been enjoying coupled with Cuomo's courage to try to tread personal waters again for his lyrics could only come from the growth and maturity that Wilson and Bell mentioned.

While the jury was still out on whether Rivers — after all the in-fighting, power struggles, membership firings and resignations, lawsuits, settlements, non-disclosure agreements, and eccentric behavior — was really ready to shed his beard and wool cap for good, his fans waited for him to stand up and take his place as the songwriter of his generation they all knew he could be.

Weezer's history alone — not to mention its back catalog — makes the foursome arguably the most distinctive, dysfunctional, tenacious, and perseverant group in the annals of popular music. And judging by the testimonials of those close to him, by the fall of 2003 it looked as if Rivers had finally reached the conclusion that there was more to life than lounging poolside with questionable confidants like Fred Durst.

That autumn, Rivers was clearly on to yet another phase in his life. For instance, he had reportedly done away with his e-mail and cell phone. In a surprise phone call to Buddyhead's Keller, Cuomo spoke of needing to "get away."

"He's been going to some place for weeks at a time to sit in a room with 150 people and meditate," Keller explained that September. "He said he's been playing all the new stuff with his band acoustically and then meeting up with Rick Rubin so he can tell him which songs suck or whatever." In support of Keller's report, a picture of a white CD cover with black letters reading "Weezer, Office Demos, 9-7-03" was posted on *Weezer.com* around this time. The twelve song titles had been blurred out.

Late that September, Cuomo even went so far as to try and bury the hatchet with Matt Sharp when he joined Brian for Sharp's show at El Sid on Sunset Boulevard in Silverlake. "That night was the first time I had seen Rivers in a very long time and we hadn't spoken in years," Sharp said soon after the reunion. "And . . . to say the least, it put a whole other layer of emotion into that evening. I knew he was there before we performed because someone brought him out to the Winnebago while we were rehearsing. And that is such a complex thing emotionally for me because there is . . . a lot of turbulent water under that bridge.

"I felt that it was a very bold thing for him to do and something that took a lot of humility for him and I know that his intentions are pure," Matt added. "But it's such an incredibly complex thing emotionally for me and that maybe it's the first step in a long line of many steps for us to really have a relationship of some sort again. It definitely made for an interesting photograph. Not only was he there, which made me self-conscious, but he was also carrying a copy of [my] EP, wearing [my] T-shirt, and had a poster in the other hand. He helped carry out the guitars for us and had very kind words about what went on that evening. But it definitely made me as self-conscious as any human being probably could ever be during the first few songs of the night, knowing that that was happening. And I think that in a strange way, it really helped that evening become a better night, a more emotionally complex thing, and brought a whole new sense of depth and a weight to the evening.

"And as far as Brian goes, we had talked about six months ago. He had been the first person to break the ice and really put himself on the line to mend some of those roads. And with all those guys, we've been through so much and I think there is some sense of family, and also a sense that something was broken and a lot of trust lost. Because what came out in that whole legal mess was the absolute last resort for me, it was the last thing I wanted to put out there, especially in public, but I was forced into that situation. It was something I had worked very hard at making sure it didn't happen but I was just left no choice. Thank God it's over and life moves on and as far as the future goes, it's a long road I think."

But five months later, on February 12, 2004, during a Sharp solo gig in the Titan Student Union at Cal State Fullerton, Cuomo's public estrangement from his former Weezer bassist officially ended. The pair shared the stage for the first time since 1997 as attendees of the gig looked on in amazement. Just two days shy of Weezer's twelfth anniversary, Rivers joined Matt for "Mrs. Young," one of their earliest joint efforts; "Time Song," a new songwriting collaboration; plus stripped-down versions of "Say It Ain't So" and "Undone."

"Rivers and I have been through more wars together standing side by side than we've fought against each other," wrote Sharp in an e-mail interview with this author a week after the event. "I guess there have been some turbulent waters under that bridge and I suppose we both have a few scars to show for it, but it's nothing the sun can't heal.

"Shows like the Fullerton show are emotionally beyond the reality of their situation," Matt continued in an interview to promote the long-awaited release of his self-titled solo album, which was finally set to drop on April 6. "It seems like the weight of everything descends upon you all at once, the loss of time, where you've been, where you've landed, heavy sadness, intense gratitude, waves of nostalgia, waves of joy, a flood of everything you can't control and then, overall, an enormous embarrassment for feeling all this over what should be such a simple thing. You tell yourself, it's just a solo show or it's just an old friend you'd lost coming back to join you to sing a few songs, but no matter what you tell yourself, it's all hopeless, so you just close your eyes and try to hold it together.

"After some procrastination on my part, we got together to talk," Sharp admitted. "It didn't take long for us to realize that there still is something there, something very powerful between us, although it's rather elusive and intangible, there is still something there that elevates us both artistically. I can only speak for myself, but since Rivers and I split off into our separate directions, I've spent a lot of time searching for a way to fill a void that was left after losing a great friend."

As for "Time Song," Sharp said it was the product of their rekindled friendship. "We've been writing every Saturday afternoon for the past couple of months now and have decided not to put a label on anything as of yet," he explained. "At this point, we're both being open to all possibilities creatively and just enjoying the process. Who knows what will come of it? But I'm not counting anything out. The only thing that is important now is that Rivers and I are doing what we should be doing, making music together. As Johnny Cash once said, 'New services to render and old scars to heal.

Life and love go on.' Ain't that the truth."

Just the same, all signs were suggesting that things had come full circle in Rivers' life. Returning to the practice of meditation — possibly at the suggestion of Rubin — Cuomo had again embraced a practice he left behind when he departed the Yogaville ashram. Was he looking to tap into deep-seated and long suppressed emotions of his youth? Was he indeed seeking internal and external solace? Was Rivers prepping Weezer to deliver the masterpiece that fans all believed the group could create?

Judging by the band's erratic past, only one thing is certain. Anything can happen in the weird world of Rivers Cuomo.

Rivers

EZBoard.com, The Cuomo Board, "Rivers Cuomo — His Middle Name,"
     Posting as "Ace"
All Music Guide
www.riverscuomo.com
Jac Zinder, "Rock Candy," *Spin*, January 1995
David Daley, "Happy Days Cancelled," *Alternative Press*, January 1997
Kate Sullivan, "Weezer's Big Makeover," *Blender*, June/July 2001
Kate Sullivan,
     www.katesullivan.blogspot.com/2002_5_12_katesullivan_archive.html
Chris Mundy, "Weezer's Cracked Genius," *Rolling Stone*, September 13, 2001
"Weezer for the Masses," *Pulse*, May 2002
Elliot Wilder, "Weezer — The Voice of a Maladroit Generation," *Amplifier*,
     July/August 2002
Justin Fisher; phone interview with author, August 21, 2002
Rick Ross; e-mail interview with author, July 2, 2003

Fury

www.riverscuomo.com
Jac Zinder, "Rock Candy," *Spin*, January 1995
Tom Beaujour, "Man of Steel," *Guitar World*, March 1995
David Daley, "Happy Days Cancelled," *Alternative Press*, January 1997
"Break, Rattle & Roll," *Vox*, September 1995
Marc Lewman, "Ol' Nerdy Bastard," *Rip*, 1997
"Cutting Classes," *Spin*, May 2001
Harry Thomas, "Not So Serious," *Rolling Stone*, June 7, 2001
"We Just Want to Be Middle of the Road and Conventional," *New Musical
     Express*, July 1, 2001
Kate Sullivan, "Weezer's Big Makeover," *Blender*, June/July 2001
Chris Mundy, "Weezer's Cracked Genius," *Rolling Stone*, September 13, 2001
BBC Radio's *Session Obsession*, September 20, 2001
Richard Cromelin, "It's Them Again, Weezer Is Poised for a Comeback," *The
     Bergen Record*, September 28, 2001
Matt Blackett, "Alt-Shred, Weezer's Rivers Cuomo Saves the Guitar Solo,"
     Guitar Player, July 2002
Justin Fisher; phone interview with author, August 21, 2002

Avant Garde

www.riverscuomo.com

Weezer.com

Tom Beaujour, "Man of Steel," *Guitar World*, March 1995

Vikki Toback, "Nerd Chic?" *The Detroit News*, August 10, 1995

Roger Catlin, "Weezer's Worry," *The Hartford Courant*, December 4, 1996

Michael Goldberg and Claire Kleinedler, "Weezer Revealed: The Rivers Cuomo Interview," *Addicted To Noise*, December 1996

David Daley, "Happy Days Cancelled," *Alternative Press*, January 1997

"Geek God of Love," *Livewire*, February/March 1997

Heckler magazine interview circa spring 1997 (transcribed to fan site www.geocities.com/SunsetStrip/Towers/6651)

Joe Matt and Rivers Cuomo, "Joe Matt, creator of Peepshow, and Rivers Cuomo of Weezer, Reveal Their Biggest Influence," *Cake*, July 1, 1997

"Odd Man Out," *Kerrang!*, May 2001

"We Just Want to Be Middle of The Road and Conventional," *New Musical Express*, July 1, 2001

Jenny Eliscu, "Rivers Cuomo's Encyclopedia of Pop," *Rolling Stone*, May 29, 2002

Michael Stanton; e-mail interviews with author, September 15, 2002; September 23, 2002

Justin Fisher; phone interview with author, August 21, 2002

Hollywood

www.riverscuomo.com

Weezer.com

Kris Stanton; e-mail interview with author, February 3, 2003

Michael Stanton; e-mail interviews with author, September 15, 2002; September 23, 2002

Justin Fisher; phone interview with author, August 21, 2002

Only in Dreams

www.riverscuomo.com

Weezer.com

www.mattsharp.net

www.specialgoodness.com

Mike's World of Weezer fan site (www-ec.njit.edu/~mxz0261)

Karl Koch Is God fan site

DGC Records Artist Biography, May 1994

Alan Sculley, "Weezer: L.A. Alternative Group Is In from the Dark," *St. Louis Post-Dispatch*, July 31, 1994

Roger Catlin, "Rivers Cuomo Returns Home with Weezer," *The Hartford Courant*, October 6, 1994

Angela Lewis, Pat Wilson phone interview, *The London Independent*, February 24, 1995

Tom Beaujour, "Man of Steel," *Guitar World*, March 1995

Mim Udovitch, "Revenge of the Nerds," *Rolling Stone*, March 25, 1995

Pat Riley, "Pat Wilson and the Weezer Way of Life," *The Buffalo News*, July 23, 1995

Michael Goldberg and Claire Kleinedler, "Weezer Revealed: The Rivers Cuomo Interview," *Addicted To Noise*, December 1996

Marc Lewman, "Ol' Nerdy Bastard," *Rip*, 1997

Paul Watkin, "Rivers Runs Through It," *Drop D*, January 1997

David Daley, "Happy Days Cancelled," *Alternative Press*, January 1997

Linda Laban, "Weezer Shows Love for Barry Manilow," *Wall of Sound*, June 3, 1997

Gil Kaufman, "Return of the Rentals Fueled by Trip to Europe," *VH1*, April 7, 1999

Matt Sharp, Gil Kaufman, SonicNet Online chat, *Sonic Net*, April 19, 1999

Karl Koch interview, Emopop.com, February 22, 2001

Jenny Eliscu, "Rivers Cuomo's Encyclopedia of Pop," *Rolling Stone*, May 29, 2002

Elliot Wilder, "Weezer — The Voice of a Maladroit Generation," *Amplifier*, July/August 2002

Adam Budofsky, "Weezer's Pat Wilson: The Unlikely Drum Hero," *Modern Drummer*, December 2002

Justin Fisher; phone interview with author, August 21, 2002

Jason Cropper; phone interview with author, April 26, 2003

Matt Sharp; phone interview with author, November 23, 2002

In the Garage

www.riverscuomo.com

Weezer.com

Mike's World of Weezer fan site (www-ec.njit.edu/~mxz0261)

Crater Face, A Space Twins Site (www.spacetwins.itgo.com/main.html)

DGC Records Artist Biography, May 1994

Roger Catlin, "Rivers Cuomo Returns Home with Weezer," *The Hartford Courant*, October 6, 1994

"Weezer: Sheds Their Sweaters," *Green Day vs. Offspring Magazine by Starline*, November 15, 1994

Tom Beaujour, "Man of Steel," *Guitar World*, March 1995

Steve Appleford, "As Funny as They Wanna Be?" *The Los Angeles Times*, May 21, 1995

John Wirt, "Weezer's Success Far Exceeded Own Expectations," *The Baton Rouge Advocate*, July 21, 1995

Alan Sculley, "Weezer: L.A. Alternative Group Is In from the Dark," *St. Louis Post-Dispatch*, July 31, 1994

Weezine #3, September 1995

Michael Goldberg and Claire Kleinedler, "Weezer Revealed: The Rivers Cuomo Interview," *Addicted To Noise*, December 1996

Brian Bell interview, Soundz.com, 1997

David Daley, "Happy Days Cancelled," *Alternative Press*, January 1997

Karl Koch interview, Emopop.com, February 22, 2001

Lauren Viera, "Hashing Out the Details," *Mean Street*, May 2001

Justin Fisher; phone interview with author, August 21, 2002

92-93

www.riverscuomo.com

Weezer.com

Alan Sculley, "Weezer: L.A. Alternative Group Is In from the Dark," *St. Louis Post-Dispatch*, July 31, 1994

Roger Catlin, "Rivers Cuomo Returns Home With Weezer," *The Hartford Courant*, October 6, 1994

Weezine #1, January 1995

Tom Beaujour, "Man of Steel," *Guitar World*, March 1995

Mim Udovitch, "Revenge of the Nerds," *Rolling Stone*, March 25, 1995

John Wirt, "Weezer's Success Far Exceeded Own Expectations," *The Baton Rouge Advocate*, July 21, 1995

Weezine #3, September 1995

Original Weezer FAQ, 1995

Mike Moore, "Weezer Feature," *Music Connection*, June 10, 2002

Electric Lady

www.riverscuomo.com

Weezer.com

Crater Face, A Space Twins Site (www.spacetwins.itgo.com/main.html)

Alan Sculley, "Weezer: L.A. Alternative Group Is In from the Dark," *St. Louis Post-Dispatch*, July 31, 1994

Arthur Staple, "Hand's on Experience; CMJ Music Marathon's Hoopla Awaits Weezer," *The Bergen Record*, September 20, 1994

Lenny Stoute, "Out of the Garage, Into the Charts," *The Toronto Star*, November 28, 1994

Roberto Santiago, "Weezer Fans Dispute Band's Opinion of Itself," *The Cleveland*

Plain Dealer, December 2, 1994

Tom Beaujour, "Man of Steel," *Guitar World*, March 1995

Steve Appleford, "As Funny as They Wanna Be?" *The Los Angeles Times*, May 21, 1995

John Wirt, "Weezer's Success Far Exceeded Own Expectations," *The Baton Rouge Advocate*, July 21, 1995

Wayne Bledsoe, ". . . Good Fortune For Weezer's Brian Bell," *Knoxville News-Sentinel*, July 23, 1995

Pat Riley, "Pat Wilson and the Weezer Way of Life," *The Buffalo News*, July 23, 1995

Weezine #3, September 1995

Original Weezer FAQ, 1995

Weezine #5, January 1996

Marc Lewman, "Ol' Nerdy Bastard," *Rip*, 1997

Brian Bell interview, Soundz.com, 1997

David Daley, "Happy Days Cancelled," *Alternative Press*, January 1997

"Jason Cropper Interview," *O. Flageul*, January 26, 1999

Knoxville News-Sentinel, August 11, 2002

Justin Fisher; phone interview with author, August 21, 2002

Linda Menasco; e-mail interview with author, September 18, 2002

Jason Cropper; phone interview with author, April 26, 2003

Ric Ocasek; phone interview with author, July 10, 2003

Brian Bell; phone interview with author, July 18, 2003

Weezer

www.riverscuomo.com

Weezer.com

www.mattsharp.net

Chris Morris, "Geffen's Modern Rock Methodology Pays Off," *Billboard*, February 12, 1994

DGC Records Artist Biography, May 1994

Original Weezer FAQ, 1995

Carrie Borzillo, "Popular Uprisings," *Billboard*, May 28, 1994

Jim DeRogatis, *Weezer* album review, *Chicago Sun-Times*, July 3, 1994

Greg Baker, *Weezer* album review, *Miami New Times*, July 6, 1994

Dan Kening, "Lush and Weezer, Sunday at the Vic," *Chicago Tribune*, July 29, 1994

Mark Pollack, "Lush, Weezer, Glam Slam, Los Angeles, Monday, August 8," *The Hollywood Reporter*, August 10, 1994

"Weezer Wins with 'Sad Song'," *Minneapolis Star Tribune*, September 4, 1994

Lorraine Ali, "Lumps of Coal Fill KROQ's Second Stocking," *The Los Angeles Times*, December 13, 1994

Rivers Cuomo, "Life in the Fast Lane," *Details*, January 1995

Jac Zinder, "Rock Candy," *Spin*, January 1995

Tom Beaujour, "Man of Steel," *Guitar World*, March 1995

James Bonisteel, "Pat Wilson Q&A," *Rad zine*, March 1995

Wayne Bledsoe, ". . . Good Fortune for Weezer's Brian Bell," *Knoxville News-Sentinel*, July 23, 1995

Gerard Mizejewski, "Weezer: Looking Beyond Today's Style," *The Washington Times*, July 27, 1995

Weezine #3, September 1995

Marc Lewman, "Ol' Nerdy Bastard," *Rip*, 1997

Claire Kleinedler, "Cool, Another Weezer Member Doing the Solo Thing," *Addicted To Noise*, June 10, 1997

Kitts, Appellant v. Utica National Insurance Group — No. 95CA006088 — Court of Appeals of Ohio, Ninth District, Lorain County, 667 *North Eastern Reporter* 2d 30, October 4, 1996

Jon Regardie, "All that You Can't Leave Behind," *CMJ New Music Monthly*, April 2001

Lauren Viera, "Hashing Out the Details," *Mean Street*, May 2001

"Cutting Classes," *Spin*, June 2001

Jim McGuinn; phone interview with author, August 16, 2002

Dave Leto; e-mail interview with author, August 2, 2003

Holiday

Michael Saunders, "A Dog of a Song," *The Boston Globe*, September 16, 1994

Eric J. Larsen, *Weezer* review, *The Orlando Sentinel*, September 16, 1994

Arthur Stapel, "Hand's on Experience," *The Bergen Record*, September 20, 1994

Carrie Borzillo, "Weezer, Widespread Panic Offer Glimpse into Rock Radio's Future; DGC Act Surprised," *Billboard*, October 1, 1994

Roger Catlin, "Rivers Cuomo Returns Home with Weezer," *The Hartford Courant*, October 6, 1994

Weezine #1, November 1994

Troy J. Augusto, "Live, Weezer, Ventura Theater, October 29th, 1994," *Daily Variety*, November 1, 1994

Lenny Stoute, "Out of the Garage, Into the Charts," *The Toronto Star*, November 28, 1994

Roberto Santiago, "Weezer Fans Dispute Band's Opinion of Self," *The Plain Dealer*, December 2, 1994

Lorraine Ali, "Lumps of Coal Fill KROQ's Second Stocking," *The Los Angeles Times*, December 13, 1994

Jay Bobbin, "Winkler Is Wearing Well," *The Albany Times Union*, December 15, 1994

"Exposure: Spike TV," *Spin*, November 2003

Stephen Thompson, "Top 5 of 1994," *Wisconsin State Journal*, December 29, 1994

Paul Corio, *Weezer* review, *Rolling Stone*, December 29, 1994

James Bonisteel, "Pat Wilson Q&A," *Rad zine*, March 1995

Weezine #3, September 1995

David Daley, "Happy Days Cancelled," *Alternative Press*, January 1997

Jim McGuinn; phone interview with author, August 16, 2002

Mike Gent; phone interview with author, April 29, 2003

Blast Off

SFTBH.COM

Weezer.com

Rivers Cuomo, "Life in the Fast Lane," *Details*, January 1995

Angela Lewis, Pat Wilson phone interview, *The London Independent*, February 24, 1995

Tom Beaujour, "Man of Steel," *Guitar World*, March 1995

James Bonisteel, "Pat Wilson Q&A," *Rad zine*, March 1995

Emma Forrest, "A Spectacled Success," *The London Independent*, March 3, 1995

Roger Catlin, "Heavy Metal Sinks . . . ," *The Hartford Courant*, March 15, 1995

Michael Mehle, "Stardom Comes — Even to Nerds," *Denver Rocky Mountain News*, March 17, 1995

Mim Udovitch, "Revenge of the Nerds," *Rolling Stone*, March 25, 1995

Steve Appleford, "As Funny as They Wanna Be?" *The Los Angeles Times*, May 21, 1995

John Wirt, "Weezer's Success Far Exceeded Own Expectations," *The Baton Rouge Advocate*, July 21, 1995

Wayne Bledsoe, ". . . Good Fortune for Weezer's Brian Bell," *Knoxville News-Sentinel*, July 23, 1995

"Happy Days Are Here Again," *What Magazine*, August 6, 1995

Vikki Tobak, "Nerd Chic? Weezer Trashes the Labels and Just Plain Rocks," *Detroit News*, August 11, 1995

Marc Lewman, "Ol' Nerdy Bastard," *Rip*, 1997

"We Just Want to Be Middle of the Road and Conventional," *NME*, July 1, 2001

"Break, Rattle & Roll," *Vox*, September 1995

Weezine #3, September 1995

Friends of P

Weezer.com

Vikki Tobak, "Nerd Chic? Weezer Trashes the Labels and Just Plain Rocks,"
  Detroit News, August 11, 1995

Maverick Records Artist Biography, September 1995

David N. Meyer, "Back in Black (And White)," *Entertainment Weekly*, October
  27, 1995

Brett Atwood, "$400 Video Sells MTV on Rentals," *Billboard*, October 28, 1995

The Tampa Tribune, October 30, 1995

Jim Minge, "Weezer Bassist Doesn't Sell His Rentals Act Short," *The Omaha
  World Herald*, November 19, 1995

Kieran Grant, "Rentals Look for Hire Ground," *The Toronto Sun*, November 25,
  1995

Roger Catlin, "Weezer's Matt Sharp Focusing at the Moment on Rentals New
  Album," *The Hartford Courant*, November 30, 1995

Maverick Records Artist Biography revised, December 1995

Michael Mehle, "Rentals Eye Long-Term Lease on Hit Parade," *Denver Rocky
  Mountain News*, December 8, 1995

Alan Sculley, "Return of the Moog," *St. Louis Dispatch*, February 2, 1996

Mark Brown, "A Band on the Run that Finally Took Off," *The Bergen Record*,
  February 9, 1996

Anne Hogan, "Obsession Drives Troubled Musician's Soul," *The Auckland Sunday
  News*, October 6, 1996

Gary Steel, "Power Popsters Make Short Work of New Album," *The Auckland
  Sunday Star-Times*, October 6, 1996

Yves Bongarçon, Interview with Rivers Cuomo translated to English from *Rock
  'n' Roll Sound No. 40*, November 1996

Jennie Punter, "Weezer Does Its Homework," *The Toronto Sun*, November 21,
  1996

Roger Catlin, "Weezer's Worry," *The Hartford Courant*, December 4, 1996

Michael Goldberg and Claire Kleinedler, "Weezer Revealed: The Rivers Cuomo
  Interview," *Addicted To Noise*, December 1996

Marc Lewman, "Ol' Nerdy Bastard," *Rip*, 1997

Paul Watkin, "Rivers Runs Through It," *Drop D*, January 1997

Tom Beaujour, "Schoolhouse Rock," *Guitar World*, March 1997

Scott Tempesta, "Weezer but Wiser," *Slamm*, June 1997

Zac Crain, "The Rentals," *The Dallas Observer*, April 1, 1999

Jake Brown, "Interview with Cherielynn Westrich," *GloriousNoise.com*, 2001

Rob Brunner, "Older & Weezer," *Entertainment Weekly*, May 25, 2001

Kate Sullivan, "Weezer's Big Makeover," *Blender*, June/July 2001

Chris Mundy, "Weezer's Cracked Genius," *Rolling Stone*, September 13, 2001
"A Weezer Pleaser," *Playboy*, October 2002
Matt Sharp; phone interview with author, November 23, 2002
Ric Ocasek; phone interview with author, July 10, 2003
Cherielynn Westrich; phone interview with author, July 19, 2003
Josue Minoz, "Matt Sharp Interview," Mattsharp.net, November 2003

The Good Life

Weezer.com
Matt Pattenden, "Preparing for Worldwide Success," *Dotmusic.com*, September
    16, 1996
Kieran Grant, "Pinkerton Secures Band Great Press," *The Toronto Sun*,
    November 21, 1996
Jennie Punter, "Weezer Does Its Homework," *The Toronto Star*, November 21,
    1996
Michael Goldberg and Claire Kleinedler, "Weezer Revealed: The Rivers Cuomo
    Interview," *Addicted to Noise*, December 1996
Roger Catlin, "Weezer's Worry," *The Hartford Courant*, December 4, 1996
Marc Lewman, "Ol' Nerdy Bastard," *Rip*, 1997
Paul Watkin, "Rivers Runs Through It," *Drop D*, January 1997
Gavin Edwards, "Rivers Edge," *Details*, February 1997
"Geek God of Love," *Livewire*, February/March 1997
Tom Beaujour, "Schoolhouse Rock," *Guitar World*, March 1997
Heckler magazine interview, spring 1997 (transcribed to fan site
    www.geocities.com/SunsetStrip/Towers/6651)
Ric Ocasek; phone interview with author, July 10, 2003

El Scorcho

Stephen Dalton, "The Glory that Is Geek," *The London Times*, August 24, 1996
Matt Pattenden, "Preparing for Worldwide Success," *Dotmusic.com*, September
    16, 1996
Christian Berthelsen, "Weezer Suit," *City News Service*, September 24, 1996
"Pinkerton's Obtains Order Against Geffen Records," *Bloomberg News*, September
    25, 1996
Valerie Kuklenski, "Pinkerton's Wants Weezer Album Changed," *United Press
    International*, September 25, 1996
J.D. Considine, *Pinkerton* review, *The Baltimore Sun*, September 26, 1996
Jeff Gordinier, *Pinkerton* review, *Entertainment Weekly*, September 27, 1996
Chris Riemenschneider, *Pinkerton* review, *The Austin American-Statesman*,
    October 1, 1996

Pinkerton review, *Billboard*, October 5, 1996

Anne Hogan "Obsession Drives Troubled Musician's Soul," *The Auckland Sunday News*, October 6, 1996

Gary Steel, "Power Popsters Make Short Work of New Album, *The Auckland Sunday Star-Times*, October 6, 1996

Rob O'Connor, *Pinkerton* review, *Rolling Stone*, October 31, 1996

Kieran Grant, "Pinkerton Secures Band Great Press," *The Toronto Sun*, November 21, 1996

Jennie Punter, "Weezer Does Its Homework," *The Toronto Star*, November 21, 1996

Michael Goldberg and Claire Kleinedler, "Weezer Revealed: The Rivers Cuomo Interview," *Addicted To Noise*, December 1996

Roger Catlin, "Weezer's Worry," *The Hartford Courant*, December 4, 1996

Marc Lewman, "Ol' Nerdy Bastard," *Rip*, 1997

Paul Watkin, "Rivers Runs Through It," *Drop D*, January 1997

Gavin Edwards, "Rivers Edge," *Details*, February 1997

"Geek God of Love," *Livewire*, February/March 1997

Tom Beaujour, "Schoolhouse Rock," *Guitar World*, March 1997

Heckler magazine interview, spring 1997 (transcribed to fan site www.geocities.com/SunsetStrip/Towers/6651)

Wayne Bledsoe, "No Hack Appeal," *The Chicago Sun-Times*, June 29, 1997

Joe Matt and Rivers Cuomo, "Joe Matt, Creator of Peepshow, and Rivers Cuomo of Weezer, Reveal Their Biggest Influence," *Cake*, July 1, 1997

David Daley, "Hide and Geek," *Alternative Press*, May 2001

J.T. Leroy, "Weezer's Pat Wilson," *New York Press*, June 27, 2001

Jim McGuinn; phone interview with author, August 16, 2002

Rob O'Connor; e-mail interview with author, April 26, 2003

Fat Mike; phone interview with author, July 1, 2003

Dave Leto; e-mail interview with author, August 2, 2003

Who You Callin' Bitch?

www.riverscuomo.com

Kieran Grant, "Pinkerton Secures Band Great Press," *The Toronto Sun*, November 21, 1996

Jennie Punter, "Weezer Does Its Homework," *The Toronto Star*, November 21, 1996

Michael Goldberg and Claire Kleinedler, "Weezer Revealed: The Rivers Cuomo Interview," *Addicted To Noise*, December 1996

Roger Catlin, "Weezer's Worry," *The Hartford Courant*, December 4, 1996

Weezine #9, Winter 1996

Marc Lewman, "Ol' Nerdy Bastard," *Rip*, 1997

Brian Bell interview, Soundz.com, 1997

David Daley, "Happy Days Cancelled," *Alternative Press*, January 1997

Paul Watkin, "Rivers Runs Through It," *Drop D*, January 1997

Gavin Edwards, "Rivers Edge," *Details*, February 1997

"Geek God of Love," *Livewire*, February/March 1997

Tom Beaujour, "Schoolhouse Rock," *Guitar World*, March 1997

Heckler magazine interview, spring 1997 (transcribed to fan site
    www.geocities.com/SunsetStrip/Towers/6651)

Weezine #10, April 1997

Angie C. & Rivers Cuomo, WFNX Web Chat, May 1997

Gary Susman, "Whither Weezer?" *The Boston Phoenix*, May 15, 1997

Claire Kleinedler, "Cool, Another Weezer Member Doing the Solo Thing,"
    Addicted To Noise, June 10, 1997

"Weezer Break Up?" *O.C. Weekly*, May 30, 1997

Scott Tempesta, "Weezer but Wiser," *Slamm*, June 1997

Wayne Bledsoe, "No Hack Appeal," *The Chicago Sun Times*, June 29, 1997

Kate Sullivan, "Weezer's Big Makeover," *Blender*, June/July 2001

Chris Mundy, "Weezer's Cracked Genius," *Rolling Stone*, September 13, 2001

Justin Fisher; phone interview with author, August 21, 2002

Brian Diaz; e-mail interview with author, June 28, 2003

Mykel & Carli

Weezer.com

Michael Goldberg and Claire Kleinedler, "Weezer Revealed: The Rivers Cuomo
    Interview," *Addicted to Noise*, December 1996

David Daley, "Happy Days Cancelled," *Alternative Press*, January 1997

Heckler magazine interview, spring 1997 (transcribed to fan site
    www.geocities.com/SunsetStrip/Towers/6651)

Letter from Karl Koch to Members of Weezer Fan Club, July 1997

"Weezer Fan Club Founders Mykel & Carli Allan . . ." MTV News. Original air
    dates August 18–20, 1997

Claire Kleinedler, "Hundreds Join Weezer in Tribute to Fanclub Members,"
    Addicted to Noise, August 20, 1997

"Weezer Fan Club . . ." *Spin*, November 1997

Knoxville News, August 11, 2002

Kate Sullivan, "Weezer's Big Makeover," *Blender*, June/July 2001

Fun Time

Weezer.com

www.riverscuomo.com

Weezine #11, October 1997

Ashok Chandra, "Weezer Breathes New Life into Career after Four Year
      Hiatus," *Daily Texan*, November 15, 2000

Matt Sharp; phone interview with author, November 23, 2002

Drew Parsons; phone interview with author, March 20, 2003

Kevin Stevenson; phone interview with author, April 2, 2003

John Horton; phone interview with author, May 19, 2003

Turn It Off, Now

Weezer.com

www.riverscuomo.com

It's All About Mikey Welsh fan site (www.geocities.com/jonaswelsh/mikeybio.html)

musicrag.com

Claire Kleinedler, "Weezer Plan New LP Without Sharp," *SonicNet*, April 13, 1998

Claire Kleinedler, "Weezer Share Songwriting Duties on Next Album," *SonicNet*,
      August 25, 1998

Zac Crain, "The Rentals . . ." *Dallas Observer*, April 1, 1999

Heidi Sherman, "The Rentals' Matt Sharp Has Come Undone," *RollingStone.com*,
      April 23, 1999

"Weezer," *Status Magazine*, July 2000

David Enders, "Weezer Sneaks into Detroit," *Michigan Daily*, September 6, 2000

Zac Crain, "Don't Call It a Comeback," *Dallas Observer*, September 21, 2000

Gil Kaufman, "Reassured by Sold Out Tour . . ." *VH1.com*, September 24, 2000

Ashok Chandra, "Weezer Breathes New Life . . ." *Daily Texan*, November 15,
      2000

Eric Himmelsbach, "In the Garage," *Revolver*, March/April 2001

"Cutting Classes," *Spin*, May 2001

"Odd Man Out," *Kerrang!*, May 2001

Richard Cromelin, "Where's Weezer Been?" *The Los Angeles Times*, May 12, 2001

Evan Schlansky, *Weezer* review, *Entertainment Weekly*, May 18, 2001

Rob Brunner, "Older and Weezer," *Entertainment Weekly*, May 25, 2001

Erik Himmelsbach, "50,000,000 Weezer Fans Can't Be Wrong," *Request*,
      May/June 2001

Interview, *Abercrombie & Fitch Quarterly*, Summer 2001

Chris Mundy, "Weezer's Cracked Genius," *Rolling Stone*, September 13, 2001

Thalia S. Field, "The Grass Is Always Greener for Rivers Cuomo," *The Harvard
      Crimson*, February 22, 2002

"Odder than Hell," *Guitar World*, May 2002

Jenny Eliscu, "Rivers Cuomo's Encyclopedia of Pop," *Rolling Stone*, May 29, 2002

Weezine Vol. 2, Issue #1, Fall 2002

Somebody Save Me
Weezer.com

Thespecialgoodness.com

Thespecialgoodness.net

Allmusic.com

Popmatters.com

Pitchforkmedia.com

Rockonline.com/therentals

The Weezer Dump fan site

Carrie Borzillo, "A Playful Attitude Marks the Return of Maverick's Rentals,"
    Billboard, March 6, 1999

Matt Sharp and Gil Kaufman, SonicNet Online chat, *SonicNet*, April 19, 1999

Rob Sheffield, *Seven More Minutes* Review, *Rolling Stone*, April 29, 1999

Jennifer Vineyard, "Weezer Brace for Return," *RollingStone.com*, February 4, 2000

Erik Himmelsbach, "In the Garage," *Revolver*, March/April 2001

Jon Regardie, "All that You Can't Leave Behind," *CMJ*, April 2001

Brad Cawn, "Nothing But Net," *The Chicago Tribune*, April 15, 2001

David Daley, "Hide and Geek," *Alternative Press*, May 2001

"Odd Man Out," *Kerrang!*, May 2001

Richard Cromelin, "Where's Weezer Been?" *The Los Angeles Times*, May 12, 2001

Erik Himmelsbach, "50,000,000 Weezer Fans Can't Be Wrong," *Request*,
    May/June 2001

Kate Sullivan, "Weezer's Big Makeover," *Blender*, June/July 2001

Jo Piazza, "Post Geek?" *The Daily Pennsylvanian*, July 19, 2001

Chris Mundy, "Weezer's Cracked Genius," *Rolling Stone*, September 13, 2001

Richard Cromelin, "It's Them Again . . ." *The Bergen Record*, September 28, 2001

Erik Himmelsbach, "Weezer Give Good Shred," *Gene Simmons' Tongue*, Spring
    2002

Jenny Eliscu, "Rivers Cuomo's Encyclopedia of Pop," *Rolling Stone*, May 29, 2002

Gonna Make My Move
Weezer.com

The Weezer Dump fan site

Jennifer Vineyard, "Weezer Brace for Return," *RollingStone.com*, February 4, 2000

"That's Not Weezer," *The O.C. Weekly*, June 30, 2000

Jennifer Vineyard, "Revenge of the Nerds," *RollingStone.com*, August 25, 2000

Riley Graebner, "All New Weezer," *The Buffalo News*, September 1, 2000

Toni Ruberto, "Weezer," *The Buffalo News*, September 4, 2000

Bobby Reed, "Weezer at Metro," *Chicago Sun-Times*, September 5, 2000

Joshua Klein, "A New Generation . . ." *The Chicago Tribune*, September 5, 2000

David Enders, "Weezer Sneaks into Detroit," *Michigan Daily*, September 6, 2000

"Rivers on the Adventure Club," *The Adventure Club with Josh*, September 12, 2000

Zac Crain, "Don't Call It a Comeback," *Dallas Observer*, September 21, 2000

Gil Kaufman, "Reassured by Sold Out Tour . . ." *VH1.com*, September 24, 2000

"Mikey Welsh Interview," *Chick Click*, March 27, 2001

Erik Himmelsbach, "In the Garage," *Revolver*, March/April 2001

Jon Regardic, "All that You Can't Leave Behind," *CMJ*, April 2001

David Daley, "Hide and Geek," *Alternative Press*, May 2001

"Odd Man Out," *Kerrang!*, May 2001

Erik Himmelsbach, "50,000,000 Weezer Fans Can't Be Wrong," *Request*,
     May/June 2001

Richard Cromelin, "Where's Weezer Been?" *The Los Angeles Times*, May 12, 2001

J.T. Leroy, "Weezer's Pat Wilson," *New York Press*, June 27, 2001

Ben Rayner, "Nothing to Weeze At," *The Toronto Star*, September 24, 2001

Ben Harvey "Rivers Cuomo Interview," wPLY, Y100, Philadelphia, December 30,
     2001

Paul Zaic, "10 Questions with Matt Sharp," *Mike's World of Weezer*, June 2002

Weezine Vol. 2, Issue #1, Fall 2002

Matt Sharp; phone interview with author, November 23, 2002

Ric Ocasek; phone interview with author, July 10, 2003

Don't Let Go

Weezer.com

Emopop.com

The Weezer Dump fan site

Zac Crain, "Don't Call It a Comeback," *Dallas Observer*, September 21, 2000

Gil Kaufman, "Reassured by Sold Out Tour . . ." *VH1.com*, September 24, 2000

"Weezer to Headline Yahoo! Outloud . . ." *Business Wire*, November 20, 2000

Steve Hochman, "KROQ Spreads Holiday Cheer," *The Los Angeles Times*,
     December 18, 2000

Natasha Emmons, "Web Works," *Amusement Business*, January 29, 2001

Dave Thomas, "Hooked on Sonics," *The Palm Beach Post*, February 23, 2001

Doug Levy, "Weezer — Roseland Ballroom," *Dotmusic.com*, March 12, 2001

Andrew Dansby, "Weezer Album Due in May," *RollingStone.com*, March 16, 2001

Jon Regardie, "All that You Can't Leave Behind," *CMJ*, April 2001

Brad Cawn, "Nothing but Net," *The Chicago Tribune*, April 15, 2001

"Cutting Classes," *Spin*, May 2001

Lauren Viera, "Hashing Out the Details," *Mean Street*, May 2001

Erik Himmelsbach, "50,000,000 Weezer Fans Can't Be Wrong," *Request*,
     May/June 2001

Don Zulaica, "Interview: Weezer Drummer Pat Wilson," *Live Daily*, May 24, 2001

Rob Brunner, "Older and Weezer," *Entertainment Weekly*, May 25, 2001

Kate Sullivan, "Weezer's Big Makeover," *Blender*, June/July 2001

"We Just Want to Be Middle of the Road . . ." *New Musical Express*, July 1, 2001

Shannon McCarthy, "Weezer: The Good Life," *Real Detroit*, September 1, 2001

Chris Mundy, "Weezer's Cracked Genius," *Rolling Stone*, September 13, 2001

Brian McCollum, "Internet at Heart of Weezer Comeback," *The Charleston Gazette*, September 27, 2001

Ben Harvey "Rivers Cuomo Interview," WPLY, Y100, Philadelphia, December 30, 2001

Kimberly Chun, "Mixing It Up . . ." *Mix*, August 2002

Ken Allardyce; e-mail interview with author, March 20, 2003

Brian Diaz; e-mail interview with author, June 28, 2003

Ric Ocasek; phone interview with author, July 10, 2003

Golden *Green*

Weezer.com

www.riverscuomo.com

Jon Regardie, "All that You Can't Leave Behind," *CMJ*, April 2001

Brad Cawn, "Nothing but Net," *The Chicago Tribune*, April 15, 2001

"Odd Man Out," *Kerrang!*, May 2001

John Santos, "Rock Stars? Sex Idols? Geeks with Guitars?" *Meltdown*, May 2001

Erik Himmelsbach, "50,000,000 Weezer Fans Can't Be Wrong," *Request*, May/June 2001

Teresa Gubbins, "Weezer's Second Wind," *The Dallas Morning News*, May 11, 2001

Richard Cromelin, "Where's Weezer Been?" *The Los Angeles Times*, May 12, 2001

Rob Brunner, "Older and Weezer," *Entertainment Weekly*, May 25, 2001

Gideon Yago, "Plan for World Domination . . ." *MTV.com*, June 1, 2001

Kate Sullivan, "Weezer's Big Makeover," *Blender*, June/July 2001

Harry Thomas, "Not So Serious Rivers Cuomo," *Rolling Stone*, June 7, 2001

The Craig Kilborn Show, CBS-Television, original airdate June 9, 2001

Lara Cohen, "Watch the Vid, Pass the H*** Pipe," *Cable World*, June 25,2001

J.T. Leroy, "Weezer's Pat Wilson," *New York Press*, June 27, 2001

"Mikey and Rivers Interview," *Terra Ocio*, June 28, 2001

Nick Duerden, "No Sweat," *Q*, July 2001

"We Just Want to Be Middle of the Road . . ." *New Musical Express*, July 1, 2001

AOL live Internet chat, July 3, 2001

Chris Mundy, "Weezer's Cracked Genius," *Rolling Stone*, September 13, 2001

Fat Mike; phone interview with author, July 1, 2003

I Wish You Luck

Weezer.com

Scott Shriner Experience fan site (www.scottshrinerexperience.cjb.net)

Weeklydig.com

Superior Court of California (Santa Monica) Case Number SC0677488

Neal Weiss, "Weezer Sued for Millions . . ." *Launch.com*, August 2, 2001

Greg Heller, "Weezer to Redo Island," *RollingStone.com*, August 14, 2001

Shannon McCarthy, "Weezer: The Good Life," *Real Detroit*, September 2001

Rivers Cuomo, BBC *Radio Session Obsession*, September 20, 2001

Andrew Dansby & Jenny Eliscu, "Weezer Ready *Maladroit*," *RollingStone.com*, January 22, 2002

Rivers Cuomo, Posting as "Ace" on Official Weezer Message Board, January 30, 2002

Steve Morse, "Weezer Wunderkind Cherishes Crimson Tie," *The Boston Globe*, February 8, 2002

Rob Brunner "Hear and Now," *Entertainment Weekly*, March 15, 2002

Lisa Wilton, "Living the Good Life," *The Calgary Sun*, April 20, 2002

Mike Ross, "Easy Weezer," *The Edmonton Sun*, April 22, 2002

Erik Himmelsbach, "Weezer Give Good Shred," *Gene Simmons' Tongue*, Spring 2002

Chris Whyte, "Weezer Story," *Mean Street*, May 2002

Kristin Roth, "Weezer: As Dope as Ever," *CDNow*, May 1, 2002

Laura Sinagra, "River's Edge," *Spin*, June 2002

Mike Saccone, "Weezin' Along," *Toledo City Paper*, September 12, 2002

Doug Elfman, "Lighten Up," *The Las Vegas Review-Journal*, September 14, 2002

Alexander Stevens, "Weezer Bassist in Painter's Paradise," *Boston Herald*, November 4, 2002

Mikey "Heroin" Blurb, *Rolling Stone*, November 28, 2002

"Side Dish," *Devil in the Woods*, July/August 2003

Broken Arrows

Weezer.com

Ben Rayner, "Nothing to Weeze At," *The Toronto Star*, September 24, 2001

Kevin Amorim, "Playing It Cool for a Warmed Up Crowd," *Newsday*, October 2, 2001

CSB #103510 Division of Labor Standards Enforcement, October 31, 2001

Rhea Cortado, "Rivers Never Run Dry," *Campus Circle*, April 29, 2002

Modern Dukes

Weezer.com

Official Weezer Message Board

Weezon.com fan site

David Daley, "Hide and Geek," *Alternative Press*, May 2001

Shannon McCarthy, "Weezer: The Good Life," *Real Detroit*, September 2001

Reverb, November 2001, HBO Television

Mary Williams, "Weezer Lets Music Do the Talking," *The Daily Bruin*, November 26, 2001

Christina Saraceno, "Weezer, Crow Rock for Their Rights," *RollingStone.com*, December 21, 2001

Ben Harvey, "Rivers Cuomo Interview," WPLY, Y100, Philadelphia, December 30, 2001

"Weezer Gives New Album a Proper Title," January 21, 2002

"Weezer: Hear and Now," *Entertainment Weekly*, January 25–February 1, 2002

Steve Lamacq, BBC1 interview, April 3, 2002

Chris Whyte, "Weezer Story," *Mean Street*, May 2002

Weezer Feature, *Rockpile*, May 2002

Matt Blackett, "Alt-Shred," *Guitar Player*, July 2002

Kimberly Chun, "Mixing It Up . . ." *Mix*, August 2002

Rhea Cortado, "Rivers Never Run Dry," *Campus Circle*, April 29, 2002

"Odder than Hell," *Guitar World*, May 2002

Dope Nose

Weezer.com

UWFTM.com

"Album Title TBA," *Alternative Press*, January 2002

"Weezer: Hear and Now," *Entertainment Weekly*, January 25–February 1, 2002

Steve Morse, "Weezer Wunderkind Cherishes Crimson Tie," *The Boston Globe*, February 8, 2002

Jonathan Cohen, "Weezer's Self-Promotion Irks Label," *Billboard.com*, March 6, 2002

Brian Hiatt, "Rivers Edge," *Entertainment Weekly*, March 22, 2002

Steve Lamacq, BBC1 Interview, April 3, 2002

"Redone — The Weezer Saga," *Rocknews.com*, April 12, 2002

Rhea Cortado, "Rivers Never Run Dry," *Campus Circle*, April 29, 2002

Chris Whyte, "Weezer Story," *Mean Street*, May 2002

Kristin Roth, "Weezer: As Dope as Ever," *CDNow*, May 1, 2002

Wes Orshoski, "Geffen's Weezer on 'Maladroit'," *Billboard*, May 11, 2002

Weezer feature, *New York Post*, June 2, 2002

Mike Moore, Weezer Feature, *Music Connection*, June 10, 2002

Maladroit

Weezer.com

Official Weezer Message Board

www.riverscuomo.com

Thalia S. Field, "The Grass Is Always Greener . . ." *The Harvard Crimson*,
    February 22, 2002

Kyle McDonald, Brian Bell interview (www.elevator.ca/brian), March 2002

Erik Missio, "Say It Ain't So," *Chart Attack*, March 6, 2002

John Sakamoto, "Anti Hit List/Alternate Top 10," *Jam Showbiz*, March 13, 2002

"Redone — The Weezer Saga," *Rocknews.com*, April 12, 2002

Gideon Yago, "Former Weezer Bassist Sues . . ." *MTV.com*, April 24, 2002

Mike Ross, "Weezer Pleaser For Fans," *The Edmonton Sun*, April 24, 2002

Rhea Cortado, "Rivers Never Run Dry," *Campus Circle*, April 29, 2002

Weezer Biography, Geffen Records, May 2002

"Odder than Hell," *Guitar World*, May 2002

Chris Whyte, "Weezer Story," *Mean Street*, May 2002

Kristin Roth, "Weezer: As Dope as Ever," *CDNow*, May 1, 2002

Corey Moss, interview, *MTV.com*, May 2, 2002

Wes Orshoski, "Geffen's Weezer on 'Maladroit'," *Billboard*, May 11, 2002

"Don't Fear the Weezer," *Spin*, June 2002

Paul Zaic, "10 Questions with Matt Sharp," *Mike's World of Weezer*, June 2002

Weezer feature, *New York Post*, June 2, 2002

Corey Moss, "Matt Sharp Preps Solo LP . . ." *MTV.com*, June 7, 2002

Ann Powers, "Maladroit Review," *Rolling Stone*, June 7, 2002

Mike Moore, Weezer feature, *Music Connection*, June 10, 2002

Matt Blackett, "Alt-Shred," *Guitar Player*, July 2002

Elliot Wilder, "Weezer — The Voice of a 'Maladroit' Generation," *Amplifier*,
    July/August 2002

Sarah Rodman, "Rivers Flows in Two Directions . . ." *The Boston Herald*, July 21,
    2002

Ric Ocasek; phone interview with the author, July 10, 2003

Take Control

Buddyhead.com

Official Weezer Message Board

www.riverscuomo.com

Weezer.com

Y100.com

Weezer Go Fishin' Video Trailer

Scott Shriner Experience fan site (www.scottshrinerexperience.cjb.net)

Erik Himmelsbach, "Weezer Give Good Shred," *Gene Simmons' Tongue*, Spring 2002

Sandy Hunter, "Marcos Siega — Reel Dealer," RES, April 4, 2002

"Odder than Hell," *Guitar World*, May 2002

"Tantrums, Beards, Paranoia," *Kerrang!*, May 2002

Chris Whyte, "Weezer Story," *Mean Street*, May 2002

Kristin Roth, "Weezer: As Dope as Ever," *CDNow*, May 1, 2002

Corey Moss, interview, *MTV.com*, May 2, 2002

Wes Orshoski, "Geffen's Weezer on 'Maladroit,'" *Billboard*, May 11, 2002

Corey Moss, "Weezer Hitting Sheds with Dashboard Confessional," *MTV.com*, May 24, 2002

"Don't Fear the Weezer," *Spin*, June 2002

Jonathan Cohen, "Strokes to Join Weezer," *Billboard*, June 5, 2002

Interview with Chris Carrabba of Dashboard Confessional, *The Palm Beach Post*, June 7, 2002

"The Ultimate Tour Guide," *Rolling Stone*, June 12, 2002

"Weezer Collaborate with Kermit . . ." *MTV.com*, June 25, 2002

Elliot Wilder, "Weezer — The Voice of a 'Maladroit' Generation," *Amplifier*, July/August 2002

Dan Nailen, "Deconstructing Emo," *The Salt Lake Tribune*, July 5, 2002

Dean Kuipers, "Oh the Angst, Oh the Sales," *The Los Angeles Times*, July 7, 2002

Gary Graff, "Popping Back Up," *The Plain Dealer*, July 12, 2002

Wendy Case, "Pop Band Weezer . . ." *Detroit News*, July 12, 2002

Alan Sculley, "Weezer, With a Twist . . ." *The Providence Journal-Bulletin*, July 19, 2002

Sarah Rodman, "Rivers Flows in Two Directions," *The Boston Herald*, July 21, 2002

Kimberly Chun, "Mixing It Up . . ." *Mix*, August 2002

Weezer Tour Report, *Rolling Stone*, August 8, 2002

Knoxville News-Sentinel, August 11, 2002

Jim McGuinn; phone interview with author, August 16, 2002

Adam Budofsky, "Weezer's Pat Wilson: The Unlikely Drum Hero," *Modern Drummer*, December 2002

Kevin Murphy, "Crazy Town's Metamorphosis," *The Arizona Republic*, January 2, 2003

Travis Keller; phone interview with author, June 2003

Brian Bell; phone interview with author, July 18, 2003

Turn Me 'Round

Ink19.com
MattSharp.net
Pitchforkmedia.com

www.riverscuomo.com

Weezer.com

"A Weezer Pleaser," *Playboy*, August 2002

"Rolling Stone Readers Top 100 Albums," *Rolling Stone*, September 30, 2002

Matt Sharp; phone interview with author, November 23, 2002

"Top CDs of 2002," *Spin*, December 2002

Pat Wilson; e-mail interview with author, December 2, 2002

Bret Begun, "How Do You Like It?" *Newsweek*, December 23, 2002

Willie McCool interview, *National Public Radio*, January 29, 2003

Steve Hochman, "Time to Return Those Favors," *The Los Angeles Times*,
    February 2, 2003

Matt Sharp; e-mail to author, February 4, 2003

"Weezer's Cuomo Tunes In AM Radio," *MTV.com*, February 11, 2003

Ashok Chandra, "AM Radio Hits the Road," *Daily Texan*, February 26, 2003

Jim Abbot, "Possibilities in Weezer Side Project," *The Orlando Sentinel*, March 7,
    2003

Alex Pappademas, "The Pinkerton Papers," *Spin*, May 2003

Gary Graff, "Cold News Story," *The Plain Dealer*, May 16, 2003

Travis Keller; phone interviews with author, May 21, 2003; June 2003

"Side Dish," *Devil in the Woods*, July/August 2003

Land, Air, Sea Review, *CMJ New Music Monthly*, July 2003

Ric Ocasek; phone interview with author, July 10, 2003

Brian Bell; phone interview with author, July 18, 2003

"Weezer Getting Personal . . ." *Billboard.com*, August 19, 2003

Travis Keller; e-mail to author, September 8, 2003

Gimme Skelter Liner Notes, Buddyhead/Nettwerk Records, Released October 23,
    2003

Josue Minoz, "Matt Sharp Interview," Mattsharp.net, November 2003

John D. Luerssen is a contributor to *Rolling Stone*, *All Music Guide*, and *Billboard*. He lives in Westfield, New Jersey, with his wife Heidi, their three young children, and two attack beagles.